W9-ARG-097

HISTORY OF RUSSIA

Sergei Mikhailovich Soloviev

The

Academic International Press

Edition

of

Sergei M. Soloviev

History of Russia From Earliest Times

SERGEI M. SOLOVIEV

History of Russia

Volume 43

Catherine the Great in Power.

Domestic and Foreign Affairs

1763-1764

Edited, Translated and With an
Introduction by

Daniel L. Schlafly, Jr.

Academic International Press
1998

The Academic International Press Edition of S.M. Soloviev's *History of Russia From Earliest Times* in fifty volumes.

Volume 43. *Catherine the Great in Power. Domestic and Foreign Affairs, 1763-1764.*
Unabridged translation of the text of Chapter III of Volume 25 and Chapter I of Volume 26 of S.M. Soloviev's *Istoriia Rossii s drevneishikh vremen* as found in Volume XIII of this work published in Moscow from 1962 through 1966, with added annotation by Daniel L. Schlafly, Jr.

ISBN: 0-87569-194-3

Composition by Diana J. Godwin

Printed in the United States of America

A list of Academic International Press publications is found at the end of this volume.

ACADEMIC INTERNATIONAL PRESS
Box 1111 • Gulf Breeze FL 32562-1111 • USA

CONTENTS

WEIGHTS AND MEASURES

Linear and Surface Measure

Arshin: 16 vershoks, 28 in (diuims) 72.12 cm
Chetvert (quarter): 1/4 arshin, 1/2 desiatine, 1.35 acre (sometimes 1.5 desiatinas or ca 4.1 acres)
Desiatina: 2,400 square sazhens, 2.7 acres, 1.025 hectares
Diuim: 1 inch, 2.54 cm
Fut: 12 diuims, 1 foot, 30.48 cm
Obza (areal): c. 10 chetverts, 13–15 acres
Osmina: 1/4 desiatina, 600 sq. sazhens, .256 hectare
Sazhen: 3 arshins, 7 feet, 2.133 m
Vershok: 1.75 in, 4.445 cm, 1/16 arshin
Verst: 500 sazhens, 1,166 yards and 2 feet, .663 miles, 1.0668 km
Voloka (plowland): 19 desiatinas, 20 hectares, 49 acres

Liquid Measure

Bochka (barrel): 40 vedros, 121 gallons, 492 liters
Chetvert (quarter): 1.4 bochkas, 32.5 gallons
Kufa: 30 stofy
Stof: Kruzhka (cup), 1/10 vedro, c. 1.3 quarts, 1.23 liters
Vedro (pail): 3.25 gallons, 12.3 liters, 10 stofy

Weights

Berkovets: 361 lbs, 10 puds
Bezmen: c. 1 kg., 2.2 lbs
Chetverik (grain measure dating from 16th century): 1/8 chetvert, 15.8 lbs
Chetvert (grain measure): 1/4 rad, 3.5 puds, 126.39 lbs, c. 8 bushels
Funt: 96 zolotniks, .903 lbs, 14.4 ozs, 408.24 kg
Grivenka: 205 grams
Kad: 4 chetverts, 14 puds, 505.56 lbs
Kamen (stone): 32 funt
Korob (basket): 7 puds, 252 lbs
Osmina (eighth): 2 osmina to a chetvert (dry measure)
Polbezmen: c. 500 g, 1 lb
Polosmina (sixteenth): 1/2 osmina
Pud: 40 funts, 36.113 lbs (US), 40 lbs (Russian), 16.38 kg
Rad: 14 puds, 505.58 lb
Zolotnik: 1/96 lbs, 4.26 grams

Money

Altyn: 6 Muscovite dengas, 3 copecks
Chervonets (chervonny): gold coin of first half of 18th century worth c. 3 rubles
Chetvertak: silver coin equal to 25 copecks or 1/4 ruble (18–19th centuries)
Copeck: two Muscovite dengas
Denga: 1/2 copeck
Grivna: 20 Muscovite dengas, 100 grivnas equals 1 ruble, 10 copecks
Grosh: 10 peniaz
Grosh litovsky (Lithuanian grosh): 5 silver copecks
Kopa grosh: 60 groshas, one Muscovite poltina, 1/2 ruble
Moskovka: 1/2 copeck
Muscovite Denga: 200 equals 1 ruble
Novgorod Denga: 100 equals 1 ruble
Novgorodka: 1 copeck
Peniaz: 10 equals one grosh (Lithuania)
Poltina (poltinnik): 50 copecks, 100 dengas, 1 ruble
Poltora: 1 1/2 rubles
Polupoltina (-nik): 25 copecks, 50 dengas
Ruble: 100 copecks, 200 dengas
Shiroky grosh (large silver coin): 20 Muscovite copecks.

Foreign Denominations
Chervonnyi: c. 3 rubles
Ducat: c. 3 rubles
Efimok: c. 1 ruble, 1 chervonets or chervonnyi
Levok: Dutch silver lion dollar
Thaler (Joachimsthaler): c. 1 ruble, 1 chervonets or chervonnyi

Note: Weights and measures often changed values over time and sometimes held more than one value at the same time. For details consult Sergei G. Pushkarev, *Dictionary of Russian Historical Terms from the Eleventh Century to 1917* (Yale, 1970).

RUSSIA'S WESTERN FRONTIERS, 1763

PREFACE

This book is an unabridged translation of Volume 25, Chapter 3; and Volume 26, Chapter 1, which are pp. 191-287, 289-293, 295, 313-408, and 584-585 in Volume XIII of the multi-volume edition of Soloviev's *Istoriia Rossii s drevneishikh vremen* (History of Russia From Earliest Times, 29 vols. (St. Petersburg, 1851-1879), published from 1962 through 1966 in Moscow.

The present translation endeavors to render the text and Soloviev's thought as accurately as possible. No attempt has been made to reproduce his style and text word for word for this would have yielded a bizarre Russianized text. The main consideration has been to make his history as readable as possible consistent with accuracy, while retaining at least something of the flavor of the language of the era. An effort has been made to find English-language equivalents for all technical terms Soloviev employs (ranks, offices, titles, legal, administrative and so forth) in the belief that English is no less rich in such terms than other languages. This is intended to smooth the flow of the narrative for the reader and to avoid marring the pages with annoying untranslated words. The exception involves Russian words which have become common in English—boyar, tsar, cossack. In all of this the translator remains painfully aware of the inevitable shortcomings that may remain.

Soloviev's pages are featureless and interminable, one long and complex sentence marching after the last. To make the text easier to follow for today's readers, long paragraphs and sentences have been broken into shorter ones. Most of the subtitles are based on the descriptive topic headings clustered at the beginnings of the chapters in the Russian edition. These headings have been moved into the body of the text as subtitles to mark and ease for the reader the transition from one subject to another. In some cases, to even the frequency of breaks in the text or to show topics not listed by Soloviev at the beginning of chapters, new subtitles have been added. Soloviev's arrangement of the material has been followed strictly.

Brief explanatory or interpretive materials have been inserted into the text enclosed in brackets, or added as footnotes to each chapter at the end of the book. All material enclosed in brackets has been added by the present editor and all material in parentheses is the author's. Emphasized words or phrases in italics are the author's.

The general policy followed in annotating has been to identify prominent personalities at first mention, and to give explanation and elucidations of less common or obscure terms and passages, assuming the typical reader to have relatively little familiarity with Russian history. If brief, these have been included in the text in brackets; otherwise they appear as numbered footnotes at the back of the book by chapters. Most of the author's own notes are not included because their highly specialized archival, documentary and bibliographic nature is of value solely to specialists who, in any case, will prefer to consult the original Russian text. In addition, most of the notes added by the editors of the edition published in the Soviet Union which also are technical in nature—fuller bibliographic citations than those in Soloviev's notes—have not been included. When the author's notes and those of the Soviet editors are included, they are so designated. All other notes are those of the present editor.

Russian personal names are preserved in their Russian form except for Alexander, Alexis, Michael, Nicholas, Catherine and Peter, which English usage has made familiar with respect to Russian historical figures, and for important ecclesiastics whose names have been recast into Latin or Greek equivalents, especially for the earlier period of Russian history. This applies to prominent individuals; Russian forms usually are used for the less prominent. Certain other names and terms have been anglicized for the sake of clarity and because they are used widely—Casimir, Sophia, Danzig, boyar, rubles, versts, Dnieper river, and others.

The editors of the edition published in the USSR frequently added patronymics and other names, and these have been retained without brackets; patronymics appearing in the original edition also have been included. Plural forms for names and terms which might be confusing have been anglicized—Vologdians rather than Vologzhane, Voguls and not Vogulichi, the Dolgorukys not Dolgorukie, and so forth. Even so, in a few cases the Russian plural form is used when this form is common. Most Slavic surnames show gender, and this has been preserved. Since an "a" at the word end usually signifies a female, Golovkin would have a wife or daughter Golovkina. The final "iia" in feminine personal names has been shortened to "ia"—"Maria" and "Evdokia" instead of "Mariia" and "Evdokiia".

Non-Russian names, locations, terms, ranks and so on are spelled according to the language native to the person or particular to the city, region or culture when this can be determined. Confusion arises at times because the text is not clear about nationalities. An excruciating example is Lithuania where at least three languages intermingled. In such cases the context is the guide used and as a last resort the Russian spelling in the text is accepted. Individuals whose names were once non-Russian but had been in Russian service for generations are named by the original spelling of the family name. Turkish, Tatar, Persian and other names and terms are spelled in the original according to accepted forms in scholarly books. In some instances, if not otherwise ascertainable they are translated from the Russian as given by Soloviev. The names of geographical locations conform to commonly accepted English usage—Podolia, Moscow, Copenhagen, Saxony and so forth.

Finally, with respect to transliteration, this translation follows a modified Library of Congress system omitting diacritical marks and ligatures, and rendering the initial "ia" and "iu" as "ya" and "yu" ("Yasnaia" and "Yury"), the suffices "ii", "skii", "skaia" and "skoe" as "Dmitry Poliansky", "Polianskaia", "Polianskoe", and the form "oi" has been replaced by "oy" ("Donskoy" not "Donskoi") for certain family names familiar in this form in English. In some cases "i" has been inserted in place of hard and soft signs, or apostrophes indicating these signs. Hence "Soloviev", not "Solov'ev". The soft sign is not indicated by an apostrophe, as in some transliteration systems, but is dropped completely.

All dates, as in the original, except where otherwise specified, are according to the Julian calendar ("Old Style"); that is, for the seventeenth century, ten days and for the eighteenth century eleven days behind the Gregorian used in the West. A table of weights and measures is included at the front of this volume for the convenience of the reader.

I would like to thank those who helped make this volume possible. Edward Kasinec and Serge Gleboff of the Baltic and Slavic Division of the New York Public Library located some of the references for the notes. The library at Washington University in St. Louis was the source for many of the other notes and also kindly granted permission to reproduce some of the illustrations. The maps and other illustrations are the work of calligrapher and artist Patricia Dresler. A grant from the Europäisches Übersetzer-Kollegium in Straelen, Germany allowed me to use the reference library and facilities of this unique haven for translators from around the world. Dr. G. Edward Orchard has been a helpful and professional editor while Peter von Wahlde saw the manuscript through to publication. Any mistakes or shortcomings are mine. As with my previous volume in this series, my deepest gratitude is to my daughters Maria and Theresa, and to my wife Shannon, and it is to them that this work is dedicated.

Daniel L. Schlafly, Jr.

INTRODUCTION

The present volume originally appeared in 1875 as Chapter 3 of Volume 25 and in 1876 as Chapter I of Volume 26 of Soloviev's *Istoriia Rossii s drevneishikh vremen*. Since 1851 the volumes appeared at the rate of one a year, and by the time he reached the reign of Catherine the Great contemporaries stood in awe of Soloviev's exhaustive research, rigorous scholarly standards and original vision. Although the jubilee planned for the publication of Volume 25 did not occur, in 1876 formal congratulations were presented from a number of individuals and institutions, including the Academy of Sciences and the Moscow archive of the Ministry of Foreign Affairs, the source for so many of the documents he cited. The tone of the Academy's address was typical. "The closer you come to our epoch, the more you have become, not just the sole, but also the most reliable, guide to bygone events. It also has fallen to you to open new paths in recent history, for which present and future researchers of Russia's past doubtless always will mention your name with respect."

Born in 1820, the son of an Orthodox priest, Soloviev received an excellent education at home, at Moscow schools and at the Moscow University, where he earned the *kandidat* degree in 1842. There and in travels in Western Europe from 1842 to 1844, he supplemented his studies of Russian history with wide reading in Western European history and culture. Back in Moscow, Soloviev completed his master's and doctor's degrees by 1848 and began a series of teaching and administrative positions, culminating in the rectorship of Moscow University from 1871 to 1877. He also tutored two sons and successive heirs to the throne of Alexander II, participated in various professional societies and directed the Kremlin Armory. While the *History of Russia* remains his greatest achievement, Soloviev also published a number of specialized studies on topics from early Novgorod to Karamzin and other historians of Russia. For a fuller analysis of Soloviev's life and work with a helpful bibliography, see Carl W. Reddel, "Soloviev, Sergei Mikhailovich (1820-1879)," *The Modern Encyclopedia of Russian and Soviet History*, Academic International Press, Gulf Breeze, Fla., Vol. 36, pp. 145-51.

The two chapters translated in the present volume cover a relatively short period at the outset of Catherine II's reign, the calendar years 1763 and 1764. Like Catherine herself, Soloviev turns his attention now to domestic, now to foreign affairs, in matters great and small. What emerges is a vivid picture of the new empress vigorously asserting her right to the throne she seized six months earlier, sorting out the the legacy of Peter III's favorites and policies and striving to fashion a Russia that would flourish under her autocratic guidance, dominate its neighbors at will and command the respect of other European powers. Recent surveys of Catherine's reign which include useful summaries of the period covered by Soloviev include Isabel de Madariaga, *Russia in the Age of Catherine the Great* (New Haven, 1981) and John T. Alexander, *Catherine the Great. Life and Legend* (New York, 1989). Both include extensive bibliographies.

At first glance these chapters seem to justify the criticism that Soloviev merely continued Karamzin's "statist" approach, as in Alexis Khomiakov's charge that Soloviev considered "not the history of Russia, nor even the history of the Russian state, but only the history of the state principle in Russia." It is true that Soloviev believed the state to be the "necessary form for a people, whose existence is unthinkable without a state," presenting the story of Russia as an organic and continuous evolution and the centralized monarchy as the natural culmination of the historical process. Thus "details and anecdotes about sovereigns and courts, and reports of what one minister said and another one thought always will remain important because the fate of an entire people, and very often the fate of many peoples, depend on these words and thoughts."

This approach initially strikes not just contemporary Slavophile critics like Khomiakov but also modern readers as one-sided, since even in military and diplomatic history we expect broader social and economic analysis, not to mention the "history from below" exemplified in the *Annales* school. Soloviev's methodology and interpretation are particularly effective in dealing with the topic at hand. While Russia was a vast and heterogeneous empire, there were neither rivals to imperial authority nor structures or entities that effectively might challenge the empress's will, even if at times they frustrated or delayed its implementation. Hence all politics ultimately was court politics, with individuals, groups, and the policies they espoused totally dependent on the monarch's will. Soloviev had ample justification for choosing the true center of power as his focus, even if he does not always range far enough afield for modern tastes.

Catherine, and the world, realized that her coup of June 28, 1762 and the murder of Peter III cast a shadow on her claims to legitimacy. But by the time this volume opens on January 1, 1763 she had consolidated her position, and dealt individually with courtiers from Elizabeth I's and Peter III's reigns quickly and decisively. Some, like Andrei Gudovich or Afanasy Davydov, were punished, while others who were too old or did not enjoy the empress's full confidence, like Nikita Trubetskoy or Chancellor Mikhail Vorontsov, were retired with generous rewards. Ivan Shuvalov was cleared of charges concerning his administration of Moscow University and allowed to go abroad. General Peter Rumiantsev, whom Catherine chided for thinking "your previous favor now will be considered a fault," was kept in service despite his links to Peter III.

The empress showed little of this confidence and magnaminity when confronting plots and conspiracies that questioned her right to the throne or challenged the Orlovs' favored position. Although relatively mild punishments were meted out to Chamberlain Fedor Khitrovo's group for promoting a half-baked scheme to displace the Orlovs, the empress was concerned enough to have a special manifesto read on the streets of Moscow threatening "morally and intellectually depraved people" making "insolent or unseemly disclosures" with the "full rigor of the law."

She was even more alarmed by Vasily Mirovich's abortive attempt to free the imprisoned Ivan VI and put him on the throne in her stead. Although it soon was obvious that the plot was the work of a disaffected loner and a few associates, Soloviev paints a vivid picture of Catherine's fear that there was "a spark hidden in the ashes, in St. Petersburg rather than Schlüsselberg" and her concern that the "scoundrels...might be able to spread their poison." We get additional confirmation of the empress's insecurity from the author's portrait of the feebleminded Ivan Antonovich, impossible to imagine as a serious rival, and his details of the elaborate cover-up Catherine ordered.

Catherine lost no time taking decisive action on a number of pending issues. She settled one of these, the vexed question of church domains, which Peter the Great, Elizabeth and Peter III considered but did not resolve, by confiscating church holdings and subordinating the hierarchy even more completely to state control. Although Soloviev admits that the "fifteenth-century solution" which confirmed Joseph of Volokolamsk's support for church possessions, "no longer was possible" and cites Catherine's concern about unrest among ecclesiastical peasants as justification for her action, he clearly disagrees with her philosophical anticlericalism. In sharp contrast to his endorsement of most of Catherine's measures, he takes no position on the issue of church domains and makes a point of praising Bishop Arseny Matseevich, whom Catherine defrocked and imprisoned for opposing confiscation, for his "courage and his persistent defense of his ideas." By the time Soloviev wrote his account it was clear that, whatever the immediate benefits of secularization, both church and state paid a high price for Catherine's enforced solution.

On another perennial issue that reemerged under Peter III, the treatment of Old Believers, Soloviev sympathizes with Catherine's policy of greater tolerance for non-Orthodox religious groups if they cooperated with state authorities. He describes how she encouraged Orthodox bishops to accommodate Old Believer rites and urged more sensitive handling of some Novgorod Old Believers who refused to pay taxes. Eventually she removed all civil disabilities on Old Belief. In another part of the empire, Catherine was not concerned at reports that a converted Kalmyk princess did not observe Orthodox fasts strictly, but was ready to take harsh measures to stop her from asserting any political independence.

Catherine tried to resolve another longstanding problem, the status of the nobility. By 1763 it was obvious that the nobility, contrary to Peter the Great's expectations, had not become the reliable source of trained and dedicated government servants that justified the privileges the state extended to them. The immediate impetus for Catherine's action was noble dissatisfaction with Peter III's manifesto of February 18, 1762, which freed them from compulsory service but did not define noble privileges or legal status clearly. Although a prominent commission to investigate the matter was convened in February 1763, the empress was disgusted when the commission's report eagerly endorsed her recommendation for "broadening noble liberties" but proposed no effective means to "encourage the greatest possible desire to serve." It was not until the Charter on the Nobility of 1785 that a comprehensive official policy was formulated, but neither during Catherine's reign nor later did the Russian nobility ever find a secure and satisfying place in the social and political structure or make a contribution to the general welfare commensurate with its privileged position.

Catherine was equally forceful in pushing for implementation of a census planned since 1761, brushing aside senators' fears that it would not be comprehensive even if major military forces were used and large amounts of money spent. Although Soloviev notes that the empress's directions to the Senate concerning the census "radiated confidence," the new effort soon bogged down in the delays, excuses and plain evasion so often the fate of imperial Russia's government initiatives.

Soloviev describes how Catherine dealt, or tried to deal, with a host of other domestic issues, whether individual cases of wrongdoing or broader issues of organization and policy. Throughout she wavered between relying on talented and dedicated individuals to accomplish reform and designing an institutional structure to achieve her goals. She had no doubt that a single authority was necessary and that she had the wisdom and energy to exercise absolute power effectively. As she put it in her instructions to the new procurator of the Senate, Alexander Viazemsky, "the Russian empire is so vast that autocracy is the only salutary form of government. All others move too slowly and allow countless special interests to fragment and divert the state's power."

Soloviev's account confirms Catherine's view of an immense state threatened by numerous "special interests," but he does not share her confidence that a stream of preemptory orders from St. Petersburg would achieve the desired effect throughout the empire. Using a variety of local examples he describes the abuses, corruption and inefficiency Catherine discovered in institutions throughout the realm, then lists the measures she and her officials took to correct them and reshape Russia along modern European lines. Her faith in centralized autocratic rule led her to pay special attention to the Senate, the highest organ of state. When in August 1763 the empress reviewed the status of directives she delivered to the Senate since her accession, she voiced her frustration that "many of her orders concerning individual petitioners or state affairs have not been executed." In addition to ordering more frequent sessions and exhorting the senators to work together harmoniously, Catherine divided the Senate into six specialized departments and introduced a procedure for resolving disputed cases.

Rational reforms dictated from above were to be applied throughout the empire. Catherine's December 1763 manifesto on the Senate envisioned "devising the proper internal procedures and creating a complete set of judicial and administrative organs. What our empire now has is totally inadequate." Even earlier, in August, she ordered changes in the College of Foreign Affairs to reduce the undigested mass of information that landed on her desk and shorten the lag in responding to Russian envoys abroad.

The greater the distance from the capital and the farther down the administrative hierarchy, the more serious and less tractable the abuses and inefficiency. Soloviev's colorful vignettes, many of them drawn from the Senate archives, provide striking evidence of the gap between Catherine's ideal and the Russian reality. Two governors were caught taking bribes. The bishop of Kolomna complained that the military governor there was "drunk day and night." Records in the Treasury College were in complete disorder, with accounts from 1732 still pending. The College of Manufactures had not submitted the required reports. The archive of the Chief Magistracy was a room "where cases are piled on the floor in bags and bundles." An army captain dragged the mayor of Mtensk out of the magistracy by force and knocked over the judges' bench.

Non-Russians, often victimized by the very officials sent to care for them, suffered even more. Guardians appointed for new converts in the Kazan government "instead ravaged them by extortion and bribery." Prince Alexander Alexeevich Viazemsky reported systematic extortion of Tatars and Votiaks by foresters and tax collectors. In a February 6, 1764 order to the Senate, Catherine noted that collectors of the fur tribute from the native peoples of Siberia "instead unscrupulously plunder and ruin all those defenseless tribute payers."

Soloviev cites other instances of disorder which in a country with a pervasive state presence also automatically involved the central government. A bitter struggle between two groups of Orel merchants escalated into mob violence with murder and arson. Agricultural and foundry peasants protested harsh treatment, while other peasants in the western borderlands fled to Poland to escape harsh landlords. Soloviev is skeptical of Catherine's optimism that maltreatment of peasants could be corrected by administrative action, at one point saying that "the answer lay not in orders but in people to implement them." Nor does he share Catherine's confidence that a modern state could be built with forced labor, commenting that "wherever the historian sees slavery he must assume people will run away and rebel." At the same time Soloviev believes Russia had no alternative, stating that "from time immemorial the Russian land had suffered from a scanty population and inadequate labor force, a shortage impossible to fill with free labor....There were no freemen, for freemen had no reason to choose such arduous and unfamiliar work."

Although Catherine's immediate reaction to these and similar abuses was to investigate, punish those caught in wrongdoing and issue detailed orders to correct the particular problem, from the outset she realized that ad hoc responses were not enough. She wrote that although "since Peter the Great's reign there have been various measures to curb these abuses and the full force of the law applied," the reality was that "coercion and bribery or, in plain words, robbery, have ruined and impoverished our subjects." With characteristic confidence she then claimed that "we have found the quickest and most effective means of eliminating this sorry state of affairs" by appointing "knowledgeable and upright people" to "all judicial positions" with "an appropriate salary."

It was in the same spirit that Catherine looked to the governors as effective agents of reform. Announcing that "I cannot provide every benefit, avert every malady, or take every precaution," she put many local agencies under the governor's authority and gave him increased latitude to deal with official corruption. He was to gather information, submit plans for improvements, promote economic development, stamp out brigandage, "protect and defend the oppressed" and, in general, be the "faithful guardian" of his government.

Catherine preferred uniform rational solutions. Certain problems might require immediate special arrangements, but these were regarded as temporary concessions. As Catherine put it in an instruction to Alexander Viazemsky, it would be "most improper" to abolish the local privileges of the Ukraine, Livonia and Finland immediately, for "these provinces and the Smolensk province should be russified by the gentlest of means." When Yaik Cossacks claimed their leader had violated their rights she dismissed him, yet several years later abolished all Yaik privileges after most of them joined the Pugachev rising. On another occasion she rebuked a state councillor for harassing customs franchise holders, although she opposed the franchise system in principle and formed a special commission to conduct a general review of commerce and the merchant class.

Sometimes a particular issue was exploited to impose greater central control. After the leader of the colony of New Serbia was removed for corruption, Catherine put the new administrators under closer supervision by the governor of Kiev and the War College. Similarly, a dispute over succession to the Ukrainian hetmanate provided the occasion for abolishing the office in favor of a Ukranian College under a Russian president, Peter Rumiantsev. As usual when trying to solve a problem through a firmer exercise of state authority, Catherine found justification for her action in the abuses which "have become endemic as a result of various imprecise foreign laws and statutes." Characteristically, she singled out the clergy, which under "pernicious" Roman Catholic influence were "infected by the insatiable lust for power which has had such widespread and deleterious consequences in previous European history." Soloviev clearly sympathizes with Catherine's policy, not only giving a lengthy summary of Grigory Teplov's memorandum describing the poverty, disorder and corruption in the Ukraine under the hetmanate, but also claiming such conditions were typical when "economic life was rudimentary and state power weak."

Catherine's vision for Russia went beyond reacting to specific problems and devising effective preventive mechanisms for them. She actively recruited foreign settlers, to this end establishing the Chancellery for the Guardianship of Foreigners with special incentives for immigrants. Although the usual delays and difficulties attended the project, this ultimately was one of the most successful of the empress's policies as talented and industrious colonists, most of them from Germany, made contributions far out of proportion to their numbers.

Soloviev paints a graphic picture of the difficulty, if not the impossibility, of reconciling Catherine's various economic goals. She never doubted that devising the right bureaucratic structure and finding the proper people to fill positions would produce the desired results. She spoke of promoting free trade yet at the same time wanted more energetic government action to stimulate development, for example, by the College of Mines to expand production and improve the quality of iron. Her solution for late repayment by merchants of loans from the Commerce Bank was to put it first under the supervision of the College of Commerce, then under Nikolay Golovin. Catherine then confidently ordered that bank supervisors "collect the overdue loans, with interest, by methods that do not ruin trustworthy merchants and hurt the treasury."

A more general problem was that government income was insufficient to cover current expenditures, let alone pay for Catherine's new projects, such as adequate pensions for state employees to reduce the incentive for bribery. Hence the regime resorted to such familiar devices as increasing the amount of copper money in circulation and raising fees on everything from heraldic paper to peasant passports. Yet Catherine would not admit the negative impact of such measures, grandly instructing the Commission for Supervision of State Salt and Alcohol Revenues to "search for means to maintain and increase income for the treasury that do not burden the people."

Why did Catherine fail to realize her dream of equitable administration, economic prosperity and social harmony? In some cases orders were ill-conceived or incompatible with other decrees. And, for all her talk of "knowledgeable and upright people," Catherine rarely looked beyond a restricted circle of courtiers when making assignments. It also was impossible to establish and maintain regular bureaucratic procedures when the autocrat intervened at will to override or alter existing structures and appoint or remove personnel. Neither then nor later did Russia have a true civil society and a genuine respect for law rather than automatic deference to superior authority. The conviction that individuals and groups had no intrinsic rights and were subject to the whim of the state or any of its officials was too deeply ingrained. It was assumed that enhancing the prestige and exercising the authority of the state automatically would insure popular welfare. Catherine never admitted that, no matter how sincere her commitment to her subjects and however zealous her efforts on their behalf, there was a fundamental flaw in ruling by autocratic decree. It was inherently contradictory to insist that her subordinates act responsibly and effectively while simultaneously executing the monarch's wishes without question. The system encouraged neither flexibility and sympathy by officials nor autonomy and energy by those subject to their authority.

In the foreign arena, to which Soloviev devotes the bulk of his narrative in this volume, Catherine's Russia was a nation with extensive interests and even broader ambitions. The conquests of the Great Northern War (1700-1721) made Russia a major power and it played this role thereafter, most recently in the Seven Years War (1756-1763). This was a position Catherine was anxious to exploit and extend. "Obviously I think Russia deserves notice," she told Baron Breteuil as the French diplomat left Russia. "I will fight when necessary...when reason tells me to."

Poland provided the best opportunity for expanding Russian power. Since the days of Peter the Great Russia intervened there more and more blatantly, so that by 1764 Nikita Panin could speak of "the role which Russia hitherto...alone has played [in Poland], one acknowledged by other powers." Soloviev, who covered some of the same ground in his *Istoriia padeniia Polshi* (History of the Fall of Poland) published in 1863, vividly describes how Catherine used Russia's self-proclaimed protectorate over Poland to take advantage of domestic weakness and division to seize opportunities as they arose. Russian strong-arm tactics used to depose the Polish-Saxon prince Karl as duke of Courland and install Ernst Biron in his stead foreshadowed those Catherine employed in Poland itself. "If the Polish court ignores the empress's friendly representations," the Russian resident in Courland Matthias von Simolin told a Polish royal commissioner, "there are, if absolutely necessary, ways to render justice to the aggrieved party." Catherine was even blunter after the Courland coup, saying she would not "allow that court [Poland] unilaterally to violate its kingdom's statutes" when August III sent forces to the frontier without prior agreement from the Sejm.

Soloviev has scant sympathy for Poland. Despite his detailed account of corruption and abuse at the lower levels of Russian life, Catherine and her leading statesmen, given occasional lapses and mistakes of judgment, are portrayed as honest, dedicated and patriotic and the Russian empire as an effectively functioning entity. In Poland, by contrast, he saw a state paralyzed by venality and factionalism at all levels of society, whose impotence justified intervention by its stronger neighbor. After describing peasant flight to Poland, for example, Soloviev writes that "as ruler of a more powerful state Catherine could not tolerate a weaker country on her border allowing continual migration from its mighty neighbor."

Promoting Russian interests in Poland was far more challenging than putting a Russian puppet on the throne of Courland. The most vivid pages in this volume are those describing Catherine's success in electing her client, Stanisław Poniatowski, king of Poland after the death of August III. This required a coordinated campaign simultaneously publicizing alleged persecution of the Orthodox minority in the Commonwealth, building a pro-Russian party among the Polish gentry, blocking rival candidates from Poland and abroad, and diplomatic initiatives in various courts to insure support of, or at least acquiescence in, Russia's choice.

Soloviev guides us through the tangled rivalries of Poland's great families, showing at every step of the way how the Russian envoys in Poland, Count Hermann Karl von Keyserling and Nikolay Repnin, used persuasion, bribery and even military force at Catherine's behest to promote Poniatowski's cause. Catherine told Keyserling that he could "give the primate up to one hundred thousand rubles to assure his personal loyalty," while Panin wrote the envoy that "[Russian] forces should be stationed nearby" when the electoral Sejm convened to insure Poniatowski's election. St. Petersburg made it clear that in return for political and financial support the new king was to induce Poland to follow Russian dictates. Panin wrote to Keyserling that "if the Commonwealth does not respect her imperial majesty sufficiently for defending a just cause, its further stubbornness will compel her to achieve by certain necessary means what recognition of her magnificent friendship and benevolence could not."

Soloviev never directly criticizes Catherine's policy towards Poland but he clearly sympathizes with Poniatowski's vain hopes for reform and, by implication, holds Russia and Prussia at least partly responsible for Poland's problems. After reading Catherine's expressions of outrage at abuses in Russia and her declarations of the need for a strong monarchy to curb disorder and achieve reforms within the empire, it is impossible not to be struck by the cynicism with which she opposed strengthening the crown in Poland or Sweden. Of course, weak and unstable neighbors meant more opportunity for Russian interference.

Soloviev makes it clear that what he calls the "great obstacles" to reform were Russia and Prussia. He quotes Poniatowski's angry response when the Russian and Prussian ambassadors warned him against trying to abolish the *liberum veto.* "What! It is our friends and allies who will not let us escape our stagnation!" After his description of the new king's impossible position, the reader can only smile at Madame Geoffrin's comment that after his election she saw "Poland rising from the ashes...in radiant splendor like the new Jerusalem!" For a modern treatment of Poland, see Herbert Kaplan, *The First Partition of Poland* (New York, 1962). Also see Norman Davies, *God's Playground. A History of Poland*, 2 vols. (New York, 1984), Vol. 1, pp. 511ff., for an account which is much less favorable to Russia than Soloviev's.

Soloviev also describes how Poland became the nexus for Russia's relations with other powers. Russia was at war with Prussia as recently as 1762, and disputes between the two countries over Saxony continued into 1763. Yet Frederick II felt isolated without allies and realized he and Catherine had common interests in Poland, paving the way for ever-closer cooperation. Soloviev's excerpts from the correspondence between the two monarchs shows how quickly they agreed to support Poniatowski's candidacy and block all reforms that would strengthen the Polish state. "Naturally I turned to your majesty when I learned the Polish king was dead," Catherine wrote to the Prussian king after the death of August III. The two powers also worked together in Sweden and Turkey, a friendship solidified by a formal alliance signed in March, 1764.

This community of interest at Poland's expense between its powerful neighbors became one of the enduring relationships in European history.

Russia and Prussia carried this policy to its ultimate conclusion in three partitions of Poland later in Catherine's reign, proposals for which already were circulating at this time. Prussia and Russia cooperated in suppressing Polish nationalism in the nineteenth century in the Convention of Alvensleben in 1863, and as recently as 1939 the Molotov-Ribbentrop pact continued the tradition begun by Catherine and Frederick. No wonder the Poles were alarmed by the 1990 talks between the Russian and German leaders, Mikhail Gorbachev and Helmut Kohl, in 1990 which paved the way for German reunification the following year.

Russia's relations with another bordering state, Sweden, had certain similarities to those with Poland. Both once were major regional powers that invaded Russia. By 1763 each lost influence and territory to its eastern neighbor and saw Russia play an ever stronger role in its domestic affairs. In Sweden as in Poland, Russia freely used bribery and pressure to support a pro-Russian party among the nobility, weaken the power of the crown and work in concert with Prussia and England to counter the efforts of its principal international opponent, France. Soloviev has a detailed description how in Stockholm the Russian envoy Ivan Ostermann prevented Sweden from opposing Russia's candidate for the Polish crown yet failed to gain decisive advantage over France and its supporters. His account of relations with Denmark is more cursory. There the foreign minister Johann Bernstorff was a friend of Catherine's and a loyal supporter of Russia whose fears that Russia would not protect Denmark against a possible Swedish threat were mollified easily.

Just as Poland was the key to Russia's closer ties with Prussia, it also was uppermost in Catherine's mind as she dealt with England. Soloviev describes how Russia sought English financial support for its efforts in Sweden as well as in Poland by portraying them as part of a general anti-French strategy. To this end Catherine delayed signing the alliance and commercial treaty London coveted, telling her chancellor Mikhail Vorontsov in February, 1764 that "we want an agreement on the future Polish royal elections before concluding a treaty of alliance."

Reaching consensus with England proved more difficult than with Prussia. Soloviev offers a comprehensive analysis how different political systems, divergent foreign policy goals, and the lack of confidence each country had in its minister in the other's capital meant limited results. If Russia could use "the empress's preoccupation with a multitude of pressing domestic issues" as an excuse for delaying treaty negotiations,

England cited parliamentary opposition in refusing requests for large subsidies in Poland. Soloviev concludes that "funds might be extracted with difficulty for Sweden because they would be used against the French enemy, but there was no asking England to throw pounds into a Poland which did not concern it." Nor was England anxious to be drawn into a possible Russian conflict with Turkey. Although Russia sent Friedrich Gross to replace Alexander Vorontsov in London, and England recalled the earl of Buckinghamshire in favor of George Macartney, fundamental policy differences between the two powers precluded any lasting ties.

Russia's relations with Austria also were dominated by the Polish question. Vienna preferred that one of the Saxon princes succeed August III and encouraged High Crown Hetman Jan Branicki to support a Saxon candidate against the Russian-backed Poniatowski and his Polish supporters. Catherine and her statesmen recognized that Austria might raise obstacles but was too exhausted after the Seven Years War to block Russia's plans. Soloviev quotes Maria Theresa's frank admission that "I cannot consider sending forces into Poland, for that might draw me into a new war when the wounds of the last one have not healed yet."

Russia also knew that insisting on dominance in Poland in conjunction with Prussia would make future cooperation with its erstwhile ally, Austria, difficult, if not impossible. Thus Nikolay Obrezkov, the Russian resident in Constantinople was rebuffed coldly when he tried to enlist his Austrian counterpart's support in opposing a Turkish-Prussian alliance. Soloviev makes it clear St. Petersburg was willing to pay the price, quoting Panin's comment that "Mr. Kaunitz [the Austrian chancellor] equates his interests in Poland with ours for nought. Any policy we adopt will create serious differences. We will lose a third of our power and preeminence if we do not control Poland."

Soloviev's discussion of Russian relations with Turkey further reflects the primary importance of the Polish question. In Constantinople, as in Warsaw, cooperation between Russian and Prussian envoys was able to win the Porte's acceptance of Poniatowski's candidacy despite strenuous opposition from France and Austria. Here, as elsewhere, Catherine was willing to use every means necessary to achieve her goals. Obrezkov was instructed to spend money to buy support for Russian aims and even to depose the Turkish vizier if he made too much trouble. Soloviev provides a step-by-step narrative of Obrezkov's skillful application of judicious bribery, flattery, bluster and dissimulation to carry the day for Russia, earning him praise from Panin for his "political insight." The author's brief description of the first Russian vessel to enter the Mediterranean suggested that Catherine looked to a more active role there. A few years later Alexis Orlov's squadron smashed a Turkish fleet at Chesme and established Russia as a major power in the region.

Aside from Catherine's failure to gain the upper hand in Sweden and win English financial support for Russian efforts in Poland, the years 1763 and 1764 were very successful for Russian foreign policy. The em-press's boldness and energy contributed to this success, but a more important reason was that the Seven Years War exhausted Prussia, Austria and France, the other major powers on the continent. With Prussia now a Russian ally and Austria neither willing nor able to make more than a token protest against Russian policies, only France offered any resistance, and this was largely ineffectual. A French ministerial report in May 1764 in effect conceded Poland to Prussia and Russia, concluding that "no direct relationship between France and Poland exists." Panin, correctly predicting that "it [France] will do nothing to thwart us except intrigue on a grand scale and spend a certain amount of money," noted that St. Petersburg might proceed in Poland more or less with a free hand.

Thus France recalled its envoy from Poland after it became obvious he could not block Russian moves there and, as we saw, failed to incite the Porte to take a strong stand against Poniatowski's candidacy. Only in Sweden was France able to frustrate Russian policy, and even there the outcome was a stalemate rather than a clear-cut victory. Soloviev's account of French policy in this period is a most unedifying depiction of a great power now too weakened to maintain its former dominance. Unable to realize its grandiose ambitions, yet unwilling to surrender them, France was reduced to petty plots and vain hopes that opposition to Catherine at home or quarrels with her new Prussian ally would succeed where diminished French power could not. Soloviev quotes French diplomatic correspondence claiming that Catherine's "tyrannical measures promote unrest rather than suppressing it," encouraging the French *chargé d'affaires* in St. Petersburg "to proceed very cautiously" in "probing the nation's sentiments and intentions," and describing Russia's alliance with Prussia as "fundamentally unsound."

Soloviev includes a brief description of Russian interests on its distant eastern frontier. Long after the expeditions of Bering and others Asia remained a peripheral concern, although the Senate's interest in commercial and security issues on the Chinese border was a portent of Russia's increased attention to the region in the nineteenth century. The College of Foreign Affairs cited "the Chinese court's unmistakable obstinacy" to plans to put boats on the Amur river, but shortly thereafter a special conference recommended strengthening Russian forces in the Far East, settling native peoples closer to the frontier and protecting Russian trade with China.

While much of Soloviev's treatment of Russia's international relations in this volume is a narration of ad hoc responses to specific opportunities and crises, particularly to those in Poland, he positions these in the broader context of Nikita Panin's displacement of Alexis Bestuzhev as the dominant figure in foreign affairs. What Soloviev describes as "the beginning of Panin's complete authority" came when Stanisław Poniatowski, whom Panin persuaded Catherine to back for the Polish crown over Bestuzhev's preference for one of the Saxon princes, was chosen king. "This deed has increased my confidence in you immeasurably," Catherine wrote to Panin after the election, "because now I see how correct all your measures were." No wonder the numerous comments and instructions Soloviev quotes from Panin reflect the assurance that he spoke in the empress's name.

Behind Catherine's and Panin's individual measures we see the emergence of the Northern System first proposed by Russia's ambassador to Denmark Johann Korff as "a prominent and forceful group of powers in the north...to oppose the Bourbon alliance...[and] Austria." Despite Russian successes in Poland and elsewhere Soloviev argues the concept behind the new alignment was fundamentally flawed. He points out that although Frederick II made an alliance focused on Poland "he wanted no part of any system with obligations to secondary powers," while England "was even more opposed to any system which offered no immediate commercial benefit."

Within a few years Panin's grand design collapsed. Prussia cooperated with Russia on specific matters elsewhere, but really was interested only in Poland, and even here pushed Russia into a partition of the latter it hoped to avoid. England and Russia were even farther apart. Common hostility to France was insufficient for a formal alliance, nor was overall policy coordinated except in isolated instances. In Sweden Russian efforts to undermine the French party were frustrated, and the pro-Russian Bernstorff's disgrace in 1770 ended Russia's dominance in Denmark. The failure of Panin's foreign policy and Catherine's suspicion of his alleged partiality for Grand Duke Paul eventually led to his fall in 1781. An excellent analysis of the Northern System is David M. Griffiths, "The Rise and Fall of the Northern System. Court Politics and Foreign Policy in the First Half of Catherine's Reign," *Canadian Slavic Studies*, IV, No. 3 (Fall, 1970), pp. 547-69. Also see David L. Ransel, *The Politics of Catherinian Russia. The Panin Party* (New Haven, 1975).

As in the other volumes of the *History* Soloviev's pace is unhurried, allowing the reader to participate in the gradual unfolding of a complex theme by citing extensive excerpts from primary sources. He once said that his narrative should be shaped by "the course of external events" rather than by abstract principles. In his treatment of both domestic and foreign affairs, Soloviev lingers on what might appear to be extraneous details, but which give the reader the context in which decisions were made and policies formulated. Thus he moves from reports of local events to the Senate's reaction to these, and then to Catherine's decisions and how they were implemented. Often, as when he describes confiscation of church lands or abolition of the Ukrainian hetmanate, Soloviev puts the issue in historical context. He lets his analysis emerge from the sources themselves, often giving pages of documentation without comment or just a summary sentence or two. His sources are so carefully orchestrated that the author's interpretation seems to be the logical and inevitable conclusion of the flow of events.

Thus Soloviev goes far beyond a simple recounting of the Mirovich conspiracy by tracing Mirovich's family background, accompanying him step-by-step as he tries to free Ivan VI from Schlüsselberg. He quotes Catherine's frantic reaction to news of the attempted coup and describes Mirovich's interrogation and execution in detail. He even tells us that when the crowd saw Mirovich's head in the executioner's hands "they all cried out at once and shuddered so hard the bridge [crowded with spectators] swayed and threatened to collapse." Similarly, Soloviev's account of Stanisław Poniatowski's ascension to the Polish throne is a mosaic of various perspectives, whether those of his Czartoryski relatives, other Polish factions, foreign powers, Russian diplomats and statesmen, Catherine herself or even Poniatowski's indulgent French patron, Madame Geoffrin. The reader is left with an unforgettable portrait of the new king as charming and talented, but painfully aware that he and his state were the helpless pawns of domestic and foreign forces.

As in earlier volumes of his *History*, Soloviev here finds most of his primary material in official Russian archives. He makes extensive use of the Archive of the Ministry of Foreign Affairs, today the Foreign Policy Archive of the Russian Federation, from which he excerpts or summarizes the reports of Russian diplomats abroad and Catherine's and Panin's replies to them, reports from diplomats of other countries, official correspondence with foreign courts, texts of proposals, and the like. The result is a panoramic survey of Russia's interests along the periphery of its vast empire, from Sweden in the Baltic to China in the Pacific.

The principal sources for domestic affairs are the Senate Archive and State Archive, with occasional recourse to the Synodal Archive. All three now are included in the Russian State Archive of Ancient Acts. There is no archival material from outside Russia in this volume. Extensive use is made of published primary sources, particularly from the *Sbornik Russkogo istoricheskogo obshchestva* (Collection of the Russian Historical Society), from which Soloviev quotes many of Catherine's writings. He draws heavily on the *Russkii arkhiv* (Russian Archive), with additional material from the *Chteniia v Obshchestve istorii i drevnostei rossiiskikh* (Materials Read in the Society for Russian Antiquities and History). Soloviev also uses the *Polnoe sobranie zakonov* (Complete Collection of Laws), with occasional items from the *Sankt-peterburgskie vedomosti* (St. Petersburg News).

Other Russian documentary publications cited include the third volume of the *Sochineniia Imperatritsy Ekateriny II* (Literary Works of Empress Catherine II) published in 1850, part one of the *Sobranie postanovlennii po chasti raskola, sostoiavshikhsia po vedomstu Sinoda* (Collection of Orders Concerning Old Belief, Compiled by the Synodal Bureau) published in 1860, the second volume of the *Zapiski o yuzhnoi Rossii* (Notes on Southern Russia) which appeared in 1857, and S.A. Poroshin's 1844 work, *Zapiski sluzhashchie k istorii e.i.v. tsesarevicha i velikogo kniazia Pavla Petrovicha* (Notes on the History of His Imperial Highness, the Tsarevich and Grand Duke Paul Petrovich). Soloviev quotes as well from the published writings of G.R. Derzhavin, E.R. Dashkova, and A.V. Khrapovitsky.

Non-Russian sources cited include the second volume of the *Memoirs of Frederick II, King of Prussia*, published in 1866; the first volume of M.E. Boutaric's edition of the *Secret and Unedited Correspondence of Louis XV*, which also appeared in 1866; Volume 3 of F. Raumer's *Essays on Recent History, From the British and French State Archives*, published in 1839; Volume 9 of the *Researches in German History*, published in

1869; the first volume of Alexis de Saint-Priest's *Diplomatic and Literary Studies*; and the *Unedited Correspondence of King Stanisław Poniatowski and Madame Geoffrin (1764-1777).*

Since these volumes appeared in 1875 and 1876, additional primary sources for this period were published, among them the two volumes of King Stanisław Poniatowski's memoirs (1914-1924) and a massive forty-six-volume edition of Frederick II's political correspondence (1879-1939). English translations of sources for topics covered by Soloviev here still are sparse, except for occasional excerpts in handbooks of selected primary documents or secondary works.

Few historians can equal Soloviev's volume of sources or the skill with which he chose and juxtaposed his citations to assemble a coherent and comprehensive picture of Russia's domestic and international situation, whether for the period 1763-1764 in this volume or its evolution over the centuries in the *History* as a whole. Admittedly his vantage point here is that of Catherine and her inner circle, and while he may disagree with particular policies he lets Catherine's priorities dictate the attention he devotes to particular topics. Yet it was precisely the people who dominate Soloviev's account who shaped the events he describes, and he succeeds brilliantly in bringing them to life on the political stage. His canvas is broad and he paints it in rich detail, yet never loses sight of the contours of the whole. His picture of the personalities and events of this short but extraordinary complex period can be savored both on its own merits and as one component of his vast panorama of Russian history.

At first sight, Catherine's empire as described by Soloviev seems impossibly remote from today's Russian Federation. Growth and confidence have given way to contraction and irresolution. The power of the central government is dwindling rather than expanding. Russia once exploited disorder in neighbors like Poland, Sweden and Turkey. Today these same neighbors are relatively stable, and it is Russia that is unsteady and unpredictable. But the Russia Soloviev portrays in this volume also had a weak civil society, a corrupt and arbitrary bureaucracy, local turmoil and a leader who believed issuing orders could solve all problems. The *History of Russia* can can be read, not just as a chronicle of Russia's rise, but also as a prophecy of its present crisis.

HISTORY OF RUSSIA

Volume 43

Catherine the Great in Power

Domestic and Foreign Affairs
1763-1764

I

CATHERINE IN POWER, 1763

CELEBRATION OF THE NEW YEAR

In Moscow the court greeted the new year of 1763 with the customary festivities. There was a special celebration of January 1 in the new capital by the sea. The commanding naval and infantry officers and the field and company grade officers attended a banquet at the home of Vice Admiral Prince Meshchersky,[1] cannons were fired and toasts raised to the empress's health. In the evening there were fireworks followed by a ball. The ceremonies celebrated awarding the title of admiral general to the empress's heir Paul Petrovich.[2] The empress was motivated by her ardent and tireless concern for the welfare of the state, an edict stated, which required maintaining the fleet in peak condition. Despite the grand duke's tender age she wanted to instruct him in state affairs, following the example of Peter the Great.[3] The former general admiral Prince Mikhail Mikhailovich Golitsyn[4] retired permanently after sixty years of service on full pay (seven thousand rubles) for life.[5]

IVAN SHUVALOV AND MOSCOW UNIVERSITY

After Golitsyn's retirement Count Alexander Shuvalov's[6] was announced, confirming the grant of two thousand souls to him "under the former and previous regime."[7] Ivan Ivanovich Shuvalov's[8] permanent retirement was opposed as a reward just for long term service. He remained in service but was permitted to go abroad because his situation at court and in the capital had become unbearable. The empress obviously disliked him, and malcontents labelled him the chief troublemaker. He must have known that those who resented his prominence at the end of Elizabeth's[9] reign were conniving against him. These malcontents, Panin[10] and Bestuzhev,[11] were Catherine's principal advisors.

Ivan Shuvalov paid a price for his fall from power. A certain Adadurov,[12] one of the greatest malcontents at the end of Elizabeth's reign, was named the second curator of Moscow University.[13] As early as December 17, 1762 Adadurov reported to the Senate that all payments Shuvalov made from university funds on credit were *illegal.* Adadurov complained that the borrowed money disbursed by Shuvalov was yet to be recovered, although payment was past due. The money was spent illegally, leaving nothing to pay either the university employee salaries due September 3 or the university's debts. Adadurov asked for instructions and wanted Shuvalov to return all university property he had, without exception, to the university chancellery. This meant written records, instruments and so on. After hearing the report the empress ordered that Shuvalov be directed to respond.

A month later his reply was ready, enumerating and justifying all expenses. Shuvalov pointed out that Elizabeth personally wrote on the proposal establishing the university that "state funds are to be disbursed at the discretion of the curators." Consequently the curators enjoyed complete confidence in their conduct of all university business. There was no alternative, because the state lacked the necessary resources, regulations were inadequate and instructions did not cover all contingencies. This was true especially at the outset when Shuvalov was more concerned with establishing and expanding the university than with following chancellery procedures to the letter. It was the only thing to do. The university chancellery was not constituted as a regulatory body because the university curators had exclusive supervision.

Shuvalov reported how he developed the university and provided everything it needed. It had a library of about five thousand volumes, not counting books distributed yearly in classes or those given annually as prizes to outstanding students. These books were worth almost twelve thousand rubles. The university had an extensive mineral collection which Shuvalov had supplied, costing at least twenty thousand rubles. It also had a laboratory and a sizable number of the most essential prime mathematical instruments. More than twenty-five thousand rubles was spent for the press, which was in excellent condition.

The university's greatest achievement was its eighteen hundred graduates since its founding, all but three hundred of them nobles, most with good marks. Ten of these now served admirably as instructors of mathematics, Latin, French and German in the Corps of Cadets. The knowledge and diligence of others now studying abroad certainly would benefit their fatherland. The recently established gymnasium in Kazan also had achieved significant results.

Finally Shuvalov pointed out that the university had an income of thirty-five thousand rubles in 1761, while expenses were just 31,675 rubles. The six thousand rubles loaned to the wife of Major General Plemiannikov, the thousand rubles to Second Lieutenant Debrini, the twenty-five hundred rubles to Count Yaguzhinsky[14] and the five hundred rubles to Councillor Kheraskov[15] would not be lost, because there were receipts, promissory notes and guarantees. The former director of the university Argamakov lent five hundred rubles to Catherine Korf. She died and the money could not be recovered. This same Argamakov took two thousand rubles for himself and died without repaying it. On the other hand Argamakov gave a lot of his own property to the university. The money lent to the actor Serini for a promissory note of 4,744 rubles could not be recovered because he had died. In conclusion Shuvalov complained that Adadurov's statement caused him grief and injury and was motivated solely by malice.

The Senate decided that Shuvalov must repay the money he lent to the actor Serini because he did not get a receipt or a guarantee. Argamakov's heirs were to be asked for the money he took. Since Shuvalov stated that Argamakov had given much of his own property to the university, the Senate referred the matter for decision by her imperial majesty. Shuvalov's complaint against Adadurov was unjustified because Adadurov only wanted to restore order. Catherine responded to the Senate's report with a handwritten order. "The university was entrusted to Lieutenant General Ivan Shuvalov by order of Empress Elizabeth. Everyone knows he founded it, and it seems he has accomplished more good than evil. There have been some irregularities because it is so new. Shuvalov should not be held accountable for the four thousand rubles given to Serini because he spent at least that much, if not more, of his own money for the new enterprise. For the same reason Argamakov should not be held accountable. Curator Adadurov is to submit a plan and a staff for the university for approval, taking income into account. If he thinks additional funds would help establish order and improve the university, he should recommend increasing the present appropriation, because minor expenditures should not prevent the greater good."

Shuvalov went abroad but remained a curator of the university he founded. The empress's circle, and educated people in general, considered him a patron of the arts. He enjoyed the same reputation abroad and corresponded with the leading European literary figure, Voltaire.[16] Shuvalov's image among some of the general public forced those who laughed at public opinion, and felt compelled to oppose it, to respect him more. Derzhavin,[17] then a soldier in one of the Moscow guards regiments, described this public opinion. When he heard that Shuvalov was going abroad, he considered asking Shuvalov to take him along to further his education. Derzhavin had an aunt in Moscow who believed Shuvalov was the leader of the freemasons,[18] who were apostates, heretics, blasphemers, disciples of the Antichrist and people who could kill their enemies several thousand versts away. The aunt gave Derzhavin a severe scolding and in the strongest possible terms forbade him to approach Shuvalov. She threatened to write his mother if he disobeyed. Derzhavin obeyed.[19]

VORONTSOV'S RETIREMENT

At the time Ivan Shuvalov, spokesman for the new learning, was sent abroad honorably, Prince Nikita Yurievich Trubetskoy,[20] a member of the old "learned guard" of Feofan Prokopovich[21] and a friend of Cantemir's,[22] was retired permanently. He received full pay instead of a pension, and a one-time sum of fifty thousand rubles. Chancellor Vorontsov,[23] still young compared to Trubetskoy, went abroad for two years for health reasons. Vorontsov never enjoyed the full benefits of his triumph under Bestuzhev because his ambition exceeded his intellectual talents. Under Elizabeth Ivan Shuvalov took the active role, while under Peter III Goltz[24] was in charge, and if not Goltz, then Volkov.[25]

Under Catherine II Vorontsov realized the empress lacked confidence in him and that his two principal advisors on foreign affairs, Panin and Bestuzhev, opposed him. Although they soon became rivals, this did not help Vorontsov. Dissatisfaction with his service conditions prevented improvement in Vorontsov's chronically poor health, which also suffered from his financial problems. He spent too much money on family issues caused by the unhappy marriage of his only daughter to Count Stroganov.[26] Thus Vorontsov always could attribute his retirement to poor health. Because he was absent for two years, retaining the rank of chancellor, responsibility for foreign affairs temporarily was entrusted to Panin. "Under the present difficult circumstances," the order stated, "her imperial majesty thought it best to entrust the supervision and direction of all College of Foreign Affairs matters to Senior Privy Councillor Panin during the chancellor's absence. He is to serve in that college to the extent his other duties permit."

CATHERINE TRIES TO IMPROVE THE COLLEGE OF FOREIGN AFFAIRS

The empress described her relationship to the College of Foreign Affairs in an interesting note dated August 21. "Our ministers at foreign courts complain that their reports are neither acknowledged nor acted on. After reading the reports there are too many items for me to give them the necessary attention, neither can I consider all the factors required for their successful resolution. Therefore I direct the members of the College of Foreign Affairs to submit proposals at least every two months, having read each minister's reports in order. These proposals shall reflect our basic interests and, with our orders appended, will provide replies and instructions to the ministers. We hope implementation of this measure will enable our College of Foreign Affairs to discharge its responsibilities most successfully. A report on this matter is to be submitted for our approval. At present the college sends nothing except reports as they are received. These await decision, which for the aforementioned reasons does not follow in every case."[27]

ZAKHAR CHERNYSHEV'S RETIREMENT RESCINDED

Zakhar Chernyshev,[28] the second general who passed through the school of the Seven Years War, was retired for reasons unknown. Apparently Chernyshev was disappointed because he thought he was being held back. When he was retired he requested an audience with the empress, anxious to make his case in person and to remind Catherine of her favor to him when she was grand duchess. After he was refused Chernyshev wrote a humble letter, asking for pardon and expressing his willingness to serve again. The following year his petition was accepted[29] and he resumed his former position as vice president of the War College.

RUMIANTSEV REMAINS IN SERVICE

The first general to pass through the school of the Seven Years War had a different fate. Rumiantsev[30] thought his career was finished under Catherine because Peter III favored him. His request for retirement elicited the following letter from the empress. "General Rumiantsev! I received your letter requesting retirement. I felt I must explain my reasons since I see you are unaware of them. You judge me by previous standards when a man's personality was more important than his merit or service. You think your previous favor now will be considered a fault which your enemies will use to their advantage. Let me say that you do not know me well. Come here, if your health permits, and you will be received with the favor befitting your rank and your services to the fatherland.

"Do not think that I want to force you back into service unwillingly, far from it. Not just a general who has done his service but every Russian nobleman has the right to decide whether to serve or to retire. I do not want to limit this prerogative, but rather confirm it without exception. I only write to you that we might understand each other and that you might see my intentions clearly. When another was sent to replace you, things seemed confused and in fact were confused. Perhaps you suspected that I did not trust you, but you should put this behind you as something I have forgotten completely."[31] Rumiantsev remained in service.

FATE OF VOLKOV, GUDOVICH, CHERNYSHEV AND TODTLEBEN

Catherine forgot neither Rumiantsev's friend Todtleben[32] nor his splendid talents. Since she received frequent complaints about the Orenburg governor Davydov[33] she decided to remove him and name Volkov to this important post. The empress's confidence in Volkov deserves notice. "The Orenburg Vice-Governor Volkov," her order stated, "is named governor there with full power, which her imperial highness entrusts to him because he can draft various reports and submit projects to her majesty."[34]

The third person often mentioned "in the previous regime" was Gudovich.[35] There was no reason to remember him or to keep him in service. We saw that the Senate recommended the villages Peter III had awarded him be taken away.[36] Catherine agreed with the Senate's opinion, the villages were confiscated, while Gudovich received ten thousand rubles in compensation![37] Andrei Chernyshev,[38] an old courtier who enjoyed Grand Duchess Catherine's special favor and suffered as a result,[39] proved unfit for service. He was retired but awarded the rank of major general.[40]

Todtleben's case was not settled until that year either. A military court sentenced him to death, but the empress realized that his plot caused the state no harm and that the criminal had spent three years under arrest. She ordered him sent abroad under heavy guard and stripped of his ranks and decorations.

CLASH BETWEEN BESTUZHEV AND PANIN

Some prominent figures from previous reigns disappeared either permanently or temporarily. Others from the same circles reemerged after momentary disgrace. The new men, on whom Catherine doted and whom she called her pupils, as yet were not in evidence. Bestuzhev and Panin were in the forefront, the former the famous chancellor of the Elizabethan era, and the latter a student of Bestuzhev's foreign policy. But when jointly they confronted the wreckage of the old system,[41] teacher and pupil fell out. Both concurred there should be no rapprochement with France, but disagreed strongly over the old man Bestuzhev's unwillingness to hear about France or Prussia. He wanted to restore the old system, the former alliance between Russia, Austria, England and Saxony, to permit the Saxon elector to reign in Poland again.[42] Panin repudiated the old system completely, planning instead a Northern alliance, a Northern *concert* or *accord,* to use the expression then current. This would unite Russia, Prussia, Poland, England and Scandinavia in opposition to a Southern alliance between France, Spain and Austria. The obstinate Bestuzhev refused to defer to his student, creating an open rift between them.

"I have settled accounts with Count Bestuzhev," Panin told the Prussian ambassador Solms,[43] "and have repaid all my previous obligations. I owe him nothing, and I do not count him among my friends."[44] Panin apparently referred to his role in Bestuzhev's acquittal, since he wrote the manifesto which announced it.[45] A little more than six months after this conversation, Panin complained to Solms about his situation, and said he wanted to eradicate what remained of Bestuzhev's influence.[46]

This influence is understandable. Catherine realized that Bestuzhev was not the great chancellor he once was, and no longer could conduct foreign policy. She knew he was obstinate and had experienced the unpleasant consequences of his stubbornness, but she could not help respecting the old man for his obstinacy. She well remembered that this same Bestuzhev was the sworn enemy of her influence, and particularly that of her mother, when it harmed the interests of the empire. Yet he came over to her side and became her most loyal ally when forced to do so by a terrible threat to the interests of the empire.[47]

Catherine indignantly rejected foreign accusations of venality against Bestuzhev. "That is a lie," she said, "Bestuzhev was as solid as a rock and never for sale." She had a different opinion of Bestuzhev's rival Vorontsov. "There never has been such a hypocrite. He sold himself to the first buyer, and every court had him on its payroll."[48] Finally Bestuzhev gained enough power that Panin ceased demanding an imperial council be established. Bestuzhev remained true to his convictions although he knew his obstinacy was annoying. He felt compelled to use every kind of flattery and servility to counter this annoyance. The old man's fear when the empress's wrath burst on him completely unexpectedly in March easily can be imagined.

II

ARSENY MATSEEVICH AND FEDOR KHITROVO

THE ARSENY MATSEEVICH AFFAIR

We saw how Catherine felt she had to show mercy to those who had transgressed against her in some way.[1] Those publicly incurring the empress's displeasure were sent away as punishment, most of them honorably and with rewards. Thus it was all the more surprising that Catherine acted very harshly, angrily and even spitefully in persecuting someone whose rank apparently deserved greater consideration. This was the hierarch of Rostov, Arseny Matseevich.[2] We observed that Catherine inherited the difficult problem of church lands from her predecessors.[3] Continual unrest among the monastic peasants brought it to the fore again. When Catherine returned the estates which Peter III placed under secular administration the hierarchs and the monastic authorities were placated, but the peasants were not.

Peasant disturbances prompted the establishment of a commission to resolve the matter. The commission was established, and naturally its first task was to collect all available information on the monastic estates. Only impartial people with no incentive to produce erroneous results could assemble the necessary inventories. A new commission appeared with new officers who recorded all church holdings. There were ominous premonitions, renewed dissatisfaction and grumbling. A proclamation, approved by the throne, said there would be no commission, but now here it was again!

Some grumbled quietly among themselves, but then a man appeared who was not afraid to raise his voice and proceeded to do so. Arseny Matseevich was one of those learned Ukranian monks first summoned by Peter I to Great Russia to fill ecclesiastical positions when he needed educated pastors able to supervise schools, but Arseny differed from the two leaders of that learned guard. He had neither Dmitry of Rostov's[4] lofty spiritual aspirations nor Feofan Prokopovich's cunning, servility and talent for living "in the world." His lack of self-control and extreme hot temper led to very unpleasant conflicts. Stories also circulated of his great cruelty.

Information about his life before Elizabeth's accession to the throne is scanty and obscure but it is clear that he never was in favor, was removed from the top ranks of the secular clergy and banished from the capital on an expedition to Kamchatka. In part this was because he supported Stefan Yavorsky.[5] Arseny was a man who would have found advancement during Anna's[6] reign difficult. The scurvy he contracted on the Kamchatka expedition undoubtedly affected his character. He was not consecrated metropolitan of Tobolsk until Anna Leopoldovna's[7] reign, so we should ignore his statement in a subsequent report to Empress Elizabeth that he had refused to swear allegiance to Biron[8] as regent.

When Elizabeth, who always protected him, ascended the throne Arseny was transferred from Tobolsk to Rostov and nominated to the Holy Synod[9] but never took his seat because he argued about the text of the oath for Synod members. Arseny went to his Rostov diocese. When the Synod ordered a feebleminded convict sent to a certain monastery Arseny wrote a report characterizing the synodal decision as indiscreet, audacious and contrary to the decrees of Peter the Great and Elizabeth. The Synod returned him a stern warning threatening that he would be stripped of his church rank and defrocked if he dared write such reports in the future.

This was in 1743. In 1745 Arseny petitioned the Synod for permission to retire to the Savior monastery in Novgorod Seversk because he had contracted *scurvy* at sea and begun to suffer headaches that year. The Synod submitted a report recommending that Arseny be allowed to retire, but he did not. In 1753 Arseny presented two books to Elizabeth: (1) A denunciation of a book by the Olonets Old Believers[10] and (2) A reply to a Lutheran polemical tract on the *Rock of Faith.*[11] When Elizabeth sent him Hungarian wine Arseny wrote that he was drinking it on her orders, adding *sal volatile* at a doctor's suggestion.

Arseny's correspondence with clergy dissatisfied with Peter III's decree on church domains and his letter to Bestuzhev during Catherine's reign on this topic have been mentioned.[12] Rostov was particularly important at the time. Crowds of pilgrims flocked there to venerate the newly-discovered relics of St. Dmitry the metropolitan and miracle-worker.[13] Although the relics were discovered under Elizabeth, only now was a shrine completed.

Catherine was determined to attend the transfer of the relics to the new shrine but her knowledge of Arseny's character made her very uneasy. This is evident in her letter to Olsufiev[14] "Since I know the Rostov hierarch's anger and lust for power, I am mortally afraid that he will erect

Dmitry of Rostov's shrine without me. Tell me what you have done about the shrine, what orders have been given and who has supervision over it. If every precaution has not been taken, then do so, to make absolutely sure the shrine is not erected without me." Olsufiev wrote to reassure her that such insolence was impossible. He had written a letter to the metropolitan, and the major responsible for the shrine would not permit such wilfulness. It would be unthinkable audacity should his grace dare intervene.

ARSENY PROTESTS GOVERNMENT SUPERVISION OF CHURCH LANDS

This correspondence continued until the end of February. At the beginning of March Arseny surprised people with another daring gesture. He sent two reports, one after another, to the Synod, at that time in Moscow, attacking the new regulations for church domains in the harshest terms. The Synod had sent account books to the diocesan chancelleries and the monasteries for recording receipts and expenditures. "Sending me the books," Arseny wrote, "disparages the hierarchy because it indicates that the hierarchy is not promoting the church's welfare energetically. The books sent to the hierarchs and heads of monastic houses as well as to treasury officials are an intolerable and unheard of burden, not just for the hierarchy but for the entire clerical estate."

Since apostolic times, Arseny asserted, church property was subject to the apostles alone and then to the hierarchy, under whose sole control and supervision it remained. No one might take church lands for other purposes. Whatever was taken must be returned at once. Not only was restoration [of church property] not contemplated, what remained was to be confiscated as well, just as was observed in the previous reign. The first to seize church property was Emperor Julian the Apostate.[15] In our case church domains have remained free since the days of Prince Vladimir,[16] not only during the reigns of pious princes but also under Tatar rule.

Under Peter the Great Musin-Pushkin[17] issued a decree on the income and management of church domains, a decree more far-reaching than any the Turks or the idolatrous Roman emperors ever promulgated. When St. Cyprian of Carthage[18] was brought to the place of execution he ordered his servants to give the executioner twenty-five gold pieces, but Musin-Pushkin's *decree would have made* this good deed impossible. Although Musin-Pushkin outdid the pagans, the church and the poor hierarchs accepted their poverty whether they liked it or not because at least they were not interrogated about gifts. Now we have entered a time of trial when people in prisons and alms houses live better than the poor hierarchs who are persecuted, not by pagans, but by self-proclaimed true believers.

The manifesto announcing the empress's accession stated that she assumed the throne to uphold Orthodoxy, which was threatened during the previous reign. It described pastors as "eager to spread the word and doing so, not with sighs, but gladly." The unbloody victims of such a painful yoke, crueller than that imposed by the Turks, how can we not sigh now? Nowhere is it written that the hierarchs must pay to establish academies. Even were there such prescription, how might they obtain the funds, all of which were confiscated? Most parish priests are desperately poor, taxed as much as peasants and must till the soil to support themselves. A priest receives no additional income even if he is a theologian or an astronomer. Certainly schools and academies are needed, but the right kind, for example, as in ancient Greece or in the West today. They should be located in important urban centers with government offices and maintained at state expense in major cities, not in mud and swamps.

The primary need was for more churches, properly maintained, but no one thinks of this nowadays. Many prefer to feed dogs than priests and monks, and acquiring the extra property of churches and monasteries takes precedence. Everything is being confiscated by claiming it is excessive. Many churches and monasteries stand empty, and the rest are desperately poor. The result is envy. Nowadays few men choose to take monastic vows, and soon there will be none at all. Without monks there can be no hierarchs, and without hierarchs what kind of piety and what kind of church would we have? God save us from a state without hierarchs! This means apostasy from the venerable apostolic church. There would be priests for a while, then they would disappear, and our state for all its academies would become heretical, Lutheran and atheist.

It is claimed that church property is not being confiscated, and the state merely is trimming the surplus. This is like Judas Iscariot who wanted to betray Jesus. When he saw the woman whose ardent faith and love led her to anoint Jesus with precious myrrh, he said "Why was not this ointment sold for three hundred pence and given to the poor?"[19] Everyone can read and understand how the Gospel would judge such an *official*. How would our prayer before God "Blessed be thy name" resound, and which petitioners would ask that we bless God's name in our land when gifts for the glory of God's name, not only ours but those of others, are taken by the state as superfluous?

The Synod received another report in the same tone, dated March 15, from Arseny, prompted by the arrival of officers to compile an inventory of church property.

ARSENY'S FATE

The Synod presented the first report to the empress, adding its opinion that it insulted imperial authority, rendering the author liable for prosecution. The Holy Synod would not presume to act without the empress's consent and left it to her to judge Arseny and grant him mercy. Obviously the Synod considered Catherine's cautious and lenient policy towards troublesome and hostile people, the sensitivity of the issue and Arseny's rank. It believed that Catherine would not pursue the matter aggressively, limiting the outcome to a reprimand, a suggestion that he request retirement and the like. The Synod was mistaken. Catherine understandably was angrier than ever before. The more obvious the difficulty of an action, the more apparent the objections against it and the more readily these baseless objections were commonly accepted, the greater her exasperation when such difficulties and objections actually surfaced. She was quite irritated by the reference to her accession manifesto and by Arseny's defiant and intimidating tone. You [Catherine] want to pass for a defender of Orthodoxy, yet at the same time you act as did Julian the Apostate and Judas. It should not be forgotten that Catherine and every reader of the period were influenced by the tendency of leading literary figures to emphasize the fanaticism and selfishness of clerics and monks,who must be curbed for the good of society.

"Holy Synod!" Catherine wrote personally, "your report presented yesterday states that the hierarch Arseny of Rostov is liable to judgment for sending a report dated March 6 to the Synod, consisting entirely of insults against imperial authority. You cannot pursue the matter further without my consent and so refer it for my consideration and compassion. I am confident the Holy Synod sees clearly that the power of all pious monarchs, among whom my deeds allow me to include myself, is exercised, not on their behalf, but for the welfare of all true sons of the fatherland, and thus must be preserved and defended.

"I noted distorted and seditious interpretations of many passages from sacred scripture and the holy books in Arseny's original report which you sent me to read and which I now return to you. Therefore, to preserve the tranquility of my faithful subjects henceforth and forever, I am handing over this hierarch Arseny, whose guilt you have acknowledged, to the

Holy Synod for judgment by the proper legally-constituted court. Whatever sentence the court renders shall be submitted to us for confirmation, leaving me free to show my leniency and my forgiveness."

BESTUZHEV'S INTERVENTION

Arseny grew frightened when he learned of the impending doom and requested permission to retire from his diocese to live again as an ordinary monk in the Savior monastery in Novgorod Seversk. It was too late, and he was arrested and sent to the synodal court in Moscow. Before his arrest he sent copies of his reports to the Synod to his confessor, Fedor Yakovlevich Dubiansky,[20] and to Count Alexis Petrovich Bestuzhev-Riumin. What the confessor did with the documents is not known, but Bestuzhev decided to intervene on Arseny's behalf by suggesting to the empress that the unpleasant affair be resolved as quickly and quietly as possible.

"(Arseny's) report to the Synod," he wrote to the empress on March 31, "is full of the most choleric insults and the greatest impertinence. Your imperial majesty's anger with him is justified. Count Bestuzhev does not take Arseny's part in any way whatsoever, and is motivated solely by a sense of duty towards a neighbor who has sinned. He dares most humbly to petition that a monarch's and a mother's mercy be shown him [Arseny] in the harsh sentence the court certainly will impose.

"Would her imperial majesty not deign to modify the Synod's judgment and promptly grant her imperial confirmation of the sentence for what clearly is a crime needing no investigation? Such a resolution of the matter would be a warning, and forestall public discussion."

His mild tone was to no avail. The previous year Catherine had written to Bestuzhev, "Little father Alexis Petrovich, help advise me!" Now his suggestion elicited a stern response. "I think no one ever has insulted a sovereign as grievously as the metropolitan of Rostov, whom the whole Synod has arrested. I do not think I have given any reason to doubt my mercy and my love of humanity. In the first place heads have rolled without ceremony or process in minor episcopal questions. I do not know how I could uphold and enhance the tranquility and prosperity of my people (not to mention defending and preserving my God-given authority) if subversives were not punished."

Of course neither Bestuzhev nor anyone else could remember when heads had rolled without ceremony or process in minor episcopal questions. Catherine's words showed Bestuzhev just how angry the empress was. "In his most humble reply," he hastened to soothe her, "your most faithful servant reports that he did not support the hierarch of Rostov in any way whatsoever. He merely added his comments to Arseny's note to St. Petersburg and was not interceding for a grave offender. He mentioned resolving the matter promptly only to curtail needless popular discussion and comment by those unaware of the particulars of the case. If thereby an old man transgressed, his motive was zeal and not insubordination, and this grieves him." "I am sorry," Catherine replied, "about your grief. I wrote to give you something to say to the person who bothered you with his request. I hope you sleep well."

THE SYNOD ACTS AGAINST ARSENY

On April 7 the Synod submitted a report. "The Holy Governing Synod," it stated, "has sufficient grounds to find the metropolitan Arseny guilty of inexcusable insults to her imperial majesty. He has violated the laws of sacred scripture and apostolic tradition. He has shown contempt for his hierarchical and general oaths and opposed the government statutes concerning church domains, enacted by her imperial majesty in 1762 and 1763, by sending his reports to the Synod, the first on March 6 and the second on March 15. Not only must the language of these reports be judged offensive to her imperial majesty, he also misconstrued the meaning of many passages from sacred scripture and various other books. He gave his own distorted interpretations of many passages from sacred scripture and various other books. These contradict the meaning and sense of these passages, specifically (here the familiar passages from the reports are cited).

"His report concludes by claiming that it was inspired solely by zeal for God and His law. Her imperial majesty has stated her views clearly enough in official manifestos and decrees to reject his request for pardon. Neither orders issued at the highest levels nor anyone else's directives provide any grounds for considering this petition. His sarcastic statements and objections render him liable to the harshest punishment. Hence, although he cites zeal as a pretext for his extremely impertinent and audacious protests mentioned earlier, he and no one else must answer for them.

"Arseny said under interrogation that he did not want his reports to cause any insult to her imperial majesty. Zeal and conscience alone prompted him to write, and he intended no duplicity. He objected, not to the orders, but to the commission's reports on which they were based. Since the commission's reports were not rejected, he did not expect his reports would be either, and certainly did not believe they would insult her imperial majesty. Since they did insult her imperial majesty, he most humbly and most obediently throws himself at her imperial majesty's feet to implore her pardon and her mercy.

"The metropolitan's testimony is false, however, because according to the clerk Zhukov's letter, copies of both reports to the Synod were sent to two prominent persons in Moscow. In 1743 the Synod sent Arseny a written reprimand because he dared use offensive and threatening language in his report to it. This reprimand clearly stated he would be stripped of his hierarchical rank and defrocked[21] if he acted so offensively and disdainfully again.

"Therefore the following sentence was passed. 'Metropolitan Arseny has committed serious crimes now and in the past, above all the present grave insult. He violated his hierarchical and general oaths as well as government statutes. For these offenses and for insulting her imperial majesty, based on Regulation 84 of the apostolic hierarchy and his 1743 reprimand, he is to be defrocked, sent to live under strict supervision in a distant monastery and deprived of paper and ink.'" The sentence was signed by Metropolitan Dmitry of Novgorod,[22] Metropolitan Timofey of Moscow;[23] Archbishop Gavriil of St. Petersburg,[24] Archbishop Gedeon of Pskov,[25] Archbishop Amvrosy of Krutitsa,[26] Bishop Afanasy of Tver[27] and Archimandrite Misail of the New Savior monastery.[28]

The frightened old man begged for mercy. His conviction was a foregone conclusion, but we do not know who insisted on the unusual procedure of including in the text of the sentence the clerk Zhukov's testimony that Arseny's sending copies of his report to an ecclesiastic[29] and to Bestuzhev was proof of his insincerity. "This sentence," Catherine wrote on the report, "strips the metropolitan of his rank and his priesthood. According to ecclesiastical regulations and other church statutes the offender remains an ordinary monk so he can do proper penance in his old age. For humanitarian reasons we shall spare him civil justice and a civil trial and shall order our Synod to send him to a distant monastery subject to a wise superior. Guidelines will be issued to prevent Arseny from corrupting weak and simple people there either orally or in writing."

The Synod named the Ferapontov monastery in the Vologda diocese as the place of exile, but on April 15 the high procurator of the Synod sent it an order specifying the St. Nicholas of Korela monastery in the Archangel diocese instead, allotting fifty copecks a day for meals.

ARSENY MAKES MORE TROUBLE

Four years passed. In 1767 Arseny was investigated again after Hierodeacon Joasaph Lebedev denounced him for saying that Catherine was not of our stock and therefore should not have ascended the throne. Arseny further was reported to have said that the heir to the throne had scrofula, and that God alone knew who would succeed him. It should be Ivan Antonovich, Ivan's father and others who were imprisoned at Kholmogory.[30] Arseny cursed the members of the Synod and said of Dmitry Sechenov[31] "I would be set free if he disappeared but he is alive, and Dmitry will do nothing without Senior Secretary Ostolopov as long as he lives. The villages would not have been taken from the hierarchs and the monasteries if Sechenov and Gavriil of St. Petersburg had not agreed."

Arseny compared himself to Chrysostom, who also was imprisoned by an empress.[32] He cited a prophecy, supposedly from a life of St. Cyril of Belozero,[33] that two youths would reign in Russia who would drive out the Turks and conquer Tsargrad [Constantinople]. The first was the grand duke (Paul Petrovich) and the second his brother Prince Ivan (who when he said this already was dead). Lebedev reported that Archimandrite Antony of the St. Nicholas of Korela monastery, the soldiers of the guard and their commander Subaltern Alekseevsky, responded to Arseny's statements as he had hoped. They believed that the two youths would rule soon, and Arseny's hierarchical rank be restored. He was guarded less strictly, he gave his blessing and was asked to preach in public.

Under interrogation Antony and Alekseevsky admitted they had been lenient, and Alekseevsky confirmed that Arseny said that "our sovereign is not of our stock and does not support our laws. She should not have taken the throne." "Arseny said this in 1763 to Captain Nikolay Durnovo," Catherine noted here, "when Durnovo came to take him to the Synod. So Alekseevsky did not make this up."

Despite this new problem Arseny still hoped to contest the grounds for his utter disgrace. On October 22 he petitioned the Archangel government chancellery to register the following statement and send it to the empress. (1) Arseny begs her imperial majesty's favor and asks that she deign to read his original report, the grounds for his sentence. Undoubtedly she would deign to acknowledge its truth. He had written a letter to Empress Elizabeth

Petrovna when he received a copy of a proposal to seize villages from the church (the original was signed by the former chancellor, Bestuzhev-Riumin, and other leading authorities, except for Count Peter Shuvalov).[34] That letter was similar to the report for which now he was being punished. When Empress Elizabeth saw that what he wrote was correct, she did not approve the original proposal when it was submitted to her. She only heeded Arseny's letter, saying she would not sign the proposal and people could do as they wished after she died. (2) Arseny thought that the Synod had sent the empress just a summary of its investigation of his report to her, but had her imperial majesty seen fit to read the original report, he certainly would not have been punished. (3) Arseny affirms even now that villages should not be taken from the church for the reasons given in his report to the Synod. It was decided "to defrock Arseny as a monk, to rename him Andrei Vral [Liar] when defrocked, and send him to perpetual imprisonment in Reval."

SIGNIFICANCE OF THE ARSENY MATSEEVICH AFFAIR

This concluded a controversy which first arose in Russia in the fifteenth century.[35] The importance of the issue made the conflict bitter and intense from the outset. Initially opinion favored monastic possession of lands with peasants. During the era of reform[36] each Russian felt free to question the necessity and the utility of everything hallowed by tradition. Hence the question of church lands grew more urgent, but as soon as the crucial issue of church structure and governance was resolved the provisional measures concerning church domains were rescinded. In some of his last instructions on the matter the Reformer [Peter the Great] envisioned new obligations and a new order of life for the monastic clergy. Even so he was confident that the new collegial form of church governance would prevent the recurrence of old abuses.

The Reformer's daughter [Empress Elizabeth] raised the issue again in the mid-eighteenth century. No one could suspect her of impiety or "thinking like the philosophes" (a quality Catherine admired in herself). Hence the fifteenth-century solution no longer was possible, and in the eighteenth century Arseny of Rostov fell for defending Joseph of Volokolamsk's position.

Whatever the historian's opinion of this position, he must acknowledge Arseny's courage and his persistent defense of his ideas. He asked for leniency and requested that his opinions be read carefully, but did not compromise his convictions to obtain mercy and avoid punishment. "I affirm even now," he concluded his petition, "that villages should not be taken from the church."[37]

CATHERINE VISITS ROSTOV

Catherine set out for Rostov in May 1763 as she had planned. The weather was bad. "Wind, cold, constant rain and the ensuing mud have made unpleasant a journey which in good weather would have been a pleasure," the empress wrote to Panin from Pereiaslavl. From the same city she wrote to Procurator General Glebov[38] "I received everything you sent, and I hope to return the latest reports to you quickly. Pereiaslavl is as boring as the weather is bad. The house where I am living is very large, attractive and full of cockroaches."

"The transfer of St. Dmitry's relics," Catherine wrote to Panin after arriving in Rostov, "occurs tomorrow. There were some miracles yesterday, and a woman was healed. Bishop Sechenov wants to seal the shrine lest the relics be stolen, but I asked that they be displayed for a while lest the common people blame me for concealing them."[39]

THE KHITROVO AFFAIR

Catherine's letters to Glebov show she was busy tending to affairs during her journey. While in Rostov she received very unpleasant news of a quarrel among major participants in the events of June 28,[40] sparked by the dramatic rise of the present favorite, Grigory Orlov.[41] The greatest irritant to those who considered their contributions equally valuable was the manner of his brother Alexis.[42] "The Orlovs' pride and their deeds," one of them, Lasunsky, said to another, [Fedor] Khitrovo, "are offensive. We expected that our common service to the sovereign would strengthen our friendship, but we see now the Orlovs are corrupt."

Catherine sheds light on the matter in an interesting note to Yelagin.[43] "You can tell the chamberlains Lasunsky and the Roslavevs[44] that I hope my reply does not offend them because they helped me ascend the throne and repair the disorder in my fatherland. It really is impossible to hand out money now, and you can attest to it!"[45] These gentlemen could be justified for taking offense when their requests were refused. They thought that the Orlovs had not been refused, and said so.

On May 24 Catherine sent a letter from Rostov to Senator Vasily Ivanovich Suvorov.[46] "Upon receipt summon Chamberlain Prince Ivan

GREGOIRE GREGORIEWITZ
ORLOFF,
Begunstigde van Catharina II.

Nesvizhsky[47] and order him to give you in writing or to write down in your presence everything he heard from Chamberlain Fedor Khitrovo. Send for Khitrovo if Nesvizhsky's testimony warrants it. If Khitrovo should be arrested, call Prince Mikhail Volkonsky[48] and Prince Peter Petrovich Cherkassky[49] to help you pursue the matter and report to me as often as feasible. I recommend you proceed as cautiously as possible. Do not stir up the city, and alert only those you have to, but be thorough and find out the real truth. Distinguish between words and deeds, and remember that the walls have eyes and ears."

Prince Nesvizhsky reported that on returning from the country he met Khitrovo, who inquired about any news. "What news," Nesvizhsky answered, "would I bring from the country?" "I have a lot of news," Khitrovo said, "and all of it bad. First, because the sovereign went to the Resurrection monastery, that old devil Bestuzhev had more opportunity to pursue the project he initiated. He wrote a petition urging the sovereign to marry Grigory Orlov, and a number of clergy and senators signed it. When Panin and Razumovsky[50] found out about it, Panin asked the sovereign if she sanctioned the petition. Although she told him no, Panin saw from her expression and gestures that she had approved it. The hetman [Razumovsky] and Zakhar Chernyshev decided to put a stop to the matter, inviting Repnin,[51] the Roslavevs, Lasunsky, Passek,[52] Teplov,[53] the Boriatinskys,[54] the Karevs, Peter and Sergei Khovansky,[55] Peter Apraksin,[56] and Nikolay Rzhevsky to join them. They agreed the petition was a bad idea and threat to the fatherland, something every patriot should stand up and oppose.

"Nothing would have come of it," Khitrovo continued, "because Grigory Orlov is stupid. That big scoundrel Alexis Orlov, Grigory's brother, is the one who started it and is the principal instigator." "I would like to ask the Orlovs if this is true," Nesvizhsky replied. "This would be a great help for us," said Khitrovo. "Check with the Orlovs as often as you can. At our meeting we decided to petition the sovereign to marry. Ivanushka[57] has two brothers, and if she refuses them she will exclude everyone else if she clings to the Orlovs. There still is time to divert her, and she will be grateful if we snatch this troublemaker from her.

"While I was on guard duty under the late sovereign [Peter III], I happened to discuss with Alexis Orlov the prospect of the sovereign [Catherine] acceding to the throne. Orlov said that Panin had drafted an agreement setting the conditions for the sovereign to assume power, and that she had subscribed to them, but Captains Roslavev and Lasunsky of the Izmailovsky Regiment rejected the agreement when it was presented to them, instead proclaiming Catherine autocrat and ordering the soldiers to shout hurrah.

"If possible," Khitrovo continued, "the Orlovs should be crushed at the first opportunity. Princess Dashkova[58] initiated me into this conspiracy. Glebov, who also was of our party, planned to give us all the money we needed."

INVESTIGATION

On May 27 Khitrovo stated under interrogation that his cousin by marriage Vasily Brylkin[59] spoke to him two weeks previously. Vasily's brother Ivan[60] told him that Bestuzhev approached Ivan with an agreement petitioning the sovereign to marry. She might choose any of her subjects she wished because the heir apparent [Paul] was sickly and as yet had not had smallpox. The clergy and some of the senators already had signed the agreement.

Nikolay Roslavev told Khitrovo that he went to Panin, the hetman and Chernyshev as soon as he heard of the agreement. They said they would not sign it. When Panin asked the sovereign if she approved Bestuzhev's agreement, she said she knew nothing about it. Panin recommended that Bestuzhev be brought to judgment if the agreement came from him. The sovereign fell silent, and that was the end of the agreement. When Khitrovo heard an agreement existed, he asked Princess Dashkova if this were true. Dashkova told him everything that Roslavev had told him, and expressed her surprise at the project's stupidity.

Catherine was displeased. "He (Khitrovo) had to be making it up," she wrote to Suvorov, "that I promised Panin I would become the ruler. Alexis Orlov could not have told him the lie Khitrovo says he heard. Order an investigation to determine whether arresting Khitrovo will alarm curiosity seekers, or if the city still is ignorant of the matter." Catherine reported on the interrogations in a note to Suvorov. "Khitrovo," she wrote, "persuaded two men to join his party. He claims that if I agreed to the proposal put forward by Alexis Petrovich [Bestuzhev], his party would confer, then inform me of its shortcomings. They would kill all four Counts Orlov unless I agreed with them.

"Khitrovo was unmasked, and after many denials finally confessed to me and asked for pardon. He named many others in addition to the two he had invited: N.P. (Nikita Panin), Al. Gleb. (Glebov), Grigory Teplov, the two Roslavevs, the two Boriatinskys, the two Karevs, the two Khovanskys, Passek and Princess Dashkova. He disavowed the testimony of the two [he had invited] and confessed to me that his only partners were the two Roslavevs and Lasunsky. Nikolay Roslavev told Khitrovo that all the others were in agreement, but that he thought the project should be postponed because things had quieted down.

"They knew their project would anger me and that, as they themselves said, it was contrary to my wishes. Hence I cannot believe they did not take steps to avert my wrath and did not see that the two Roslavevs and Lasunsky must be banished or arrested. When Khitrovo was arrested Passek and Boriatinsky told the Orlovs there was talk in the city of plans to kill the Orlovs and depose me. When I asked them [Passek and Boriatinsky] where they heard these stories, at first they said from a sergeant, but then one said from a grenadier and another from an unidentified servant. It was obvious that they suspected something was afoot or, in other words, knew that there was."[61]

CATHERINE ACTS

Since "things had quieted down" the project was pointless, and everyone merely repeated earlier talk. Proposing an unrealistic scheme against the Orlovs without coordinating it with other measures was impractical. It still was uncertain how those who plotted contrary to the empress's will planned to avoid her wrath. The only result was a decision to banish the Roslavevs, Lasunsky and Khitrovo. Only Khitrovo was sent to his estate, which was in the Orlov district. Lasunsky and Alexander Roslavev were retired with the rank of lieutenant general, the former in 1764, the latter in 1765.

The more clandestinely the project was conducted and the more doubtful its consequences, the more discussion it caused. At the beginning of June a manifesto *On Silence* was read on the streets of Moscow to the sound of drums. "It is our will," the manifesto stated, "that each and every one of our faithful subjects devote himself exclusively to his calling and his duty, avoiding any insolent or unseemly disclosures. Contrary to every expectation and to our extreme regret and dissatisfaction, we hear that morally and intellectually depraved people have appeared. They care nothing for the common good or general tranquillity and have been infected by strange opinions that do not concern them. Although their information is false, they attempt to seduce others who are weak-minded...If our maternal admonitions and solicitude do not move their depraved hearts and do not guide them on the path of true happiness, I will order that we pro-ceed with the full rigor of the law against every one of these ignoramuses."[62]

Archbishop Amvrosy's letter of March 12 to Bestuzhev illustrates how Catherine tried to stop popular gossip. "The high procurator of the Synod[63] proposed an imperial order that offices and public remembrances for the dead for the former emperor Peter III be held on his birthday in the Archangel cathedral. If you do not deign to permit us to perform offices for the dead, popular discussion may take a different tone from that of the manifestoes. The holy church even might be subject to abuse from Old Believers."

Bestuzhev made the proposal. "God has ordered that prayers be said for evildoers," Catherine wrote on the report, "especially for a wayward soul. If there are no remembrances for the dead it will be rumored that he is alive." Rumors circulated anyway. Ensign Voinovich of the Moldavian Hussar Regiment reported that on September 7 he went to the quarters of Lieutenant Colonel Yezdemirovich in the St. Elizabeth fortress. Yezdemirovich said that he had been with Melgunov's[64] valet Ivanushka the previous evening. Ivanushka told Yezdemirovich that Guards Major Roslavev had been Melgunov's guest, and told Melgunov the former emperor was alive and had been sent to Sliushin (Schlüsselburg).[65] This was done because Orlov wanted to marry the sovereign.[66]

III

ADMINISTRATIVE REFORMS

FOUNDING OF THE PAULINE HOSPITAL

Catherine finished her journey at Yaroslavl. "I like the city of Yaroslavl very much," she wrote, "and think it ranks third among the cities I have seen in Russia."[1] Her last act during her stay in Moscow was to establish the Pauline hospital. As stated in the decree, this was at the request of the heir apparent Paul Petrovich, and was to be free. Procurator General Glebov's suburban residence was purchased to house the hospital.[2]

CATHERINE REBUKES THE SENATE

The empress left Moscow on June 14 and arrived at Tsarskoe Selo on the evening of the nineteenth. From there she made a triumphal entry into St.

Petersburg on June 28, the first anniversary of her accession to the throne. Catherine met with the Senate eight times that year, four in Moscow and four in St. Petersburg. The Senate departed Moscow after hearing this order from the empress. "Honorable senators! I cannot say that you lack patriotic concern for my welfare and that of the realm in general. I must tell you in a spirit of sympathy, however, that matters are not being resolved as successfully as we would wish. The sole reason for this is disagreement, hostility and envy in the Senate. One member finds another's project intolerable, so they divide into parties and look for occasions to inflict mutual harm.

"What is the cause? It is nothing more than unbridled malice and dissension. A notable source of discord is some members' tendency to belittle other members' projects, even useful ones, solely to block things they did not originate. Such instances should be judged on their merits, because not everyone is equally talented."[3]

The senators were admonished even earlier, in March, about certain improprieties. When the Senate heard a case about wrongdoing in the Irkutsk liquor franchise, it ordered Senator Sumarokov[4] to recuse himself because he held a liquor franchise in Bakhmut province. This was to comply with Peter the Great's directive that a judge recuse himself when his situation was the same as the petitioner's or the respondent's, lest this interest affect his decision. For example, a judge should not hear a case concerning a grievance over confiscated property if the judge had a similar grievance somewhere else. Sumarokov resented the decision and complained to the empress that the recusal order was illegal. It did not apply to him because no one had accused him of wanting the [Irkutsk] franchise.

"The Irkutsk liquor franchise," Catherine wrote in response to Sumarokov's petition, "and the liquor franchise in Bakhmut province are not the same, because one is in Siberia and one in Russia. The Senate shall follow Peter the Great's directive in individual disputes without making any trouble. If cases involving franchises are problematic, the Senate can deal with it."[5] Catherine did not want to be involved with franchises.

CATHERINE RESTRUCTURES THE SENATE

The Senate received the following order in St. Petersburg. "Her imperial majesty has been informed by the procurator general of the status of all orders signed since her accession to the throne until today, August 5. She has observed that many of her orders concerning individual petitioners or state affairs have not been executed. Other orders still are under consideration.

Her imperial majesty is all the more anxious that her ceaseless efforts to benefit the state and assure the orderly administration of justice achieve the success she desires. Therefore the Senate is ordered to meet afternoons three times a week until all cases are resolved." The order was issued on August 20. On September 4 Catherine announced in the Senate that only one session a week would be held instead of three, since so many cases had been considered. She also heard that the chancellery personnel had a fairly heavy work load.

The empress complained again in September about the Senate's "terrible slowness,"[6] but she wanted to do more than complain. On April 17 an order was issued "to the consultative assembly on noble emancipation"[7] about dividing the Senate into departments. "Thus the Senate would not consider just one case a day but resolve as many cases as there are departments designated."[8] "It cannot be denied," a manifesto issued December 15 stated, "that every state's welfare rests on the peace and prosperity of its citizens. The rulers of states will enjoy genuine tranquility only when they prevent their subjects from being exhausted by various projects, particularly those initiated by the authorities.

"This is achieved only by devising the proper internal procedures and creating a complete system of judicial and administrative organs. What our empire now has is totally inadequate. Primary attention must be paid to the Senate which, in addition to appeals, receives a variety of cases from throughout the realm with requests for their resolution. The vast number of cases so overwhelms the Senate that it cannot resolve them in the time allotted."

The Senate consequently was divided into six departments, four in St. Petersburg and two to replace the Senate bureau formerly located in Moscow. Domestic and political matters were assigned to the first department and judicial ones to the second. The third department was responsible for the Ukraine, the Baltic provinces, Finland, the Academy of Sciences, the university, the Academy of Fine Arts, the police and so on. The army and navy were assigned to the fourth department. The fifth department in Moscow assumed responsibility from the existing Senate bureau there for all state affairs. The sixth department, also in Moscow, dealt with judicial matters on the model of the second department in St. Petersburg.

SENATORIAL PROCEDURES

The procurator general continued to serve in the first department, with a chief procurator named for each of the other departments. Cases were to

From an engraving by J.B. Fosseyeux, 1788

be decided unanimously. The chief procurator informed the procurator general of the point at issue if the members disagreed or if he himself had doubts. He then forwarded the case to the first department, summoned all available senators from the other departments and presented the matter for general consideration. When the senators of the first department disagreed, the matter was laid before a general assembly. If even then the senators were not agreed, or if no law applied to the case at hand, the procurator general presented the entire file to the empress along with his and the other senators' opinions.

REORGANIZATION OF OTHER GOVERNMENT BODIES

The College of Justice, the College of Hereditary Estates, the College of Audits and the Chancellery of Justice were divided into departments like the Senate, and for the same reasons. The College of Audits was split into five departments because the number of unaudited accounts had grown to the point where millions in state funds were unaccounted for. In certifying accounts the College of Audits was to ensure that income matched expenditures, and take special care that all monetary and other disbursements were done legally. The Chancellery for Siberia, the Chancellery for Inquiries and the Bureau for Old Believers were abolished.[9]

On August 20 her imperial majesty issued a signed order that Chamberlain Count Fedor Orlov[10] be present whenever the Senate transacted business, particularly at meetings. He was to have a place at the procurator general's desk so he could audit the cases presented and discussed, as well as read, and occasionally write his own summaries of current business. Orlov thus would gain a valuable knowledge of affairs and would serve her imperial majesty more competently and more effectively in the future.

CATHERINE COMBATS OFFICIAL CORRUPTION

Catherine requested the Senate to make a special effort to root out abuses in local government, especially bribery. She cited the case of the Kaluga military governor Miasoedov when reprimanding the Senate for failing to reach agreement. There is an interesting note from the empress to Procurator General Glebov on this case. "Convoke a plenary session of the Senate on the Miasoedov case when I arrive in the city. I personally intend to hear each senator and have the gentlemen of the Senate reach agreement. Otherwise people will say that one or another of them is tearing me to pieces."[11] An indication of her great interest in the case was that Catherine was alarmed by rumors that senators tried to influence her privately.

Miasoedov, his colleague, his secretary and his clerk were accused of taking bribes on contracts and pleaded guilty. Miasoedov and his colleague were stripped of their rank and exiled to the country. The secretary was reduced to copyist in perpetuity and exiled to a distant city, while the clerk was flogged and sent as soldier to a remote garrison.[12]

Catherine was just as concerned about the case of the Smolensk governor Arshenevsky,[13] accused of taking bribes. Here the senators disagreed again, which caused more comment, eliciting the following note from Catherine to Glebov."You are called weak if you do not punish people and harsh if you do," she wrote. "Arshenevsky should remain stripped of his rank until I arrive. I shall present these thoughts to the Senate and reduce the sentence. I hope the offender, or those with a bad conscience or who failed to write me or advise me concerning the case, will be discredited. Some belittle any matter on which they are not consulted like an oracle, but then people generally pay no attention to oracles."[14] Catherine continued to believe that many had a bad conscience. When she learned that Tver had burned she wrote to Glebov "Do what you can for these unfortunate people. I think many will not be sorry that almost all the files were burned."[15]

Senators Prince Yakov Shakhovskoy[16] and Count Skavronsky[17] presented letters to the Senate they received from Bishop Porfiry of Kolomna.[18] The bishop complained that the Kolomna military governor Ivan Orlov[19] was drunk day and night. He rarely came to the chancellery and even there was drunk. The cases of more than one hundred prisoners still were pending. Orlov forbade anyone to leave the chancellery or the city, yet on his own authority went to Moscow for a masquerade.

KRYLOV AND THE IRKUTSK MERCHANTS

These were new cases, but an old case involving the famous Irkutsk investigator Krylov still was pending. We saw that Krylov's investigation found Irkutsk merchants guilty of misappropriating one hundred fifty thousand rubles of state funds.[20] When Krylov's own violent crimes were revealed the merchants testified that their confessions were extorted under torture and that Krylov had acted on behalf of the former chief procurator Glebov, now procurator general. Glebov suddenly began selling alcohol in Irkutsk. The merchants testified that a significantly higher price was set than in the previous decade, and that Glebov wanted to pay much less for the state distilleries than the merchants' appraisal. Sending Krylov thus was Glebov's personal revenge against the Irkutsk merchants.

The entire Senate was as guilty as Glebov because it handled the case improperly in allotting the franchise tavern income to Glebov without the necessary documentation. When Glebov reported the Irkutsk merchants' abuses, appending his personal complaints, the Senate initiated an investigation. Not only was the chief procurator barred from intervening in state affairs, redress of grievances was ordered from offices specified by law. Krylov was dispatched by the Senate bureau and reported directly to the Senate, which awarded him one thousand rubles for this irregular conduct, thus encouraging illegality in the future. The Senate did not forward the petition of Wolff, the vice-governor of Irkutsk, to Empress Elizabeth and did not order an investigation into how the seal on the petition was cut off. When the Irkutsk merchants admitted embezzling state funds, Krylov on his own authority forgave them a sizable amount. Since some of the senators involved in these irregularities had died and others retired, the empress issued a manifesto at her coronation pardoning those still living, a bad conscience their only punishment.

GLEBOV'S DISGRACE

Catherine saw how little Glebov cared about the proper conduct of affairs or the interests of the state. Although the matter was illegal from start to finish, he regarded it merely as an occasion to falsify his own reports and to divert the extra franchise income from the state treasury to himself. It was recommended that he be stripped of his ranks and subjected to additional punishment. Thanks to the same [coronation] manifesto of amnesty, he was barred permanently from holding office but retained the rank of procurator general. Krylov was spared the death penalty since he had spent considerable time in chains, but was flogged with the knout in Irkutsk and sentenced to life at hard labor.

The empress noted that these verdicts occurred before the legally-prescribed investigation was concluded. "Since," she said, "we were able to get a clear picture of the affair from the information at hand, we deemed it proper to reach a decision based on the obvious facts of the matter rather than follow legal procedures by reopening the investigation. The Irkutsk merchants already have suffered considerably, and summoning them here to present evidence and testify would burden them even more."[21]

EXTORTION BY VORONEZH GOVERNOR PUSHKIN

Traces remained of an old case involving abuses by Pushkin, the governor of Voronezh,[22] a matter Peter III had ordered hushed up. Captain Kara confessed that in 1758 Registrar Savinov told him that Pushkin gave orders for Kara to make the inhabitants of Biriuchia collect one thousand rubles for the governor. If they complied Pushkin would look kindly on them. They collected the money voluntarily and sent it to Voronezh. Pushkin then ordered the inhabitants of Biriuchia to pay their respects to Vice-Governor Koshelev, whereupon the Biriuchia authorities gave Koshelev three hundred rubles. Finally Pushkin demanded five hundred rubles from the same Biriuchia settlement lest it be ravaged by military units passing through it. Assessor Veniaminov confessed that he gave Pushkin three hundred rubles and the adjutant one hundred rubles of the money Veniaminov received from forest inspections.

PRINCE VIAZEMSKY'S REPORT ON THE KAZAN CHANCELLERY

Prince Alexander Alexeevich Viazemsky[23] was sent to pacify the peasants in and investigate the administration of the iron foundries.[24] "After I left Kazan," he reported, "I tried to gather information in various villages about the activities of the Kazan chancellery. Everywhere I confirmed the reports of bribery. I also found out how much was collected last year from each native tributary peasant[25] for gifts to chancellery employees before the next tax roll[26] was drawn up, and how much foresters collected for each visit. Two hundredmen[27] from the Tatar village Agryzy confirmed that nine or ten copecks per male serf were paid for tax rolls and even more by the Votiaks,[28] a simple and conscientious people.

"Foresters collect three or four copecks per male serf on each visit to the Tatars and four or five copecks from the Votiaks. I asked why they made such large gifts. The answer was that some years ago their hundred[29] took a stand and gave the forester nothing, whereupon he reported that they had cut down oaks from a forest preserve. The government chancellery rejected their explanation and fined them eight hundred rubles. They contributed now because, even though the forester found no oak timber, he found oak runners when he examined their sleds and reported to the government chancellery that oaks were cut down.

"I found as much corruption on my journey from the government of Siberia to the government of Orenburg as I did elsewhere. Court Councillor Kaptiazhev was the worst. It was rumored that he refused to pay his subordinates unless bribed. The Simbirsk nobility is quite indignant about the former military governor Prince Nazarov, whereas the current military governor is more acceptable. Nazarov tried to sow dissension among the nobles and then resorted to bribery on an unprecedented scale. He was prone to robbery and bribery, and tortured people ruthlessly."

ABUSES IN THE OREL CITY GOVERNMENT

Eighteenth-century Russian history records that cities did not suffer at the hands of military governors alone. A resident made powerful by wealth, a "loud-mouthed peasant"[30] to use the old expression, felt no need for restraint when dealing with the weakest members of society, particularly after becoming magistracy president,[31] a city's highest position. The president created a powerful party and counted on its support, but sometimes encountered another loud-mouthed peasant with his own strong party in the city, who did not want to step aside. A terrible struggle then erupted between these eighteenth-century Boretskys, and their parties' armed attacks on each other made the parallel with Great Novgorod even more striking.[32] The participation both of prominent and ordinary citizens in the conflicts also was reminiscent of Novgorod. We should not fail to mention an interesting example of this kind from the period under discussion.

A rich merchant, Dmitry Dubrovin, was magistracy president in Orel. The Chief Magistracy removed him from office after citizens complained of his violent ways. The opposition party, which apparently engineered the whole affair, exploited its triumph by naming its leader Kuznetsov president, but Dubrovin and his party refused to concede. Dubrovin's son Mikhailo, a prominent citizen and director of customs, sent a petition on his father's behalf to the Senate. The petition claimed the Chief Magistracy acted improperly by removing his father from the presidency after he was denounced by the Orel merchant Nikolay Kuznetsov. Kuznetsov testified that Mikhailo Dubrovin had a liquor warehouse and tavern in Orel.

This same Nikolay Kuznetsov in league with his brother Stepan insulted and ruined the entire merchant estate when Stepan was president. Mikhailo Dubrovin submitted a petition signed by 142 Orel merchants as proof. In this petition President Dubrovin testified that Kuznetsov caused disorder and ruined the merchant estate now just as he had in the past. Consequently the merchants wanted to deny Kuznetsov merchant status, whereas Dubrovin continued to protect the merchants. Kuznetsov's accusation that young Dubrovin had a liquor warehouse was false because Mikhailo abandoned it. In conclusion, the merchants requested that Kuznetsov's petition be ignored, that he be expelled from the merchant estate and that Dmitry Dubrovin be named president.

This petition to the Senate was followed by one from one hundred and fifty Orel merchants stating that Kuznetsov was a fine man and a merchant of the first class. He paid his own taxes in full and the taxes of those in need or who had died, and he had receipts to prove it. Therefore they asked that

Kuznetsov not be expelled from the merchant estate nor any credence given Dubrovin's statement, because his petition was improper. Dubrovin's petition was signed in the markets, in shops and on the street without consulting the merchants of the first class. It was presented under the pretext that it would benefit the merchant estate, and people were given no chance to read it.

When the Senate received these contradictory petitions it ordered a commissioned officer and a member of the Moscow magistracy sent to Orel. When they reached the city they were to assemble the leading Orel merchants of the first and second classes, excluding Dubrovin and Kuznetsov, and obtain signed statements from them indicating whether they wanted Dubrovin or Kuznetsov as president.

For some reason the mission was not sent, and the Orel rivals settled matters themselves. Dubrovin became president again, and Kuznetsov's case from the previous year was revived. On February 5, 1763 about two hundred men gathered to rob the free homesteaders' administration office.[33] They killed the guards and went to the home of the Orel merchant and cloth manufacturer Kuznetsov. That night the crowd moved on, breaking down the gates of the guard house, taking a conscript from it, and freeing the other prisoners. Kuznetsov's factory workers and foreman participated in the robbery. Orel free homesteaders reported that their fellow free homesteaders fled their regular duties and hid from Kuznetsov, intending to burn their promissory notes.

Misfortune befell the apparently triumphant Dubrovin at the end of the year. The procurator general gave the Senate a packet with Dubrovin's petition written on three scraps of paper. Dubrovin complained that he was seized without cause by the Orel government chancellery, evidently solely as a result of intrigue by the Kuznetsovs. Given neither paper nor ink, it took him eight days to collect scraps of paper to write this petition. The Senate directed the Senate bureau to learn from the Orel provincial chancellery why Dubrovin was held under such strict guard, and why he received no paper and ink.

The Moscow governor general Soltykov,[34] whose jurisdiction included the government of Orel, provided an explanation. On November 17 Soltykov reported that Dubrovin "was responsible for oppression, robbery, murder and misappropriation of funds in Orel. The Chief Magistracy therefore removed him from office, but he obstinately continued to exercise his official duties. During this *insolent* exercise of authority

Dubrovin's comrades plundered and destroyed Kuznetsov's factory and drove off, beat and maimed its workers.

"Kuznetsov complained to the Senate bureau, which ordered Davydov, colonel of the cuirassier regiment in Orel, the Orel military governor and a deputy from the Chief Magistracy to make a complete investigation. To stop the unrest and restore order, Dubrovin and his accomplices were to be taken into custody and the city patrolled regularly. Since the cuirassier regiment was absent on maneuvers large groups of rebels continued to roam about with loaded guns and clubs, killing and maiming anyone who disagreed with them. Dubrovin's son Mikhailo went with six men to the military governor's house, threatened to beat him and demanded that the governor free the senior Dubrovin.

"When his demand was refused Mikhailo fled to Moscow, where on my orders police arrested him and five accomplices. Gendarme General Yushkov[35] told me yesterday morning that on the third day, the fifteenth, he saw Dubrovin with Senator Vorontsov (Ivan Larionovich).[36] That evening the gendarme general reported to me that Dubrovin had escaped police custody."

PROBLEMS IN MTENSK

At the same time the empress ordered a special commission established to investigate complaints from Mtensk. The Mtensk military governor Yemelianov objected that the merchants treated him rudely. Captain Ovinov of the Murom Infantry Regiment complained that the Mtensk magistracy had seized his and a grenadier's swords. The magistracy retorted that Ovinov entered the magistracy with a detachment, dragged the mayor out, almost cut the magistracy personnel to pieces with drawn swords and knocked over the judges' bench with its mirror and fixtures.

ABUSES IN COLLEGES

Such coarseness in outlying regions is understandable if all too evident in instructions issued by the colleges. The nobleman Prokofy Demidov complained to the empress that a College of Mines order unjustly slandered him in abusive language, calling him a spiritual menace and a total reprobate. Catherine instructed the Senate to determine whether the college had decided Demidov's case correctly. It was reprimanded for using insulting language and ordered to recall all orders that were abusive.

EFFORTS TO REFORM ADMINISTRATIVE CUSTOMS

It was the state's responsibility to eliminate this coarseness by combatting it in the civil administration and the judiciary. Elizabeth's attempts to limit torture have been described earlier.[37] Further progress was inevitable under Catherine, who paid careful attention to European thinkers. At her first appearance in the Senate in 1763, she stated that an honest confession was elicited more effectively by mercy and admonition than by severity and torture, especially when filling out the details of various cases. Blood should not be shed unless circumstances required it. Torture might be applied when other means were exhausted but not in small towns,[38] which must send their criminals to provincial and government chancelleries.

The greatest care possible must be taken lest the innocent unjustly be tortured with the guilty. Everyone put to torture first must be exhorted to confess by a learned priest. A special exhortatory manual should be compiled for cities without learned priests. "The innocent must not suffer with the guilty," the empress said, but the innocent always suffered with the guilty because an innocent wife and children were punished by confiscation of a criminal's property and then sent out into the world. Catherine also mitigated this kind of judicial brutality.

THEFT OF BESTUZHEV-RIUMIN'S DIAMONDS

In addition to the Glebov case the Senate resolved another unfortunate affair. The senior secretary of the Senate Brianchaninov and Secretary Weymarn were convicted of taking Count Bestuzhev-Riumin's diamonds and gold snuff-box when he fell from power. The empress confirmed the sentence passed on the offenders. Brianchaninov was to be stripped of his ranks and brought to the square facing the Senate and the colleges. There he was to stand for a quarter-hour at a pillar with the inscription on his chest "bribe-taker and violator of oaths." Then he was to be imprisoned for six months and forbidden to take any public or private position in the future. In respect for Lieutenant General Weymarn's title and years of service his punishment was limited to stripping of his ranks, bread and water for two weeks, prison for six months and being barred from serving again. Their property was divided among their wives and children as prescribed by law.

CATHERINE NAMES A COMMISSION ON THE NOBILITY

On this occasion the offenders' property was not confiscated and instead was given to their families, but this was a unique occurrence. The nobility wanted a statute abolishing confiscation permanently. They were dissatisfied with Peter III's manifesto freeing the nobility from compulsory service because it was incomplete and unclear.[39] Catherine said in a note to Nikita Panin that the nobles grumbled because their freedom was not confirmed, and wrote that "we should not forget to act on this."

Action was taken by naming a commission on the nobility. Its members were Field Marshal Count Bestuzhev-Riumin, Hetman Count Razumovsky, Chancellor Count Vorontsov, Senators Prince Yakov Petrovich Shakhovskoy and [Nikita] Panin, General-in-Chief Count Zakhar Chernyshev, Prince Mikhail Volkonsky and Adjutant General Count Grigory Orlov. Teplov was named chief secretary. On February 11 the commission was summoned to her imperial majesty's private quarters. Catherine entered and gave Teplov a handwritten order, which he read aloud to the assembly.

"The former emperor Peter III," the order said, "granted the honorable Russian nobility freedom but in several areas this act restricted that freedom more than the fatherland and our service needs might require. Since then both the state and the education of noble youth have changed. Therefore we order you assembled here in our court to examine this act and confer among yourselves how to improve it. What specific regulations should we issue for the Russian nobility that it might receive from our hand a new pledge of monarchical favor for its posterity? A prudent policy must have a firm foundation. Hence, while broadening noble liberties, you are to draft articles encouraging the greatest possible desire to serve, and to aid us and our beloved fatherland."[40]

BESTUZHEV'S PROPOSALS

We are aware of the elderly Bestuzhev's thoughts at the commission. To encourage service, he suggested that those who served a minimum of seven years receive precedence over those who did no service. Without service they might not buy land, and must defer to the lowest commissioned officer. Otherwise nobles would be careless in their work and relapse into their former idleness. Bestuzhev proposed that noble rights include a prohibition against being placed under guard without a preliminary hearing, and exemption from torture or confiscation of property. In court a noble must be allowed to choose another noble for his attorney. Nobles must have unlimited authority over peasants and serfs. Peasants and bondsmen might neither testify against their masters nor have their petitions or denunciations concerning their masters received.

Measures must be enacted to prevent nobles from wasting time idly and carelessly in their villages after leaving service. They must elect members to take turns serving as district councillors to supervise the districts of the various noble corporations. After the Senate received notice of the nominees and approved them, the district councillors would undertake everything necessary to further the state's interests and the nobles' welfare, including settling quarrels among nobles. They would promote their corporation's interests and be advocates for oppressed or offended nobles in local district courts. To discourage further idleness, nobles might choose worthy men from their number to serve as governors' assistants, military governors and military governors' assistants.

Bestuzhev understood that Catherine's instruction to the commission was intended to encourage nobles to serve after service no longer was compulsory. "A prudent policy requires a firm foundation. Consequently, while expanding noble liberties, articles must be drafted promoting the greatest possible desire to serve for our benefit and that of our beloved fatherland." The commission's report reflected Bestuzhev's requests that it deal with noble rights, but ignored everything he said about nobles in the countryside doing some kind of service. Instead the report expanded on the notion that the only restriction on noble liberties be ambition *already inculcated* by education.

THE COMMISSION'S REPORT

"The nobility," the report said, "already has such high aspirations that for nobles who have lived in the age of enlightenment or were born in this era to revert to the former distaste for service is unthinkable. Since each strives to find a position for his son or relative, there scarcely are enough places for those who wish them. Each admitted to service, particularly in your imperial majesty's reign, gratefully acknowledges how indefatigably the most gracious sovereign labors on behalf of the fatherland and how carefully she watches over it. A worthy noble seeking distinction is incapable of sluggish service."

Deceitful phrases could not soothe Catherine's wrath at such a false picture of the existing nobility, and it was reflected in her remarks at various places on the report. The commission recommended, for example, that nobles might travel abroad and enter the service of foreign powers, saying that "nothing so perfects a military man's knowledge of his profession, and nothing better fosters courage and ambition than a host of good examples, models and experiences." Catherine wrote in the margin

"N.B. and nothing is more beneficial than loafing in theaters and taverns, for example, in Paris." Where the commission said that "everyone doubtless agrees that a noble who serves in many (foreign) armies is considered a competent general," Catherine wrote, "he is a vagrant."

The empress was dissatisfied with the commission's report and did not resolve the matter until 1785. Information she received in the meantime about Russian nobles' conduct abroad only confirmed her opinion that the commission was too hasty. "Prince Alexander Mikhailovich," she wrote to Vice-Chancellor Prince Golitsyn,[41] "I have been asked to recall Dmitry Mikhailovich Matiushkin[42] from Paris where he has been leading a totally ruinous and debauched life. I foresaw it all, but no one listened to me. I order you to write to have him leave at once." This was not the only example.

POLICY TOWARDS OLD BELIEVERS

Peter III's January 29 [1762] manifesto concerning Old Believers[43] required review as well as his Manifesto of Freedom to the Nobility. The Old Believers were guaranteed religious freedom, and religious persecution of Muslims or pagans was prohibited. Great hopes were aroused among the Old Believers, who now submitted new requests to Catherine. The question was referred to the Holy Synod, which delayed action because of the issue's importance and complexity. "Alexander Ivanovich," wrote the empress on February 28 to Glebov, "rouse the bishops of Novgorod and Pskov to act on the Old Believers. Just today I received a petition from those people (that is, Old Believers)."[44]

Bishops Dmitry of Novgorod and Gedeon of Pskov submitted their opinion. "The pastors of the Russian church," they wrote, "have made and continue to make every effort to preserve the community of faith, and not just in matters of dogma and ritual. They wrote many books presenting the real truth, but with only minor results. Next the pastors were inflamed by zeal to condemn the Old Believers and sever them completely from the church, but this approach also failed. Like skilled physicians who try another remedy to cure an illness when the first has no effect, we are contemplating another way to gather the lost sheep. Now they want to return, but preserve some of their rites, such as seven Communion loaves, the two-fingered sign of the cross and so on. They promise to obey the church in everything else and to accept our priests.

"The first question is whether we can allow this, because these rites have been condemned by the synods. Our opinion is that the condemnation applied to the essence of the rites rather than to the rites themselves. The Old Believers were condemned for their opposition to the holy church, for willfully breaking with it and even more for the various insults and attacks many of them directed against it. Our reasoning is as follows. If the condemnation were based on rites alone there would be grounds for considering it invalid, something occasioned by excessive zeal. Since the Apostle Paul stated that the law can be changed if need be, does changing rites and customs necessarily mean changes in belief? Let them be of one mind with our Orthodox church in all save their rites. Hence there is no doubt that they be accepted by and united with our Orthodox community, and let God take care of the rest. This is our opinion. For this reason we trust our other brothers and fellow pastors of the holy church will agree with us. Our judgment will have added weight when the council concurs, and doubtless the entire church will rejoice over the salvation of its excommunicated children."

Two other bishops, Gavriil of St. Petersburg and Amvrosy of Krutitsa, presented a separate opinion. "Receiving the Old Believers," they argued, "and retaining them without coercion is possible only on the same basis as the currently-registered Old Believers, allowed everything they demand. This means permitting them to build separate churches, have their own priests and books in the old print and live according to the same rites as they now do abroad. Sanctioning that would be wrong. All intelligent people believe that allowing syncretism or a variety of faiths in an autocratic state is harmful, for nothing so binds subjects to their sovereign as a common faith. On the other hand, religious differences definitely pose a great danger. To avoid this, in the past many sovereigns exterminated religious dissenters when they appeared and continue to do so today.

"If they are allowed to build separate churches and have their own priests, it follows that they will be permitted to have their own hierarchs not consecrated by us. Consequently the Old Believers either will receive our hierarchs who have been expelled or have run away, or institute their own hierarchy. The church in Russia thus could split in two. Attention also should be paid whether some deception lurks here. Might this not be the occasion for Old Believers living abroad to request the same conditions and privileges as those here at home? If those abroad return to Russia we see no need for them to enjoy total freedom and to live and worship as they please. It is true that in the Russian empire non-Orthodox Christians are allowed public churches and Muslims their mosques, but that is no precedent for Old Believers because these other religions pose no threat to our Orthodox Christians."

This complex problem was not resolved, although the way already was prepared for the so-called community of faith. On September 15 the Senate and the Synod held a joint meeting to deal with an issue presented in a signed order. Because the census decree failed to specify the taxes the secret Old Believers must pay, the Senate in joint conference with the Synod was to decide. The Synod said that Old Believers' tax obligation was a secular matter and hence the business of the Governing Senate. Those who did not shun the Orthodox church, received the sacraments from Orthodox priests and merely used the two-fingered sign of the cross should not be excluded from the churches and the sacraments.[45]

COLLEGE OF CHURCH LANDED PROPERTY ESTABLISHED

The report of the commission on church lands led to the establishment of the College of Church Landed Property. It was to administer church lands, set economic affairs in order, increase income and collect dues in cash and in grain. It was charged as well with keeping official records for diocesan chancelleries, monasteries and other clerical property, and for higher schools in the dioceses and lower schools in the monasteries. The college was responsible for supplying food and money in specified amounts to invalids' residences and for supervising invalids. Court Tutor Boris Kurakin[46] was named president of the new college.[47]

GRIGORY POTEMKIN ASSIGNED TO THE SENATE

We saw that one of the Orlovs, Count Fedor, was assigned to the Senate to acquaint him with its transactions.[48] A second prominent participant in the events of June 28,[49] Grigory Alexandrovich Potemkin,[50] was sent to the Senate for the same reason.[51]

UNREST AMONG FOUNDRY PEASANTS

It was hoped that transferring the monastery peasants to the College of Church Landed Property would halt the turmoil among them. A similar transfer of the iron foundries with their assigned peasants was intended to pacify them as well, but this proved more difficult. The impossibility of including all private foundries necessitated other measures, particularly since other peasants also were restive.

Prince Viazemsky reported that peasants were assigned to foundries by force at the foundry owners' request. Elected peasant representatives[52] selected foundry workers by household rather than by village and hamlet.

This procedure excluded some fit for labor, creating great hardship and inequality. Those selected had to work far more to feed themselves and their families than peasants who remained on the land, causing the foundry peasants great burdens. The duties were so onerous that a peasant simply could not finish his daily tasks with or without a horse. Since the soul tax was based on the total number of registered male serfs, those registered as able-bodied paid the taxes for all. The result was gross inequality, terrible burdens and devastation for the peasants. Assigned peasants sometimes lived as far as four hundred versts from the foundries, so over a year laborers wasted considerable time. The foundries did not profit and the peasants were ruined.

Consequently the College of Mines was directed to inform all foundry owners that the peasants did not rebel on their own. In simple-mindedness they trusted evil plotters, and these were to be punished. Because the peasants bore heavy burdens and their pay in no way was commensurate with their labor foundry owners could not ask the peasants to pay for the damage they inflicted, and most seek some kind of peaceful settlement. The foundry owners profited nothing from the complete ruination of the assigned peasants.[53]

OTHER PEASANT DISTURBANCES

We learned that disturbances were not confined to foundry peasants nor to a specific eastern border region. In the spring news came that Tevkelev's peasants rebelled in the Ufimsk region. Order was restored and fourteen peasants and a retired soldier living there were named the chief instigators. The Senate ordered the peasant ringleaders punished at the landlord's discretion, then restored to peasant status, while the soldier was to be flogged mercilessly in public. At midyear the Senate learned that six hundred peasants of the Bezhetsk district of the Novgorod lands belonging to her imperial majesty's confessor Dubiansky, the Princes Meshchersky and other landlords had rebelled, refused to submit and opposed a military detachment sent against them.

VIAZEMSKY TO INVESTIGATE CORRUPTION

Viazemsky's reports showed how officials took advantage of peasants, particularly non-Russians.[54] Viazemsky was commissioned by the sovereign personally to investigate corruption and report directly to her. Lieutenant Colonel Svechin, sent to the Kazan government to inspect oak groves, reported that the state peasants were being mistreated and ruined by foresters, chancelleries and officials on various assignments. This took the following forms (1) Foresters collected between three and six copecks per male serf and forest hundredmen a ruble from each village. (2) Clerks and soldiers sent to collect dues at harvest time took one or two copecks from each male serf and a ruble or more from each village for accepting declarations and issuing various permits. (3) When appeals to control bootleggers, robbers and brigands were submitted to the chancelleries at soul tax payment time, a village was charged two or three rubles for each appeal. Otherwise payment for the soul tax was not accepted. (4) When the soul tax was collected, officers and clerks took ten or fifteen copecks per male serf from every rural district. (5) Fifty copecks were charged for each passport with a seal. (6) People were forced to work on boats carrying copper up the Volga, mostly without pay. (7) Chancellery messengers took food and supplies without payment. Although these travellers had no business to transact with local inhabitants they displayed documents of one kind or another, threatening dire consequences. Since the local people were illiterate, understanding nothing, they paid.

The Senate demanded to know why such conduct was tolerated. It demanded a report on the matter to determine the penalty for the Kazan chancellery and a separate list of of those complaining of chancellery abuses for the present and past years, and the satisfaction accorded them. If no decision was reached, what caused the delay?

PEASANT FLIGHT TO POLAND

In western areas peasants continued to try to cross into Poland. Novgorod landlords reported that for many years numerous peasants and household servants abandoned their villages at the instigation of Gavriushka, a fugitive conscript of Polish origin. This year, 1763, he incited at least one hundred families numbering about five hundred males and females to flee. The Senate offered a reward of three hundred rubles for anyone who found Gavriushka, but with no assurance of success.

There was a search for the cause of the problem and effective means to combat it. Peter Ivanovich Panin[55] proposed measures to stop the flight abroad, citing the reasons for it (1) Clerical severity and various demands from the clergy and the civil authorities on Old Believers for money. (2) Conscription in villages nearest the border and some landlords' practice of taking men from families in their own villages and selling them to take the place of conscripts from other landlords' villages. This ignored the grief and pain of the families left behind, who saw conscription as death and perpetual exile. (3) The extraordinarily harsh conditions conscripts endured on their way to their regiments and the heavy financial burdens laid on them. Conscripts, already distressed by separation from family and friends, were employed for personal ends rather than sent to the military. Even in the two capitals [Moscow and St. Petersburg] conscripts were assembled before their quarters were ready. They spent days in bitter cold and nights in hot public baths. This was a terrible sight for their families and an example of what future conscription held in store for their children. (4) Landlords enjoyed unlimited power, and their unbridled love of luxury drove them to collect dues from their subjects. Serfs were forced to labor more than what was required across the nearby frontier, labor beyond human ability. (5) The increase in the price of salt and alcohol made their sale more difficult, ignoring the fact that they were cheaper and readily available across the border. (6) Injustice and negligence in public affairs due to endemic corruption, particularly in outlying areas. (7) City officials were chosen for their usefulness to the dignitaries dispatching them rather than for ability to discharge their responsibilities.

A manifesto was issued pardoning the fugitives and welcoming them to return. Another appeal was made for foreign colonists and to Old Believers. It was broadcast widely in neighboring states, yet those without assets who responded found closed doors. Settlers were best attracted by the special supervision of a senator or minister, one for foreigners and one for Old Believers. Information about these authorities must be disseminated abroad so that people wanting to resettle might turn to them directly for help and protection.

Returning Old Believers were to be assessed two rubles seventy copecks a year, divided into three payments. Landlords were to receive one hundred rubles for each male serf who refused to return but only for actual runaways, not for their fathers and grandfathers. Instead of levying conscripts from villages and cities within seventy versts of the frontier, one hundred rubles were to be collected for each conscript needed and the money used to enlist freemen in hussar regiments. The barbaric practice of selling private peasants as substitutes for conscripts from other villages, a practice springing from insatiable love of luxury, must be prohibited. Peasants might not be sold except as families.

A new law must be enacted with truly effective provisions for the best possible care of new peasant conscripts and the best possible consolation for the families from whom they had been separated. A statute valid throughout the realm must be drafted to regulate peasant dues and services to landlords, and its contents sent to the governors as secret directives not to be revealed to the general public. When entire villages or families fled from landlords or rebelled, detachments to pacify and apprehend them must be sent without fail at the landlords' request. In such cases the governors were to assign reliable people to investigate how the landlords exercised their authority, whether they conformed to the provisions of the statute or treated their peasants too harshly.

If it was found that landlords exceeded statutory provisions, they must be summoned to government chancelleries and told to desist. If their peasants subsequently complained to the government, the villages of such landlords must be confiscated and administered by the crown. Henceforth governors must supervise offending landlords carefully and report violations to the Senate. Landlords must not compel peasants to work more than four days a week, nor plow more than one desiatina of good land, mow more than three stacks of hay nor cut more and one and a half sazhens of firewood in a twenty-four hour period. Quitrent must not exceed two rubles. Town governors[56] in border districts must have a good European education in addition to specific qualifications for the post.

DIFFICULTY OF PEASANT REFORM

These views did not make it any easier to resolve this difficult issue. Catherine knew the causes of the misfortune and considered ways of eliminating it, but in vain. It was easy to say a decree should be issued to entice conscripts into service and ease the pain of separation for their families, but there was no mention of actual wording. Educated people who insisted others ought to be educated should have known that Peter the Great ordered peasants taken from oppressive and rapacious landlords. The answer lay not in orders, but in people to implement them, and these did not exist.

It was hoped that such educated people would appear, but in the meantime the commission on noble liberties dismissed the issue of nobles' responsibilities to the state and the obligations of landlords who did no service. Instead it discussed how a Russian noble should serve "in seven hordes[57] for seven kings," and said that nobles raised with this sense of honor needed no other inducement to serve. Breeding was innate, and could not developed further. Meanwhile the commission's senior member demanded unlimited authority for landlords over peasants. Even though Panin's proposal spoke forcefully of the harm this unlimited power caused, he recommended a secret statute specifying what landlords ought to require of peasants!

CATHERINE CONSIDERS A MORE GENERAL REFORM

As Catherine heard all these opinions she became convinced more and more that effective measures to improve the people's lot were possible only if enacted as part of a coordinated policy of general government restructuring. All interested parties should be heard, not just particular individuals. It was not until later that this student of eighteenth-century European political theory developed her plan for a commission representing all estates to draft a new code of laws.[58]

CATHERINE ACTS TO COUNTER FLIGHT TO POLAND

As ruler of a much more powerful state Catherine could not tolerate a weaker country on her border allowing continual migration from its mighty neighbor, and so taunted Poland with complaints and demands. The empress issued an order to the Senate in August 1763 saying that many Russian fugitives in Poland engaged in large-scale brigandage on her imperial majesty's domains. The Poles ignored our complaints, encouraged flight [from Russia], held runaways by force and refused to surrender brigands. In Moscow the Senate recommended sending special military units to seize brigands and fugitives secretly. A similar recommendation was made to her imperial majesty earlier, but she postponed action in order to maintain friendly relations with her neighbor.

Now her imperial majesty saw that leniency and moderation were hurting and ruining her subjects, and so authorized the dispatch of military detachments. As a result of this order Major General Maslov was sent with a force across the Polish border. He returned on October 7 with 1,015 males and 512 females, 1,527 in all.

FORGED IMPERIAL ORDER CIRCULATED

That month [October 1763] a forgery, purportedly an order from the empress to the Senate, was circulated. "It is time to eradicate corruption. It is my fervent wish that tranquillity prevail. Our nobles have flouted the laws of God and of the realm, thereby causing the Russian state great harm. The monarchs who were the ancestors and forefathers of the Russian state granted the nobles hereditary estates and money, but the nobles forgot that they truly were members of the first class and protest against obeying as they formerly did in Russia. Under the benevolent reign of the monarch Peter the Great, the nobles faithfully honored the laws of God and rigorously observed those of the state.

"Now justice has been banished completely, totally excluded from Russia. No one wants to hear that the Russian people and little motherless children are orphans. Will not those nobles perish and face divine judgment? God will judge them and His retribution shall be meted out to you in due measure as well. Catherine."[59]

NEW CENSUS PROPOSED

Preparations began at the end of 1761 for a new census. "I went to the Senate," Catherine described how the matter was resolved, "some time after my return to St. Petersburg in June 1763. The senators were discussing a new census, a necessity because the last was twenty years ago. They asked me to order a new census of the whole empire, including military units not previously counted, estimating that it would cost at least eight hundred thousand rubles. In their discussions the senators mentioned the countless responsibilities the government would incur in conducting a general census, the fugitives in Poland and abroad to be counted and the vast military forces needed. They thought it would be a hardship for the empire, but considered it beneficial.

"For a long time I listened to everything they said. When finally it was time for a resolution, the gentlemen senators fell silent. I asked why such a large military force and so great a burden on the treasury were necessary. Was there an alternative? They told me things were done this way in the past. I responded that I thought a public announcement could made throughout the empire for each settlement to send a list of its inhabitants to the proper military governor's chancellery. The chancelleries would send the lists to the governments, who in turn would forward them to the Senate.

"Four senators rose to tell me there would be countless omissions. I told them to penalize omissions, but they replied omissions existed despite harsh penalties already imposed for them. I then said a pardon should be granted at my request for all previous instances of omissions, and that settlements be instructed to add those formerly omitted to the current census lists. Here Prince Yakov Petrovich Shakhovskoy said angrily that this was unjust and equated the guilty with the innocent. I declared forcefully that I would have no omissions and that anyone who tolerated them was usurping my authority.[60]

"Alexander Glebov, who was procurator general at the time, listened from his desk to the whole discussion. When he saw how angry Prince

Shakhovskoy was, he leapt out of his chair and came over to me. He asked me to tell him I wanted a census conducted, which I did readily. He ordered everything written down and the details worked out. This was done, and the census was conducted without troops and without hardship. There are no omissions, neither is there any mention of them."[61]

The record of the matter in the Senate protocols is dated February 10, [1763], which means that the Senate was in Moscow and had not returned to the capital. In the empress's presence the senators heard how the census was discussed in 1761. On December 20, 1761 the Senate sent directives throughout the realm for lists of male serfs to be collected by the chancelleries of governments, provinces and military governors when the soul tax was paid. This was to be done within five months of the issuance of the directives, *but without sending special inspectors*. Some lists already were collected. Later the Governing Senate learned that, contrary to regulations, chancelleries in the cities deceived, burdened and obstructed submission of lists. As a result on July 31, 1762 the Senate stopped collecting lists pending a formal order.

Since it was absolutely necessary to complete the census the empress directed all lists be collected. There were several procedures: (1) To obviate all possible burdens in submitting lists, those responsible were allowed, once the list was compiled, to submit them in person or send them with the name of the governor or military governor written and printed on the packet. To avoid mistakes, printed sheets were to be sent free of charge to all churches for distribution to the people. Anyone was free to buy eight sheets for a copeck, and priests could use the money received for church needs. (2) Anyone who concealed information would be dealt with most severely. Landlords would be stripped of their ranks and no longer accounted men of honor. Bailiffs and elders would be treated as prescribed by law.

Taxpayers and laborers were not to be omitted from the census or allowed to emigrate. Fugitives were to be returned and appeals made to attract voluntary colonists. These measures were intended to increase the number of taxpayers and replenish the depleted state treasury. "The Riga military commanders have not been paid for ten months," Catherine wrote to Glebov in February, "the common soldiers for eight and the other ranks for six. There are loud complaints, and we cannot require obedience from a soldier serving without pay. Many officers sent to retirement in Russia have not received even a quarter-copeck of their pension, and are forced to leave."[62]

EFFORTS TO INCREASE STATE REVENUE

Even though pay was in arrears, the need for raising official salaries to prevent corruption was recognized. The Senate received an order to find one and a half million rubles for state institutions. The Senate also deliberated how to make up the loss caused by lowering the price of salt by one grivna a pud. It decided salt must be sold at the former price of forty copecks a pud and the new income assigned to state institutions.

The Senate decided that these fees go to state institutions. (1) Thirty copecks for each pail of liquor and five copecks for each pail of beer and mead sold at taverns. This should amount to 452, 565 rubles for liquor and 182, 557 for beer and mead, a total of 635,122 rubles. The Senate observed that "these purchases are voluntary and hence no burden on the people." (2) Three and a quarter copecks from the duty on registering real estate contracts and the same amount when contracts are written and executed. (3) Fees for permission to sell beer and kvas. (4) Fees from inns. (5) Fees on promissory notes. (6) Fees on official petitions. (7) Fees for renegotiating leases at higher prices for warehouses, shops, smithies and other commercial properties. (8) Fees from industrial mills. (9) Fees from factories. (10) Income from higher charges for peasant passports. (11) Fees for licenses. (12) Fees for diplomas. (13) Fees for marriage certificates. (14) Fees for stamping drinking vessels. (15) Fees for renegotiating leases for grain mills. (16) Higher fees from secret Old Believers. (17) Fees for manufacturing glue for government sale. (18) State institutions were to collect two copecks for each ruble paid to collectors when the soul tax is deposited. (19) Income from doubling charges for heraldic paper.

CATHERINE ORDERS GOVERNMENT RESTRUCTURING

A manifesto was issued [by Catherine] on December 15 based on the Senate's material. "To our great distress and deep regret, daily experience makes us realize that many of our loyal subjects' cases are not resolved quickly and fairly as provided by law. This occurs in various courts, particularly those far from our residences. Coercion and bribery or, in plain words, robbery, have ruined and impoverished our subjects. Granted that since Peter the Great's reign there have been various measures to curb these abuses and the full force of the law applied, the results fell short of expectations. Total ignoramuses and incompetents received assignments because neither judges nor their subordinates were investigated carefully enough. Further, officials routinely were sent on assignments with inadequate support. They received daily rations, but no additional salary and little else. Like paupers in a poorhouse they had just enough for food but not enough to conduct business. In reality each looked to his own interests, ignoring the common good.

"We have found the quickest and most effective means of eliminating this sorry state of affairs. Knowledgeable and upright people must fill all judicial positions. Each must receive an appropriate salary sufficient for support above the poverty level. Therefore we have established and confirmed new state institutions, not just for colleges and chancelleries, but for governments, provinces and cities. These accord with the particular circumstances of each post and the kind of business that comes before it."[63]

PROBLEMS WITH THE SALT TRADE

The new state institutions refused to lower the price of salt. The Senate reported that the treasury paid less for the more desirable salt from Perm than for salt from Elton.[64] Perm salt was delivered to the barons Stroganov and the Peskorsk monastery in Nizhny Novgorod for 8.1 copecks. Since they stored the salt in their own warehouses, there was no further cost to the treasury. The state bore the entire expense of producing and storing Elton salt, which because of transport problems cost seventeen copecks a pud delivered from Elton and Pletsk to Nizhny Novgorod.

Therefore the Perm producers should be paid ten copecks a pud to pay for sawmills to allow the transport of salt in boats of planks sawn rather than hewn by axes. They were not to be held to a quota but allowed to produce as much salt as they wished. More salt thereby would be delivered to the Salt Bureau at a cheaper price. When the bureau must reduce salt delivery or stop it altogether, it was to inform the producers a year before the next saltboiling. When producers planned to reduce deliveries they were to notify the bureau a year in advance to allow it to stockpile other salt. Both Pletsk and Elton salt were supplied.

The Medical Bureau said that Pletsk salt was suitable for salting meat and fish. The Orenburg governor Volkov claimed that Pletsk salt was the best in the world, although the Chief Salt Bureau reported that both big and little lumps of Pletsk salt were full of dust, and some contained dirt, trash and sand. The sand could not be removed completely nor dust picked out of the smaller lumps. The Senate ordered salt sent to it for testing, and directed Volkov to visit the mine to assess salt quality and whether it came dirty from the mine or was contaminated from carelessness during transport.

PROBLEMS WITH CUSTOMS FRANCHISES

Commercial and financial issues went hand in hand. Catherine gave her views on commerce in a letter sent from Moscow on June 10 to Ivan Ivanovich Nepliuev.[65] "Holders of customs franchises have complained that State Councillor Yakovlev has invented ways to oppress not just them, the franchise holders, but commerce in general. The authority vested in Yakovlev and his assistants is to be exercised only in conformity with our directives, and he is not to act in a way to destroy thriving commerce. You know that as a rule commerce flourishes when it is free and unfettered, and that we never intended such harsh treatment of commercial franchises. Only prescribed procedures are to be followed.

"The primary concern is that somehow the treasury receives the agreed amounts from franchise holders. Since the franchise holders are the experts in trade and commerce, they should be allowed to collect duties any way they wish. The nature of commerce is such that a single hour of maladministration can injure credit established over many years, which once lost is difficult to restore. Therefore have this matter investigated by the Senate bureau immediately."[66]

In this instance Catherine felt obligated to defend customs franchise holders although in general she opposed the franchise system. The Senate reported that the Karachev merchant Sulov wanted to pay the state sixty thousand rubles a year for a six-year franchise to sell Russian and foreign playing cards. "May the devil take him and his franchise," remarked Catherine. "You [the Senate] are frightening all the merchants, and it is said the Senate favors franchises." At the end of the year Nepliuev, Prince Yakov Shakhovskoy and Count Münnich.[67] were ordered to investigate commerce in the Russian empire and the merchant class. This commission was important enough that the empress wanted to participate in it and put it under her sole authority and protection. Teplov was named chief clerk.

CONSULS IN POLAND AND PERSIA NAMED

A consul was needed in Poland, and the Senate picked the Smolensk burgher Davydov. Following the precedent for consuls in Persia, the Senate fixed Davydov's salary at five hundred rubles a year, with an additional fifteen hundred rubles from the merchant estate. "Remember," Catherine wrote on the report, "that the Astrakhan merchants voluntarily gave the consuls in Persia a salary, which we supplemented with five hundred rubles. He [Davydov] should have two clerks, or perhaps only one to avoid needless expense." The Senate named the Simbirsk merchant Ilia Igumnov consul to Persia at the request of the Moscow and Astrakhan merchants, directing them to choose a second consul for Persia as well.

DEBATE OVER COPPER MONEY

An argument broke out in the Senate when some members wished to increase the supply of copper money in circulation, but Prince Yakov Shakhovskoy was opposed. "I disagree with Prince Shakhovskoy," wrote the empress. "I do not believe the consequences will be as dire as he predicts if the amount of copper money in circulation is increased in proportion to the population of our empire rather than on the basis of sixteen rubles from each pud [of copper]. Everyone knows how little money, especially copper, now circulates in our empire. Since the days of Tsar Alexis Mikhailovich[68] there were never more than five rubles per person.

"It would be no great calamity if private citizens transferred their money through letters of exchange instead of taking it in wagons from city to city. This requires large state banks in various locations, but banks cannot be established without sufficient money. A bank is nothing more than a safe repository for money. The unfortunate existence of banks for copper money is not a good precedent. Laws must eliminate bad precedents, not be determined by them. As the guardian of laws, the Governing Senate's primary obligation as long as I live is to prevent harm."

FOUNDLING HOME ESTABLISHED IN MOSCOW

Betskoy[69] proposed establishing a foundling home in Moscow. Since state finances were problematic, his idea of using voluntary contributions was received warmly. Prince Yakov Shakhovskoy, [Nikita] Panin and (Senior Privy Councillor) Count Münnich accepted and approved the proposal, stressing that "the establishment and maintenance of the home depends solely on voluntary public donations and must not impose the slightest burden on your imperial majesty's government or subjects."[70]

MEDICAL PROBLEMS ADDRESSED

Adults needed care as well as children. Procurator General Glebov informed the Senate there were 671 patients in the St. Petersburg general hospital, more than two wards of whom had contracted syphilis from loose women. Glebov suggested that all military units question everyone with this disease how he contracted it. The women were to be found and examined and, if syphilitic, treated at state expense, then resettled in Nerchinsk or somewhere else when cured. Soldiers' wives must be returned to their husbands, who would give receipts and guarantee to support them and keep them from loose living. Serf and other women were to be sent to their masters. The Senate confirmed Glebov's proposal, adding that special care be exercised lest women be defamed unnecessarily. At the end of the year a separate college of medicine was established to improve medical care. Retired guards captain Baron Alexander Cherkasov[71] was named first president of the college.

IV

PROVINCES AND BORDERLANDS

FIRES IN STARAIA RUSA, TVER AND USTIUZHNA

The new government soon had to deal with a common Russian calamity. Staraia Rusa burned down on April 22. Tver was destroyed on May 12 by a fire which consumed 852 dwellings and killed thirty-three people. The chancellery, the palace and the chancellaries of the archbishop and the military governor were burned. The Senate decided to lend victims of the fire one hundred thousand rubles interest-free for ten years and supply another one hundred thousand rubles' worth of stone building materials. The two hundred thousand rubles were to be raised at no cost to the treasury by minting an additional sixteen rubles from each pud of copper. Victims were exempted from the soul tax for three years. Free bread was to be distributed to those unable to work. Only stone houses built to specifications might be allowed in the city. Wooden houses were permitted in the suburbs if there were gardens, kitchen gardens or passageways between them. Open spaces would be set aside for squares in the city and suburbs. Betskoy was sent to Tver to supervise reconstruction. Ustiuzhna burned on June 25.

MISTREATMENT OF SIBERIAN NATIVE PEOPLES

The border regions demanded considerable attention. For one hundred and fifty years there were continual complaints about mistreatment of Siberian native peoples. The same descriptions of oppression recurred in every reign, as for example in a signed order the Senate received on February 6.

"We know that the fur tribute is collected in a most burdensome and irregular manner from local inhabitants throughout the Siberian government and Irkutsk province. A better way of putting it is that Siberian nobles, cossacks and junior boyars sent to collect the fur tribute take not the prescribed amount but instead unscrupulously plunder and ruin all those mute and defenseless tribute-payers. These include Yakuts, Tungus, Chukchi, fraternal cossacks (Buriats) and others."[1] The Senate was ordered to send Guards Captain Shcherbakov to Siberia to combat these evils.[2]

REGULATION OF KAZAN SETTLERS

Since 1736 retired non-commissioned officers and enlisted men were settled according to the Roman system[3] in the Kazan government on the Zakamsk line and in the neighboring small towns of Novoshashminsk, Zainsk and Tiinsk. During that period 1,477 adults with 3,489 male children settled there. They lived profitably on fertile land on which they paid no taxes. Every ten homesteads established more than five years was required to erect a homestead for new settlers to ease their circumstances and stabilize their life. Settlements were limited to one hundred homesteads.

New settlers received twenty to thirty chetverts of land, military rations for the first two years, rye, oats, and eight rubles in cash. They could not spend the money themselves. Instead they gave it to designated reliable people assigned to buy all their necessary equipment. Settlers' children were exempt from military conscription and the soul tax "to allow the settlers to become more firmly established and economically secure." It was decided to found settlements on the same model in Siberia and since the land was empty, the state would pay to build houses for settlers.

RECRUITMENT OF FOREIGN COLONISTS

When Catherine decided to attract foreign colonists,[4] Peter Panin recommended especially trustworthy people to supervise arrangements for them. Negative rumors about Russian administration of justice discouraged all but a few from wanting to settle there. An order to the Senate signed July 22 established the Chancellery for Guardianship of Foreigners, with Adjutant General and High Chamberlain Count (Grigory) Orlov as president. Foreign settlers were to appear before this chancellery when they arrived in Russia to state whether they wanted to be enrolled as merchants, burghers or artisans, or become colonists and live in small settlements on open arable land. All were to be free to practice their religion as they saw fit. Colonists might have as many pastors and other ecclesiastics as necessary and build churches and belfries, but not monasteries. Proselytizing Christians of other denominations was strictly prohibited, but conversion and enserfment of Muslims was permitted.

Settlers who cultivated the land were exempt from all duties, taxes and service for thirty years. City dwellers enrolled in St. Petersburg, in Moscow or on territory acquired by the Treaty of Nystadt[5] were exempt for five years and those in other cities for ten. Each colonist received a three-year interest-free loan, which could be extended for seven more years. Individual colonies and settlements were granted self-government, and Russian authorities were forbidden to intervene in colonists' internal affairs.[6]

SLAVIC COLONISTS IN NEW SERBIA

At the time the Chancellery for Guardianship of Foreigners was established, changes in the governance of the Slavic colonists who settled in New Serbia[7] under Elizabeth were required. The famous leader of the colony, Khorvat, began to cause trouble in the Ukraine. At first St. Petersburg gave no credence to complaints against him, but even in Elizabeth's time an inquiry had to be ordered.[8] On March 21 [1762] under Peter III a commission was established to investigate the Khorvat affair, although it was rumored that he forestalled it at the time by making sizable gifts to prominent people.[9]

The matter was reopened under Catherine. It was found Khorvat illegally spent 64,999 rubles of state funds, which sum the treasury was to recoup by selling Khorvat's holdings. He was removed as administrator of New Serbia and replaced by Lieutenant General Melgunov. Brigadier Zorich, who knew the colonists' mores and customs, was named to assist Melgunov, who in turn was subject to the governor general of Kiev. The War College was to supervise the New Serbian Corps, since it consisted of professional soldiers. Only a few emigrants came from peoples hitherto specified in official decrees (Serbs, Bulgars, Wallachians and Macedonians). Consequently orders were issued to receive fugitives returned from Poland, Little Russians, Great Russians and all nationalities "to settle and develop to the greatest extent possible those lands now barren, making them an effective defense line. Their proximity to the border requires this."[10]

TURMOIL IN THE YAIK COSSACK ARMY

Although the Zaporozhian and Don regions were quiet, the old cossack way of life with all its customs and pretensions found an echo far to the east in the Yaik area.[11] Early in 1763 a commission directed by Major General Brachfeldt was established in the town of Yaitsk to investigate cossack leader Borodin, accused of collecting excessive payments from the cossacks and withholding their salaries, powder and shot. The commission also was charged with reviewing arbitrary conduct by Loginov, a cossack officer who improperly and inappropriately commented on orders sent to the Yaik cossack army. The issue was raised when cossacks complained about the War College to the empress. At the same time the sultan of a minor Kirghiz[12] horde asked the chancellor [Mikhail Vorontsov] to remove Borodin and replace him with someone honest and intelligent.

When Borodin's removal became known on the steppe, two Yaik Cossacks appeared in Moscow with a letter to the chancellor from the same Kirghiz sultan. "Some of our requests," wrote the sultan, "have been granted. I am most gratified that Andrei Borodin has been dismissed. I hear, however, that the War College has named a unit officer, Mogutov, a newly-arrived peasant, as cossack hetman. Ever since forty cossacks founded the town of Yaitsk, the Yaik cossack army always has chosen one of its number hetman. The cossacks will be insulted deeply and offended grievously if put under Mogutov's command. I, my brother and the whole Kirghiz-Kesek people will be displeased. If I did not inform your excellency of the cossack army's ruination and the bitter tears, it would receive no satisfaction."

When the chancellor forwarded the letter to the empress she wrote "I already wrote to the president of the War College when other cossacks sent me a petition describing the college's violation of their customs and liberties. It is impossible the Kirghiz are interceding on their behalf."

SECURITY MEASURES ON THE EASTERN FRONTIER

Catherine believed Russian forces on the eastern frontier were insufficient to force the steppe peoples into submission. "Mikhail Larionovich!" she wrote to the chancellor. "The Orenburg governor wrote me that the Kirghiz are delaying and harassing foreign merchants on the road to Orenburg. Have the college take suitable measures at once to deal with the Kirghiz and put a stop to these delays and this harassment. The best policy," she added, "is to arrange to pay them for escorting the caravans."

The Kalmyks[13] also were unruly. The widow of Khan Dunduk-Ombo, a figure from Elizabeth's reign,[14] was baptized with her three sons, taking the name Vera. In 1762, citing her advanced age and poor health, she asked to return to her native steppe. She was permitted to live with her son Alexis in Yenotaevsk, although forbidden to enter the steppe. The supervisor of the Kalmyks, Brigadier Beketev, was ordered not to let her go to Kalmyk settlements or to have dealings with Kalmyk clergy or consort with them.

Beketev reported that since her arrival in Yenotaevsk the princess did associate with Kalmyk clergy. Judging from the Kalmyk ceremonies in her house, he doubted she was committed firmly to Orthodox Christianity. Although she fasted during the first week of Great Lent, she ate meat from the second week on, even during Holy Week. "When Princess Dondukova [sic] and her sons lived in the Corps of Cadets," Catherine wrote on the report, "she always ate meat, and the corps doctors knew she could eat no fish. Take the utmost care to prevent legal interference in possible methods of placating the Kalmyks."

Beketev related the rumor from Yenotaevsk that Prince Iona Dundukov soon would issue a decree naming his mother Princess Vera supreme ruler of the entire Kalmyk people and her son Alexis khan. Ubasha, the current holder of the khanate, was to keep only his hereditary settlement. Rumor also had it that the Kabardian[15] leader Kasay and a company of Cherkess[16] planned to join Princess Vera at Yenotaevsk.

"These intrigues seem well advanced," the empress wrote. "Instruct the supervisor or commandant at Yenotaevsk to watch mother and son lest they leave as did before." A letter was sent Princess Vera threatening to remove her to Moscow if she did not keep quiet. A memorandum from the College of Foreign Affairs recommended moving the Dundukovs from Yenotaevsk to Moscow. The princess would be paid three thousand and her son Alexis one thousand rubles a year. Each also would receive one thousand male serfs from Russian villages as compensation for the settlements granted the current holder of the khanate.

Earlier Catherine named Volkov governor of Orenburg.[17] She expressed complete confidence in him even though he initially declined the post, citing the great popularity his powerful rival, Major General Tevkelev, a Muslim, enjoyed among the non-Russian population. The empress ordered the vice chancellor [Alexander Golitsyn] to discuss Kirghiz affairs with Tevkelev, but Tevkelev said he could not give an opinion until he knew whether the empress wanted to send him to the eastern frontier. If sent he would state his plans, but could not make suggestions for someone else. He also boasted about his previous service.

"His statement indicates he is eager to go to Orenburg," the College of Foreign Affairs reported. "Perhaps he wants to be supreme commander there, although his Muslim faith makes this less than proper." The empress told the vice chancellery to leave Tevkelev alone, noting that Volkov received enough salary at his disposal to stay where he was.[18]

TROUBLE OVER SUCCESSION TO THE HETMANATE

Bad news arrived from Kiev at the very end of the year, on December 27, to be exact. Tumansky, a senior clerk of the General Army Chancellery (a brother of the general secretary), came to Kiev on magistracy business in the middle of December. After he left it was discovered he made certain statements to the metropolitan of Kiev and the archimandrite of the Caves monastery. The archimandrite said Tumansky was circulating a petition urging that one of the sons of the present hetman Razumovsky be chosen and confirmed as the new hetman. The archimandrite refused to sign the petition, and the metropolitan said that "imperial favor alone shall determine who is worthy to be hetman." General Secretary Tumansky was the only [regimental or general] officer who signed, although all of the colonels did, with the exception of the colonel of the Chernigov Regiment Miloradovich. Tumansky and two colonels, Gorlenko and Khovansky, drafted the petition.

The petition said that since Bogdan Khmelnitsky's time new men [not from previously prominent families] were chosen hetmans, creating disorder. Therefore the hetman always must come from the family displaying the greatest loyalty to Russia. This would protect the paramount interests both of her imperial majesty and the whole empire, preserve the previously confirmed Ukrainian laws, liberties and privileges, and spare the people terrible hardship. Next came praise for Razumovsky. He was trustworthy beyond question, his domains in Great Russia were as extensive as those in the Ukraine and his sons would imitate their sire's qualities and laudable conduct. The present hetman's sons should succeed him as hetman just as Yury Khmelnitsky was chosen hetman in gratitude for his father's service.

The colonels and regimental officers met at Glukhov to discuss the search to a new hetman and heard the petition read in the general chancellery. After they heard it some said it was a good idea, but the majority remained silent. "It may seem like a good idea now," General Judge Dubliansky said, "but what will happen in the future? It is impossible to know what will happen, and so I will not sign." At these words everyone left the chancellery one by one. They were summoned to reconvene the following day. At that meeting all colonels signed except for the colonel of the Chernigov Regiment [Miloradovich], whereas none of the regimental and general officers signed except for the general secretary [Tumansky]. "This document I cannot sign," said Quartermaster Kochubey. Lieutenant Skoropadsky said "Even if he [Tumansky] is my superior, I will not sign." "Since they [the other officers present] have seniority," said Standard Bearer Apostol, "let them sign." "I agree with Skoropadsky," said Standard Bearer Tarnovsky, and with that the meeting broke up.

V

COURLAND

BIRON'S TRIUMPHAL ENTRY INTO MITAU

These events on the southwestern frontier were all more unwelcome because Polish affairs required special attention. Simolin[1] wrote to the empress January 11, 1763 describing Biron's triumphal entry into Mitau. The duke's carriage was followed by more than fifty carriages of Courland nobles. A Russian battalion greeted Biron with drum rolls, music and cannon fire as he passed. "I dare say," Simolin wrote, "this city never witnessed such happiness and joy. Every possible source of sound was employed so vigorously that all conversation was drowned out. Church bells rang despite Prince Karl's[2] orders in addition to the shouts of the populace, discharge of weapons and military music." The general jubilation was dampened because the previous prince still occupied the palace, forcing Biron to stay with the merchant Fermon.

POLAND OPPOSES BIRON AND RUSSIA

As many as five hundred noblemen and noblewomen presented themselves to Biron. Only the chief aldermen and members of the court party, about twenty in all, failed to appear. Simolin notified the chief aldermen that the empress would be pleased were they to demonstrate their respect for, love of and obedience to their sovereign [Biron]. They expressed their gratitude for the favor the empress had shown their fatherland and their deep regret that they were unable to attend Duke Ernst Johann. Prince Karl strictly forbade them to do so, and as his subjects they had sworn allegiance to him.

That very day they received an edict from Karl's father the king, ordering them and the entire land to remain loyal to his son. They were not to deal with Duke Ernst Johann or foreign courts without risking loss of life and property. The king instructed Prince Karl not to allow himself to be expelled from Mitau. Other nobles petitioned Simolin to ask the empress if Prince Karl somehow might be induced to leave Mitau before the so-called fraternal conference was convened on January 30. Since the chief aldermen and local authorities were bound by their oaths of allegiance, Karl's presence would confuse and obstruct the conference.

The royal commissioner Castellan Lipski[3] visited Mitau to support Prince Karl against Simolin, and a second military commander, Plater, was expected shortly. Simolin told the chief aldermen to avoid contact with the Polish commissioners. Since the empress acknowledged only Ernst Johann as duke of Courland, she refused to recognize any chief aldermen who served anyone else. The threat worked, and Baron Offenberg quickly submitted to Biron. Others explained to Prince Karl that if he could not defend them, they could conduct no local business against Biron's opposition. Although they preferred postponing matters until the next Sejm,[4] the prince threatened them in the king's name and ordered them to do their duty.

The unfortunate chief aldermen now turned to Simolin, requesting he assure Biron they were prepared to execute his orders loyally and faithfully when they released from their oaths and no longer must fear the king's wrath and retribution. They would forsake Prince Karl should the empress give them a direct order, and also thought it wise were the prince to depart Mitau as soon as possible.

Simolin then told Commissioner Lipski the empress recognized no other duke in Courland but Ernst Johann. Lipski began by saying he knew no justification for Russia's authority over Courland, since presently he was accredited with plenipotentiary powers to Prince Karl. On his arrival he learned that Biron made a triumphal entry into the city and he observed a large Russian force in Mitau. The Russians relied on force alone, whereas his only weapon was the law. Simolin replied that he was not present to demand an explanation of Lipski's behavior but simply to proclaim the empress's wish to safeguard the rights and privileges of the Polish Commonwealth and the Baltic duchies.

I do not dispute," Simolin continued, "that your only weapon is the law, which your side has violated. The empress is obligated by treaty to uphold the law in a neighborly spirit as her predecessors did. It is not in your interest to do anything to harm these lands and their laws. When the Polish court ignores the empress's friendly representations there are, if absolutely necessary, ways to render justice to the aggrieved party." Lipski remained unconvinced and repeated his intention to obey his instructions. To block him Biron followed the nobles' advice to order the chancellery and ducal law courts sealed. This brought the government to a complete standstill.

FRATERNAL CONFERENCE CONVENES

Many nobles assembled in Mitau on the day appointed for the fraternal conference. The morning it opened Lipski ordered copies of the royal rescript forbidding all dealings with Biron posted in all public places. The Lithuanian Grand Master of the Hunt Zabiełło[5] and General Lewicki came to Mitau to be present at the church where the nobility was to gather before the conference, ready to protest all recent Russian actions. Simolin reported that he ordered all copies of the rescript removed because he feared some of the nobles were vacillating and cowardly. He reminded Lipski of the empress's declaration, demanding he not meddle in Courland affairs not of his concern. Heartened by these measures, the directors [of the conference] elected the pro-Russian Heyking of Durben as director, but without the customary noise and shouting. The next day they went to pay homage to Biron.

Simolin ordered Lewicki expelled from Mitau to Lithuania because the nobles felt threatened when he initiated proceedings to bring the matter before Polish courts. The assembled nobles urged the chief aldermen as their elder brothers to join them, for without them the conference would fail. Except for Baron Offenberg, the chief aldermen claimed illness and did not attend. They told the nobles they could not participate in the conference as long as Prince Karl was in Mitau. Better the nobles petition the king [of Poland] describing recent events and requesting he release the province from allegiance to Prince Karl. Some nobles agreed, but as Simolin put it, he did not want to leave the conference to face so difficult a task alone.

BIRON AND RUSSIA'S VICTORY

Biron arranged a meeting where the nobles proclaimed Courland's desire to remain in the Polish Commonwealth yet acknowledge only Biron as their duke. Since only one of the chief aldermen refused to recognize Biron, while the quorum for transacting business was three chief aldermen, Biron now was considered the actual ruler of Courland.

Prince Karl continued to live in the palace, while Biron stayed in a private home. Since Biron did not join Simolin in trying to persuade the nobles to insist Prince Karl vacate the palace and request the empress's protection, the nobles also abstained. "They have been instilled with such respect for their laws," wrote Simolin, "that they regard this step as a clear violation." Eighteen supporters from Prince Karl's villages dined with him on the evening of April 15 at the residence of Elder Korf, where he bade them farewell. Certain of his speedy return, they promised to remain loyal to him. Then early the next morning Karl and his entire court departed for Warsaw, leaving the two Polish senators, Plater and Lipski, to protect his interests. The moment Simolin heard the prince was gone he sent Lieutenant Colonel Schroeder to secure the palace. This was done, and Senators Plater and Lipski left on July 14. Biron now had a clear field.

CONFLICT WITH POLAND

These developments necessarily exacerbated relations between the Russian and Polish courts. "You should write to Count Keyserling,"[6] Catherine wrote to Vorontsov on February 21, "that under the present circumstances I am quite surprised to hear an army is assembling along the Polish frontier near Courland and Lithuania. I will not remain indifferent, nor will I allow that court unilaterally to violate its kingdom's statutes. The king is not permitted to assemble an army on a foreign border unless the Sejm agrees. "If that army aims to disturb the lawful duke of Courland Ernst Johann, I will inform the king that I do not recognize such exercise of royal authority without the Sejm's permission. I will consider any step which excludes the Commonwealth a violation of Polish liberty. I guaranteed this liberty,[7] and I intend to defend it. I will protect Duke Ernst Johann as an unjustly persecuted sovereign."

August III[8] sent Borch[9] with plenipotentiary powers to intercede with the empress on his son's behalf, but Borch was not allowed to present himself to the empress or begin negotiations with the chancellor or vice chancellor. Courland was a purely Polish affair. Because the Polish Commonwealth refused to recognize the Russian imperial title there were no direct relations between Russia and Poland, and Borch could not be accorded the plenipotentiary status given him by August III as king of Poland. Borch could not discuss Courland as Saxon minister either, because as elector of Saxony August III had no rights in Courland.

"Mr. Borch could be told," Catherine wrote Vorontsov on February 24, "that all these problems are irrelevant. I will not change my mind about

Courland because justice is on my side. Personally Borch is acceptable, but absolutely not in his official capacity. His king's blindness is surprising. August III's love for his son is destroying the legality and violating the statutes of his kingdom. Even more astonishing is that the king seizes every occasion to say my actions are dictated by this or that piece of intelligence. He could be told that approaching the matter legalistically[10] is a greater affront to my dignity and that I intend to stay the course with all the means God gave me."

Keyserling reported plans to bring action against Duke Biron, the Lithuanian chancellor Czartoryski[11] and the Lithuanian table attendant Poniatowski,[12] the last-named because during Elizabeth's reign he negotiated to allow Russian forces into Polish territory. "The Polish court must not be so eager," Catherine wrote upon hearing this, "to try the table attendant for inviting Russian forces into Poland. The king also should be tried for making similar overtures on Saxony's behalf."

"Under the present circumstances," wrote Keyserling at the beginning of February, "we must expand our circle of friends. Clearly the Polish court does not wish to distribute titles and rewards to help us do this, thus we must find our own methods. Because the primate[13] is the dignitary closest to the king and plays a crucial role during an interregnum, I will make every effort to gain his sympathy and friendship. Primate Potocki[14] formerly received fifteen thousand rubles' pension annually, and if your imperial majesty agrees, this pension might be divided to give the primate and the Lithuanian hetman Massalski[15] eight thousand rubles a year each. As far as I know neither presently is obligated to any foreign power. To prevent this, perhaps your imperial majesty would have the appropriate directives concerning pensions sent to me immediately."

"It is common knowledge," the chancellor [Vorontsov] noted on the report, "that money and pensions must be distributed to succeed in Poland. Would your highness authorize Count Keyserling to give three thousand ducats now with the expectation of an annual pension thereafter to each person he designates? Count Keyserling also should offer a sizable sum to Hetman Branicki[16] to convert him." "It is so ordered," the empress wrote. "Count Keyserling will supervise the matter. Obviously he cannot give if his pocket is empty."

KEYSERLING PROPOSES RUSSIAN ACTION

"The Senatorial Council[17] will convene soon on February 23," Keyserling reported on February 4, "and some senators already are here. A sizable attendance is predicted because there will be a major effort to find a majority in the Senate to sanction what otherwise would be illegal and unjust action in Courland. In the Commonwealth today the court always can rely on a majority in a [senatorial] session. Although the *pacta conventa*[18] stipulate that titles and awards be given soley for service and proven merit, for over twelve years they have gone exclusively to those who wholeheartedly approve court measures. Blind obedience has replaced any kind of service.

"It is easy to determine how far the current government of this free Commonwealth has deviated from its original form to something approaching an aristocracy, which little by little could acquire absolute power. Were the present king otherwise inclined and were his ministers more intelligent, more capable and more powerful, strengthening royal authority would be easy. Only at Sejms can the Polish gentry talk about its rights, but because sessions continually are disrupted the gentry have no way to rectify violations of law and liberty. The Polish gentry apparently is unaware that the Sejm is the bulwark of liberty. For more than twenty years they have been accustomed to seeing the Sejm disrupted, leaving them nowhere to discuss their rights. Now the liberty of the nobility is nothing but a meaningless expression.

"A state's liberty is secured by power whereas power at present is parcelled out to those who heed the court's desires and pay no attention to the state's directives. This was demonstrated when Courland was handed over to Prince Karl without the Sejm's concurrence, a clear violation of the 1607 constitution.[19] The opposition party was impotent, merely saying that the king and the Commonwealth rather than Russia must decide Courland's fate.

"I say that Russia does not intend to decide anything. The issue was resolved when the 1736 constitution gave Courland to Duke Biron,[20] and your highness never will permit one fraction of the Commonwealth to reverse the will of the whole. After a decision is made, there is nothing to decide. I have heard that an extraordinary session of the Sejm will be convened in May after the current session of the Senatorial Council. It might help if your imperial majesty ordered her forces on the Polish border be prepared to march."

VI

THE POLISH QUESTION

CATHERINE CONSIDERS POLICY TOWARDS POLAND

Forty-eight of the sixty Senatorial Council members recognized Prince Karl as the lawful duke of Courland and decided to institute criminal proceedings against Biron and his followers. When Catherine learned of this she wrote Vorontsov to "Tell Mr. Borch that I have seen nothing from his king but the grossest insults, and nothing from Borch but what his court instructed him to do (which also referred to the declaration about the imperial title). I therefore order him to leave within forty-eight hours, and if he does not, I will have him expelled. Add that the Senatorial Council's decision is the cause of this step. Clearly the Poles intend to make me change my friendly policies, although the Saxon ministry acted with its usual impropriety and insulted the Commonwealth and me equally. They should know that I will defend Duke Ernst Johann and Polish liberties with all the God-given means at my disposal."

CZARTORYSKIS INTERVENE

The Czartoryskis took advantage of the friction. Keyserling's report shows how much they influenced the old man. They induced him to warn his court that the *liberum veto*[1] in the Polish Sejm was a threat. The Czartoryskis needed to persuade the Russian court little by little to extend them the help they needed for the changes they deemed necessary. Meanwhile they insisted on a confederation.[2] "King August III's name," the Czartoryskis' memorandum to Keyserling stated, "will be invoked in the confederation proceedings. Grammont told Louis XIV 'We [Grammont[3] and the Prince de Condé] waged war with Mazarin to fulfil our obligations to your highness.' The same should be said to August III."

To ensure the success of the confederation the Czartoryskis asked Catherine to create a commission with a budget of fifty thousand ducats to compensate Poles for their losses in the last war.[4] An arms depot should be established in Smolensk and wagons prepared, in which weapons should be taken to Sklów, the estate of Rus military commander, Prince Czartoryski. Another arms depot was needed in Kiev, to transfer arms to another Czartoryski estate at Międzybóż. One hundred Russian artillerymen and four hundred hussars should be put under the confederation leaders' command. The Czartoryskis wrote that fifty thousand ducats would be only the first of many similar payments. They did add that "we have no intention of giving orders to the great soul [Catherine] who undertakes nothing without completing it and who knows very well that sufficiency of means reduces the labor expended."

CATHERINE POSTPONES ACTION IN POLAND

The "great soul" wished no such drastic action, particularly since it entailed sizable Russian outlays. Irritated by the Polish court's feeble petitions and threats, Catherine wrote Keyserling on April 1. "Tell the Poles unequivocally that if they dare seize any friend of Russia and send him to Königstein[5] I will people Siberia with my enemies and turn the Zaporozhian Cossacks loose. The cossacks want to send me a delegation for permission to avenge the insults the Polish king has inflicted on me."[6]

A letter to Keyserling written July 14 struck a different tone. "I see our friends are enthusiastic and ready to form a confederation, but I do not see why a confederation is needed while the Polish king lives.[7] The plain truth is that my coffers are bare and will remain so until I put my finances in order, something that I cannot do overnight. My instructions are to restrain our friends,since my army cannot launch a campaign this year. It is crucial that you do not take up arms without my permission. I do not want to be drawn in farther than my interests require." Additional instructions were sent on July 26. "In my last letter I directed you to keep our friends from forming a confederation prematurely. At the same time you may promise them our support for any reasonable course of action before the king dies. After that we will intervene openly on their behalf."

A note Catherine sent the vice chancellor [Alexander Golitsyn] concerning a petition from a certain Baron Linsingen shows how carefully she watched her money "Resolve his claims to his and my satisfaction. Placate the wolves and protect the sheep, and by sheep I mean ducats."

RUSSIAN PLANS FOR THE POLISH SUCCESSION

Catherine judged any decisive action before the king's death premature. She was concerned when she learned at the beginning of the year that the king was gravely ill, and a conference was convened immediately.

Bestuzhev insisted that August III's son, the future Saxon elector,[8] be put on the throne, but his opinion was not accepted. Instead it was decided to promote a Piast[9] (a native Pole), specifically the Lithuanian table attendant Count Stanisław Poniatowski. Should this fail his cousin Prince Adam Czartoryski,[10] the son of Prince August,[11] who was the Rus (that is, Galich) military commander would be the choice. Strict secrecy must be maintained. Thirty thousand troops were to be stationed on the border with another fifty thousand in readiness.

"The Polish king's age and poor health," read an instruction Keyserling received on February 8, "are powerful incentives for appropriate and timely measures on our part when his highness dies. These will give the throne to a Polish king who actually promotes Russian interests instead of hindering them. We foresee no benefit if any Saxon prince becomes king. The weak constitution of the present elector[12] obviously makes him unacceptable to the Poles. Prince Xavier[13] would be beholden totally to France, and under the present circumstances we could expect nothing from Prince Karl save hostility and ill-will towards our empire. In our opinion no other foreign prince is fit to be king, so we should choose a Piast and hold him in readiness.

"Investigate all princely houses and outstanding Polish dignitaries thoroughly, gathering as much information as possible. Then recommend to me whom you judge most suitable and most likely to support our state interests, either a foreign prince or a Piast. We believe making a foreign prince king would perpetuate the Polish Commonwealth's current division and weakness. This is detrimental to our interests. A German prince would give us greater influence in German affairs. He also would have his own domains and sufficient private income not to need subsidies from foreign powers and thus be dependent on them. We would not have to burden our treasury by subsidizing him. Since we cannot find a suitable [German prince], a pro-Russian Piast would be a better choice. There will be no final decision until we receive your report.

"The necessary preparations have been made to support the designated candidate forcefully when the present king dies. A corps of thirty thousand is ready to march into Poland as soon as the order is given, and a large sum has been set aside. You should make every effort to ingratiate yourself with the primate and other prominent and influential Poles. Assure them of our imperial protection and assistance so that when the time comes we can count on their cooperation to bring us success. Naturally we will extend our military and financial support.

"Since these preparatory measures, which cost the treasury a great deal, are taken solely to promote our interests, it is appropriate we receive advance assurance from the new candidate that our empire will benefit. You realize this means implementing the provisions of the peace treaty between the two states to fix the borders and return lands seized from our subjects by the Poles. In addition many thousands of our subjects who have fled to Poland and Lithuania must be returned to Russia, and future fugitives neither accepted nor concealed. Polish and Lithuanian inhabitants of the Greek[14] faith now suffering intolerable oppression shall have complete freedom to practice their religion and conduct services. Property confiscated from them and churches given to the Uniates[15] should be returned. All this can be done by a king acting more in accordance with the laws."

A very confidential instruction specifying action to be taken at the king's death was sent as well. "Assure all Poles in our name of our friendship for and good will towards the Polish Commonwealth. Because we always felt honor-bound to uphold its liberties and constitution, we will do our best to maintain them. It is in the Commonwealth's interest that a true patriot, sufficiently talented and virtuous, be chosen king. Our nominee is the Lithuanian table attendant Count Poniatowski or Prince Adam Czartoryski. Each possesses the merits and virtues proper to a sovereign, and each is known to be loyal to our empire. We shall use our entire God-given strength to maintain one of them on the Polish throne. The Commonwealth also must realize that we have a real interest in the Polish royal election and are entitled to a role in it. If our recommendation is not accepted with due deference, their fatherland inevitably will be ruined."

Keyserling reported on March 9 that the French had spread rumors of the king's fatal illness to ascertain the policy of the Russian court in the election of a new king. The king had recovered, and since he lived moderately he might survive several more years. Should matters remain unchanged in Poland, France undoubtedly would play its usual role in Polish elections, especially if in the interim the dauphin[16] succeeded his father. Time would be lost by Russian efforts to extricate the Prussian king[17] from France's snares and convert him to Russia's interests, which in this case were the same as Prussia's. France already was active in Vienna. A Bourbon princess was married to the archduke, and the current policy would prevail as long as Kaunitz was in command.[18]

Keyserling wrote that allowing the Saxon prince to become the next king of Poland would be dangerous because many Poles wanted to replace the elective with an hereditary monarchy. A powerful Polish king never would be in Russia's interest. If rich he could live on his own resources. Were his hereditary domains far from the Russian border he would pay little heed to Poland and none to Russia, even if he owed his crown to Russia. Gratitude was a rare virtue today. Russia could have no use for a foreign prince on the Polish throne connected by birth and interest to the great and powerful houses of Europe. Thus Keyserling, considering Russian interests, knew of no foreign prince suitable for the Polish throne. A Piast, more precisely a Piast friendly to Russia, would remove all these obstacles.

Catherine replied that she was very glad the king had recovered and possibly might live for several more years. There might be serious and well-nigh inescapable problems if he did not, particularly if other powers intervened. "We agree with you," wrote Catherine, "that we must bring the Prussian king in on our side here and wean him from France. We must give this further consideration, and since the Polish king now has recovered, we have enough time to do so."

POLICY DEBATE AFTER AUGUST III'S DEATH

Keyserling was wrong in suggesting the king would live longer. On October 6 Catherine learned from him that the king had died. "Don't laugh at me for leaping out of my chair," Catherine later wrote [Nikita] Panin, "when I learned the Polish king was dead. I heard the Prussian king leapt up from the table." A conference met at once in the empress's private apartments with Count Bestuzhev-Riumin, Nepliuev, [Nikita] Panin, Count Grigory Orlov, Vice Chancellor Prince Golitsyn, Privy Councillor Olsufiev and the vice president of the War College Chernyshev.

Bestuzhev again cited reasons for preferring the Saxon elector. The first was that he was named under Elizabeth, and the Viennese, French and even the Saxon courts informed of the choice. Second, no native Pole or Piast, no matter how wealthy or distinguished, could survive without the help of foreign powers. A hostile state would give him money, and he would turn on Russia. Third, any foreign prince would be a threat to Russia, particularly one from the rising house of Brandenburg.[19] Fourth, Peter the Great had tried to keep the Polish crown in the Saxon line(?).[20] Fifth, the Saxon elector would be elected easily. The Poles certainly were ready to choose him, and so the expense would be minor.

It was known the Poles looked to two foreign princes, Charles of Lorraine[21] and the count of Hesse-Cassel.[22] Vienna was promoting the both unsuitable for Russia. Therefore another foreign prince or Piast must be chosen immediately. Because he would owe his crown to the empress alone and depend on her completely, Russia could have full confidence in him. If her imperial majesty did not desire the Saxon elector as her candidate, it made no difference whether he was a member of another foreign house, or even another Saxon. All were better than a Piast because of the annual subsidies required to keep a Piast on the throne.

Bestuzhev knew only two capable and reliable Piasts, Prince Adam Czartoryski and the Lithuanian table attendant Count Poniatowski. Poniatowski would be much more reliable because Czartoryski's great wealth made him unwilling to depend completely on Russia. Although Bestuzhev presented Poniatowski's advantages, he cleverly hit a sore point by emphasizing that choosing the Saxon elector was the only way Russia could avoid great expense. Despite this the conference did not agree on the Saxon elector as the Russian candidate, instead reaffirming its previous choice for Polish king.

Since Keyserling was quite elderly and often ill, the conference decided to send a minister plenipotentiary to Warsaw to assist him. Catherine named Major General Repnin,[23] formerly minister to the Prussian court. The empress said that even though in private correspondence the Prussian king assured her he would not interfere with her plans in Poland, she personally would write to his highness to confirm his stance and also would write the Roman empress [Maria Theresa][24] to convert her. An army was to be stationed on the Polish frontier ready to march the moment orders were issued. Since secrecy was impossible under normal chancellery procedures, the empress had Count Chernyshev prepare a directive giving him sole responsibility for executing the plans.

CHERNYSHEV PROPOSES ANNEXING POLISH TERRITORY

The secret project Chernyshev submitted to the empress was read at the end of the meeting. Russia should annex Polish territory to create a more regular and more secure border along the Dnieper and Dvina rivers.

Although in many respects the project's benefits far outweighed any foreseeable difficulties of execution, it was agreed to table it until Russian forces made their first move elsewhere. "Our frontier," Chernyshev concluded, "ought to be the Dvina, linking it from Polotsk [Połock] to Orsha [Orsza] with the Dnieper as far as Kiev. On the near side of the Dvina we should seize Kreuzberg, Dünaburg, all of Polish Lithuania, Polotsk and

Polotsk province, Vitebsk and its province and from the village of Ula to Orsha. Orsha also should be taken, together with Mogilev, Rogachev and all of Mstislav province on the near side of the Dnieper down to our present borders."

Chernyshev believed Russian troops could seize these districts during the Polish royal election. Polish treaty violations and Poland's failure to comply with legitimate Russian requests provided the justification. The next day a rescript was sent to Keyserling repeating the previous directive that a Piast must be elected king who would owe his throne to Russia and be prepared to fulfill previous Russian demands.

"If a lesser amount is not sufficient," Catherine wrote, "Count Keyserling may give the primate up to one hundred thousand rubles to assure his personal loyalty."

Keyserling stated that to accomplish Russia's goals certain orders be issued and preparations made. (1) Reach agreement with the Berlin court and act in concert with it. (2) Dash foreign candidates' hopes for the crown before the electoral Sejm met by excluding them from consideration by the dietines. (3) Push for an agreement between the Czartoryskis and Potockis to prevent a rift during the election and the opposition party from looking to a foreign power. (4) Because the country will experience upheaval during the interregnum the Poles must be made to recognize they would derive no benefit from electing one of their elderly men for a short reign. Thus the crown hetman [Jan Branicki], the Kievan military commander [Potocki] and many other old men with one foot in the grave should be excluded from the list of candidates. (5) There are rumors in Poland of plans to make the Commonwealth a powerful state, which would not enhance the security of Poland's neighbors. Should we reach agreement with the Prussian king and inform the Poles that Russia and Prussia will block any such transformation? The empress approved everything.

POLISH GENTRY PARTIES

To understand the following narrative, the parties the Polish gentry formed on the death of August III must be described. We know that "the family," as the Czartoryski princes and their relatives were called, led a party which wished to reform the Polish constitution, abolish the *liberum veto*, increase royal power and make the monarchy hereditary. In short their goal was to strengthen Poland and rescue it from the dreadful turmoil which led other powers to ignore it. Because the bulk of the Polish gentry, eager to preserve

Teigel sculpsit

A POLISH GENTLEMAN.

Published according to Act of Parliament. Jan.y 1st 1784. by T. Cadell in the Strand.

its ancient rights and liberties, resisted reform, magnates opposing the family always found strong support.

The family was led by two brothers, Prince Michał, the Lithuanian chancellor and August the Rus (Galich) military commander. August's son Prince Adam, who was general of the Podolian lands, ranked third, followed by four of his Poniatowski cousins. Kazimierz[25] was a crown property magistrate, Andrzej[26] a general in the Austrian service, Michał,a cleric,[27] and the famous Stanisław the Lithuanian table attendant.

Other members of the family included Michał's son-in-law, the Lithuanian high notary Ogiński,[28] the Lithuanian hetman Massalski, his son the bishop of Wilno,[29] the Lithuanian crown treasurer Flemming,[30] the Pomeranian military commander Mostowski,[31] the Inowrocław military commander Andrzej Zamoyski[32] and crown frontier commander Stanisław Lubomirski.[33] The party's strength derived from its unity and above all from the Czartoryskis' ability to find talented and educated men. Zamoyski, a leading example, was the first to insist on improving the lot of the rural population. Electing a king from the Czartoryski party would make it easier to achieve the reform they wanted.

The high crown hetman Jan Branicki led the other party, which preferred one of the Saxon princes, and if this proved impossible, Branicki himself. Here they counted on Austrian and French assistance. This party did not oppose reform as long as someone besides the Czartoryskis implemented it.

Another party gathered around the wealthy Potockis. It was large but lacked a clear political focus. Despite its numbers it lacked standing because it had no capable members. The same was true of the party headed by the Wilno military commander Prince Radziwiłł,[34] the richest man in Lithuania. His simplicity and courtesy could sway a crowd, but he had no other talent for party leadership. Slow-witted, totally uneducated and prey to first impressions, he was so taken with his wealth and status that his impetuosity knew no bounds. Hence he always was ready for drastic measures.

The Cracow military commander Wacław Rzewuski[35] wanted to enlarge the army but did not want to contemplate any violation of sacred Polish traditions. His talents made him the leader of the remnants of the former Saxon party at court. High Crown Marshal Bielinski,[36] Court Marshal Mniszech,[37] Bishop Sołtyk of Cracow[38] and Bishop Krasiński of Kamieniec[39] also were members.

Predicting which party would dominate the royal election was easy. It would be the most unified with the more capable members, men who understood that foreign powers must be involved. Neither help nor hindrance might be expected from France or Austria, whereas Russia alone had both the desire and ability to install its candidate. This was the view of the Czartoryski party. During the interregnum the primate Władysław Lubienski was the most important man in the Commonwealth. Although initially he tried to be impartial, he had to go along with the Czartoryskis.

RUSSIA'S POLISH ALLIES APPROACH KEYSERLING

When the king died the Lithuanian hetman Massalski and his son the bishop of Wilno went to Keyserling, accompanied by the Lithuanian referendary General Sosnowski.[40] They asked the ambassador directly whom the empress preferred in the royal election, saying they would support him. Would the empress prefer the Saxon elector on the throne, or would she rather have a Piast? Did the Prussian king consent to a Piast? Keyserling replied that the empress wanted a Piast and that the Prussian king agreed. The hetman promised strong support for all who as true sons of the fatherland worked to realize her highness's plans for her own and the fatherland's welfare.

The guests then presented a memorandum stating that fifty thousand ducats would be needed in Lithuania for the forthcoming dietines and the convocation Sejm, plus twenty thousand ducats for the army. The electoral Sejm required one hundred thousand ducats. They and their Russian friends would manage the funds, distributing them to the lesser gentry to assure a majority. Keyserling informed his court that he did not think they should be given that much, although it was obvious the election would go more easily if Russia's friends gained control of the convocation Sejm, where issues were decided by majority vote.

THE SAXON ELECTOR ENTERS CONTEST

The new Saxon elector announced his candidacy for the Polish throne and wrote to the Russian empress asking for her endorsement, but was refused. "It is apparent," Keyserling reported on November 17, "from your highness's response to the Saxon elector and his wife how disinclined your highness is to help them gain the Polish crown. Despite this, their adherents tell us that, *although the Russian empress's statement does not meet the*

Saxon court's expectations, there still is hope for Russia's consent. [Nikita] Panin noted on the report that "there is no question that the underlined passage gives a complete picture of the policy of the Saxon court and its allies. They are trying to implement it now." "They are deluding themselves in vain," Catherine added.

Keyserling told Hetman Branicki that the empress refused to help the Saxon elector because she wanted a Piast. Branicki replied that he respected the empress's intentions, yet did not want to be committed to a particular candidate. "Undoubtedly he wants to be the candidate," [Nikita] Panin noted on Keyserling's report. "Then let him promote himself," Catherine added, "for he poses no threat. There will be an immediate split among the Saxon party and its allies. Count Keyserling cleverly has led him into a trap."

The Saxon elector named Branicki commander of the Saxon forces stationed [in Poland] to protect royal possessions and castles, making him a Saxon general as well as hetman of the crown army. This step, moves by the Kievan military commander Potocki, and Prince Radziwiłł's military preparations in Lithuania prompted the Czartoryski family to petition Keyserling that the empress send eight hundred to a thousand Russian troops to protect them. The Czartoryskis noted that the crown hetman and the Kievan military commander openly defied the law by accepting foreign troops, even though they claimed these troops were under their command and in their pay. Russia's friends could not be blamed should they solicit foreign assistance purely in self-defense. Meanwhile a declaration was needed in the empress's name, announcing her wish to see a Piast on the Polish throne. Some courts were trying to convince the Poles that Russia and Prussia already had concluded a treaty to partition Poland.

REPNIN'S INSTRUCTIONS

Prince Repnin was sent to assist Keyserling with instructions to speak and act in concert with him. Repnin was told to make every effort to induce Poles loyal to Russia to petition the empress, and her alone, to insure free royal elections. It would be best if the primate participated. "Thus," the instructions stated, "we not only will promote our interests but also can intervene directly in this crucial matter."

Candidate Poniatowski would receive an annual pension of three thousand ducats. Keyserling also was to pay Poniatowski's entire debt in three installments, so that by the end of 1764 he would owe nothing.

Poniatowski must realize beforehand that he must pay for these favors. "At an opportune moment," Repnin's instructions said, "skillfully and decorously suggest to him (Poniatowski) that our special benevolence for him allows us to grant him substantial sums with no regrets. Not content with this, we are determined to confer on him the greatest honor anyone ever might expect, bending our entire God-given strength to the task. Naturally this will burden our loyal subjects, bringing grief to our maternal heart. Thus we have every reason to expect and to demand his gratitude and loyalty.

As partial repayment for our benevolence he will continue to provide us complete information about his herculean exertions to gain the throne. We also want our many boundary disputes with the Poles settled in our favor. Throughout his reign he shall consider Russian interests his own and be certain to make every effort to promote them. He must cherish the unwavering personal trust we have in him, never refusing to further our interests.

"With a permanent peace treaty as a basis, he must do everything possible to return our fugitives, stop the robbery and brigandage tolerated by the Poles and safeguard our coreligionists' rights, liberties and freedom to conduct their customary worship services. In particular not only must he halt the confiscation of more churches and monasteries with their lands and possessions, at the first opportunity he was to return everything previously taken. He is to obtain the Commonwealth's recognition of our imperial title and confirmation of Duke Ernst Johann of Courland's right to his principalities, perhaps during the current coronation Sejm.

"Formal recognition is needed, specified in the constitution if possible, that the Commonwealth depends on Russia to prevent violation of its freedom and laws. The key point is a precisely worded formal request in it (the constitution) for our perpetual guarantee to preserve the legally established government structure, freedom and integrity of the entire Commonwealth."

REPNIN AND KEYSERLING IN WARSAW

Repnin's first report on arriving in Warsaw discussed the death from smallpox of Poniatowski's main rival, the new Saxon elector. "This," Repnin wrote, "is completely in your highness's interest. The Saxons will be disoriented completely." "This is the best of all possible worlds," he said later in the report. "The Saxon party is split between Prince Xavier and Prince Karl (brothers of the deceased elector), and a quarrel is expected between them. Hetman Branicki is contemplating the crown, and should Prince Xavier lose hope, he will support the hetman because Branicki is old and might die soon."

Meanwhile Keyserling reported that Saxon supporters were not confined to Warsaw. "The primate told us (him and Repnin) in strict confidence," he wrote the empress, "that he was informed by Mercy[41] of the latter's correspondence with Bestuzhev, who utterly opposes the empress's plans for Poland." "Obtain their letters either here or there," Catherine wrote on the report.

RELATIONS WITH PRUSSIA

Massalski's first task was to learn from Keyserling whether Russia and Prussia had agreed on the royal election, and he was told that they had. How did it come about? The previous year's bad feeling between the two courts continued into the new year. Berlin still was upset that Catherine extended her protection to Saxony. Vorontsov tried to reassure Solms on this point.

"Personally," he said, "the empress is not committed enough to Saxony to declare war on your sovereign over it. I fear lest Bestuzhev, who still hates your king and still retains great influence over the empress, in time might overcome her preference for peace." Solms suggested to Vorontsov that were he, the chancellor, to join forces with Panin they could defeat Bestuzhev. Although Panin was obligated to Bestuzhev, his gratitude stopped short of sacrificing his own peace plan for Bestuzhev's sake. Vorontsov promised not to request retirement that winter.

RAPPROCHEMENT WITH PRUSSIA OVER POLAND

The unfriendly exchanges between the Russian and Prussian courts ended with the peace between Prussia, Austria and Saxony.[42] The rapprochement Frederick so ardently desired now became a reality. "After the war," he wrote in his memoirs, "Prussia found itself isolated with no allies. Hostility and hatred replaced the former alliance with England. It is true that no one attacked the king (Frederick),[43] but neither was there anyone to defend him. This cannot continue.... Negotiations have begun with Russia for an alliance...."

Poland provided the impetus for rapprochement. On February 8 a directive was sent from Moscow to the Russian ambassador in Berlin Prince Vladimir Dolgoruky.[44] The empress and the Prussian king must be candid with one another, working in concert through their ministers in Poland. Their goal is the maintenance of order and elevation to the throne of a mutually acceptable king. Dolgoruky was to inform Frederick II that the empress did not want to impede free elections but rather to preserve and protect them based on the Russian guarantee of 1716.[45]

"These proposals," the directive read, "shall suffice for now, and our subsequent resolutions will depend on circumstances and our knowledge of the Prussian king's intentions, which we should make every effort to ascertain. Of particular interest is the possibility he plans to place one of his brothers or a German prince loyal to him on the throne." This is exactly what Frederick II expected. "When the king heard what I had to say," Dolgoruky replied, "he seemed quite satisfied that he now understood your imperial majesty's intentions. He told me the time had come to act in Poland because recent letters informed him of the Polish king's terminal illness. He also said that he did not care who the next king of Poland was. He can accept your imperial highness's choice readily, provided all princes of the house of Austria are excluded, and he hopes your imperial majesty concurs. His preference is that a native Pole rather than a foreign prince to be elected king.

"The king then said that because your imperial majesty had her partisans in Poland and he his, united they could have decisive influence in the kingdom. This he would consider most advantageous, since just having ended a long and very bloody war he had no wish to start a new one. I told the king that your imperial majesty desires only peace and concord, and thus feels obligated to obtain a comprehensive agreement with him through private and personal correspondence. The king replied that he thought this would resolve the issue more quickly and more surely. As I left, the king added that he had some ideas about an alliance with your imperial majesty that could insure long-term stability throughout Europe."

CATHERINE AND FREDERICK CORRESPOND

An exchange of letters began. Frederick informed Catherine that Vienna suspected Russia's views on Poland. He asked her not to be alarmed by Vienna's concerns because Vienna had no money and Maria Theresa was in no position to start another war. "You will reach your goals," Frederick wrote, "if you dissemble somewhat and have your ambassadors in Vienna and Constantinople refute the false rumors current there. Otherwise your cause will suffer. You will put your candidate on the Polish throne without going to war. This is a hundred times better than again plunging Europe into the abyss it only now escaped.

"The Polish outcry means nothing. There is nothing to fear from the Polish king because he can barely maintain an army of one hundred

FREDERICK THE GREAT

After a picture by H. Ramberg

thousand, although the Poles can make alliances and this should be prevented. The Poles must be neutralized lest they act soon enough to impede our plans." Frederick wrote that he wanted a Piast on the Polish throne. Catherine replied that she did also, except that the Piast not be an old man with one foot in the grave. Then new currents and intrigues from various sides would appear in expectation of new elections.

In April Dolgoruky reported his second conversation with Frederick. "The empress writes," said the king, "that she does not want a Bourbon elected to the Polish throne. I do not think any assistance to Versailles or Vienna is required. Besides, as I already have written the empress, I agree with her completely, except that I prefer a native Pole. Great caution is required, and an effort made not to reveal the empress's intentions prematurely. I am very doubtful this is possible. When I was in Saxony and met with the royal family the crown princess told me the empress was trying to have Prince Czartoryski elected king of Poland. I said this was nonsense and that the king still was healthy. This was not the time to think about his successor. Like the empress I did not intend to prevent the Poles from conducting free royal elections."

Frederick then discussed the alliance he wanted with Russia. "The empress," he said, "cannot oppose this alliance, since her desire for peace is well known and this alliance is the best guarantee of peace. Although the Viennese court has made peace with me, it will start a new war as soon as it puts its domestic affairs in order, but when it learns about my alliance with Russia it will not hazard it. The courts of Versailles and Stockholm already have proposed an alliance with Prussia, but I gave them a courteous and noncommittal answer while awaiting the empress's decision."

Frederick made it clear he needed an alliance with Russia because it would lead to an agreement on Poland. Frederick wanted a Piast, but his ambassador in Warsaw Benoît,[46] more experienced and more observant than Keyserling, realized the Czartoryskis would exploit their success by instituting reforms incompatible with Russian and Prussian interests. "I tell Count Keyserling again and again," Benoît wrote to his king, "that Russia and Prussia have the same interests in Poland. It is to neither's advantage to let the Commonwealth become a major power threatening both courts. Keyserling gave me his word of honor Russia would prevent this."

Benoît realized that prevention required cultivating people with whom Russia and Prussia inevitably would clash later. "The Czartoryskis', and particularly Table Attendant Poniatowski's, only goal," he wrote the king, "is reforming the Polish constitution. They will initiate reform as soon as a confederation is organized, which they hope Russia will support." Although Keyserling favored a confederation, Benoît, fearing general war, opposed it and advised his king to remain neutral. If Russia and Prussia cooperated, all Europe would realize they were profiting at Poland's expense. Frederick told Benoît to keep his distance from this commotion, but not to give Russia any reason to suspect Prussia of any contrary action.

RUSSIA AND PRUSSIA COORDINATE POLICY

Prince Dolgoruky learned of the Polish king's death on September 26 from the foreign minister Count Finckenstein.[47] "This situation," Finckenstein said, "makes me very sorry there is no treaty of alliance between Russia and Prussia. A treaty would justify joint action by the king and empress in the eyes of other states." Dolgoruky replied that the empress was reviewing the proposed defensive alliance the king sent her, and that the Russian side soon would have a counterproposal. "Although there is no treaty yet," Dolgoruky added, "I hope the king will not repudiate his stated intention to cooperate fully with the empress in the Polish royal election. That is what he told me, and that is what I have communicated to the empress." The king," Finckenstein replied, "reaffirms his previous intentions. His only wish is that an alliance treaty be concluded as soon as possible."

On October 11 Dolgoruky again discussed an alliance concerning Poland. The minister [Finckenstein] explained that the new Saxon elector had written the king to inform him of his candidacy for the Polish throne. He hoped Prussia would not oppose him because Poland would be much stronger under a Piast. Maria Theresa also was promoting the Saxon elector. It was time for the king to ask for the empress's decision and to conclude an alliance treaty as soon as possible. The king then could give the other powers clear answers on Poland.

As soon as August III breathed his last, his daughter-in-law, the wife of the new Saxon elector, sent Frederick II a letter asking him to help her husband gain the Polish throne. She also asked Frederick to mediate between her husband and Russia, offering to do everything possible to satisfy Russia. Frederick sent a copy of the letter to St. Petersburg and wrote to Catherine that "If your imperial majesty now reinforces her party in Poland, no state can take offense. If an opposition party emerges, just have the Czartoryskis request your protection. If necessary, this formality provides the pretext for sending forces into Poland. I think that if you inform the Saxon court you cannot consent to the Saxon elector's election as king of Poland, Saxony will do nothing and not intervene."

This letter crossed with a letter from St. Petersburg. "Naturally I turned to your majesty when I learned the Polish king was dead," Catherine wrote to Frederick. "Since we agree a Piast should be chosen, we now must make that clear without further circumlocutions. I propose to your majesty that Piast who, thanks to all we have done for him, owes more to your majesty and to me than other family members. If your majesty agrees, he is the Lithuanian table attendant Count Stanisław Poniatowski.

"Here are my reasons. He has a better chance of winning the crown than any of the other claimants, and so will be more indebted to those from whose hands he receives it. Any of our party's leaders who attained the throne probably would attribute it to his own administrative ability and not to us. Your majesty tells me that Poniatowski is penniless, but I think the Czartoryskis will like having one of their relatives on the throne and will maintain him accordingly. Your majesty, do not be surprised by troop movements on my frontiers, since my policy calls for them. I abhor any disorder and wish devoutly that this important matter be resolved peacefully."

Frederick replied that he agreed and shortly thereafter directed his minister in Warsaw to work on Poniatowski's behalf in concert with Keyserling. Reports from Warsaw said that the French and the Saxons were using every possible intrigue to have the Poles reject a Piast, but Frederick was not alarmed. He was certain the leading magnates would agree immediately if together the Russian and Prussian ministers explained their sovereigns' wishes. Vienna would not intervene in the elections if the formalities were observed.

Frederick anticipated the empress's desires concerning the Porte by ordering his ambassador in Constantinople[48] to act in both courts' interest. When the Turkish ambassador[49] arrived in Berlin he would be persuaded that electing a Piast king of Poland fully served the sultan's interests. "For my part," Frederick wrote, "I will spare no effort to reassure people and will use all my power to insure that everything goes peacefully and without bloodshed. I congratulate your imperial majesty in advance for the king you are giving Poland."

The king took the opportunity to emphasize that he considered Poniatowski's election already decided. Catherine sent him a present of Astrakhan melons. Frederick responded to this kindly gesture (on November 7). "Besides the rarity and superlative flavor of the fruit," he wrote, "above all I cherish the hands from which I received it. There is a great difference between Astrakhan melons and Polish Sejms, but you have managed to embrace both. The same hands which send melons also bestow crowns and safeguard European peace."

NEGOTIATIONS FOR ALLIANCE

All this generosity and kindness presumed the speedy conclusion of an alliance. St. Petersburg desired every conceivable advantage during the interval, concluding an alliance only at the very last minute. "Only the empress and I favor the Prussian system," Panin told Solms at a masquerade in October. "I support this system not for its general advantages, but because I see it bringing the greatest possible benefit to my court and the greatest possible glory to my sovereign. The Viennese court has many friends who support the old system, but I oppose them stoutly and need assistance. There is one king, your sovereign, who can help me by endorsing my sovereign's views completely."

"Cooperate with us in Poland," St. Petersburg said, "and you can expect the alliance as a reward," while Berlin said "first conclude an alliance, then we will work together in Poland." St. Petersburg did not want an alliance. "Ordinarily the empress listens to everybody," Solms wrote to Frederick, "thus subjecting herself to diverse influences. Disloyal people have found the weak point which they exploit at every opportunity, convincing her that one or another of her actions displeases the people. Her fear of losing the nation's love has made her timid." Since Catherine thought it premature to conclude an alliance with a single power, she would balk all the more at an alliance with Prussia, a policy too reminiscent of the previous reign.[50] If this were so, why put Poniatowski on the Polish throne?

Berlin opposed all cooperation with Russia in Poland, which meant following Catherine's wishes there and working with Austria in Turkey. There was an interesting encounter between Dolgoruky and Finckenstein when this policy became clear. The Turkish ambassador Frederick mentioned finally arrived in Berlin. Finckenstein informed Dolgoruky that the king, at the ambassador's request, intended to draft a proposal for an alliance treaty between Prussia and the Porte. Dolgoruky thanked Finckenstein for his frankness, but remarked that St. Petersburg would be surprised and displeased to hear of an alliance between the Porte and Prussia.

Although the alliance was directed against Austria alone, it had many implications for Russia, which must maintain close ties with Vienna regarding the Porte. The security of both countries and the defense of all of Christendom were at stake. Consequently it would please the empress greatly if, in the common European interest, the king declined an alliance with the irreconcilable enemy of all Christian peoples. Prussia stood in no need of an alliance that would scar the king's reputation and arouse suspicion by harming Christian sovereigns, particularly our allies, and consequently it must be refused. Refusal befitted the honor and status of the Prussian state and its current frank and friendly relations with the empress. Prussian acquiescence clearly would signal the alliance now being concluded between Russia and Prussia.

Finckenstein then prevented Dolgoruky from saying anything more with the irrelevant comment that the Landgrave of Hesse [Friedrich II] had arrested an agent of the Dutch Republic. This irregular comment convinced Dolgoruky that the king and his ministry wanted no more talk of refusing the Turkish alliance. Consequently Dolgoruky told Baron Ried[51] about the alliance so Vienna could oppose it in Constantinople.[52]

AUSTRIA, RUSSIA AND PRUSSIA

Vienna could not accept Russian policy either before or after the Peace of Hubertusburg.[53] On January 2 a directive was sent to Prince Dmitry Mikhailovich Golitsyn[54] in Vienna. "Count Solms, the Prussian ambassador here," it read, "told our ministry that personally his king wished neither war nor conquests. Prussia would withdraw its troops from Saxony on Russia's recommendation if Vienna made peace with the Prussian king after the evacuation was completed. The king would not return Saxony to the Polish king unless Prussia retained all its prewar domains.[55] You are to make the Prussian minister's statements known to the Viennese court. Inform the ministry orally and in friendly confidence, using the occasion to ascertain whether Vienna wants peace on these conditions."

The chancellor [Kaunitz] told Golitsyn the Prussian king should be concerned about returning what he had seized instead of talking about his conquests. This was the sole explanation advanced. When Golitsyn suggested the empress was prepared to mediate in peace negotiations between Austria and Prussia, he was told that peace would be concluded quickly or negotiations broken off. Peace was concluded and discussion of Poland began.

In March Golitsyn, at the empress's directive, after asking strict secrecy be observed, handed Kaunitz a proposal concerning Poland. Because the old Polish king's death was imminent, the empress had begun to consider his successor. As yet there was no final choice, confirmation of which awaited free elections, but it was well to have a suitable candidate ready. Hence the empress, in a spirit of friendly candor, asked the empress-queen who would advance the common interests of both imperial courts. The Austrian ambassador in Warsaw absolutely must be instructed to cooperate fully with his Russian counterpart.

Count Kaunitz assured Golitsyn that Maria Theresa was delighted and very flattered to learn of Empress Catherine's friendly candor. Since as yet Austria entertained no intentions or plans concerning Poland, he could not respond, but asked if the Russian court had a particular candidate in mind. Golitsyn said Russia had no candidate and the empress only wanted free elections and intended no intervention unless Polish liberties and laws were threatened.

Meanwhile rumors of a Russo-Prussian alliance caused great alarm in Vienna, leading Mercy to raise the issue in St. Petersburg. Golitsyn was instructed to assure Kaunitz everything was concocted by malcontents envious of the concord between the two imperial courts and were trying to sow dissent. No such treaty existed, and none had been proposed. When Golitsyn asked Kaunitz for a copy of the imaginary treaty and its source, Kaunitz replied there was no copy and that rumors were from various quarters. The Prussian king had hinted at and commented on the treaty and had done so on purpose.

Kaunitz said that Maria Theresa desired one of the Saxon princes be chosen in Poland if free elections were possible. August III's recovery ended matters for the time being, then after he died Golitsyn had an audience with Maria Theresa on October 12. Among other comments Maria Theresa emphasized she would be most gratified if Empress Catherine supported the new Saxon elector for the next Polish king. Moreover she hoped and expected the royal elections would proceed peacefully and in accord with Polish law.

Further declarations and correspondence between the two empresses made it clear that Vienna's primary concern was for free elections. If the Austrian candidate, the Saxon elector, lost a completely free election, the empress-queen would agree to a Piast king on condition he gave absolute assurances that a Polish partition during his reign was ruled out. In conclusion Vienna thought it unnecessary and dangerous to assemble Russian troops on the Polish frontier, for this might upset other interested powers.

Golitsyn reported that Vienna again was disturbed to learn of an alliance treaty between Russia and Prussia, of the continual correspondence between Catherine and Frederick II, and of the frequent dispatch of couriers. "Your majesty has demonstrated," Panin wrote on Golitsyn's report, "that she acknowledges a natural community of interest with the house of Austria. An alliance with the Prussian court could upset the Austrians when the Prussians ask us to participate in their confiscations. On the other hand a Prussian alliance is nothing new and is crucial now, given the strong Russian interest in an orderly royal election."

When Golitsyn reported that Kaunitz stressed the absolute necessity of both imperial courts safeguarding Polish rights and prerogatives, Panin noted "Mr. Kaunitz equates his interests in Poland with ours for nought. Any policy we adopt will cause serious differences. We will lose a third of our power and preeminence if we do not control Poland."

In an attempt to forestall a Russian rapprochement with Prussia the Viennese court warned St. Petersburg about Prussian ties with Turkey. This prompted the empress to remark that "this was nothing more than simple jealousy, but eventually everyone will realize we will not be led by the nose." Until the end of the year Catherine hoped she might manage Polish affairs without a Prussian alliance, although Panin continued to recommend it. The empress was encouraged in her belief because Austria and France did not raise major obstacles.

FRENCH POLICY IN THE POLISH ELECTION

As early as February Catherine instructed Prince Dmitry Alexeevich Golitsyn,[56] *chargé d'affaires* at the French court, to ask the ministry casually whether there were any French candidates for the Polish throne. Golitsyn replied that as far as he knew France had designated one of the Czartoryskis. "Your information," read a memorandum Golitsyn received on April 4, "more or less confirms what Count Keyserling reported from Warsaw.

"Keyserling said the French assured the Czartoryskis of his most Christian majesty's[57] favor. He is prepared to render them every assistance should they demonstrate genuine loyalty to France and not allow greater Russian influence in Poland. The French have made identical overtures to the Poniatowskis and the Czartoryskis, leading inevitably to the conclusion that France desires to insure a future Polish king loyal to France alone and hostile to Russia." After August III recovered Golitsyn was told not to raise the Polish question, rather to gather intelligence assiduously about the French court's inclinations and intentions regarding this crucial matter.

French reports do not support Golitsyn's comments about the Czartoryskis. Apparently he interpreted the French desire to promote the Czartoryskis' plans for reform as a wish to see one of them on the throne. In fact Breteuil[58] did propose his government cooperate in reforming the Polish constitution to strengthen Poland. "It is frightening to think," he wrote, "that giving an office or land to this one rather than that one turns almost all Poles against the common welfare and the defense of liberty. I know that powers committed to upholding their republican form of government find such conduct quite distasteful (dégoûtant). The more I consider Russia and its ambitious ruler, the more I am inclined to believe we must pity Polish blindness and rescue the aristocracy from a morass of greed."

The French representative might pursue this policy in Warsaw, but Versailles took a different view. "My greatest wish," wrote Louis XV[59] on March 17 (New Style), "is that the Poles be able to conduct royal elections freely. I also would like to have one of the dauphine's brothers (one of the Saxon princes)[60] chosen, preferably Xavier. If the Poles prefer the Prince of Conti,[61] I will not oppose him. The other princes of our house are unsuitable."

On a previous occasion the king described France's general policy and in particular its Polish policy. "No one knows better than I that we concluded a disadvantageous and inglorious peace, but that was the best we could do in our present misfortune. I say that if we continue the war, next year's peace would be worse. As long as I live I will not abandon the alliance with the empress (Maria Theresa), neither will I forge close ties with the Prussian king. We shall manage with our own resources and be prepared lest our present enemies swallow us. This does not mean resuming the war. Unfortunately the Polish throne is vacant for the moment, but luckily the king is recovering after his operation. We will do what we can in the new election, but we cannot start a war over the Polish throne with the pitiful sums we have left."

A ministerial report on Polish affairs was read in the royal council on May 8 (New Style). "It should be determined," the report said, "whether it is in France's political interest to intervene in Polish affairs. Poland's distance from France is sufficient reason for a negative answer, and the present system necessitates one. Talk of a Polish partition is useless. The real interest of the potential partitioning powers lies in protecting Poland from this possibility. Poland is surrounded by Austria, Prussia, Russia and Turkey.

"These four powers who envy and compete with each other are Poland's defenders rather than its enemies. Each has a clear material interest in protecting Poland since each most fears another's advantage at Poland's expense. Thus France can make these four powers responsible for preserving Poland. Partition is possible only under unusual circumstances, and would be preceded by bloody wars. The [French] king would be involved, but gain nothing. Finally, even presuming the improbable event that all four powers agree to partition Poland, or that unusual circumstances allow one of them to seize some Polish district, it still is doubtful that French interests would be affected.

"Now the concern is that Russia and the Prussian king agree to take some suitable Polish territory, but this goes counter to Austrian and Turkish interests and is contingent on their watchfulness. France has no cause for alarm if they fail to intervene. The agreement between Russia and Prussia to extend their domains cannot last. Such expansion brings them closer, increasing each's fear of the other, arousing jealousy and culminating in hostility. The balance of power in Northeastern Europe would depend on these two powers alone.

"The partition of Poland opens vast prospects where idle dreamers can wander but wise politicians must not risk going astray. Our position should be clear, forthright, credible and unambiguous. Polish revolutions do not affect France. Either they benefit it or cause very minimal harm. The proper conclusion is that no direct relationship between France and Poland exists. If it does, it is so dim, so obscure and so contingent on unusual and unlikely circumstances that concerning ourselves with it is unwise. Such concern would come at the expense of other matters which merit the full attention of the king and his ministry and entail expenditures truly beneficial and necessary for the preservation of the French monarchy.

"It must be admitted that a sizable sum would be required should the king decides to give some candidate the Polish throne. Payments will not stop with the elections since the [Polish] king will need support later. There is danger the [French] king's dignity and resources will be sacrificed for a matter in which major exertions offer scant hope even of minor success. Nor is there any assurance that an issue of no concern to France might not incite a general war. Such a war would be difficult to extinguish and is to be avoided at all costs." This report offers a complete explanation of French conduct in Poland at the time.

"I can attest," Golitsyn wrote on October 2, "that this court has not taken a clear and steadfast position on the new Polish king. If your imperial majesty now is disposed to conclude a timely agreement with the French on this matter, the occasion is favorable for many reasons. (1) The recent war and a weak government have exhausted France. (2) The treasury is bare, the debts are extraordinary and new sources of revenue are nowhere in sight. (3) Although France uncharacteristically has said nothing about Poland, it will intrigue against any measures your majesty takes. (4) France feels, however, that it has little hope of countering these measures. It might argue somewhat for its views, but in the end gladly agree to everything your majesty proposes. This would demonstrate that France has great influence in Poland and that without its consent nothing can be done in Europe."

"Prince Golitsyn makes a reasonable case," [Nikita] Panin wrote on the report. "Now that a system is in place here the dignity of your majesty's exalted empire requires acting openly, not through prominent intermediaries. Undoubtedly France will be pleased, will look out for us and will respect us for taking the lead."

After learning of August III's death the duke of Praslin[62] met with Golitsyn, speaking to him as a friend and not as a minister. "I do not believe the rumor," he said, "alleging that the empress and the Prussian king have agreed to seize some Polish provinces and divide them among themselves. In that case the king as a guarantor of the Treaty of Oliva[63] must speak out. Naturally he wants his ally and close relative the Saxon elector on the Polish throne, but he will not use force to achieve this. He does hope the elections will be free."

Golitsyn passed Praslin's statement on to the Russian court. "The dauphin and his wife are doing everything possible," he added, "to induce this court to support their brother the Saxon elector more forcefully, but I can assure you their efforts are in vain. France's straitened domestic circumstances have forced Versailles to maintain almost total neutrality. Until now it has rejected a strong role." "Other factors must be considered," Panin noted on the report. "The Polish king will not be chosen for another year, so from time to time France will reassess the Polish situation. Perhaps its policy will change and its ambassador in Poland begin to speak out. He and the elector are members of the same party and have identical supporters. Obviously he will not abandon them. With the elector's agreement France might throw in two or three million livres to support its candidate, either in a surprise move or by exploiting a confused situation. Then France would negotiate, particularly if it sees weakness in the opposition and an opportunity to reassure its Polish friends."

On December 9 Golitsyn informed the French ministry in confidence of the empress's decision to support a Piast. She hoped the king of France would instruct his ministers in Warsaw and Dresden to cooperate with the Russians. Praslin promised to report this to the king, remarking that Poland would be denied the freedom to choose its own king. The ambassador's, Count Keyserling's, utter rejection of the Saxon elector's candidacy was contrary to Russia's stated intention of preserving the Polish Commonwealth's rights. France advocated complete freedom for the Commonwealth to elect whomever it wanted, whether a Piast or not.

The French court did not change its mind even after the Saxon elector died. Praslin told Golitsyn that the king could not support a Piast were foreign candidates excluded. This was not a free election. In responding to the empress's confidential message [that she supported a Piast], the king could not deny his continued preference for the Saxon elector. The elector now deceased, one of his brothers should be chosen. The king promised to follow a policy of suasion and good offices instead of force, unless the resort of other powers to force compelled him to follow suit. "France is being candid," Panin noted on Golitsyn's report of the French response. "It will do nothing to thwart us except intrigue on a grand scale and spend a certain amount of money. When the election comes, even if the only candidates are Piasts, it will foment its intrigues and distribute its money to prevent being excluded from Polish affairs."

BRETEUIL'S FAREWELL AUDIENCE

France's relations with Russia during Catherine's first year on the throne stabilized to the point where a high-ranking French representative was not required in St. Petersburg. Besides, Baron Breteuil outranked Prince Golitsyn, the Russian representative at the court in Versailles. Breteuil had a farewell audience with Catherine in Moscow before leaving for his new assignment in Sweden. "You will oppose me in Sweden," Catherine said. "I am certain of it." Courtesy prompted the ambassador to insist that the empress's assumption was mistaken and that since her accession Europe was at peace under the aegis of the Russian sovereign.

"You think," said Catherine, "that Europe looks to me? That statesmen pay me any respect? Obviously I think Russia deserves notice. I have the best army in the world, I have money, and in a few years I will have much more of both. I tend to prefer war to peace but am restrained by justice, reason and love of humanity. Preserving peace is my constant hope, yet like Empress Elizabeth I do not have to be pushed into war. I will fight when necessary, and I will fight, not from a desire to please, but when reason tells me."

The empress then turned the conversation to her ministers' incompetence. "Fortunately," she said, "I am consoled by my hopes for the young, and I spare no effort to please my people." Turkey was the next topic. Breteuil mentioned that French influence there could benefit Russia. "Do you think," the empress objected proudly, "that you have more influence with the divan[64] than I do?" Breteuil described France's long-standing friendship with the Porte, made possible by the great distance between the two, and recalled French services to Russia when Empress Anna concluded the last peace with Turkey.[65] "Russia," replied Catherine, "waged war brilliantly, and the peace would have been even more brilliant had the

Austrians acted in good faith. The Austrians tied our hands then, and Peter III paid the price.[66] We shall even the score."

BÉRENGER'S VIEW OF RUSSIAN POLICY

Bérenger,[67] who remained in Russia as *chargé d'affaires* after Breteuil departed, reassured his court about Russian and Prussian plans to expand at Poland's expense. "Polish partition is a dead issue," he wrote in December. "Perhaps I should believe the Russian ministers' claim that they never dreamed of violating Poland's integrity, or perhaps they are deterred by open and unanimous opposition from other powers. The only certainty is that Russia plans no aggression now. When I discussed the matter with the vice chancellor [A.M. Golitsyn], he said that Russia's interests required preserving Poland's integrity scrupulously and preventing any other power's gains at Poland's expense. The minister said the empress's intentions were pure, adding that the Prussian king's might be less so. Russia would oppose all such views the moment they appeared."[68]

VII

RELATIONS WITH OTHER POWERS

RUSSIA AND MONTENEGRO

Although apparently Prussia, Russia and Austria presented no problems, Turkey might be incited by others and hence was more dangerous. Obrezkov's[1] initial reports stressed the Porte's peaceful intentions. In April he sent an interesting depiction of Montenegro.[2] "The Montenegrins are enduring and will continue to endure Turkish and Venetian oppression. The reports of Metropolitans Savva and Vasily Petrovich to the Holy Synod described this oppression. The root of the problem is the latter hierarch's inability to get along with any of his neighbors. I was able to talk with various people, including Roman Catholics, Greek-Russian Orthodox[3] and Montenegrins. All express equal praise for Hierarch Savva and equal criticism of Vasily. They predict that if Savva dies, Vasily's recklessness and discontent soon will ruin the Montenegrin people utterly.

"The state chancellor's [M.L. Vorontsov's] letter responding to the Petroviches' report advised them to live in peace with all their neighbors. This was timely counsel, worth affirming for the Montenegrins' future welfare. The hierarchs asserted that the Venetian republic is spending money to establish a Uniate[4] hierarchy in the surrounding areas. Yet it is common knowledge that the Venetian republic does less than any other Roman Catholic power to induce its peoples to acknowledge papal supremacy, instead permitting complete freedom of conscience. Clear proof is that the islanders of Corfu, Zante and Cephalonia suffer no persecution in their practice of Orthodoxy. I will explain this to the patriarch of Constantinople[5] although this probably will avail little because everyone knows he will do anything for money."

TURKISH POLICY TOWARDS POLAND

Alarming reports began to come from Constantinople after the middle of the year. In July Obrezkov obtained the instructions to the Porte's envoy to Berlin indicating Turkey's desire for an alliance with Prussia. During the envoy's stay in Poland he was to tell the Poles the Ottoman Porte would continue to aid and protect the Polish Commonwealth, and tolerate no violation of its ancient rights and liberties. When the present king died the envoy was to consult Prussia's ministers on Polish affairs and inform Prussia the Porte was determined never to tolerate an Austrian prince on the Polish throne.

"Previous Turkish participation in Polish affairs," Panin wrote on the [Turkish] instructions Obrezkov relayed to St. Petersburg, "has been based on Polish initiatives and complaints and the Crimean khan's[6] representations. Hence the Porte is convinced Consul Nikiforov[7] has orders to continue trying to win the Crimean khan over. Whatever happens in the Polish Commonwealth, the khan can be useful in keeping the Porte from aiding the Poles now or later. At present timely action is more feasible, using the khan rather than the Porte. There will be no additional expenses, for the consul already has sent the khan gifts."

RUSSIA NAMES A CONSUL TO THE CRIMEAN KHAN

Panin's remark shows that the Russian court had achieved its longstanding wish for a consul in the Crimea. On February 20 the Kievan governor general informed the College of Foreign Affairs he had sent Lieutenant Bastavik with letters to the Crimean khan. The khan told Bastavik he was willing to accept a Russian consul but was unable to present the matter to the Porte until the Russian government wrote him personally. Bastavik then asked the khan's senior court officials how the governor general might thank the khan for his favors. They dictated a list of presents to him, consisting of thousands of ducats, furs and a carriage with horses.

"For God's sake," the empress wrote to the chancellor on April 9, "be quick about assigning someone to the Crimea. You can promise any volunteer enormous benefits. Obviously I will begrudge nothing for such important and vital service." It was a month before a candidate was found, and on May 9 the empress wrote to Vorontsov again. "Mikhailo Larionovich, please get Nikiforov underway faster. Do what you can to give him all the presents he wants lest inaction frustrate this serious and important matter. I cannot thank God enough for our previous success. May God continue to show us His kindness!"

RUSSIA, TURKEY AND POLAND

Constantinople learned of August III's death on October 20. That very day the grand vizier was deposed and Mustafa Pasha,[8] twice previously grand vizier, replaced him. In 1756 Obrezkov was instructed to promote Mustafa's removal and sent ten thousand ducats to accomplish this. The money remained unspent because Obrezkov was not involved in the transfer of power. The resident [Obrezkov] judged Mustafa as exceedingly malicious and cunning as well as the most competent Turkish army commander. "The new vizier," Panin noted on Obrezkov's description of the events, "perhaps will oppose us less when he realizes that our policy has changed towards Vienna and its relationship with Poland."

Obrezkov was sent a directive (1) Suggest to the Porte the advantages of distinguishing our interests from those of the Austrians in Poland. (2) Given the Viennese court's firm alliance with France, Spain and all the Italian powers, detaching itself from this alliance would be as beneficial for Turkey as it has been for Russia. (3) Proceed carefully, approaching only those in a position to restrain the Porte. Spend your money with this in mind. (4) If the Porte cannot be restrained, use the money to depose the vizier if he makes trouble.

A diplomatic struggle began in Constantinople. The French ambassador Vergennes[9] told the Porte it must intervene in Poland, where Russian domination was intolerable. The Prussian ambassador Rixen claimed the Russian agreement with Prussia over Poland was in Poland's best interest and requested the Porte not to allow itself be snared by the French or anyone else. To do so would award the Polish crown to the house of Saxony for the third time, thus making it hereditary.

Obrezkov's promise of a handsome gift persuaded the Porte's translator to talk. The translator said France and Austria agreed that if a Saxon prince could not be put on the Polish throne, the duke of Parma's[10] candidacy would be promoted. He was Archduke Joseph's[11] father-in-law and a close relative of the French king. Were he king, all Catholic powers, the pope, the entire clergy and the Jesuits would begin restricting the Polish Commonwealth's freedom.

The Russian and Prussian representations convinced the Porte to inform the Prussian ambassador it favored the Russo-Prussian agreement allowing the Poles to elect one of their countrymen king. Obrezkov spent three thousand ducats to induce the Porte to repeat this to the French ambassador and to order the Crimean khan and the hospodars of Moldavia and Wallachia[12] to abide by the Porte's decision. The various intrigues conducted at these rulers' courts made this step necessary.

RUSSIA OPPOSES FRANCE IN SWEDEN

A major diplomatic conflict developed between Russia and France on the Northern European peninsula. "It is impossible to imagine," Ostermann[13] reported on March 28, "that in its present exhaustion the Swedish court will attempt to intervene in Polish affairs unless so induced by France. France pays the Swedish court enormous subsidies and continues its current policy of bribing Swedish government officials." On August 26 Ostermann related that France had offered Sweden a new ten-year defensive alliance on condition that France pay Sweden a million livres in 1763 and one and a half million a year thereafter for the duration of the alliance. In return Sweden would furnish France six ships of the line and six frigates. France would return the vessels or the cash equivalent when the alliance expired.

"The French proposal to the Swedish court," Panin wrote on the report, "could be communicated to the court in London in confidence through the English ambassador here and our minister in London. This would draw the English court's attention to and make it more jealous of the French court. In addition it would lead England to respect us, recognize the need for close cooperation with our court and help make this a reality. As a result the proposed commercial and defense treaties will be more favorable and more beneficial."

The Swedish Senate decided to ask the French for larger subsidies, as much as four million livres, postponing any new agreements until they were paid. Both the Hats and the Caps[14] were dissatisfied with France. "We are at the limit," one *loyal* senator told Ostermann. "It seems France is in no position to satisfy our demands, so we are forced to convoke an extraordinary session of the Riksdag. The French party wants this, but contradictory measures adopted by state officials during the last Riksdag have caused considerable popular discontent. There is talk of reviewing and amending the fundamental laws. Loyal patriots find themselves without support. They have no direct contact with the English court because England has no ambassador here.

"Everything seems to suggest Russia's unwillingness to intervene in our domestic affairs. Self-preservation forces these patriots to accept the current unpromising situation. I must say it would be a great help if your empress offered the loyalists some minimal support and protection, thereby undercutting Sweden's new ties with the French court and enhancing Russia's popular reputation. If the empress agreed to offer the Swedish court three hundred thousand rubles, or even less, I swear on my honor that the nation would follow the empress's advice. The ministry and the French party would not dare impose a new French yoke on the people."

Ostermann passed on the loyal senator's suggestion. "It will be tricky," he added, "to open an extraordinary session of the Riksdag during the current national debate. In the first place Swedes of all classes want to review and amend the fundamental laws, which for some time they have blamed for all the unrest. Three prominent men are promoting this, General Count Fersen,[15] State Secretary Baron Hermansson[16] and Colonel Sinclair.[17] They agree completely and boast endlessly of the queen's full support. Second, state funds are exhausted totally. Third, confused exchange rates have brought foreign trade to a standstill, causing the state great hardship. Fourth, the nobles and burghers openly hate each other. Fifth, the cost of living is intolerable.

"The people blame everything on a faulty government system and imbalance between the three centers of power; namely, the king, the Senate and the state officials. The Riksdag's principal task obviously is to restore balance, and there is no telling which side will prevail. I am supposed to preserve equilibrium between the parties by suggestion, but suggestion alone is not enough. When France ends financial support of the French party, it will join the court party. Then the old Bonnets (Caps) will be like sheep without a shepherd and gradually will disappear. The court party will have sole power, and it is hard to predict the outcome."

"It is unlikely," Panin noted, "that the Swedish nation will transfer its affection and loyalty to us, for since time immemorial it has blamed the Russian empire for the loss of its power and influence in European affairs.[18] This particularly is so in its present exhaustion. Sweden still will feel the full weight of the French yoke and, wanting to break free, will hearken to our views."

News arrived from France of a decision to give Sweden three million livres in a series of payments. Then Louis XV informed the Swedish government of his plans for Poland after August III died. The king wanted the Saxon elector on the Polish throne, but this was contingent on free elections. If the lot fell to a Piast he would not block it. If anyone considered dismembering the Polish Commonwealth he would oppose it with all his might, calling on his allies to join him. Therefore he wanted to know the Swedish government's thoughts on the matter, since preservation of the Polish Commonwealth was in Sweden's vital interest.

Sweden replied that the Swedish king, recognizing the importance of preserving the Polish Commonwealth's liberty, constitution and integrity, agreed completely with the French king. Hence he did not intend to prevent free elections and would be very pleased if the Saxon elector received the crown. "The Swedish reply is most discreet," Panin noted.

Meanwhile St. Petersburg decided it should give the Swedish government the unpaid subsidy of three hundred thousand.[19] When Ostermann heard the news from his court he informed the well-known *loyal* senator, who said the offer should be delayed until the Riksdag met. Otherwise, the ministry would use the opportunity to cover financial obligations, take the money and not convoke the Riksdag. From St. Petersburg word came that the empress had announced her support for electing a Piast in Poland. The Swedish king replied that the issue of royal elections had arisen so recently that taking a position was difficult. Of course, he said, this was a matter for the Polish people, who alone must decide between one of theirs and a foreigner.

RELATIONS WITH DENMARK

Korff[20] wrote about Denmark's[21] role in Poland. It would give no one military aid no matter how great the subsidy offered. Denmark's finances were in disarray, and Sweden was a greater concern. "Apparently France is showing less interest in Sweden," Foreign Minister Bernstorff[22] told Korff. "Therefore neighboring courts have an interest in recognizing Sweden's dangerous position now. Prudence dictates precautions against the gathering storm. History teaches that autocratic Swedish kings have caused prolonged and bloody wars"[23]

In the present matter, remarked Korff, Russia and Denmark must decide things in advance. "We already considered this," Bernstorff answered, "but how shall we begin? We hear from all sides, even from Stockholm, that the Swedish queen [Louisa Ulrika][24] is looking to forge close friendship with the Russian empress, thus involving her on behalf of the queen's house. I will not investigate the truth of these reports further, but already they are public. In such delicate circumstances are we acting responsibly if we propose an agreement to our sovereign which the empress easily can repudiate? Because of her great power she has less reason than Denmark to fear Sweden. What will happen when we are the first to propose an agreement? We only will bring the irreconcilable wrath of the Swedish court down on our king!"

"This fear is groundless," Korff answered. "The empress's policy is based on her empire's national interest. Your ambassador in St. Petersburg Baron Osten[25] may make a highly confidential proposal for an agreement should you wish to learn the empress's position on Sweden." Bernstorff promised to consult with his colleagues, and at his next conference with Korff reported that the king had given Osten the commission Korff suggested. Bernstorff also said the king had instructed his minister in Warsaw to cooperate with the Russian minister concerning the Polish elections.

VIII

ANGLO-RUSSIAN RELATIONS

NEGOTIATIONS FOR AN ENGLISH ALLIANCE

The English ambassador Buckinghamshire[1] made strenuous efforts to sign an alliance and commercial treaty at an early date. As we have seen, Russia was more cautious.[2] "I think the English ambassador will respond satisfactorily," Catherine wrote the chancellor [Vorontsov] on February 15. "We want an agreement on the future Polish royal elections before concluding a treaty of alliance. I have suggested this to the ambassador repeatedly, but no one knows what his court thinks. If he says his court is in full agreement I will respond, when I have the opportunity, that these general terms are unsatisfactory unless the English minister in Warsaw is directed to cooperate with my ambassador."

On March 8 Buckinghamshire met in Moscow with the chancellor [Vorontsov] and vice chancellor [Golitsyn]. He complained his court criticized him for not doing enough to obtain an alliance. Vorontsov and Golitsyn responded that Buckinghamshire himself could attest how greatly the empress valued the English king's friendship. The sole reason the renewal of both treaties was postponed was the empress's preoccupation with a multitude of pressing domestic issues. It appeared these would give her no time to deal with foreign affairs until the court returned to St. Petersburg.

On April 22 Buckinghamshire related that his sovereign the king had instructed his resident in Warsaw to cooperate fully with the Russian ambassador, particularly if the king died. On July 8 Buckinghamshire presented a memorandum. "My sovereign the king," it read, "has postponed his request to renew the alliance because the court will spend a little more time in Moscow. Since he is convinced the court already should be in St. Petersburg, he has instructed me to convey his regret to the empress personally, and to her ministers, that nothing has been accomplished. An alliance between the two peoples is predestined by nature, an alliance advantageous for both and so necessary to preserve peace in Europe.

"It is hoped Russia will consider the matter carefully, for the alliance is long overdue. Delaying conclusion of the alliance diminishes both powers' credit, meanwhile powers opposing England and Russia are using this delay to advantage. The English court is making more effort for a Russian alliance than one with anyone else. It realizes the importance of this alliance for both peoples, and not just for them but also for the sake of their obligations to other powers. The king is unable to understand the Russian court's policy of postponing a defensive alliance until there is general peace in Europe. Besides, there is no reason not to conclude a commercial treaty, something Russia needs more than England.

"There are no grounds for reproaching the king. He has demonstrated his esteem for the empress in every way possible by satisfying her wishes in the Polish question and all other matters. His first and best basis for [foreign] policy must be a genuine alliance with Russia. With it in place it will be easy to create a wise and sound system which serves our mutual interests and preserves order in Europe. When we cooperate and speak with one voice our discussions with other courts will acquire serious weight. Our statements will be noted and respected."

This strong declaration prompted a draft proposal for an alliance treaty. When England requested an alliance so urgently, saying bluntly that a Russian alliance was the first and best basis for policy, it was unlikely to refuse satisfacion of Russia's demands. The empire's finances were not in an enviable position. The Polish elections required sizable expenditures, and wealthy England must help. An alliance lent more incentive for England to help Russia in Sweden where the opponent was France, which always was England's primary concern.

To these ends Russia included two secret articles in its draft treaty of alliance with England. The first stated the English minister in Warsaw would cooperate with his Russian counterpart when August III died, making every effort to place on the Polish throne someone acceptable to both courts. Since this required money, the English king promised to keep a large sum in Poland to achieve their common goal, and the empress would do the same. Developments in Poland might compel the Russian empress as a neighbor to employ force to promote the intentions of both contracting powers. If so, the English king undertook to provide the empress five hundred thousand rubles as soon as Russian troops entered Poland.

The second secret article noted that the Russian and English ministers in Sweden would work in concert to weaken the party supported by other states, and to maintain a balance between this and the opposing party.[3]

England found both articles absolutely unacceptable. Buckinghamshire was to tell the Russian ministry that England found it awkward to participate in quarrels over the Polish royal election, thereby risking involvement in a new war. The ambassador also objected to a third article. Turkey was named as one of the powers whose attack on Russia obligated England to come to Russia's aid. "Our ministry," Buckinghamshire said, "cannot accept this provision, which would put our commercial company in the Levant[4] in a very unfavorable position. The moment the Porte learns of the treaty, it will destroy English commerce in its domains completely."

The vice chancellor [Golitsyn] objected that were Turkey not named. France could not be, and neither alliance partner benefitted if no one were named. When Buckinghamshire attempted parallel negotiations for a commercial treaty Russia decided to extract more concessions from England by making a commercial treaty contingent upon an alliance one.

The slow pace of treaty negotiations obviously made things difficult for the Russian minister in London, Count Alexander Vorontsov.[5] The English ministers told him European courts were talking about Buckinghamshire's failure to conclude the treaties, attributing it to French influence. England's reputation was being damaged as a result. Credence was given to these opinions by newspaper reports that Baron Breteuil, the French ambassador to the Russian court, enjoyed special privileges.

The secretary of state for foreign affairs, the earl of Halifax,[6] told Vorontsov that Berlin might join an Anglo-Russian alliance readily. It faced a difficult situation since Vienna and Versailles remained allies. Lastly it was for the empress to permit other courts to join the alliance, for London would follow her lead completely.

VORONTSOV'S PROBLEMS IN LONDON

Count Alexander Vorontsov had to deal with another unpleasantness as well. His uncle Count Mikhail Larionovich Vorontsov ceased conducting foreign affairs and went abroad. Before he relinquished his duties he clashed with Buckinghamshire, who sent him a letter stating that the king promised Vorontsov two thousand pounds sterling to compensate Vorontsov for his losses when English privateers captured his possessions. This generosity could not be extended until England and Russia had concluded and signed a commercial treaty favorable to England. Vorontsov began to shout about insult and dishonor. Buckinghamshire expressed to the chancellor his profound regret about the matter, saying he was overzealous and begging him most persuasively to forget it. That was the end of the matter.

"Your excellency easily can imagine," Count Vorontsov wrote his uncle on July 30, "my feelings about Lord Buckinghamshire's unprecedented behavior. However meager I judged his talents, I could not conceive his recklessness would extend to the perversity and insanity he displayed in this strange letter. I can assure your excellency that his court justifiably is very dissatisfied with him. Today his majesty the king approached me. He wanted to say he had reason to be most displeased by his ambassador's conduct, particularly regarding his letter to you. He asked me to tell you Buckinghamshire's instructions did not sanction his behavior. He also assured me that your integrity was common knowledge, and that no one here [in London] would dare make such a strange proposition to you and hope to succeed. The ambassador acted out of ignorance."

PANIN BELITTLES VORONTSOV

Count Vorontsov's situation in London grew even worse when August III's death brought the Polish question to the fore. St. Petersburg sought strong English support for Russian plans in Poland, whereas England wanted no part of a matter so foreign to English interests. Hence all the Russian ambassador's representations were doomed to failure. Vorontsov found it very unpleasant to tell the empress of these failures, particularly when the man now directly responsible for foreign affairs disliked Vorontsov intensely.

Panin's notes on Vorontsov's reports expressed this aversion. Once Vorontsov wrote that none of his representations to the English ministry had much success since the death of the [Polish] king. "It would have been a good bet they would fail," Panin noted here, "because they were poorly conceived and clumsily executed." Where Vorontsov made the customary apology that, for all his zeal to serve the empress, his knowledge and skill were not equal to the task, Panin remarked "How true!"

Vorontsov related that he went to the country to discuss matters with the famous Pitt,[7] formerly prime minister and now leader of the opposition. Vorontsov was eager to draw him out on Poland and learn England's position on a question that should concern all European great powers. According to Vorontsov, Pitt responded with his customary eloquence, but guardedly. "I bet he [Vorontsov] talked down to him, not showing the proper respect," Panin remarked.

PITT'S VIEWS ON FOREIGN POLICY

The gist of Pitt's remarks was that there was every indication the Prussian king would coordinate his efforts with Russia in the Polish elections. Pitt believed England should support both states' demands enthusiastically. England valued their friendship highly, although it was hard to specify the exact form English cooperation might take. There were a number of circumstances to consider, which as a man out of power for two years he could not know.

Vorontsov wrote that he was assured by a mutual acquaintance that Pitt was very surprised the present ministry had done nothing on the Polish question. Pitt asked the acquaintance why the ministry had not sent a courier to St. Petersburg with an offer of good offices as soon as it learned of August III's death. Such a proposal also would assure Russia about possible French intervention. In the event of French intervention England would do everything possible to block France and also try to destroy it completely. Pitt also said that were the ministry to continue its present Polish policy he would speak out in the House of Commons, expressing his amazement that the court was so indifferent to such an important issue. "He [Pitt] is deceiving and lying," Panin wrote here. "No sensible man ever said a prominent court should send another court a courier offering its good offices. Courts do this only when misfortune strikes. Then it is a magnanimous gesture, but base and mean in the former instance."

VORONTSOV'S EFFORTS TO WIN ENGLISH SUPPORT IN POLAND

Vorontsov was supposed to ask the English ministry[8] to transfer its resident Wroughton[9] from Dresden to Warsaw. Vorontsov slipped by saying in a letter to the earl of Halifax that satisfying the empress's request in this matter might expedite the Russian alliance England wanted. This prompted a memorandum from the empress. "In general," she wrote, "we have reason for satisfaction with your ardent and zealous service. We cannot, however, conceal our surprise at the French translation of your communiqué to the earl of Halifax. You must realize the impropriety of the conclusion where, after discussing the English resident's transfer from Dresden to Warsaw, somehow you made this a condition for speedier conclusion of the treaties now being negotiated with England.

"We are asking a trivial and inconsequential favor of the English. England does not care whether its minister is in Dresden or Warsaw because he can serve equally well in either location. With this request you have obligated us in a matter involving our empire's honor and welfare. We will not conclude treaties with England or any other power unless both sides benefit. This is the most important issue, but there also is your totally unwarranted addendum to the French translation of your communiqué [to Halifax]. It is completely unfounded and does not square with your solemn pledge to the earl of Halifax never for any reason to utter a falsehood. You never were instructed in writing to attach such a condition, nor could you ever be. Since you said it was true, you have exposed the court's credit and yours to unnecessary censure. Duly noting our justifiable amazement at this, we are convinced excessive zeal led you astray. Therefore it is appropriate to insist you take precautions by proceeding more circumspectly. Do not send unnecessary written communications, particularly when oral statements might suffice."

Vorontsov labored to set things straight yet contradicted himself as he did so. Although he said his added comments merely were compliments, in no way obligating Russia, he insisted they induced the English court to transfer Wroughton from Dresden to Warsaw. London cared so little about Poland that otherwise it would not have fulfilled the Russian requests.

RUSSIA SEEKS ENGLISH SUPPORT IN SWEDEN

At the end of November Vorontsov noted that for a long period England had not participated in general European affairs. Because St. Petersburg needed England's cooperation in Sweden as well as Poland, Catherine instructed Vorontsov to approach the English ministry in a spirit of friendly candor. He was to call its attention to France's proposal for a subsidy treaty, and induce England to send an ambassador to Stockholm soon. Vorontsov replied that this fully accorded with England's interests.

Although it had made peace with France, the British ministers must realize the Franco-Spanish alliance was directed against England alone, which would be attacked at the first opportunity.

Even so, Vorontsov had to say that stationing an ambassador in Stockholm was insufficient. Unless subsidies were promised his presence would not prevent Sweden's alliance with France. It was known England never gave anyone subsidies in peacetime, and was less likely to do so during the current ministry, which dared not ask the nation for any amount. The ministers were more frightened by the rising tide of opposition at home than by all the political events in Europe and all the alliances aimed at England.

"At times other important political considerations," Catherine wrote on this report, "deter us from greater efforts to block or similarly to interrupt a development prejudicial to our interests. That requires prudent attempts to find and employ ways of thwarting completion of such a development. This is how, in concert with England, we must deal with the new Franco-Swedish alliance. Blocking the alliance would require enough bribery to convoke an extraordinary parliamentary session and cause a revolution in the Swedish government. England's subsidy would have to be sufficiently large for Sweden to cope successfully with all its problems and weaknesses. Both of us have other concerns, making cooperation on either of these agreements impossible. Therefore we must work together to create a party at that [the Swedish] court with enough national standing to weaken and immobilize that alliance. I have discussed the matter at length with the English ambassador, and any English minister who goes to Stockholm also could give Count Ostermann new instructions."

ENGLISH POLICY IN POLAND

On December 16 Vorontsov informed his court of his conversation with the earl of Sandwich,[10] Halifax's successor in the Northern Department of Foreign Affairs. Speaking for the king, Sandwich told Vorontsov instructions to the new English resident in Warsaw specified two concerns. He was to ensure free elections and protect the Polish Commonwealth against any seizure of its territory. Vorontsov expressed his surprise at this declaration. It was unnecessary to mention protecting the integrity of Poland's domains, because Russia already declared it had no intention of dismembering Poland. Poland's integrity depended on the Russian declaration, for if the Russian empress wanted a Polish district how might the English resident Mr. Wroughton save the Commonwealth? Catherine was very pleased with Vorontsov's reply. "This is a praiseworthy response," she wrote on the dispatch. "It could not have been said better."

IX

THE MIROVICH CONSPIRACY

PLANS FOR MONUMENT TO CATHERINE

It was almost two years since the Senate resolved to erect a monument to the empress. The project was assigned to the Academy of Sciences[1]. Now the Senate ordered the Academy to report progress toward construction of this monument to the eternal glory of her imperial highness. The Academy replied that there was no progress because the St. Petersburg Commission for Stone Construction had not informed the Academy of the location of the monument. The Senate then directed the Academy to prepare two proposals for monuments, one on Vasilievsky Island opposite the Academy and the colleges, and the other in the square facing the new stone Winter Palace. The Academy reported that Professor Stählin[2] had seven designs for monuments and that Professor Lomonosov[3] had promised to draft one.

THE CONSPIRATOR

While the Academy was busy with plans for Catherine's monument two officers devised a scheme to dethrone her in the name of Ivan Antonovich,[4] a prisoner in Schlüsselburg.[5] We saw that the empress had ordered efforts made to persuade Ivan to become a monk,[6] and these were underway. "In my opinion...," an undated note by Catherine stated, "he must be kept in confinement to protect him permanently from harm. He should take monastic vows now and move to a monastery that is not too near and not too remote, preferably one not a center for pilgrimages. He is to be guarded there as he is now. Find out if such places exist in the Murom woods, Kola or the Novgorod diocese," but the plan "to protect him permanently from harm" was too late.

When Karl XII[7] was approaching the Ukraine, Fedor Mirovich was colonel of the Pereiaslav Regiment. Mirovich and Mazepa[8] joined Karl XII and after the Swedish king's defeat Mirovich found refuge in Poland, leaving a wife and two young sons, Yakov and Peter, behind in the

Ukraine. The children went to their first cousin once removed, the famous Colonel Pavel Polubotok[9] in Chernigov, with whom they lived until 1723. That year Polubotok took them to St. Petersburg then was imprisoned shortly thereafter, leaving the Miroviches without a guardian. Empress Catherine I[10] sent them to study at the Academy of Sciences but they left the Academy when their scholarships were terminated, either for cause or on some pretext. Somehow or other they managed to remain in St. Petersburg.

In 1728 Peter Mirovich petitioned Princess Elizabeth Petrovna[11] that he live in her house, and she took him in as her secretary. The next year he went with the princess to Moscow, taking his brother with him. Yakov Mirovich was named secretary to the Polish ambassador Count Potocki, with whom he went to Poland. In 1731 Yakov returned to Moscow where he married one Akisheva of the merchant class. In 1732 both Miroviches fell into the hands of Secret Chancellery[12] and were sent to Siberia, where they were enrolled as junior boyars. They were punished because Peter Mirovich made a copy of an order concerning Polubotok which he used to write a letter to his treasonous father in Poland. Consequently Peter was barred permanently from going to the Ukraine and Yakov from travelling to Poland.

In 1764 Yakov's son Vasily Mirovich[13] was a second lieutenant in the Smolensk Infantry Regiment. He was oppressed by his past and present, yet lacked the strength to deal with his burdens. He considered himself a man of distinguished ancestry who must hide his lineage because his grandfather was a traitor. Vasily chafed at his low military rank which he felt doomed him to obscurity, and was offended that senior officers treated commissioned officers from the nobility the same as those from other ranks. A further blow came when efforts to better his financial status and that of his three sisters ended in failure. Mirovich petitioned for the return of at least part of his grandfather's confiscated property and for a pension for his sisters, but both requests were refused. His search for some escape led to a masonic lodge[14] where he took to the mysticism like opium.

MIROVICH LAYS HIS PLANS

The memory of June 28[15] was a terrible temptation for people like Mirovich. The unhappy and angry man was haunted continually by the question "If they succeeded then, why can't we succeed now?" On April 1, 1764 Mirovich resolved to find a way to free Ivan Antonovich from Schlüsselburg and proclaim him emperor. He confided in his friend

Lieutenant Apollon Ushakov of the Velikie Luki Infantry Regiment. Ushakov agreed to help Mirovich and agreed it would be safer to keep the plan secret. On May 13 Mirovich and Ushakov had a requiem sung for themselves in the Nativity of the Virgin (Kazan) cathedral.

Catherine's plans to visit the Baltic region that summer had been announced. The conspirators decided to start an uprising a week after the court left St. Petersburg. While Mirovich was officer of the guard at Schlüsselburg, Ushakov, posing as a courier, would come by sloop and give Mirovich a manifesto in the name of Emperor Ivan Antonovich. After the soldiers heard the manifesto and rallied to Ivan, he would be freed, taken by sloop to St. Petersburg and landed on the Vyborg side.[16] Ivan than would be taken to an artillery unit which would revolt as the Izmailovsky Regiment had on June 28, 1762. On May 25 the War College sent Ushakov to take some money to General Prince M.N. Volkonsky[17] and on the way he drowned in a river. Mirovich nevertheless stuck to his plan and decided to carry it off by himself at the appointed time.

CATHERINE LEAVES ST. PETERSBURG

Catherine was the first sovereign since Peter the Great to travel in Russia on state business. We noted that she went from Moscow to Rostov in 1763.[18] Although that journey had a religious purpose, she used the opportunity to continue north to Yaroslavl. Now she traveled west to inspect the Baltic region. She particularly wanted to see the Baltic port of Rogervik which had occasioned a great deal of discussion and cost considerable money and effort. Although the empress went on state business, grenadiers said she was going to Riga to marry [Grigory] Orlov[19] there and make him prince.

Catherine left St. Petersburg on June 20 and travelled via Yamburg to Narva, where she was greeted with festivities. Count Grigory Orlov responded in Russian to German speeches by the Estonian knights and the Narva burgomaster.[20] The empress went from Narva to Reval, where another festive reception was held. Triumphal gates bore the inscription, "To Catherine, peerless mother of the Fatherland (Matri Patriae incomparabili)."[21]

On June 26 Catherine wrote from Reval to Ivan Nepliuev,[22] who was left in charge of affairs in St. Petersburg. "People here are very happy with me and do not know how to express their pleasure. I was invited to dine with the knights and the next day with the burghers. Approval is heartfelt and genuine." She went from Reval to the Baltic port [Rogervik] on June

30. "When I arrived," she wrote [Nikita] Panin from Rogervik, "the glorious Baltic port was not at all glorious. I hope you are in good health. Already I am bored with roaming around so much." Catherine was delayed by sand and extreme heat, forcing her to travel forty versts on foot and postponing her arrival in Riga until July 9. Although she responded graciously to the salutations she received amidst the festivities and public rejoicing, Catherine was preoccupied by a letter from Panin describing the *extraordinary events* in Schlüsselburg.

FIRST NEWS OF ATTEMPTED COUP

At that time Panin was living in Tsarskoe Selo with the grand duke and heir to the throne [the future Paul I].[23] He received a report from Schlüsselburg written July 5 by the commandant Berednikov. "Vasily Yakovlev, the son of Mirovich, a second lieutenant in the Smolensk Infantry Regiment, was officer of the guard in the fortress this week. At two in the morning he mustered the entire guard and ordered them to load their weapons. When I heard the clatter and the weapons being loaded, I left my quarters and asked why the troops were being mustered and weapons loaded without orders. Mirovich rushed up to me and hit me on the head with a musket butt, exposing the skull. 'He is the villain,' he shouted to the soldiers, 'who is holding the sovereign Ivan Antonovich prisoner in the fortress! Seize him! We must be ready to die for the sovereign!'

"They seized me, and I was kept under arrest until five in the morning. Soldiers were told to restrain me by holding on to my gown. While I was being detained Mirovich twice attempted to lead his men with loaded weapons against garrison forces commanded by Captain Vlasiev and Lieutenant Chekin. Mirovich's troops fired many shots and were fired upon in reply. Mirovich brought a six-pound cannon to the barracks where the prisoner [Ivan Antonovich] was held.

"I do not know what happened next because I could not see. Later Mirovich led Captain Vlasiev and Chekin under guard before the ranks of soldiers, and his troops carried in the nameless prisoner's dead body. After mustering all the soldiers he kissed the cross[24] and told them he alone was guilty. He ordered drums to sound first reveille then forward march full. At that point I cried out to arrest him, which was done. After he was arrested I found manifestos, orders and copies of oaths he had written himself."

INVESTIGATION

When Panin received this report he immediately sent Lieutenant Colonel Kashkin to Schlüsselburg with orders to conduct a thorough investigation and to interrogate Mirovich. At the same time he notified the empress in Riga. Catherine received Panin's report on July 9 and answered him the same day. "I was astonished when I read your report of the extraordinary occurrences at Schlüsselburg. Wonderful is God's providence and inscrutable His ways![25] The only thing I would add to your excellent instructions is that the guilty should be punished without publicity, but also without any efforts at concealment. (There is no way to keep something that involved more than two hundred men secret).

"Have the nameless prisoner given a Christian burial quietly at Schlüsselburg. I am afraid there is a spark hidden in the ashes, in St. Petersburg rather than Schlüsselburg, and the longer it takes to reach the [imperial] residence the better. When it does reach St. Petersburg the matter can be made public. Therefore have a directive prepared for Lieutenant General Weymarn[26] of the division there to conduct an investigation and give the directive to him. He is an intelligent man and will not exceed his orders. Give him the papers he needs for his information, but keep the rest yourself until I come.

"I am very curious to find out whether Lieutenant Ushakov was arrested and whether others were involved. Apparently they had a plan. Show Weymarn this letter or anything else he needs for guidance. The Schlüsselburg commandant, the loyal officers and Mr. Weymarn's forces deserve a sign of my favor for their loyalty. There must be an inquiry into the disciplinary status of the Smolensk Regiment."

REPERCUSSIONS IN ST. PETERSBURG

Meanwhile Ivan Nepliuev, who remained in command in St. Petersburg, informed Panin on July 8 that although the events in Schlüsselburg were known in the capital there was no malicious talk. Then at three in the morning Teplov[27] arrived in Tsarskoe Selo with a letter from Nepliuev. The letter said St. Petersburg was quiet, particularly because people believed that "the phantom [Ivan Antonovich] on whose behalf the villainy was instigated" was dead. Teplov told Panin that Nepliuev also wanted him to give Panin an oral message. "If I were you I would bring the rebel Mirovich to Tsarskoe Selo as quickly as possible. I would torture him secretly to extract the names of his accomplices. If he were my prisoner I would ask him point-blank who approved his rebellion because it is unthinkable such a petty figure could launch so vast an enterprise on his own. Exposing these accomplices requires torture."

"Why did Ivan Ivanovich [Nepliuev] not put this in writing?" Panin asked Teplov. "I did ask him," Teplov replied, "to write you a letter or give me a note with his requests to you, but Nepliuev said he stood by what he said and motioned to Prince Alexander Alexeevich Viazemsky,[28] who was with him at the time." Panin wrote to the empress about his conversation with Teplov. The same day, the tenth, Nepliuev also wrote to Catherine that Mirovich should be tortured.

EYEWITNESS TESTIMONY

It also was on July 10 that Kashkin arrived in Riga and gave Mirovich's first statement to the empress. "I decided on April 1, 1764," Mirovich said, "to commit my crime. I was motivated by these reasons (1) When I was at court I saw that staff officers and other state officials were given free access to her imperial highness whereas others, such as commissioned officers, were not. (2) When operas were staged which her imperial highness deigned to attend, I was excluded. (3) Staff officers do not accord officers from other ranks the same respect as those from the nobility, even if their honor merits it. (4) I asked for whatever portion of the property confiscated from my ancestors her imperial highness might vouchsafe award me but the resolution prescribed that the petitioner has no claim and that the Senate should so inform him. A second plea to obtain a pension for my three sisters also was rejected. I wanted to free the sovereign Ivan Antonovich and present him to the artillery regiments."

Testimony by Mirovich and other participants in the affair provided additional information. At first Mirovich wanted to reveal his plans to Vlasiev. He met with this officer on July 4 and said "Will you ruin me before I launch my project?" Vlasiev interrupted him and said "If your project might ruin you, I do not want to hear about it." Then Mirovich tried to convince the soldier Pisklov, who said he would agree if the other soldiers did, and recruited two other soldiers. Later Mirovich won over the soldier Bosov and three corporals. Some refused at first but finally said "If everyone else is for it, I am too."

Mirovich decided to act quickly, fearing Vlasiev would guess the nature of the venture he raised with him and it would be reported somewhere.

At two in the morning Mirovich ran into the soldiers' guardroom from the officers' quarters shouting "To arms!" He called the soldiers to attention and ordered them to load their weapons. When Berednikov came in, Mirovich grabbed the collar of his tunic and placed him under guard. He and his unit then went to the garrison detachment's barracks. When challenged "Who goes there?" Mirovich answered "I am going to the sovereign!" There was a volley from the garrison. Mirovich ordered his men to return the fire, then ordered them to retreat lest Ivan Antonovich be shot.

The detachment joined him, asking "Tell us why we are taking action." Mirovich read the sections of the manifesto in Ivan's name he thought were more likely to sway the soldiers. When he read "The sovereign and I salute you!" he started shouting to the garrison detachment that if they began shooting they would be answered with cannon fire. Seeing that threats were to no avail, Mirovich ordered the cannon dragged off and again sent word to the garrison that he would open fire. The garrison forces answered that they had laid down their arms. Mirovich and his troops burst into the barracks. Since it was dark he sent for candles, and when they were brought he saw a man's body lying on the floor in the middle of the barracks. He had been stabbed to death. Mirovich looked at Vlasiev and Chekin who were standing there and said "You scoundrels! Have you no fear of God? Why did you shed innocent blood?"

"We had orders to do so," the officers answered. "Why are you here ?" "I came on my own," Mirovich said. "We," the officers continued, "were doing our duty, and we were under orders. Here they are!" They gave Mirovich a document, which he did not read. Soldiers came up to him to ask if he wanted them to stab the officers to death. "Don't bother," he answered. "It's no use now. They are right and we are wrong." After he said this Mirovich went up to the body and kissed it on the hand and foot. He ordered the soldiers to place it on a bed and carry it out of the barracks to the parade ground. Everything then happened as Berednikov described it to Panin.

Vlasiev testified that Mirovich's statements on July 4 made him suspect sinister intentions. After consulting with Chekin he sent a report to Panin, but the courier's departure was delayed by the commotion on the fifth. They killed Ivan Antonovich when they learned the cannon was being loaded. When he was questioned, Vlasiev thought he should conceal the fact that he and Chekin had a written order not to let Ivan Antonovich out of their custody alive. He testified they told Mirovich that "Whoever did this to him (Ivan) was acting under orders." "But," Vlasiev added, "no one ever gave me such (an order). Since I did not have one, there was nothing to show. We were talking about an order concerning the death penalty."

DESCRIPTION OF IVAN ANTONOVICH

Their testimony about the deceased repeated what was known from earlier reports. He was in very good health with no physical handicaps except for a serious speech impediment. Strangers found him almost completely unintelligible, and even his constant companions had difficulty understanding him. He could not pronounce words without holding his hand on his chin. He had no food preferences and ate everything greedily and indiscriminately. In eight years they had not seen a single indication of intelligence. He asked himself questions which he then answered. He said that his body was that of Prince Ivan who had been named Russian emperor, but that the prince left this world long ago.

Now he was a heavenly spirit, St. Gregory to be exact, and therefore considered everybody else vile creatures. He said they displayed their vileness and uncleanness by bowing to each other and to the holy icons, but heavenly spirits like himself bowed to no one. He wanted to become a metropolitan and asked God for permission to bow when praying as did a metropolitan. He had a savage temper and could not bear to be contradicted. He was illiterate, could not remember anything, and the only prayer he knew was the sign of the cross. He spent all his time walking around or lying down, sometimes laughing loudly as he went.

CATHERINE'S REACTION

On July 10 before Kashkin arrived, Catherine wrote to Panin, half in French and half in Russian. The letter reveals how concerned she was. "Nikita Ivanovich! I cannot thank you enough for your astute and forthright measures to protect me and the fatherland in the Schlüsselburg affair. My heart grieves when I think about it. Many, many thanks for your measures. Obviously they were sufficient. Providence gave me proof of its mercy by guiding the matter as it did. Although the evil has been nipped in the bud, I am afraid that vague rumors might cause great trouble in a big city like St. Petersburg.

"God punished those two scoundrels for the vile lies they wrote in their spurious manifesto against me, yet they might spread their poison (or least that is a possibility). My proof is that the day I left St. Petersburg a poor woman found a forged letter on the street saying the same thing as the manifesto. The letter was given to Prince Viazemsky (who had replaced Glebov[29] as procurator general) who has it now. These officers [Mirovich and Ushakov] must be questioned whether they wrote and disseminated the letter. I am afraid of other repercussions because it is said this Ushakov had connections with many lesser court officials.

"In the end we must rely on the Lord God, and I cannot doubt that He has deigned to reveal this terrible endeavor in its entirety. I am not staying here one hour more than necessary, although naturally I will not give the impression I am hurrying back to St. Petersburg. I hope my return will be a big help in eliminating all the slanders against me. You will recall Soloviev's report that an officer was insulted, and there have been more than twelve similar cases since Great Lent. Please investigate whether they (Mirovich and Ushakov) were implicated in this.

"Although I am writing you everything in this letter without reservation, just as it occurs to me, do not think I have succumbed to terror. I will not exaggerate what in fact is a desperate and foolhardy coup. Nevertheless, we must get to the bottom of it to find out how far the foolishness has spread. That way it can be stopped immediately, to protect innocent ordinary people."[30]

Catherine's letter of July 11 to Panin reflects less than total satisfaction with Kashkin's interrogation. "Although your remarks indicate that Mirovich had no accomplices, such a determined criminal is an unreliable witness. The matter must be pursued intelligently and rigorously. The brother of the drowned Ushakov must be questioned to learn if he shared his brother's ideas. I also want to know if there were any accomplices in the artillery (where they wanted to present [Ivan]), and am the more interested because I heard the artillery commander is very unpopular. I am trying to return to St. Petersburg even sooner than I had intended to conclude this matter quickly and cut off any more foolish publicity."

Catherine was still to visit Mitau despite her rush to reach St. Petersburg. Biron[31] went to Riga and implored the empress to visit him in the residence bestowed on him through the generosity and munificence of her highness, his most gracious savior and protectress. Catherine also needed to visit Mitau to demonstrate she was not being frightened into a hasty return to St. Petersburg. On July 13 she set out for Courland, where she was greeted at the border by the duke [Biron] and his two sons. In the Mitau palace Biron on his knees kissed his munificent benefactress's hand and thanked her for her visit.

"The duke," Catherine wrote Panin, "received me magnificently when we returned to Riga, quickly had a medal struck to commemorate the reception and distributed money to the people. The local people waited for my arrival from Mitau until one in the morning, and as soon as they saw my carriage conducted me with shouts of '*Vivat!*' to my residence. I am telling you this to show that the Livonians are beginning to accept their conquerors."

Catherine still was preoccupied with Schlüsselburg amidst the festivities in Mitau and Riga. On July 16 she wrote Panin on the way from Riga to St. Petersburg. "How I wish God would reveal the other conspirators, if there are any, and I how I pray to the Most High that this affair does not destroy innocent people. I saw no sign of confederates when I read the villain's calendar and notes, but one page was proof enough he wanted to kill me. It is impossible to believe they did not broadcast their ideas in St. Petersburg because since Holy Week the events have been the subject of numerous almost identical reports which insulted my honor."

"I have only praise," her July 18 letter to Nepliuev said, "for your care in directing a discreet investigation of Mirovich's relatives. If they were not involved in the affair there is no reason to arrest them. As the proverb says, 'My brother, but my own idea.' Anyway, I do not wish to have the innocent suffer."

TRIAL AND EXECUTION

The empress returned to St. Petersburg on July 25. After Weymarn's investigation of Mirovich failed to produce anything new a special court was constituted from the Senate, the Synod, dignitaries from the three highest-ranking classes and the presidents of the colleges. On August 25 the court sent a deputation to the empress asking her permission to act by majority vote without consulting with her. "In a matter concerning personal insult to us," Catherine wrote on the report, "we will grant the offender our most gracious pardon. This is a matter which affects the state's integrity, the common welfare and general tranquility. We assign this case to the full authority of our assembled loyal subjects as recommended by the report on this matter submitted to us."

As the ballots were being collected to determine whether the court should pass sentence, High Procurator Soimonov[32] started to tell the president of the College of Medicine, Baron Cherkasov[33], that some clergymen said Mirovich should be tortured. Acting Procurator General Prince Viazemsky came up and in a commanding tone forbade Soimonov to say anything further about the clergy's opinion and asked Cherkasov to respond at once if sentence should be passed. Cherkasov quickly replied that it should, then on September 2 presented a written opinion that Mirovich must be tortured to determine who had joined him or incited him.

"It is absolutely necessary," he wrote, "that the criminal give a full accounting under torture, not just for the living but also for future generations. I am afraid, however, that we cannot rely on our stage machinery, which is propelled either by outside forces or by the actors themselves." This angered the assembly, which petitioned Catherine to protect it from Cherkasov's insults. Cherkasov had to apologize and explained that he made his statement in good faith but that the assembly took offense. Drafting the sentence was assigned to Adam Vasilievich Olsufiev,[34] Procurator General Weymarn and Emme,[35] the president of the College of Justice for Livonian and Estonian Affairs. The Synod members stated that as clergymen they could not sign a death sentence but acknowledged that Mirovich deserved the most extreme punishment.

The death sentence was carried out on the morning of September 15 in the Obzhorny market on Petersburg Island. There is a tradition that Mirovich went to the scaffold resolutely and reverently. Derzhavin[36] left an account of the popular reaction to the death penalty, to which they were not accustomed in Elizabeth's reign. "People standing on housetops and bridges could not avoid seeing the execution and kept waiting for the sovereign to pardon him for some reason or other. When they saw the head in the executioner's hands they all cried out at once and shuddered so hard the bridge swayed and threatened to collapse."[37]

The soldiers who joined Mirovich in Schlüsselburg were forced to run the gauntlet and were dispersed to remote garrisons. Vlasiev and Chekin each received seven thousand rubles reward and release from service while continuing to receive their pay. They signed a statement not to importune the empress for money under pain of loss of honor and property, always to live distant from densely populated areas and never to appear together in a group. They further agreed never to engage in any state business, particularly chancellery affairs, and not to travel to the capital cities unless absolutely necessary. When a trip was necessary, they were not go together. They were to remain silent about the famous occurrence.

X

DOMESTIC POLICIES, 1764

VIAZEMSKY NAMED PROCURATOR GENERAL OF THE SENATE

The empress was present at four Senate sessions before she travelled to the Baltic provinces and three after she returned. The Senate revived after it was divided into departments. We observed that after the Krylov affair was investigated Procurator General Glebov could not keep his important post.[1] "For various reasons," read an instruction the Senate received on February 3, "having to do with Procurator General Glebov, her imperial highness commands that henceforth the post of procurator general be filled by Quartermaster General Prince Alexander Viazemsky."

Catherine sent Viazemsky secret handwritten instructions which began with a very unflattering evaluation of Glebov and also attacked his benefactor Prince Peter Ivanovich Shuvalov.[2] In her sally against Shuvalov she gave vent to exasperation over past events so strong that it was totally inappropriate in instructions to a new procurator general. "The current procurator general's tenure was marked by wrongdoing, avarice and corruption, earning him a wretched reputation. He was less than candid and frank with me. Thus I am forced to replace him, and these same traits tarnish and nullify his talent and zeal for service.

"I should add that while still a youth Glebov knew the late Prince Peter Shuvalov and spent a brief time with him. This contributed substantially to his later misfortune. Glebov was Shuvalov's puppet and came to be guided by principles which profited them but brought no benefit to society. The result was his greater bent for secrecy than for candor, and many of his dealings were concealed from me. My confidence in him diminished accordingly. There is nothing worse for society than a procurator general who is not completely frank and candid with his sovereign, and nothing worse for a procurator general than a sovereign who lacks full confidence in him. Since his office requires him to oppose the mightiest, his sole support is the sovereign's power.

"You should know with whom you will be dealing. You will be coming to me as daily events require. You will find that I want only the greatest glory and happiness for the fatherland and wish only the prosperity of my subjects, whatever their calling. My only goal is to preserve tranquillity, contentment and peace at home and abroad. As long as you demonstrate your loyalty, industry and total candor, you will enjoy my complete confidence. Above all I love the truth, so do not be afraid to speak the truth or to argue with me if it brings about good results. I hear that everyone considers you an honest man, and I hope to prove to you that at court such people live happily. Let me add that I do not demand flattery. My only requirement is that you be candid in word and forceful in deed.

"You will find there are two parties in the Senate. For my part sound policy demands paying them the proper respect, and they will disappear all the sooner. Failure to do so will reinforce them. I merely watch them carefully and employ people for one or another project according to their ability. Both parties will try to lure you to their side. In one party you will find honesty but limited vision, in the other broader but perhaps not always useful perspectives. Someone might have spent a long time in some land and therefore always presents his favorite country as a model for policy while criticizing everyone else. This ignores the fact that a nation's domestic institutions are based on its mores.

"You do not have to favor one side over the other. Be courteous and impartial, listen to everyone, think only of serving the fatherland and acting fairly, and proceed directly and resolutely to the truth. When you have doubts, ask me and have full confidence in God and in me. If I am pleased with your conduct I will not betray you..."

CATHERINE'S COMPLAINTS ABOUT THE SENATE

"The Senate and all other state institutions have changed since they were created. There are various reasons, including some of my predecessors' administrative neglect, but the biases of those who staffed them are even more to blame. The Senate was established to execute the laws referred to it although it frequently passed laws and distributed ranks, offices, money, villages, in fact almost everything. This encroached on the laws and prerogatives of other judicial offices.

"I happened to hear in the Senate that the senators wanted to question a certain college merely for daring to present its opinion to the Senate. I refused permission and told the gentlemen present that they should be glad the law was being observed. Such persecution has so paralyzed the lower offices that they have forgotten completely the regulation requiring them to protest unlawful senatorial directives, first to the Senate and then to me. The lesser officials' servility is indescribable, and no good can be expected until this evil is rooted out. The state suffers because they observe chancellery procedures and cannot imagine any alternative. Having exceeded its authority, the Senate has difficulty accommodating itself to prescribed procedures.

"Perhaps these examples will inspire the other members[of the Senate], although this will be a lifelong task. The Russian empire is so vast that autocracy is the sole salutary form of government. All others move too slowly and allow countless special interests to fragment and divert the state's power. A single sovereign commands the resources to combat every evil and identifies the general welfare with his own. Everyone else, in the words of the Gospel, is but a hireling."[3]

VIAZEMSKY ASSUMES POST

Viazemsky began his new assignment with a misstep. On January 30 there was disagreement in the Senate when nine senators proposed that the general master of petitions accept only those petitions listed in his instructions. Other petitions must go the Senate for distribution to departments by the senior secretary as specified by law. The other five senators believed that the general master of petitions should receive all petitions. On February 13 these opinions were read in the Senate in the empress's presence. Despite attempts to reach an agreement, no senator changed his position. Prince Viazemsky referred the question to the highest level, then stated that he agreed with the five senators that all petitions proceed to the general master of petitions. "The general master of petitions," Catherine wrote on the report, "should follow his instructions, but petitions should be received by departments."

On July 30 in the Senate the empress announced her decision denying requests of descendants for return of their ancestors' confiscated property, the same response Mirovich received. In 1727 property of Skoropadsky's[4] widow was seized. We know that Skoropadsky's daughter married Count Tolstoy. His heir Guards Second Major Count Tolstoy petitioned to have Skoropadsky's property returned to him and his relatives. "Since these possessions were confiscated," Catherine ordered, "and given to others by imperial orders, the petition is baseless, and the current owners will retain possession."

MORE MONEY IN CIRCULATION

The empress's instructions to Viazemsky read in part "The expanse of our empire necessitates increasing the amount of money in circulation. The Department of Money's figures show a maximum of eighty million [rubles] in silver now, which amounts to four rubles or less per person. Various remedies have been tried, resulting in the use of copper money. This has caused numerous complaints but is a necessary evil until there is significantly more silver in the realm.

"Efforts must be continued to eliminate coins of different weights with the same value and those of the same weight and metallic content but of various values. More silver must be imported, for example, for the grain trade, as the Commission on Commerce and other commissions have been told. I cannot say anything more about silver directives because it is a very delicate question and will upset many people. Still you should look into it thoroughly." At the very beginning of the year instructions were given to mint twenty-two carat gold coins worth exactly fifteen times as much as the silver. Each imperial (ten rubles) would weigh three zolotniks and 3/44 dolias [about thirteen grams] and a half imperial weighing one zolotnik and 47/88 dolias [about 6.5 grams]. The silver coin would be eighteen carats.

STATE FINANCES

Income for 1763 was 16,507,381 rubles, rising in 1764 to 21,593,136 rubles. Despite the increase, meeting state needs remained difficult. The College of Commerce reported to the Senate that the Academy of Fine Arts requested payment for the previous January and February of 3,333.33 of the twenty thousand rubles it was to receive annually from customs duties. Because for the past three years there were problems with the customs duties, they were farmed out for six years starting in 1764 for 176,000 rubles annually paid in advance. One hundred and fifty thousand rubles of this sum was appropriated for the Cabinet of Her Imperial Majesty and twenty thousand for Moscow University. Since the one hundred fifty thousand rubles were appropriated for the Cabinet before the treasury received the customs duties or the advance payment [for the farmed out customs duties], the College of Commerce did not have another twenty thousand for the Academy of Fine Arts, nor did the Senate presume to decide the matter, but referred it to the empress, who ordered the funds released.

PUBLIC WORKS

An imperial order appropriated 10,400 rubles of the Commerce Bank's interest earnings for a canal between the Volkhov and Sias rivers. Field Marshal Münnich[5] reported there was very little money for work at the Baltic port [Rogervik]. The forced laborers were utterly destitute for they had received neither clothing nor shoes this year. Münnich requested 30,751 rubles to maintain the prisoners and 16,131 rubles for material under contract or delivered. The Admiralty College had released thirty thousand rubles, to be used only for harbor construction and pressing needs, and he, Münnich, did not dare ask for more.

The Senate responded that the thirty thousand rubles released by the signed order was solely for unavoidable expenses, maintaining the forced laborers and furnishing them shoes and clothing. Before the purchase order for materials was issued Count Münnich was forbidden to enter contracts, and this prohibition now was reaffirmed. He was to inform the Senate of contracts made for materials and their prices.

A few days later Münnich supplied the Senate a report from the Chancellery for the Ladoga canal that the canal was in total decay. The Senate responded that Münnich relied solely on the canal chancellery's report without inspecting the canal himself. Because restoration of the Ladoga canal was a major government concern, Münnich must be instructed with the Senate's recommendation that he inspect the Ladoga canal personally, if his health permitted, and forward the Senate an estimate [for repairs] with his suggestions.

DISORDER IN STATE INSTITUTIONS

The Novgorod governor Sievers[6] requested his chancellery be enlarged, but the Senate refused. This economizing was necessary because in August the Office of State Accounts requested authorization for a loan of two hundred fifty thousand rubles from other state offices until the governments delivered the funds it was due. The Senate ordered the amount requested sent from the Department for the Distribution of Copper Money. In October the Senate decided to inform the empress that the Office of State Accounts was so short of money that it needed seventy-two thousand rubles from the College of Church Landed Property.

The Senate reports furnish a picture of the extreme disorder in the Treasury Bureau. Accounts dating from 1732 to 1753 still were pending, ignored by new officials after the former died. During fires they were shuffled together indiscriminately with other documents and transferred from place to place. Since 1753 the college was unable to arrange its records properly, no matter how hard it tried to review and revise them. Because some pages in books were moldy, others were ripped and most documents and copies were missing, all efforts were in vain.

The Senate submitted a report suggesting the unsorted files be sealed and kept in the archives for reference. It added that the college's statements revealed that cases pending at deaths of officials were not handled by their successors, who should have organized them promptly. This was not done. The Senate lamented the chaos now prevailing in the college and could not imagine such carelessness and negligence in the future. It was obliged to caution the Treasury College to exercise great care to safeguard files and prepare accounts on time.

The empress mentioned the disorder under the stablemaster's administration in a letter to Yelagin.[7] "Ivan Perfilievich! Repnin[8] had Stablemaster Naryshkin[9] give me a report of their needs and asking for money.... Please investigate their management or mismanagement.[10] You should know that I learned from the procurator of the Office of State Accounts that they received everything, or, to put it better, grabbed it. I gave orders they were not to receive any more (they do not know this). All day long Repnin receives every powdered petty nobleman with nothing on his mind but foppery."[11]

"The present system for salt and alcohol," the empress's instructions to Prince Viazemsky read, "weighs heavily on the people. There are so many bootleggers it is almost impossible to punish them all. Entire provinces are under their sway, and there is no stopping them. It would not be a bad idea to look for ways to ease the people's lot." On March 23 the Commission for Supervision of the State Salt and Alcohol Revenues was established. "Your first obligation," the instructions to the commission stated, "is to ensure that the alcohol and salt revenues are not interrupted. Search for means to maintain and increase income for the treasury that do not burden the people."[12]

EFFORTS TO REFORM BANKS

The Senate received two imperial orders concerning banks."(1) When state banks are established individuals may invest their money at interest. Many will benefit, including the Foundling Home. Her imperial highness wishes to allay all apprehension of individuals and to bolster a bank's credit. Hence she decrees that individual deposits be maintained separate from state funds and earn the same interest. They are not to be disbursed should orders for this be sent, nor held in the treasury. Like state funds they are to be lent at interest, adding the interest to the capital, or returned to the depositors at their request, or to the Foundling Home. They are to be returned on demand before term without delay. All this shall be observed faithfully. If perchance there is an instruction which contradicts this, even if signed by her imperial majesty, it shall not be obeyed and shall be forwarded to her imperial highness.

"(2) Since many merchants have been remiss in paying their debts to the Commerce Bank, and some cannot be counted on to pay, on March 4, 1764 her imperial highness ordered this bank placed under the supervision of the entire College of Commerce. The bank was capitalized at five hundred thousand rubles. Now it is reckoned to have a total of 802,720 rubles, including capital. This includes payments not yet received for some loans which are due, and more than 382 rubles in overdue loans. This gives her imperial highness reason to believe the bank will lose a substantial amount of capital.

"Her imperial highness does not believe supervision of the bank by the entire college is a satisfactory remedy. It is a waste of time when many people attempt to ensure that collection of state debts follows chancellery procedures. Besides, strict observance of regulations precludes any leniency in cases where investigation shows that prudent extensions will benefit the treasury and not ruin the merchant. Therefore her imperial majesty orders the Merchants' Bank placed under the direction of Chamberlain Count Nikolay Golovin.[13] He and President Yevreinov[14] of the College of Commerce shall collect overdue loans, with interest, by methods which do not ruin trustworthy merchants and hurt the treasury."

OTHER STATE INSTITUTIONS

The Senate had to remind the College of Manufactures that in 1724 Peter the Great directed it to report to the Senate twice a year on the condition of factories and workshops, what was being produced where and if production had increased.[15] The College of Mines was directed to make every effort to establish and expand the manufacture of iron and steel and improve the quality to match the [Austrian] Styrian factories. The Ekaterinburg steel used for muskets is inferior to Styrian steel, while little money is spent to improve on the scythes made at the Demidov factories,[16] which are worse than the German.

The vice president of the College of Manufactures Sukin[17] stated that nothing was done in that college to fulfill a number of Senate directives, and that a response to a signed order to gather information on manufacturing and trade was yet to be made. The president of the College of Manufactures, the famous Volkov,[18] noted that the college continued to grant concessions for new factories without consulting him. He demanded that the college cease its presumptions and secure his approval. This was not for his sake but for that of the law and of her majesty. The Senate asked the college to respond. Prince Dolgorukov wanted permission to manufacture crystal. The college replied that it had discussed the matter, but could not grant permission to Prince Dolgorukov because it had not made a final decision.

CONDITION OF CHIEF MAGISTRACY BUREAU

Prince Meshchersky, the new vice president of the Chief Magistracy Bureau, reported these shortcomings upon taking office. (1) There was no register of pending cases. (2) There was no list of the laws specifying procedures for the Chief Magistracy. (3) Nor was there a list of convicts. (4) There was nothing specifying the duties of the registrar and the archivist. (5) The cash funds lacked a register. (6) The protocols were not in folders. (7) There was no indication of the number of merchants supervised by the bureau nor of their assessments. (8) The archive was a room where case records were piled on the floor in bags and bundles. (9) Cash funds were safeguarded merely by placing the strongboxes in the judicial chambers. (10) Soldiers were supposed to guard cash funds and convicts, yet twenty convicts escaped and only now were reports being made about escapes the previous year. (11) Secretary Taushev was too old to perform his duties, and Secretary Petrov was unable quickly to decide on bills of exchange requiring speedy resolution.

Twenty-five merchants complained to the Senate that the College of Commerce did not name the merchant Sushenkov a grader of hemp and linen. The college requested satisfaction for this libelous petition since Sushenkov was not named because there already were three superfluous graders. The Senate directed that Sushenkov be told that there was no vacancy. He was to apply to the College of Commerce when one occurred.

FIRST RUSSIAN VESSEL IN THE MEDITERRANEAN

The appearance of the first Russian vessel in the Mediterranean in 1764 was a milestone in the history of Russian foreign trade. Previously no Russian vessel, either military or commercial, had gone beyond Cadiz.

Vladimirov and other Tula merchants founded a company to trade directly with Italy by way of the Mediterranean. On her own initiative the empress built a thirty-six-gun frigate for the company. The frigate, named *Hope for Success*,[19] departed Kronstadt on August 11 bound for Leghorn under the command of Captain Pleshcheev. It bore a cargo of Russian goods (iron, Russian leather, sailcloth, tobacco, caviar, wax and rope). The company's factor in Leghorn, the Kazan merchant Ponomarev, sent word to St. Petersburg that the frigate arrived safely in Leghorn on November 20. On November 24, St. Catherine's day, a solemn liturgy was held in Slavonic in the Greek church in Leghorn. It was celebrated by the frigate's chaplain in ornate vestments sent by the empress to the Greek church.

TRADE ISSUES

A signed directive was sent to the College of Commerce. "*To benefit the merchants* the college is to furnish printed lists of prices for goods, called current prices, which college shall receive two hundred rubles for the necessary expenditures from our Cabinet."[20] This was presented as a new policy, forgetting that it repeated Peter the Great's prescriptions. *To benefit the merchants* the empress ordered a Russian edition of *A Description of Amsterdam's Commerce* sent to every merchant guild free of charge.

The new Commission on Commerce, remembering one of Peter the Great's measures, likewise confirmed that it was most necessary and expedient for young children of merchants to travel on business to famous states and cities. When a merchant wished to place his son in a merchant's shop in foreign lands for several years to acquire theoretical and practical knowledge, this is a praiseworthy and useful service to the fatherland and shall not be prohibited.[21]

SERFS FOR MERCHANTS

Before the Astrakhan merchants dispatched their sons to study in foreign shops they petitioned to the Senate through their magistracy for permission to purchase people to work for them. The merchants would pay their soul tax. Distances were so great that they could not conduct business without buying people. The Senate allowed the merchants to keep those already purchased, but not buy any more (except baptized Kalmyks).[22]

The Astrakhan governor was told to investigate whether in the future they might purchase people from landlords for use as sailors. His report to the Senate must list present seagoing vessels of the merchants there and how many sailors were needed for these vessels. The Senate gave the merchant Fedorov permission to keep three men he bought to train as sailors on condition he build oceangoing vessels immediately. Otherwise he must sell these men to someone authorized to keep them.

FUGITIVES

Since time immemorial the Russian land suffered from scanty population and an inadequate work force, a shortage impossible to fill with free labor. The warrior needed land to support him, so laborers had to be bound to it. A factory was to be built, so peasants must be assigned to it. Seafaring had to be promoted and oceangoing vessels constructed, so serf sailors must be provided. There were no freemen available, for freemen had no reason to choose such arduous and unfamiliar work.

Wherever the historian sees slavery he must assume that people will flee and rebel. It was learned that in 1763 eighty-four peasants and dependents fled across the border from their landlords in the Rzheva Pustaia and Zavolochie districts, whereas five hundred fugitives returned voluntarily from Poland. These arrivals had to be moved farther east because there was no room for them in their former districts. There was no vacant land in the Pskov crown districts, and peasants even were leasing plowland and hayfields for high prices from *Pskov Cossacks*, landlords and monasteries.

Despite harsh Russian measures to repatriate fugitives from Polish territory, the military governor's chancellery for Rzheva Pustaia and Zavolochie wrote that thieves, brigands and runaway soldiers from Poland were slipping past the forest outposts. They attacked landlords and peasants, stole property and cattle, incited people to flee to Poland and guided them across the border. The chancellery reported an unusual number of fugitives and thieves this year.

The estates of Prince Radziwiłł[23] in the Polotsk [Połock] and Nevel [Newel] districts were the principal sanctuaries in Poland for fugitives and brigands. The city of Nevel belonged to Radziwiłł and its governor Bobiatinski, who under the pretext of rendering the Russian state a service, rounded up Russian runaway families one or two at a time and took them to the border. He refused to hand them over unless he received twenty or thirty rubles per family. Meanwhile he might accept ten or twenty fugitive Russian families while surrendering one. Bobiatinski also sent his peasants into Russian forests to fell and carry off timber.

POLICY ON TENANT FARMERS

We saw that Peter the Great tried but failed to enserf tenant farmers in the North.[24] The current attempt also was unsuccessful. The First Department of the Senate stated that allowing taxpaying peasant tenant farmers to leave one master for another was senseless and ought to be prohibited. They must stay where they are and assigned the status of crown taxpaying peasants. Land bought by merchants contrary to regulations ought to be confiscated unless it was granted and duly recorded. In the plenary session [of the Senate] everyone said that there had been no objections to present policy because only the very poorest taxpaying peasants became tenant farmers. It was necessary merely to ensure that peasants were tenant farmers of their own volition. Senators Yakov Shakhovskoy[25] and Adam Olsufiev of the First Department remained adamant.

EFFORTS TO CURB MILITARY EXPLOITATION OF PEASANTS

The empress knew that troops on the march exploited peasants, forcing them to perform wasteful work, as is seen from the following note to Count Chernyshev,[26] the vice president of the War College. "Order a thorough inquiry" it read, "into the matter described in the attached letter. If the account is correct, be sure you make an example of proper discipline so our men stop preying on our own people. Perhaps you could make them do something useful, such as building bridges across swamps or draining the St. Petersburg marshes."

NEW CENSUS IS DELAYED

Although Catherine's description of the directions she gave in the Senate about the census radiated confidence,[27] it was not going well. At the beginning of March the Senate reported that couriers were dispatched January 16 on the highest authority. They were ordered to send the Senate forms with summarized lists of the population figures submitted so far. Only the courier from the Astrakhan government had returned, and it was obvious from the reports submitted from various governments that in many localities very little had been done to collect information. The Siberian government chancellery wrote that the government was too vast to gather material quickly.

The following month the empress ordered announcements made in all governments, insisting in the strongest terms that all outstanding census forms be delivered by September 1 without fail. Material from some localities disclosed survivals from pre-Petrine times among the population. The Velikie Luki chancellery reported receiving census forms from the sons of cossacks and cavalrymen and other ranks who were exempt from local taxes, while others were obligated to pay and were liable for the soul tax. The Senate ordered that the soul tax be paid for all peasants belonging to the sons of cossacks and cavalrymen. The governor must inform the Senate why these individuals, contrary to regulations, were allowed to have peasants.

CATHERINE'S INSTRUCTIONS TO GOVERNORS

Such painful news about regional disorders, particularly remote ones, convinced the empress to concentrate power in the hands of the governors. Because there were not many governments at that time, she hoped to find enough trustworthy people. We have an interesting letter she wrote to Yelagin. "Listen, Perfilievich! Before the week is out bring me the [completed] instructions or regulations for governors, the manifesto against swindlers and the Beketev case, all of them separately. If you don't, you are the laziest man in the world. No one drags out assignments the way you do."[28]

Perfilich finally brought the *Instructions to Governors*, which were promulgated April 21. The instructions began with the obvious fact that "the whole cannot be perfected if its components remain in disorder and disarray. The governments are the principal components of the state as a whole, and it is they which most need improvement." The empress promised to implement these improvements in time, but meanwhile considered laying out new guidelines for governors her primary obligation. The governor was defined as someone given a trust by the sovereign, a leader and the master of the entire government area. "Many firm measures concerning the iniquity of corruption and the vileness of bribery have been promulgated," the instructions read in reference to bribery. "It is our special hope now that each of our faithful subjects will feel that our maternal mercy towards them is reward enough to shun that vile sweetmeat, attractive only to knaves and those blinded by insatiable greed. If, despite our expectations, an enemy of the fatherland of this kind appears in a government and is implicated directly in any kind of bribery, the governor may remove him from office immediately and on his own authority have him tried in the appropriate court."

Under extraordinary circumstances such as fire, famine, floods, plague, serious brigandage, or popular disturbances, the governor assumed supreme authority over the entire population of the government, state employees and civilians alike, until the situation returned to normal. The instructions addressed the concentration of power in the governor's hands. "Since our empire is so vast I have not visited all governments and provinces with their various climates and diverse advantages. If I am absent, I cannot provide every benefit, avert every malady or take every precaution.

"Therefore all local agencies in every government, except Moscow and St. Petersburg, not subject currently to the government's chancellery, henceforth are placed under the governor's supervision. This includes all civil authorities such as customs, magistracies, border commissions and gendarme and courier services. The governor shall be the faithful guardian of the government we have entrusted to him. The reports and other material which local agencies submit concerning their duties and procedures will provide him detailed and comprehensive information. He will protect and defend the oppressed who live too distant to present their complaints to higher authorities."

"The governor's firsthand knowledge of all matters and circumstances affecting his government will lend him understanding and insight. Thus, taking into account the talents, trade and manufactures of the inhabitants of his government, he can plan various ways to serve both our interests and the common good. He is to present these to our Senate and to us. If disorder, outright negligence or legal shortcomings slip in, he can correct and avert them with like representations. It is his duty as master to answer for and give an accounting of his government just as he cannot plead ignorance or inattention."

"The governor was to travel around his government every three years to verify that his orders were being executed properly. He must pay attention to agriculture "as the sole source of the state's wealth and prosperity, and to expand each government's and province's production for export." The governor was to improve roads and stamp out thieves and brigands. The language of the instructions shows how widespread brigandage was. "With a sense of maternal grief we enjoin each governor to use every possible means and exercise every possible care to eradicate those who do such damage to the fatherland and all mankind. Expose and destroy their refuges."[29]

CONTINUED CORRUPTION

An order of 1672 prohibiting military governors being named to localities where they had villages was revoked.[30] At the end of the year the Valuiki military governor Klementiev was stripped of all ranks for bribery. Lieutenant Colonel Svechin, sent to inspect oak forests in Kazan government, reported that guardians appointed for new converts instead ravaged them by extortion and bribery. These were Court Councillors Zeleny and Sokolnikov, Majors Larionov, Voroponov and Lazarev, Titular Councillor Miakishev, Lieutenant Alekseev, Ensigns Yashkov and Shiplov and Registrars Gavrilov and Cheadaev. The Senate ordered the Kazan governor investigated. Earlier the guardianship was terminated and the Bureau for New Converts abolished.

The state continued to insist that corruption could be dealt with by new government institutions. Yet these were inadequate if an official felt the need to save for a rainy day, old age or illness. He saved at the expense of petitioners and subordinates. A consistent policy meant pensions, which now were granted for thirty-five years' service, less in case of illness.

CONFISCATION OF CHURCH DOMAINS

The Commission on Church Lands, or Clerical Commission, completed its work in 1764.[31] The empress approved the commission's report in an order to the Senate on February 26. It listed 911,000 monastery peasants, excluding the Ukraine and the Kharkov, Ekaterinoslav, Kursk and Voronezh governments, where the census was taken later. Each peasant paid fifty copecks quitrent annually for a total of 1,366,299 rubles. Since regular payments must be made to diocesan chancelleries in compensation for their peasants, the dioceses were divided into three classes. Novgorod, Moscow and St. Petersburg were in the first class, eight in the second class and fifteen in the third. 149,586 rubles were allotted annually for all dioceses.

There were 728 monasteries and 219 convents for a total of 947. Most of these owned no inhabited land, some had only a few peasants while others had a great number. The monasteries and convents with peasants, and hence entitled to regular compensatory payments, became state-supported institutions, divided into three classes. There were fifteen monasteries in the first class, forty-one in the second and one hundred in the third. It was decided these monasteries would receive 174,750 rubles a year. The convents also were divided into three classes and allotted thirty-three thousand rubles annually. Monasteries and convents without peasants were left, as before, to their own resources. Only 161 remained, the others were closed or converted to parish churches.

Each diocese maintained an almshouse with a specified number of residents depending on the diocese's class. Living in almshouses were 765 males and females. Since each was to receive five rubles a year, the College of Economy was to allot 3,825 rubles annually for them.

Housing retired soldiers in diocesan chancelleries or monasteries was rejected."While the clerical authorities maintain these retired soldiers properly, they find living quietly under clerical rule and supervision very difficult. Besides, pensioners with wives and children find it hard to exist on the amount they receive. Their children are forced to roam the world, either supporting themselves by working for others or enrolling as soul tax paying peasants for landlords." It was decided to send retired soldiers to thirty-one specified cities rather than to monasteries. There for the first time they would be assigned lodging with the inhabitants, and paid.

Commissioned officers from the Guards received one hundred rubles, non-commissioned officers twenty, and corporals and rank-and-file soldiers fifteen. Lieutenant colonels from army regiments received one hundred twenty rubles, majors one hundred, captains sixty-five, lieutenants forty, second lieutenants and ensigns thirty-three, non-commissioned officers fifteen, and rank-and-file soldiers ten. It was calculated there were 4,353 retired soldiers requiring 80,600 rubles. Qualifying for this *perpetual sustenance* were subaltern officers with fewer than twenty-five male serfs, captains with fewer than thirty, and staff officers with fewer than forty, including property held in their wives' names.

A soldier's widow under forty whose property did not exceed these limits was awarded her husband's annual pension in a one-time payment. If she were over forty and did not want to remarry, she received one-eighth of her husband's pension until she died. Boys under twelve and girls under twenty were eligible for one-twelfth of their father's pension. At twelve boys would go to school, while girls received a dowry equal to their father's annual pension when they married. When a girl could not marry because of illness or a handicap she received one-twelfth of her father's pension for life. To support widows and children, 34,400 rubles were allotted.[32] Since the commission was unable to discuss the seminary system, this issue was postponed.

CATHERINE'S CONCERN FOR RETIRED SOLDIERS

The empress justified confiscating monastery lands in part because some of the extra funds could be used to support retired soldiers. Naturally she was distressed when she heard that the decree did not make it clear that unless the lands were confiscated, invalids would be reduced to beggary, nor was she satisfied by an official denial of this report. At the end of November she sent a secret instruction to Captain and [Guards] Lieutenant Durnovo of the Semenovsky Regiment.[33] "You are to go to Moscow. If, contrary to orders concerning invalids, any retired soldiers who formerly lived in monasteries still are there, take charge of them. It is rumored here that the Clerical Commission's figure for invalid soldiers in monasteries is too low, and that hundreds of them are roaming around Moscow hungry.

"When I wrote to Count Soltykov[34] he denied this, but Mikhail Baskakov saw some of them begging. I am dispatching you now to learn the truth and to find out about these soldiers. Was there any correspondence with them and were they reassured I would not abandon them? Send me a list [of these soldiers] and give the same list to Count Soltykov, whom I already have ordered to give each man two rubles at the first opportunity.... From Moscow go to Alexandrov Village as if on pilgrimage to find out if any old men not under state care are there, and if so how many, and what they need. Assure them I will care for them immediately, and return here."[35]

PROBLEMS WITH OLD BELIEVERS

Old Belief constantly needed attention. Thirty-five peasants from the village of Liubach in the Medvetsk rural district of the Novgorod government gathered in the peasant Yermolin's hut and announced they would set themselves on fire. Lieutenant Kopylov was sent with a detachment to dissuade them by promising that if they enrolled as Old Believers and submitted a declaration to that effect, they were free to go home without being punished for meeting. Although an archimandrite and an archpriest were sent to exhort them, the Old Believers responded "Your faith is false, but our faith is the true Christian faith. The four-pointed cross is a snare, and we revere the eight-pointed cross. There are many errors in your Scripture. If you come to destroy us, we will not surrender but will do as the Lord wills. If you do not come to destroy us, we do not wish to burn. Give us a rescript from the sovereign's hand that we may live as before, that there will be no twofold tax here[36] and that we will not be forced to enter the [Orthodox] churches."

The peasants dug a well in the courtyard and burned candles day and night in the courtyard and the hut. Twenty-six more males and females arrived and locked themselves in with the others. On August 20 the Old Believers asked Kopylov permission to get cabbages and other vegetables from the garden, which he granted. Twenty men and women came out of the hut with guns, spears, axes and clubs, gathered cabbages and other vegetables, returned to the hut and locked themselves in again. The next day they went out to the field to harvest beans. They sold their cattle, clothing and other property for a pittance or gave it to charity. The grain was not harvested and went to waste. Kopylov urged them several times to harvest the grain, but they answered "Let him who wishes harvest, but the Lord will feed us without it."

The Senate decided to request the empress to order the detachment to arrest them quietly and exile them to Nerchinsk. "Choose the most sensible and well-behaved Old Believers from those living there," Catherine wrote on the report, "and send someone to try to reason with them. If they will not listen, proceed as recommended." The Novgorod governor Sievers reported that in carrying out the order he found some suitable people in Novgorod who went to the locked-up Old Believers twice and finally convinced them to disperse to their homes and enroll as taxpayers.

We saw that the Senate regarded Rzhev Volodimerov as a hotbed of secret Old Believers.[37] Now it wanted Burgomaster Nemilov and Aldermen Vidonov and Voloskov dismissed from their magistracy offices for tolerating secret Old Believers and other offensive and insolent behavior. They, other merchants and the Old Believers were to be sent for interrogation as the Tver bishop [Afanasy][38] requested. The Senate referred the matter to the Novgorod governor. The Old Believers rejected their fellow believers to whom the bishop had sent the detachment, whereupon Vidonov cursed the monks as lechers and adulterers. When the priests came to Vidonov at Easter with icons, he put the altar icon of the Mother of God on his shoulder and sang a vulgar ditty. He ordered the townswoman Voloskova to join in, and both danced around with the icon.

The bishop of Tver Afanasy ordered the Rzhev cathedral archpriest Ivan Alekseev to supervise the secret Old Believers, which he did with a vengeance. The Old Believers resented him for this and three of them, Ivan Menshoy, Kliment y Chupiatov and Mikhailo Orlov, bribed Second Lieutenant Korobin and the retired sailor Shevarin, who worked for the Rzhev alcohol franchise holders. These five went with soldiers from the franchise and tavern employees to the archpriest's house at night. Claiming they had come to seize illegal vodka, they broke down the gates and doors, shut the archpriest and his wife up in a hut and forced the locks of the storeroom. The group stole eighty-four rubles in cash and forty-two rubles' worth of provisions, as well as a keg of vodka the landlord Rukin had left with the archpriest for safekeeping. After severely beating the archpriest, his twelve-year-old daughter and a young serving girl, they tied the archpriest's hands, put a woman's tunic dress of the kind worn by Old Believers on him and took him to the alcohol franchise building. Later they moved him to military governor's chancellery and placed him under guard.

Bishop Mefody of Astrakhan[39] reported that the Old Believer Gavrilov, apprehended in Dubovka, stated that he wanted to remain an Old Believer until he died. The Dubovka archpriest and an army clerk tried to force him to bow before an icon of St. Dmitry of Rostov.[40] Gavrilov knocked the icon out of the clerk's hands and struck him, causing the icon to fall to the ground. He was sent to the government chancellery, which decided the criminal should be burned, but since capital punishment no longer was imposed he was to be flogged and exiled to the Nerchinsk factories.

The Synod determined that the Old Believer Gavrilov's defiance occurred when the archpriest and the clerk tried to force him to bow before the icon and was not premeditated. Therefore they were the more culpable, the archpriest more so as a cleric. The archpriest and the clerk also were drunkards. The diocesan bishop was to give them an ecclesiastical penance, while the government chancellery was to deal with Gavrilov as with any other unregistered Old Believer.[41]

XI

UKRAINE AND THE EASTERN FRONTIER

SORRY STATE OF THE UKRAINE

"The provinces of Ukraine, Livonia and Finland," the empress's instruction to Prince Viazemsky read, "are administered in accord with their privileges. It would be most improper to abolish them all suddenly, but it is downright stupidity to label these privileges foreign and deal with them on that basis. These provinces, and Smolensk province, must be russified by the gentlest of means so they cease to be wolves looking to the forest.[1] This will be easy if wise administrators are chosen for these provinces. When the hetmanate falls vacant in the Ukraine, try to ensure the hetmans disappear once and for all and that no one receives the office."

This instruction undoubtedly was written after news arrived of competition for succession to the hetmanate in the Ukraine.[2] If this was not the source of Catherine's determination to abolish the hetmanate, it certainly strengthened her conviction that "the hetmans disappear once and for all."

Naturally she looked for guidance from a man who knew Little Russia well and who often had spoken of the confusion there. This was Teplov, who now was commissioned to draft a memorandum on the problems in the Ukraine. According to Teplov it was not justice and statute that determined government practice there but cossack officers with power and influence and educated people who deceived the illiterate. Consequently the number of free farmers shrank dramatically and the serf population increased. When the Ukraine came under Russian rule it had less than half of its present population, and significantly more free peasant households. The free cossacks were enserfed by officers, other officials and wealthy individuals.

A census made by Russian officers when Hetman Skoropadsky died listed 44,961 free households, of which no more than three thousand were distributed to landlords by 1750. This was a very small number considering the increase in population, although the present hetman Count Razumovsky[3] still could not find four thousand free households. He was told that all the other peasants fled to Poland, where reliable reports indicated that peasants subject to Polish lords were much worse off than in the Ukraine. The Polish lords treated peasant land as their own and collected whatever dues they wanted.[4]

The officers and other rich people bought all the state lands from the peasants, who as free men could sell themselves and their land. Every purchase must be registered in the local government office and signed by the local hundredman. There were many cases of falsification, as for example when a hundredman who took office in 1745 signed for a purchase made in 1737. The cossack officers were well aware of these abuses, but since they were doing their best to transfer state lands into private hands they did nothing to stop them.

Able cossacks always bought exemption from service, while the unfit preferred to live as peasants to avoid service and not have to go on campaigns. This change to peasant status was so rapid that the cossack way of life was finished. Another reason was that a man who remained a cossack paid higher taxes on his land, as much as a ruble or more, while as a peasant with no land in his own name he was taxed only two copecks or an altyn, the same as other *dependents.*[5] Cossacks constantly importuned landlords to buy their lands, thus freeing them from going on campaigns.

There were no boundary lines in Ukrainian cities, settlements, villages, hamlets, farmsteads or plowland and hayfields on farms. Everything was based on tradition and deeds, most of which were forgeries. Now the strong swooped down on the weak and simply took the land. People were murdered in these raids, leading to prolonged and exhausting trials. Cossacks who were not serfs were scattered far from their hundredmen, under the power of various landlords. The hetman's proclamations clearly said that landlords lacked jurisdiction over cossacks and their lands in villages and settlements belonging to the landlords, but what recourse did a poor helpless cossack have in his village or hamlet against a hundredman and a powerful landlord?

Cossacks built houses for hundredmen, cut hay for them and furnished them transport, not to mention other exactions. Hundredmen were chosen in the following manner. As soon as it was known a hundredman had died, even before the hetman was informed, the regimental commanders sent their own man to govern the hundred until a new hundredman was chosen.

This man had no doubts the hundred was his. When he arrived he rolled out some kegs of vodka for the illiterate cossacks, paid off the priest and the sexton, collected the drunks' endorsements, and the election was over. The candidate gave a few ducats to the commanders and was confirmed in his post.

Teplov also described the education of future hundredmen. The best families taught their sons how to read and write Russian, then sent them to Kiev, Pereiaslav or Chernigov to study Latin. As soon they acquired a little learning their fathers enrolled them as clerks. Then they became hundredmen, although the cossacks who elected them never had heard their names before.

Freedom of movement was a great curse for the people of the Ukraine. Poor noblemen sank deeper into poverty, the rich grew more powerful and the peasants turned into drunks, loafers and beggars who starved to death in a land blessed with fertility. The wealthy had a way to settle their lands. A servant was sent to recruit peasants from poor landlords by promising less onerous duties. This was an easy task because a poor landlord demanded more work from his peasants than a rich one. At other times a rich landlord erected a large wooden cross on his vacant land. On it the literate could read how many years' exemption from all quitrent and labor on the lord's land the new settlers would have, while the illiterate would be informed by word of mouth.

Lazy peasants never failed to learn where a new cross was erected to attract people to a settlement. When they found out, they chose the place that promised the greatest benefits. The peasants did absolutely nothing while exempt, listened for the latest news in the settlement when their term was up, and looked for a new cross. They spent a lifetime going from cross to cross, taking their families with them and never working anywhere. To make it easier to leave secretly, they took no household goods with them. The moment landlords learned peasants were planning to move, they seized their property, claiming it was acquired on the lord's land.

This was the way of the lesser landlords. The powerful had numerous other ways to keep peasants on their land. Thus in the fertile Ukraine the cultivator starved, the poor landlord grew more impoverished, the rich landlord gained more subjects and the state watched its income shrink daily.

"This at best is a general description of sad state of the Ukrainian people," Teplov concluded his memorandum. "If a clearer picture is needed, a look at the administration of justice, the execution of the sovereign's orders and the regional economy will furnish a host of examples. Although Peter the Great thought long and hard about these problems, the terrible hardships the Ukraine endured before him could not be corrected overnight. The many projects initiated by that wise sovereign began to make an impact, but there was insufficient time to complete them. That great monarch's death brought everything to a halt, and no one has given a thought to them since."[6]

This interesting memorandum is supported by material starting from the seventeenth century which we have included in our history. It provides a clear explanation of developments in Western Europe during the transition from the ancient to the medieval era. Since economic life was rudimentary and state power weak, small farmers became subject to the largest. The memorandum also shows that peasant movement to the North was halted when the government realized that the poor landlord in service must be protected from the enticements and crosses of the rich.

ABOLITION OF THE HETMANATE

Perhaps Teplov's memorandum finally convinced the empress to end the disorder in the Ukraine, beginning by abolishing the hetmanate. Ferment over succession to the hetmanate furnished the pretext. Otherwise it would have been difficult to take the office away from Razumovsky, who had demonstrated such loyalty under difficult circumstances. Even so, it took time. Catherine's note to N.I. Panin has been preserved, unfortunately undated. "Nikita Ivanovich! I saw the hetman and I was able to explain things to him. He told me everything he told you and finally asked me to relieve him of this difficult and dangerous office. I replied that I had no reason to doubt his loyalty and would discuss the matter in more detail with him later. Please ask him in my name today or tomorrow to put in writing what he told me." In a second note to Panin she said "Please conclude this matter of the hetmanate more quickly."[7]

Finally the hetman requested to be relieved of office. "I have devoted all that I possess," he wrote, "to the sacred person of your imperial highness, to whom throughout my term of office I have displayed my loyalty and devotion. I now find that my further tenure in the office of hetman might impinge on my supreme obligation in life. Therefore I make bold to petition your imperial highness most humbly to relieve me of this onerous and dangerous duty. Most gracious sovereign! Your highness, deign take notice of my large family's situation. With them I throw myself at the monarch's feet in the confident hope that this expression of my candor and fidelity will extend your imperial majesty's charity and generosity to me and my children. Otherwise their education, maintenance and placement will be a great burden to me."

COLLEGE FOR THE UKRAINE ESTABLISHED

The empress referred the hetman's petition to the College of Foreign Affairs. "Take advantage of Razumovsky's petition as much as possible," the college responded. "There are a number of important political reasons why the nature and history of the hetmanate in the Ukraine render it totally inconsistent with the state's interests. Governance of the Ukraine needs to be entrusted to a trustworthy and prominent person when the hetmanate is abolished. He is to have four Russian and four Ukrainian assistants.

"Formerly the Russians sat on the right and the Ukrainians on the left, which led Ukrainians to the harmful conclusion that their people were totally different from ours. To disprove this assumption all Ukrainian ranks are to be equalized with ours, and all members will sit together in the college, ranked by seniority. The most capable Ukrainian members would be Quartermaster General Kochubey,[8] General Secretary Tumansky,[9] Lieutenant General Zhuravka,[10] and General Standard Bearer Apostol.[11] The procurator of the college shall be a Russian."

RUMIANTSEV NAMED PRESIDENT

On November 10 the Senate was given a signed order establishing the Ukrainian College to replace the hetmanate. General Count Peter Alexandrovich Rumiantsev[12] was named president, and the individuals recommended by the College of Foreign Affairs were named as the Ukrainian members. The empress designated Major General Brandt[13] and Colonel Prince Platon Meshchersky[14] to fill two of the Russian seats and left the choice of the other two to the Senate. Lieutenant Colonel Alexis Semeonov became procurator. Count Rumiantsev was to pick the clerical employees. The College of Foreign Affairs' recommendation that ranks be equalized was confirmed.

The order described Rumiantsev's authority. "We designate the president of the Ukrainian College commander-in-chief in the Ukraine and as such with the same powers as a governor general. In the college he will function as president with the right to administer justice and mete out punishment. In other matters, such as maintenance of public order, ensuring the general safety and executing the laws, he will have gubernatorial powers. This means we find him particularly deserving of this position. The Zaporozhian Host[15] will come under the authority of this Ukrainian administration."[16]

CATHERINE'S INSTRUCTIONS TO RUMIANTSEV

The empress sent the new Ukrainian commander instructions with an extensive description of his duties. "Everyone knows," the instructions read, "that the Ukraine is vast, its population large and its fertility great. Its favorable climate makes it superior in various ways to many other parts of our empire. Despite this, everyone knows that its people have derived little benefit or income from these advantages, above all at the end of the hetmanate. Widespread disorder, mismanagement and an indescribable confusion of civilian and military administration have become endemic as a result of various imprecise foreign laws and statutes.

"The courts and the rest of the justice system are abusive and choked with pernicious delays. Spurious privileges and liberties acquire the force of law, often to the great detriment of the actual statutes. Migration from place to place destroys the common people and landlords alike. There is universal aversion to agriculture and other ordinary labor. The innate hatred of Russia so apparent there will demand your constant attention and special concern."

Rumiantsev was to have an accurate and detailed map of his government as well as plans and sketches of cities and major buildings. "Books of these maps, plans and sketches should be compiled. That cannot be done quickly, but nothing will be accomplished if a start is not made."

He must use his civil authority to help the clergy insure observance of divine law. "You are well aware that genuine fear of God is the primary means for eliminating tendencies to vice and inclinations to evil, while inculcating good morals and honesty. Keep careful watch on the bishops and their subordinates lest in their incorrigible lust for power they exceed their jurisdiction through various subterfuges. Sometimes they exercise spiritual authority in the secular sphere, spreading notions among a simple and superstitious people which benefit themselves but disturb the general welfare..."

"It is well known that the theological principles most often taught and applied here [in the Ukraine] are the pernicious work of the Roman clergy. The local clergy are exposed to them in seminaries in the Ukraine and across the border in Poland and thereby infected by the insatiable lust for power which had such widespread and deleterious consequences in previous European history. Therefore you need to have a complete and detailed picture of the local clergy's power, their holdings and their income..."

"It is absolutely necessary that those consecrated bishops and archimandrites be men of true humility and genuine spirituality, whom we can expect to be reasonable. I recommend that you find them in advance of need and thus present our own candidates for hierarchical and abbatial vacancies. Attach a description of their talents, ideas and way of life.

"The government and you must learn the size of the Ukrainian population...and be sure you present your opinion how and on what basis a complete census of Ukraine is to be conducted. When cultivators continue to move from place to place the tax base is shaky and cannot always produce the budgeted amount. Therefore you must make every effort using all appropriate means to induce your people to stop this migration once and for all... We think that when landlords and farmers consider this migration impartially they must realize that it works to their common detriment. Landlords obviously do not benefit from instability and flux in agriculture, and disruption of the rural economy. Farmers only dream of freedom and do not understand that it is much more to their and their descendants' advantage to be obligated to agricultural labor in permanent settlements. Stability does not mean loss of freedom. Even though peasants in many European states are free men not bound to the land, they remain where they are because it is in their interest to do so."

Because the land was extraordinarily fertile Rumiantsev was instructed to pay special attention to fledgling industries. He was to increase tobacco production, plant more mulberry groves and improve sheep raising. He was to strive to preserve the forests, maintain the road system and keep a closer watch on the courts to ascertain from public and confidential sources whether anyone was being mistreated.

"The last point that should be mentioned," Catherine said in conclusion, "is that establishing a new administration for the Ukraine is a political issue. As mentioned, Ukrainians secretly harbor hatred for us, while we habitually resent them covertly. This trait is most evident in their officers, who fear their illegal and greedy willfulness will be curbed at some point. This makes them try harder to stir up hatred in the ordinary people, frightening them with the gradual but ultimately total loss of their rights and liberties.

"Of course the current change of government makes it all the harder for them to continue their wicked ways in secret. Stopping the former disorder and establishing better institutions threatens their fickle ways and personal profit. Keep discreet watch on those officers, especially those who keep low visibility to avoid having their nefarious schemes detected and thwarted promptly. In time people's eyes will be opened, and they will realize how relieved and how much better off they will be with greater stability, freed instantly from the tortures of a swarm of petty tyrants. Right now you have a number of opportunities to eliminate these unnecessary threats more quickly if you proceed tolerantly, impartially and benevolently, thereby winning the people's love and devotion."[17]

A note of November 15 from Catherine to Rumiantsev reveals that her instructions also assigned Teplov to him. "Count Peter Alexandrovich! *With these* I am sending Teplov to you so you can discuss the Ukraine further with him."[18] The instructions clearly were written under Teplov's influence. Teplov's role in abolishing the hetmanate made some think he betrayed Razumovsky, and it was said it was he who reported the succession intrigue. There was a story that when Razumovsky arrived at the palace from the Ukraine Teplov met him with a big embrace, prompting Grigory Orlov to say "And he betrayed him with a kiss."[19]

REORGANIZATION OF NEW SERBIA

The hetmanate in the Ukraine now was abolished definitively whereas another administrative change already was implemented that spring. New Serbia, a military colony established in Southern Ukraine under Elizabeth, was transformed into a government. When Nikita and Peter Panin[20] saw Lieutenant General Melgunov's[21] report of the change, they suggested to the empress that the new government be called the Catherine government.

Even so she wrote on the resolution, "Name it the government of New Russia." Catherine endorsed the Panins' recommendation that the corner bounded by a line from the upper Ingul river to the locality Orel and the

Siniukha river along the Polish border be included in the government of New Russia. Formerly this steppe land was Zaporozhian territory.

Melgunov was named director-in-chief of the new government, with instructions to spend every winter in St. Petersburg to report on his progress. Since success was to be measured by the speed with which this empty district was populated, prospective settlers were offered incentives. Each was to receive permanent hereditary title to his allotment (twenty-six desiatins if there were forests, thirty desiatins if not), permission to sell salt and alcohol, and exemption from duties on the import and export of wares. Whoever enlisted in a regiment received thirty rubles free and clear, and each Russian and foreign subject who enrolled as a settler received twelve rubles.

Anyone could obtain as much land as he wished with the proviso he establish settlements on it. No one could acquire hereditary title to nor purchase more than forty-eight allotments. Settlers were exempted from taxes for a period of six, eight or fifteen years at the director's discretion, taking into account the fertility and amount of settlement on the land in question. To preserve the forests, settlers were to use stone or adobe for houses and construct earthen walls instead of wood for fences and gardens. Only those who planted and grew trees could have distilleries. Permission was given to import vodka from Poland. Whoever planted trees obtained hereditary title to the grove.

The last section of the announcement dealt with schools. "All children are to go to school to learn reading, writing, arithmetic and the law. Foreign languages and other subjects are to be offered to anyone who is interested or has enough talent. Children of the poor are to be supported by the state. Those who are able will be charged, but no one will have to pay to learn.

"Institutions for girls are to be established. It will take considerable effort by women of good morals to correct coarse and brutal customs. Beginning with childhood, women should become familiar with household management and all the proper crafts. There shall be a hospital for children and the elderly as well as foundling homes maintained by the state lest poor innocent children wander uncared for around the settlements."[22]

The segment detached from so-called Zaporozhian territory was not the only addition to the government of New Russia. Also joined was the Catherine province, which consisted of steppe land beyond the frontier where there were Russian settlements, extending from the mouth of the Ust-Samara to the mouth of the Luganchik river, including New Serbia and Vodolaga.[23]

SETTLEMENT UKRAINE GOVERNMENT ESTABLISHED

At the end of the year the empress approved a recommendation by Senators Prince Shakhovskoy, [Nikita] Panin and Olsufiev that all military settlements be converted into the Settlement Ukraine government. Hitherto, the recommendation stated, "cossack military service was supported by relatives and dependents, to whom supplies were distributed annually for each cossack's maintenance and equipment, but with no way to assure equal shares or regular payment. At the time of distribution or later many people's supplies often wound up on the landlords' domains or disappeared some other way. Since these [relatives and dependents] sometimes were left with as little as half the proper amount, they found it a great burden to provide all the necessary maintenance and equipment for the cossacks."

This interesting report shows how primitive social structures like clans and payments in kind survived in Russian border regions. In addition to relatives there were hangers-on, here called helpers and dependents. The new government had 154,808 relatives, dependents and neighbors, each paying ninety-five copecks. The 328,814 Cherkassians (Ukrainians) subject to various landlords and officers paid sixty copecks each. Here, too, people moved about freely. The governor, military governor and procurator were to be Russian, while the assistants to the governor and military governor would be chosen from the officers serving there.[24]

CONDITIONS ON THE EASTERN FRONTIER

The eastern frontier also required constant attention. "Ever since the order on state institutions," Bibikov[25] reported from the Kazan government, "I have heard that judges here in the government chancellery and in various bureaus have refrained from taking bribes and corrupt behavior. Whatever corruption exists is practiced more discreetly, and secretaries and clerks are less blatant about demanding bribes for transacting business. They say openly that abuses will recur as long as their salary is fixed. The military governor and several secretaries have told me that their previous income was more than four times greater than their present salary. It is rumored widely among the secretaries and clerks that the common people were accustomed to giving bribes in the past and will not protest making presents in the future.

"The current governor Prince Tenishev has been in office about eight years and before that was vice governor. He is satisfied with what he collected previously and has refrained from taking bribes, but he is not intelligent enough for the job. Since he follows the secretaries' advice on cases, they and the clerks can lay the usual burdens on petitioners. Collegiate Councillor Kudriavtsev and Procurator Vorontsov cannot handle any matter except by signing their names. It is said the only difference is that Kudriavtsev is corrupt while the procurator is honest.

"Court Councillor Kozhin is an assistant to the governor in the government chancellery and also director of the Kazan gymnasium. He not only is totally honest but also does everything he can to ensure that matters are decided according to the laws and without delay. Since nobody helps him, he realizes there practically is no way to stop the chronic disorder in affairs or harassment by the secretaries."

POLICY TOWARDS NEW CONVERTS

As early as the beginning of 1763 the empress heard a petition read in the Senate from new converts in the Kazan, Cheboksary and Kozmodemiansk districts. They requested exemption from the draft, that their children be admitted to schools, that they not pay the newly-imposed soul tax and that Court Councillor Sokolnikov or someone else be appointed to shield them from government officials. The empress ordered the Senate to confer with the Synod. It took a long time to decide the matter since it was whole year before the conference report was approved.

The report consisted of five articles. (1) Non-Christians did not have to pay the taxes levied on new converts, nor must they do military service lest they be forced to run away. A further justification was that, except for a small minority, most of the non-Christians had been baptized. (2) After a three-year exemption new converts would pay the same taxes as state peasants and have the same obligations, except for payments in place of military service. (3) New converts would have no special office or protectors and are subject to the chancelleries of the governor and military governor. (4) The Senate and the Synod recommended that schools not be established for new converts because the Synod knew that most of their children were uneducable. "Do not deny them schools," the empress wrote on the recommendation. "Let those who wish send their children to schools or parish churches, but no one should be forced to do so." (5) Three missionaries would be assigned to convert non-Christians in the Kazan diocese, two each to the Tobolsk, Irkutsk and Tambov dioceses, and one each to the Nizhny Novgorod, Riazan, Viatka and Astrakhan dioceses.

PROBLEMS IN SIBERIA

Beyond the Urals a commission named to reapportion the fur tribute[26] learned some distressing news. The Yakutsk Cossack sergeant Bazhenov said that he went to six fur-tribute Tungus[27] settlements to collect horses, and was forced to pay the military governor Lebedev one hundred fifty rubles for this commission. Lebedev testified that Bazhenov voluntarily brought him the one hundred fifty rubles, which he took because his salary was not paid, leaving him destitute. He also took money, without any coercion, from others sent to collect the fur tribute. He had to do this because the lack of necessities made life very expensive there. It cost him one thousand five hundred rubles to travel the nine thousand versts to Yakutsk at his own expense. Lebedev was stripped of his ranks and barred permanently from any role in state affairs.

Siberia long was home to a peculiar kind of business. Burial mounds were excavated in hopes of finding valuables buried with the deceased in ancient times. When the government learned that excavation of burial mounds or Dzungarian cemeteries was prohibited, it asked the Siberian governor Chicherin[28] for an explanation. Chicherin replied that this *burial mound business* on the steppe was forbidden under threat of harsh punishment because enemies profited thereby to capture or kill Russians.

EXPEDITIONS TO THE FAR EAST

In May the Senate heard an interesting description of expeditions to Kamchatka and contacts with China along the Amur river. The first expedition to Kamchatka in 1724 was led by Captain Commander Bering,[29] who later reached the coast of North America. An expedition under Captain Spanberg[30] went to Japan, where the people showed an interest in trade, but supply problems cut it short in 1743 pending new government orders.

At Peter Ivanovich Shuvalov's suggestion, the Senate decided in 1753 to ask the Siberian governor Miatlev's[31] advice about resuming expeditions. Miatlev said the first task was expanding grain production in the Nerchinsk district and sending grain to all fortresses and forts on the northeastern coast, and on the Ingoda, Argun and Amur rivers. The College of Foreign Affairs objected that the Amur was ceded to China by treaty[32] and suggested a search for a suitable location at the confluence of the Ingoda and Argun for building boats.

It also recommended learning whether the Amur was deep enough for oceangoing vessels. If so, they could be constructed there and permission obtained from the Chinese court for free passage by Russian boats on the Amur. If the Amur was too shallow, Peking might agree to construction of a small fortress and wharves at the mouth of the river. A new expedition might gain the allegiance of peoples not previously subject to another power.

Based on this proposal the Senate determined that the College of Foreign Affairs obtain from the Chinese court free passage on the Amur. It was to seek a suitable site at the confluence of the Argun and Ingoda for building boats, and employ the sailors and geographers left in Siberia after the Kamchatka expedition. Two vessels capable of navigating the Amur and then the open sea to Russian ports should be built and outfitted with all necessary equipment and provisions. When the Chinese court granted free passage on the Amur the vessels immediately would conduct a detailed survey of the Amur and surrounding areas.

Councillor Bratishchev was not sent to Peking until 1756.[33] When he returned in September 1758 the College of Foreign Affairs reported to the Senate that the Chinese court refused to allow Russian ships on the Amur. The Chinese emperor's response was in a document issued by the Chinese tribunal on September 23, 1757. "Russia never has been allowed to transport grain anywhere on the Amur nor will it be permitted to do so now." Bratishchev's journal describes the emperor's response as reported by Second Major Jacobi, who accompanied him to Peking. When the emperor read the Russian request to open the Amur to Russian ships, he said "Russia is dissimulating by petitioning for navigation rights after it has ordered the ships prepared. This means it will proceed even if permission is denied."

The Senate took the matter up again in 1764 and requested information from the College of Foreign Affairs. "Although the college," its report stated, "remains convinced that free Russian passage on the Amur is necessary and useful, the Chinese court's unmistakable obstinacy makes it impossible for the college to resubmit its petition."[34]

XII

PONIATOWSKI BECOMES KING OF POLAND

RUSSIA PROMOTES PONIATOWSKI'S CANDIDACY

Events on the Vistula diverted attention from the faraway Amur. The Polish royal elections necessarily affected the empress's relationship with her principal advisors on foreign affairs, Bestuzhev-Riumin[1] and Panin. Bestuzhev's insistence on keeping the Polish throne in the Saxon line shook Catherine's confidence in him whereas Panin's complete agreement with Catherine's views increased his standing. Keyserling's[2] report of Bestuzhev's opposition to Catherine's policies dealt the final blow to "little father Andrei Petrovich," and thereafter he played no significant role in public life until he died on April 10, 1766. Panin held sole responsibility for foreign affairs, although without the title of chancellor.

On December 24, 1763 Keyserling and Repnin[3] sent the empress her candidate Count Poniatowski's[4] demands. (1) The future king would receive an annual subsidy and a guarantee he would keep the throne. (2) The Guards regiments and some light infantry would be under the king's direct command and not the hetman's [Branicki's], as formerly was the case. (3) The king retained authority to distribute offices and rewards.

"While these points," the envoys wrote, "are not important in themselves, nevertheless they seem premature. In as much as it is absolutely necessary for your imperial highness and the Prussian king[5] that Poland's fundamental laws be safeguarded, it follows that the royal prerogatives be protected as well." The elderly Branicki[6] was the young Poniatowski's only rival. "There are no new candidates for the throne," Repnin wrote. "Hetman Branicki is the only one. There is considerable domestic turmoil, but since no state is promoting it, it soon will subside on its own.

"If the other parties lose hope of success they might be convinced to yield to our friends. If we can avoid foreign candidates and the convocation Sejm excludes them from the list of candidates, everything is won. Our friends are anxious about the royal army and Branicki's armed partisans. Their fear of possible treachery is well-founded, but your majesty's gracious support alleviates their other concerns. A crown hetman's party is possible only through alliance with the Wilno military commander

Prince Radziwiłł,[7] whom your majesty knows to be a fool governed only by caprice. I think we should drop any pretense with these gentlemen and speak to them bluntly should they insist on remaining under arms. As far as the Kievan military commander (Potocki)[8] is concerned, I think he is beginning to test the waters but still has his haughty tone and grandiose pretensions."

REPNIN RECOMMENDS RUSSIAN INTERVENTION

This was written on January 12 and by February 27 Repnin said Russian forces must move into Polish territory. "Our candidate and his family are satisfied with your highness's favors and are not disturbed by the false rumors the opposing party is spreading. Military intervention remains necessary to pacify the parties and convince the lesser gentry that our enemies are wrong. The crown hetman [Branicki], embittered by his setbacks in the dietines, also is promoting his party in them by force, wantonly violating laws and oaths. The Wilno military commander [Radziwiłł] has resorted to violence after promising to behave reasonably. Unless we take a strong stand, these open violations will unleash terrible disorder and civil war. Intervention by your majesty's forces will make them more cautious.

"There is a new candidate, the crown steward Prince Lubomirski,[9] who declared his intention to the primate.[10] The Kievan military commander [Potocki], who is in league with the steward, stated that he and his friends gladly would vote for a magnate [Lubomirski] whose lineage, wealth and personal character made him so worthy of the crown. In fact he is one of the richest men in the country. Our partisans always have been devoted to him and he to them." "Your majesty," Panin noted on the description of Lubomirski, "will remember this character. He was here to salute your ascension to the throne." Catherine added her own comment "You cannot put a saddle on a cow."[11]

Terrible party strife erupted in the dietines, making bloodshed unavoidable. "The hetman and his party," a report from Vienna stated, "are using considerable coercion in the dietines. These outrages and the open and constant use of military force either will give the hetman's opponents victory or an excuse to call for Russian aid. The Russians will come and, more importantly, will be seen by the people as the defenders of liberty."

The Czartoryskis[12] realized they could not compete with the hetman's party, which controlled the royal [Polish] army and the Saxon detachment.[13] They immediately petitioned the empress to send two thousand cavalry and two infantry regiments to aid them. Panin wrote a *remark* to the empress about this plea. "A thousand light infantry are ready and will move when the Polish commissioners come. This is enough to deal with the Saxon forces, but since our friends want to spend as little as possible and rely instead on our resources, here is my humble opinion: Assemble another thousand men as they request, but write to Count Keyserling in advance to ensure that our friends are more vigilant.

"They could bring down national mistrust on themselves and scorn on us by introducing foreign forces prematurely. Their opponents could use this to get more money from foreign powers to strengthen their position, creating trouble for us from that quarter. It might be better to stay with our first plan to drive the Saxons out of Poland without dissembling or delaying. We should have our forces on the border march and turn loose the thousand cossacks who are ready to go.

"Then our policy should be to use loyal magnates' forces, in cooperation with the Prussian king, to defeat the contentious opposing factions with the help of our money, our standing and our influence in affairs. When we oppose their plans they will fear us, especially when we have complete freedom of action. We will have this freedom if we proceed cautiously and prudently, not jumping the gun." "I agreed completely with these suggestions," Catherine wrote on the report, "and followed almost all of them after I read the memorandum."

A Russian detachment remained in Polish Prussia after the Seven Years War to guard supply depots left there. General Khomutov[14] was to lead it into Poland, marching quickly either to Warsaw or to Białystok, the crown hetman's residence, as a warning to him. "It is true," Repnin wrote Panin, "that the force is small, but for Poland it is sufficient. I am sure that five or six thousand Poles are no match for Khomutov's detachment and would not think of opposing it.

"The Prussian king sent word through his envoy that St. Petersburg should have sole direction of the undertaking. He could be hoping to avoid any serious involvement in Polish affairs. I should mention that our Polish friends would not like to see the Prussian king's forces on Polish soil. They are pinning all their hopes on our sovereign, and they want to see her play the primary role, the Prussian king relegated to a secondary one."

RUSSIAN FORCES ENTER POLAND

Internecine Polish strife grew worse. The Austrian ambassador Mercy[15] fed the flames, making countless promises to persuade Russia's opponents to stand firm. Keyserling and Repnin ordered Khomutov to stop at Zakroczym, fifty miles from Warsaw. Repnin wrote to Panin to inform him of this and urged him to conclude the alliance with Prussia quickly. Were Frederick II to declare he would not tolerate an Austrian move into Poland, they [Russia's opponents] would reject the idea, and Mercy's malicious proposals would be treated with the contempt they deserved.

Repnin also requested that Russian forces march into Lithuania to strengthen the confederation organized to oppose Radziwiłł's party. Two columns entered Lithuania, one commanded by Prince Volkonsky going through Minsk, the other led by Prince Dashkov (the husband of the famous Catherine Romanova)[16] moving towards Grodno.

SUPPORT FOR PONIATOWSKI ORCHESTRATED

On April 20 (New Style) twenty-six Polish magnates signed a letter to the empress. "We are as patriotic as any of our fellow citizens. We are distressed to learn some people are unhappy that your imperial majesty's forces have entered our land and they feel they can protest to your majesty. We grieve to see that our fatherland's laws cannot restrain these false patriots. Our liberties are besieged from all sides, particularly from the use of troops to block voting at the latest dietines.

"Force also threatens the convocation and electoral Sejms, where we would have been powerless to oppose the government's army, which oppresses rather than defends the state. Then we learned your highness sent a Russian army to protect our interests and our liberty. Every loyal Pole endorses this army's goal and applauds its intervention in our country. We feel obligated to express our gratitude to your imperial majesty." Among those who signed were Ostrowski (the bishop of Kujawy),[17] Szepticki (the bishop of Płock), Zamoyski,[18] five Czartoryskis (August, Michał, Stanisław, Adam and Józef),[19] Stanisław Poniatowski, Potocki, Lubomirski, Sułkowski,[20] Sołłohub, and Wielopolski.

Every effort was made to enhance Poniatowski's standing among the Poles. At Repnin's suggestion the Prussian resident [Benoît][21] wrote Frederick II that the table attendant should be awarded the Order of the Black Eagle.[22] The order was sent so quickly that Repnin and Poniatowski were in a quandary. They were waiting for the Order of St. Andrew[23] to be sent to the table attendant, who promised not to wear the Order of the Black Eagle before the Russian order was received. Circumstances forced a change of plans. When the other candidate Hetman Branicki suddenly arrived in Warsaw, Poniatowski donned the Black Eagle to divert attention to himself.

"This sign of the Prussian king's preference," Repnin wrote, "has strengthened our position. The Order of St. Andrew must be sent to Poniatowski to favor him further. He wants it desperately, but dares not request it."

RUSSIA MOVES TO CONTROL THE CONVOCATION SEJM

At the end of April envoys (deputies) and various lords began to arrive in Warsaw for the convocation Sejm, each as was customary bringing a certain number of armed men. Radziwiłł had a force of three thousand and Crown Hetman Branicki a large detachment as well. The Russian army erected camps in Ujazdow and Solec to reinforce the *family*. The Czartoryskis also had their own forces. When the Sejm opened May 7 (New Style), Warsaw was occupied by two hostile armies ready for battle.

The Czartoryski party appeared at the Sejm, but its opponents were absent. Since early morning they conferred with the hetman [Branicki], finally signing a protest that the presence of a Russian army violated national rights. When their attempt to disrupt the Sejm failed, they demanded a confederation be formed in Warsaw at once. Branicki demurred, pleading fears for his safety in the capital and left Warsaw to form a confederation in a more suitable location. He wasted time in idle talk while Dashkov's Russian detachment pursued him from Lithuania.

Repnin was able to join Dashkov at a minor skirmish between the latter's forces and the hetman's rearguard twenty-one miles from Warsaw. "I can affirm," Repnin wrote about the engagement, "that our army could not have been braver or more determined. The enemy fled so rapidly that we could not follow up our success, especially since our forces made an extraordinary effort to cover twenty-one miles in three days and could not continue the pursuit. It also should be noted that no one could have been more diligent and energetic than Prince Dashkov."

Repnin also heaped praise on Poniatowski. "He is as loyal and as grateful as one could find anywhere. He was the first in the Sejm to urge that the sovereign [Catherine] be thanked for her kindness in sending Russian forces to defend the Commonwealth. He also blocked a measure for the dietines to use majority rule rather than unanimous consent, even though it had almost universal support. He acted on this as soon as we asked him."

Repnin painted a different picture of Poniatowski's countrymen for Panin. "My omission of particular details about the situation here does not come from laziness or negligence but a fear of lying or seeming to lie. Your excellency cannot imagine how untrustworthy almost every member of the nation is. Whatever is said to be true, sworn to and witnessed today, turns out to be totally false tomorrow."

Both envoys, Keyserling and Repnin, wanted the treaty of alliance with Prussia completed as soon as possible. Repnin wrote Panin on May 25 when they finally received it. "When I showed the full text to the envoy (Keyserling), he asked only that both sides refrain from assuming new obligations without a general agreement. I remembered your excellency's position on the former treaty with England that dependence on another crown must be avoided as much as possible. I tried to convince Keyserling, and although I am not certain, I think I finally succeeded.

"I trust that all matters entrusted to us will be brought to successful conclusion, except that it will be extremely difficult, if not impossible, to reestablish the former rights of dissidents.[24] I do not see it is in our interest to attempt to present our views on this point. Restoring the dissidents to their previous crown offices will enhance the Prussian king's power as well as theirs. Since there are no prominent people of our [Orthodox] faith remaining, we will profit little from an improved status of dissidents. No foreign court must be stronger here than us." Neither envoy wanted the dissident issue to handicap the Czartoryskis or to obstruct their primary goal of electing Poniatowski king.

RESULTS OF THE CONVOCATION SEJM

The convocation Sejm, which ended in June, established a general confederation [for Poland] which joined the Lithuanian confederation to constitute the royal confederation. The Rus [Galich] military commander Prince [August] Czartoryski was chosen marshal. It was decided to bar foreign candidates from the royal elections. The new king must be a Roman Catholic of noble lineage on both his father's and mother's side.

The Czartoryskis tried to initiate reforms at this Sejm by establishing a military and a financial (treasury) commission. The hetmans and the chief financial officers (crown treasurers) now were merely chairmen of the new commissions, reducing their power and giving the king more effective control over military and financial affairs. The military commission was ordered to bring the regiments to the strength specified in the statute of 1717. In fact the number of men under arms already had increased.

Although reforms had begun quietly, they still were minor. The Czartoryskis used Russian money and Russian forces to reach their goal, and the Sejm repaid Russia by recognizing the Russian sovereign's imperial title. The confederations publicly expressed their gratitude to the Russian empress and sent the crown high notary Count Rzewuski[25] to St. Petersburg as token of it.

Meanwhile the Russian army pushed the *family's* powerful enemies out of Poland once and for all. After leaving Warsaw with the hetman [Branicki], Radziwiłł parted company with him. While trying to reach his home territory of Lithuania he clashed with the Russians at Słonim. Radziwiłł crossed the Dnieper at Mogilev into Moldavia with two thousand cavalry, but Prince Dashkov overtook his infantry and artillery at the village of Gavrilovka and captured them. Radziwiłł moved from Moldavia into Hungary and thence to Dresden. The Russians also forced Hetman Branicki out of Poland, in his case into Hungary.

POSSIBLE RIVAL TO PONIATOWSKI

In the midst of these successes Repnin told Panin he suspected the Russian candidate had a rival, none other than Poniatowski's uncle Prince August Czartoryski. "I am afraid," Panin wrote, "that Czartoryski wants the crown himself, but hides it because he fears failure. I am wary of his indifference to important obligations and his listlessness in the face of pressing business. He never starts anything without prodding and has to be told ten times before he does it.

"We wanted to have voting by proxy in the royal election while allowing the lesser gentry to decide this for themselves to avoid insulting them. Many provinces exercised this freedom and did not form voting blocs, although there were blocs in provinces where Prince Adam [Czartoryski] had more influence, notably the Rus (Galich) and Sandomierz provinces. He took one thousand ducats from us for the Galich dietine, but when a confederation opposing us emerged there, we investigated. It turned out that Czartoryski did not send the money to Galich because he feared he would have to do the same elsewhere. The Prussian ministers and I warned the ambassador (Keyserling) a number of times, but he thinks everyone is as decent and honorable as he is and does not want to think there are people who say one thing while believing another.

"Since the elections are approaching perhaps the empress should state her intentions clearly in an edict we should read to our friends, especially

STANISLAW AUGUST PONIATOWSKI

Last king of Poland

After a picture by Le Brun

the Czartoryski princes. The edict could say that the empress is committed irrevocably to the table attendant [Poniatowski], and that she will extend her protection and show her favor to all who stand by him. He is sure to succeed because the empress will support the table attendant and his adherents with all her God-given strength, defending him and his party against opponents of any family or status. Such an edict will delight our true friends and frighten those who might take the other side.

"Forces need to stationed nearby, and orders already have been given to have between seven and eight thousand men three miles from here before the Sejm opens. "For God's sake," Panin concluded his letter, "consider this confidential. The ambassador [Keyserling] knows nothing of this letter, and I would give anything to keep him from suspecting I was suggesting something without his knowledge. I would forfeit his friendship and trust if he did."

"In my opinion," Panin wrote on the letter, "it would be better for the family [the Czartoryskis] or their friends to announce our candidate before we act on his behalf. It is immaterial whether we wait until the elections, when something better might appear" (that is, let the envoys use their own judgment). "I think," Catherine noted on Panin's comment, "we should not announce a candidate, allowing us always to say that the Commonwealth acted freely."

RUSSIA OPENLY FOR PONIATOWSKI

Despite Catherine's unwillingness to reveal her candidate, *here* [in Warsaw] it was decided not to hold back any longer. On July 27 Keyserling and Repnin visited the primate, where they also found the Prussian ministers, the Czartoryski princes and many other lords. Keyserling told the primate plainly before the entire assembly that the empress wished to see the Polish throne go to Count Poniatowski, whom the ambassador would recommend in her highness's name to the entire nation at the electoral Sejm. The Prussian ambassador said the same thing in his sovereign's name, and the Czartoryskis recommended their relative, thanking both courts for their favor to their family. Repnin justified this step as necessary to end the confusion of the large undecided bloc, who were unsure which of its friends Russia wanted as king. There were rumors that the table attendant was merely a stalking horse for the Rus military commander [August Czartoryski].

The Russian court's preference for Stanisław Poniatowski inspired a proposal that the Russian empress marry the new king after his election.

It is interesting that Poniatowski's supporters and his Czartoryski uncles urged him to promise he would wed a Catholic when elected king. Poniatowski refused and complained to Repnin, asking him to write to Panin not to force him to marry. He said he did not want marriage, which was not a requirement, because Poland was not a hereditary state. Word of the proposed marriage reached as far as Constantinople. The Porte was alarmed and stated that it would consent to any suitable Piast as king, except for Poniatowski. It was decided to include a provision in the electoral conditions (pacta conventa)[26] that if the king married, it must be to a Catholic.

ELECTORAL SEJM CHOOSES PONIATOWSKI

The electoral Sejm opened quietly on August 16 and concluded quietly on August 26. The Lithuanian table attendant Count Poniatowski was elected without the slightest opposition, astounding the Poles who said that such a peaceful election was unprecedented. During his stay in Paris Poniatowski was close friends with the famous Madame Geoffrin,[27] about whom more will be said later. He corresponded with her and never called her anything but *maman*. He sent her the following description of his election. "There was such remarkable peace and quiet at this vast assembly that all of the prominent ladies of the kingdom were at the field where the election was held without experiencing the slightest discomfort. It was a joy to be proclaimed king by all of my people who were there, women as well as men. This happened because when the primate approached the women's carriages, he was gracious enough to ask them whom they wanted as king. Why were you not there? You could have hailed your son."

It is easy to imagine Geoffrin's joy when she learned that the brilliant young Pole she had favored in Paris had been elected king. "The future passes before my eyes, just as in the epic poems,"[28] she wrote him. "I see Poland rising from the ashes, I see it in radiant splendor like the new Jerusalem! O my dear son, my adored king! How happy I will be to see you the wonder of all Europe!"

St. Petersburg was just as pleased. "I salute you and the king we have made," Catherine wrote Panin. "This deed has increased my confidence in you immeasurably because now I see how correct all your measures were." This was the beginning of Panin's complete authority. Catherine, who also corresponded with Geoffrin, wrote her when Poniatowski was elected. "I congratulate you on the triumph of your son. I do not know how he became king, except that certainly it was the will of Providence. His kingdom should be congratulated even more because the Poles never have had anyone able to bring them greater human happiness. I am very glad to hear that your son conducts himself magnificently. I leave it to your maternal tenderness to guide him on the right path if need be."

PONIATOWSKI'S RELATIONS WITH CATHERINE

Geoffrin's correspondence with her beloved little boy naturally mentioned his relations with "distant lands" and their ruler [Catherine]. We have noted the widespread rumors abroad of Poniatowski's marriage to Catherine,[29] which Geoffrin mentioned in a letter to the new Polish king. "She (Catherine) is dealing with a number of matters which will need some time to resolve. I maintained that you did not see her (when Catherine travelled to Livonia),[30] and now I am sure you will not marry her, which makes many people unhappy. The interpretation here is that since her throne is not secure, she will abdicate in favor of her son and marry the Polish king."

Poniatowski was concerned, not about marriage, but his relations with the sovereign who put him on the throne. As soon as he was elected he went contrary to her interests by soliciting the friendship of the court most hostile to Russia. "I really need your advice," he said in the letter to Geoffrin describing his election. "My greatest wish, which I desire more than you can imagine, is the French king's friendship. If France wants good relations with me, I can assure you I will meet it halfway."

The disparity of interests was even greater in domestic matters than in foreign affairs. The happy delirium of Poniatowski's election wore away, and he had to confront his difficult position. Great obstacles blocked his plans to reform Poland and strengthen royal power. "Oh, I know very well what I ought to do," he wrote his mama Geoffrin, "but it is terrible! Patience, caution and courage! Once again, patience and caution! That is my motto." In regard to Catherine he wrote "*Over there,* people are very intelligent, *over there...* Already they are striving very hard to be intelligent. The most precious metal is there, but a skillful hand and a good heart are needed to fashion it. These they never have been willing to apply, but fate and, perhaps, preference might accomplish great changes!" What made Poniatowski think that intelligence was not guided by a good heart *over there*?

RUSSIAN SUBSIDIES

Keyserling did not survive Poniatowski's election for long. As early as the beginning of August Repnin informed Panin that the ambassador was very ill, and he died on September 19. Repnin wanted to use the 85,566 ducats

KING STANISLAW PONIATOWSKI

COAT OF ARMS

remaining in the ministerial funds for people who were promised payments. Each month three thousand ducats were alloted to the Rus military commander [August Czartoryski], three hundred to maintain Ogińskis'[31] soldiers and twelve hundred to get the king established and support him until the end of the coronation Sejm, since he would have no income until then. Of the eighty thousand rubles due the primate, seventeen thousand ducats remained to be paid to him and four thousand to his chancellor.

In addition to these sums, the empress's "special benevolence and friendship" prompted her to give Poniatowski one hundred thousand ducats primarily to furnish his residence. The poor king's only possible response to these kindnesses and presents was to send his benefactress a box of truffles, but this demonstrated his gratitude for the crown. Repnin quickly raised the issue of a new treaty between Russia and Poland but the Poles, recognizing that it would be unfavorable, protested vigorously. Since Russia wanted to guarantee the Commonwealth's present status, the Poles expressed their fear this would allow Russia unlimited intervention.

TENSION OVER DISSIDENTS

Dissidents were the most difficult issue, one Catherine could not postpone. As early as 1762 Georgy Konissky[32] told the Synod that [Roman Catholic] *missionaries* were imprisoning and robbing people who wanted to remain Orthodox. He heard from an ordinary citizen that the Pope wrote the king and the Lithuanian chancellor [Michał Czartoryski] not to grant Orthodox bishops privileges any longer and to drive the present bishop out with whips. Konissky said that because [his opponents] planned to intercept his letters, it would be dangerous for him to return to Mogilev, and there was no help for the church there. He asked to be relieved of his diocese and assigned to live quietly in a monastery with provision for support. His hearing and sight had been harmed by his stay in White Russia, and he also suffered from frequent headaches.

In February 1763 the Synod presented a memorandum asking Catherine to protect Orthodoxy in Mogilev. It claimed Konissky would be in great danger if he went there, and urged that no Orthodox bishop be sent to that diocese [Mogilev] until her imperial highness's special patronage was extended there. For obvious reasons[33] no decision was reached. The Synod sent another report that Konissky was going from Moscow to St. Petersburg to request his situation be resolved. Konissky was not the only one who complained. Metropolitan Arseny of Kiev[34] wrote that Potocki, the prefect of Trembowla, had given four Orthodox churches to the Uniates,[35] and that fourteen churches were taken from the Orthodox in Pinsk.

Consequently Keyserling and Repnin received an order from the empress on April 5, 1764. "You already know about the oppression of our coreligionists and other dissidents in Poland, so there is no need to describe it. No one is unaware that both groups are persecuted equally by the Roman clergy, which has robbed dioceses, monasteries and churches of almost all the rights and many privileges granted them. The Roman clergy's intrigues and abuse of power have reached the point of repudiating their leading fellow citizens simply because they profess a different faith.

"Not wishing this evil to become established, nor wishing to fail to act during the current interregnum, we order you to proceed on the basis of our existing general instructions. Make every effort both at the present convocation Sejm and at the future coronation Sejm for our fellow Orthodox and other dissidents jointly to defend the formal act of 1599.[36] All their previous rights and privileges must be spelled out by law, and henceforth their persons, property, diocese, monasteries and churches protected from any attack by the Roman clergy. As far as possible, everything seized should be returned.

"We rely on your skill, judgment and utilization of favorable circumstances to put these instructions into practice. A loyal [to Russia] confederation, if one materializes, would be especially desirable. It will be much easier to overcome blind subservience to the clergy and the hatred of those professing a different faith in a particular segment of the nobility." "I have two more things to recommend to you," Catherine wrote Repnin on October 17, "dissidents and borders. Remember, both matters affect my glory. Both are in your hands, so act in accordance with your orders and instructions." The word *remember* had to make Repnin despair.

Repnin thought that popular enthusiasm would make the dissident issue difficult. "I do not think," the envoy wrote, "that they (the dissidents) can made equal to the Catholics except by force. My hopes are limited to obtaining free practice of their religion and the right to have their own prefects in place of judicial authorities." "It goes without saying," Panin replied to Repnin, "that in discussing dissidents we must give primary consideration to our coreligionists. In addition to the aspirations shared by other dissidents, they have their own complaints which deserve the same careful attention.

"I do not think we ever can restore to the dissidents at one fell swoop everything they have lost. It will be enough if they achieve a certain equality of rights and privileges in the Commonwealth and have complete security against new threats. Should the current oppression persist, the dissidents, including our coreligionists, might be eliminated completely to the irreparable detriment of our state interests. There is no need to go into detail here how satisfying the dissidents will benefit our fatherland and enhance its standing, and in particular redound to the glory of her imperial highness.

"Formal conditions specified by treaty are sufficient to persuade the king and the leading magnates to follow this policy. They must be told that her imperial majesty, at no profit to herself, spared neither effort nor treasure to safeguard the Commonwealth from the upheaval, the civil disorder and the other evils these bring in their wake in a troubled and critical time such as previous interregnums generally have been. She now has every right to demand and expect the king and the entire Commonwealth to express their gratitude by taking concrete measures to protect, defend and render justice to a certain group of their fellow citizens. This will bring as much honor now to Poland as it does glory to her imperial highness. Despite solemn treaties, Poland's fundamental laws, the common rights of a free nation and a multitude of royal privileges, these citizens though blameless now endure a servile yoke for the sole reason that they profess different Christian faiths, faiths in which they were born and raised.

"Your excellency is free to add to these points anything you consider appropriate. If it is absolutely necessary when all else fails, a warning should be given. Should the Commonwealth not respect her imperial majesty sufficiently for defending a just cause, its further stubbornness will compel her to achieve by certain necessary means what recognition of her magnificent beneficence and friendship could not. To this end her imperial majesty will maintain the same forces on its (the Commonwealth's) territory now being maintained at great expense solely to benefit and serve the Commonwealth. It should realize that oppression is destroying the liberty and equality of some of its citizens. If this threat must be used, your excellency must support his words with deeds by having our forces stay longer in Poland. Thus fear will exact from the Poles what kindness could not achieve."

RUSSIA OPPOSES POLISH REFORMS

Whereas Russia's main concern was the dissidents, the king's and the *family's* was reform. They desired to introduce two major reforms immediately at the coronation Sejm. The first was majority voting in the dietines. The second was to end what now was being called the *liberum rumpo* [right of disruption]. Hitherto each separate question in a Sejm required unanimous consent. Yet one deputy's protest of any question in effect dissolved the Sejm and nullified all its previous decisions.

In effect, neighboring courts, particularly Russia, must agree before these reforms could be instituted. Stanisław August planned to convince Catherine that reforms were a prerequisite for success in the dissident question. "I will not offer you lengthy expressions of unwanted gratitude," the king wrote the empress (November 4). "Not only are you above all that, but I also would be hard put to find words to express my feelings. Let me call your attention instead to my character, which you know well. You realize the value I place on gratitude, which to you is measureless, although equalled by my devotion. Perhaps you would venture to say to yourself 'My dearest and truest friend now is king. He is allied with me as much by integrity and personal inclination as by common interest.'

"Fortunately your virtues and laudable impartiality enabled me to do my duty by you and my state. I want Poland to be free just as you do, which is why I wish to rescue it from the total anarchy now reigning here. Most of the ardent patriots are so sick of anarchy that they are beginning to express an audible preference for an absolute monarchy over a harmful and shameful individualism, if thereby more genuine freedom can be achieved.

"I want to save them from disappointment, possible only if the dietines are reformed. The dissidents are one part of the citizenry over whom I rule, as is your wish. Your highness's strong interest in their fate impels me to support them in a Catholic people which perhaps is too jealous of their obvious privileges. For success here, as anywhere else, there must be more order in the Sejm, and this cannot be achieved without improving the dietines. Thus my interests coincide with those of your highness."

Since *over there* they were very intelligent, *over there*, even if they were guided by a good heart, it was suggested to the king that reforms were premature. Stanisław August apologized and wrote (December 13) "I take the liberty of imagining her imperial majesty's acknowledgment of the sacrifice I made for you at the Sejm as the strongest proof of my boundless esteem for you. I sacrificed what was dearest to me, because what I wanted most of all were majority voting and abolition of the *liberum rumpo*. Since you did not want them yet, they were not even proposed.

"I think I am correct in assuming that my actions will dispose your highness more favorably in the future. The desire to please you as well as my own inclinations impelled me to do for the dissidents what you requested. Your ambassador will tell you how this was met with fanatic outcries. There was such bitterness in the Senate that some wanted even the primate sacrificed when he ventured a mild suggestion on the question. I expect that your majesty's keen sense of justice will lead her to realize that I cannot and ought not risk anything further after this experience."

REPNIN'S REPORT ON DISSIDENTS

The ambassador reported his disappointment with the results of the Sejm, particularly on the dissident question. "Only the dissidents were more humiliated than I," Repnin wrote on December 6. "I soothed and threatened on their behalf, but I have to admit there is little hope. Passions are running so high that neither reason nor fear has any effect." After this gloomy preface Repnin reported on December 13, "The Sejm has confirmed the 1686 treaty,[37] not by an act but in the constitution, as well as a border commission and negotiations for a new alliance. A new basis has been established for a mutual guarantee of the two powers' territory and of the rights, privileges and liberties of the Commonwealth.

"I know that this guarantee is not yet complete (that is, the resolution concerning it not yet put in final form), but still the Poles cannot deny they have been instructed to have it approved by the entire Sejm. This constitution will have the same validity as an act I sign (on behalf of the empress) and cannot be nullified by foreign powers. I think the main reason for [dissident] opposition to the act is their wish to use the existing guarantee to convince the dietines and the Sejm to agree to measures already proposed. For another thing the dissidents neither want this guarantee from the Prussian king, nor do they want to commit themselves to the alliance with him which I wanted specified in the act. None of them trusts him in the slightest.

"I have done my best to counter these objections, yet realize that hitherto it has been in vain. If I have not carried out to the letter my orders from the highest authority, it is because it simply was not possible. What was accomplished derived from threats that the army would remain here. This constitution can achieve the same desirable results as an act. I must give credit to the king for his complete devotion to the most gracious sovereign and his wholehearted espousal of her concerns.

"To accomplish all our goals I had to tell the king and, in confidence, some of the magnates, that I would receive no orders to evacuate the army until our court's desires were met, including those for the dissidents. When I saw that neither fear nor exhortation had any effect, I hoped that appealing to the nation's sense of gratitude would succeed. That is why I agreed when the king asked if he could announce publicly that our forces were withdrawing. This did nothing for the dissidents because people did not want to listen when the dissidents' leader presented his case.

"They raised such a furor that, forgetting any deference to the king, they all leapt from their seats demanding that whoever dared formulate a project on behalf of the dissidents and present it to the marshal of the Sejm be called before them. The king, the primate and a few of the reasonable members dared not utter a word in the face of these excesses. The king and the primate were afraid to take responsibility for the project, although it was they who gave it to the marshal. To put a stop to the attacks they claimed that the project originated with the ministers of foreign powers.

"This did halt the noisy proceedings, and no one ventured to say anything more in opposition. The opponents would not allow the proposal to be read, shouting like madmen that previous Sejms had settled the dissidents' status and no changes were to be made. The indescribable yelling only stopped when they felt they were under no compulsion to amend the dissidents' status.

"That morning before the proposal was made I saw that the king was undecided and almost fearful. I gave him a memorandum on the dissidents, as did the Prussian, Danish and English residents, to encourage him to raise the issue, but at noon he informed me that it would be better to restrict the project to generalities. This I considered pointless and sent him a note naturally insisting that the proposal already was introduced and that, although the Sejm had been extended just for two days, there was enough time to adopt it. He sent me a note back asking that the project be kept secret from everyone except her highness, but I replied that I must follow my instructions, which is why the proposal was made as described earlier.

"As I had planned, I was then near the Senate, where I had my informants who reported everything to me immediately. I sent a message at once to Prince Adam Czartoryski that although the king told the nation our forces were leaving, he knew I could not do that unless the dissident issue was heard and decided. The king was terrified when he heard this and took up the dissident cause again. Since he was afraid to speak himself, he ordered the marshal of the Sejm to continue to raise the issue, which was done several times but, as reported earlier, to no avail.

"I shall write to Generals Stoffel[n][38] and Rennenkampf[39] to return to their quarters in Russia as directed by her imperial majesty. As I mentioned, the king is quite concerned lest they remain, and importuned me to have them leave. I told him that my instructions did not sanction this, particularly since there was no success regarding the dissidents, yet this genuine solicitude for our court's policies convinced me to assume responsibility myself. I flattered him by saying that the most gracious sovereign, assured of his sincere devotion and friendship, would approve..."

"I acted out of zeal to achieve the goals of our exalted court and had great success in confirming the treaty. The only setback was that the dissident issue turned out so badly, and I cannot take any comfort in that. I see now that religious enthusiasm is the most dangerous thing in the world and creates more difficulties than anything else. The old treaty should be observed and a new one concluded. The rights of the dissidents must be addressed and efforts made to improve their status and protect them from slander as far as the king is able. In persuading him to act he must be led to abandon the notion that the army was ordered to withdraw for the sake of the dissidents. It should be stressed that Prince Dolgorukov's corps will not withdraw completely for precisely this reason. I intend to send this corps to the Wilno barracks because it is very expensive to maintain here and certainly no longer needed."

"I see now," Repnin wrote, "that religious enthusiasm is the most dangerous thing in the world." Stanisław August echoed this thought in letter to his *maman* Geoffrin. "Oh dear *maman*, popular prejudices are terrible! Some of them I overcame at the Sejm, but many others I could not. You will praise me because reason triumphed, although I shed a lot of blood in the process. The slightest effort to assist non-Catholics sparks a fanatical outcry. I could combat my opponents directly but prefer to show respect rather than silencing them abruptly.

"I am taking a different road which is longer and less obvious, but which in the end will allow me a humanitarian policy towards the dissidents. The dissidents have done themselves and me the greatest disservice by spreading the rumor that I want to give them complete equality with adherents of the predominant religion [Roman Catholicism]. Never will this occur to me and never will it happen."[40] The storm gathered rapidly, and in their confusion neither the king nor Repnin wished to admit the terrible danger, nor did they see the beginning of the end.

XIII

RELATIONS WITH OTHER FOREIGN POWERS, 1764

CLOSER LINKS WITH PRUSSIA

Russia's links with Prussia, based on Poniatowski's accession, inevitably became stronger. General Gadomski,[1] whom the Polish Commonwealth sent to the Prussian king with news of August III's death, saw Prince Dolgoruky[2] several times with information on conversations with Frederick II about the election of a new king. Frederick told Gadomski plainly it would be better if the Poles chose a Piast, and that he would coordinate all his steps in Warsaw with the declarations issued in the empress's name. Since she already had recommended Count Poniatowski, Frederick thought the Poles would find it in their own interest to agree.

The king added that the rumors circulating in Poland that he planned to send an army corps there were totally baseless. They were concocted by his enemies to discredit him and confuse public opinion. He had no intention of violating Polish liberty in any way. He would be compelled to send forces into Poland only if the Viennese court dispatched its forces there first. This he could not ignore, and would respond in like manner. Hence he advised the Poles to forestall Vienna's moves as threats to their stability.

"It seems," Dolgoruky reported, "that Mr. Gadomski agrees the Poles should endorse the proposals made by your highness and the Prussian king. He told me that although Prince Xavier[3] is promoting his election [as king of Poland] secretly and has a sizable party, the Poles will choose their own stability over this prince's cause."

Dolgoruky held a conference with Finckenstein[4] at the beginning of April. The Prussian minister told him some of the Polish magnates secretly were trying to persuade Mercy to announce one of the Austrian princes as a candidate for the Polish crown and to say that this be the end of all parties in Poland. If a Piast were chosen, parties were inevitable. Mercy had given no answer yet, but the king already had written to Count Solms[5] in St. Petersburg on the subject so the empress might be informed.

Finckenstein added that his highness thought he should write to the Russian resident in Constantinople [Obrezkov][6] about this. The courts of

Vienna and Versailles were trying to upset the Porte about the actions of the courts of St. Petersburg and Berlin in Poland. Since Austria and France were telling the Porte that Polish liberty was in grave danger, the Russian resident could suggest that, on the contrary, it was the Viennese court that was trying to weaken Polish liberty by its prince's open candidacy. This the Porte would not permit, and would put less faith in the overtures of the Austrian and French envoys after it found out. That same day Dolgoruky sent word to Obrezkov in Constantinople.

Frederick II's letters to the empress continued to promise success in Poland. "Since I know this (Polish) nation well," the king wrote on February 16, "I am confident you will obtain what you want from the Poles by appropriate distributions of funds and unambiguous threats against intriguers. I think threats and general proclamations should be used only if all forms of magnanimity, suggestion and private counsel have been tried. This will deny Poland's neighbors any pretext for intervening in what you consider your business."

On April 7 Frederick wrote that France and Austria would use clandestine intrigue rather than force to oppose Catherine in the Polish royal election. The only danger was that their intrigues might rouse the Porte. "As far as the Poles are concerned, sending in a Russian army and issuing forceful proclamations against Hetman Branicki and Princes Radziwiłł and Lubomirski will cool their ardor."

"Most Poles," Frederick wrote, "are proud, vain and base[7] when they think they are not in danger, but grovel when threatened. I do not think there will be any bloodshed unless some nobleman's nose or ear is cut off in the Sejm." "The Poles have received some money from the Saxon court," Frederick wrote on May 12. "Those who want money are making a certain amount of noise, but that will be the end of it. Your highness will accomplish her project, and you can trust this oracle more than Calchas."[8]

Meanwhile Frederick was displeased when Benoît[9] in Warsaw issued a statement identical to that of the Russian envoy. "A statement should say only that the king does not wish to expand his domains at Poland's expense," he ordered his minister informed, "not directly requesting a Piast be chosen. Although the king agrees with the empress on this, he wishes to avoid the suspicion that he wants to interfere with free elections." Although the king also agreed with the empress on the dissidents, he ordered Benoît told "Do everything you can under the circumstances for the dissidents, yet not let our affection for them jeopardize the issue."

ALLIANCE WITH PRUSSIA

Berlin waited impatiently for the alliance treaty to be concluded with Russia. In his reports to the king Solms attributed the delay to the press of business at the Russian court and its usual slowness. The desired treaty finally was signed on March 31. Each state guaranteed the other's European domains. In case of an attack against one of the contracting powers, the other initially was obligated to use its good offices to end the conflict. If these were unsuccessful, after three months the ally upon request was to furnish ten thousand infantry and two thousand cavalry. If desired both states could agree to increase this number and to use all their forces for defensive purposes.

The first secret article stated that if an attack was at a distant location, a sum of four hundred thousand rubles might be supplied instead of troops. For Russia this would be from Turkey or the Crimea, and for Prussia from across the Weser. The second secret article obligated the allies to cooperate in Sweden to maintain a balance between the opposing parties there. In the event of a threat to the existing Swedish governmental structure, the allies would agree on ways to avert the danger.

The [Prussian] king guaranteed the grand duke's [Peter III's] Holstein possessions in the third secret article. The allies were bound by the fourth secret article not to allow changes in the Polish constitution and to counter and defeat all efforts to do so, even by force. In a separate article the allies pledged to protect the dissidents and persuade the king and the Commonwealth to restore their previous rights. They were to wait for a suitable opportunity if this proved impossible, but at a minimum were to try to prevent oppression of the dissidents. The duration of the treaty was eight years, and it could be renewed before its expiration.

Dolgoruky reported that Finckenstein informed all foreign ministers orally about the treaty, including the existence of a secret article on Poland. Dolgoruky also informed all foreign ministers about the treaty. Since he was closer to the English ambassador Mitchell[10] than to the others, Dolgoruky read him the entire treaty, including the text of the secret article [on Poland].

"Dolgoruky deserves a reprimand for this," Panin wrote in the report. "On what authority did he dare discuss the secret convention? Besides, the whole report is incorrect. To assert that the Berlin court told all foreign ministers about the secret Polish article is impossible because it was agreed here that only Vienna and London would be informed." The strong reprimand was justified. Dolgoruky replied that he did not consider it necessary to conceal the secret article from the English ambassador. It was decided in St. Petersburg to inform the London court, and Dolgoruky was instructed to deal openly with Mitchell.

AUSTRIA AND THE TREATY WITH PRUSSIA

The Austrian ambassador Ried[11] suggested to Frederick that Maria Theresa wanted a public declaration from Prussia that in restoring order in the Polish Commonwealth Prussian forces would not enter Poland before those of other powers. The king, displeased with Ried's statement, replied "I already informed the Viennese court about the treaty I concluded with the Russian empress. Now I am obligated to cooperate with her completely. Hitherto the empress has done nothing to violate her promise to protect the liberty and rights of the Polish Commonwealth, and there are no grounds to protest the presence of Russian forces in Poland. The alliance between Prussia and Russia is a natural one, for as the Polish Commonwealth's closest neighbors it is in our interest to join forces and together to preserve Poland's freedom and fundamental laws."

The king ordered Finckenstein to tell Dolgoruky immediately about his conversation with Ried so Dolgoruky could report to the empress, adding Frederick's comment that all Polish unrest was caused by Vienna's initiatives. In fact when the crown hetman Count Branicki halted three miles outside Warsaw after leaving the capital, the Austrian ambassador Mercy visited him and persuaded him to stand firm.

PRUSSIA OPPOSES POLISH REFORMS

In autumn the new Polish king's efforts to institute reforms aroused great concern in Berlin, especially since Frederick II received reports from St. Petersburg and Warsaw that the Russian court was indifferent to and even favorable towards these efforts. Solms wrote from St. Petersburg that the Polish ambassador Count Rzewuski gave a memorandum to Panin asking the empress's approval for limiting the harm done by the *liberum veto* in the matter of the *liberum rumpo*. Panin was ready to agree, suggesting that a Poland without a chaotic Sejm and with its commerce, justice system and police in order could be a useful ally, replacing Austria in dealing with the Turks. Solms received an order from Berlin. "God save us," it read, "from promoting Rzewuski's proposal!"

From Warsaw Benoît also sent disturbing news that Russia was regarding the Polish reforms too lightly. Originally Repnin's stance was quite inconsistent, and he began to take the issue seriously only when Benoît told him how important it was for the Prussian king. When Repnin raised the question with Stanisław August the king was greatly offended and began to speak with a zeal Repnin never had seen in him before: "What! It is our friends and allies who will not let us escape our stagnation!" "The Poles," Benoît wrote, "will seal their own doom by such conduct and force their neighbors to destroy Poland some day. Should they introduce the English form of government, their vast domains will incite too much fear."

"Many prominent Poles want to abolish the *liberum veto* and replace it with majority voting," Frederick wrote Catherine (October 30). "This plan is of great importance for all Poland's neighbors. I agree there is no cause for alarm with King Stanisław, but what will happen after him? If your highness agrees with this change of course, you may regret it, and Poland might become a danger to its neighbors. Should the old laws of the state, which you guaranteed, are upheld, we always will have a way to make changes when we find it necessary. The best policy is to keep the Russian forces there until the Sejm is adjourned, to prevent the Poles from yielding to the first rush of enthusiasm."

According to Solms, Panin repeatedly emphasized that keeping the Poles in barbarism was too harsh. Yet Frederick's letter made a strong impression on Catherine, who refused to approve the reforms. "Panin scowled," Solms wrote, "but concealed his disappointment. He hoped for glory as the man who restored Poland."[12]

Poland's third neighbor also was very interested in everything that happened there. On January 29 the Austrian envoy Prince Lobkowitz[13] told the vice chancellor [A.M. Golitsyn] that the empress-queen [Maria Theresa] wanted to know whom Russia preferred for the Polish crown in order that the two sides reach a timely agreement. The information promised as yet was not forthcoming, while the Russian and Prussian ministers' declaration in Warsaw violated previous assurances that the Commonwealth would be allowed to conduct free elections. The exclusion of foreign princes [as candidates] contradicted these assurances. If Russia sent forces into Poland to support its candidate, Vienna as an important entity and a close neighbor could not be indifferent. If some foreign power imposed a king on Poland, frustrating free elections, Vienna would be compelled to intervene. Were a Saxon prince freely chosen for the Polish throne, did the empress intend to respond with force?

RUSSIA AND AUSTRIA AT ODDS IN POLAND

At a conference on February 3 Lobkowitz again asked whether the empress might oppose the election of a Saxon prince. The Viennese court desired this prince chosen in a free election and did not plan to support him by force, hoping that the empress also would refrain from force on behalf of her candidate. It might help restrain hotheads in Poland were both imperial courts to make a timely agreement endorsing free elections. When Lobkowitz inquired about the empress's response to his proposal, he was told no decision was made and that the matter was not urgent.

In a note from the vice chancellor to all foreign ministers on March 29 the Russian court reported widespread disorder in Poland and attacks by the crown hetman Count Branicki, the Wilno military commander Prince Radziwiłł and their associates. The empress, albeit unwillingly, might be compelled to send part of her army into the Commonwealth to protect loyal patriots and preserve order in neighboring districts.

Lobkowitz remarked that he knew nothing of Hetman Branicki's use of force and that Prince Radziwiłł was innocent of the charges in the Russian note. In general he, the ambassador, strongly deplored Russia's failure to limit its interest in Polish affairs to specific objectives. Knowing his own court's desire for peace, he feared disruption of the tranquillity so prized by all. The vice chancellor replied that Branicki's attacks and Radziwiłł's excesses were beyond question. The Russian court's intentions remained unchanged, which were to safeguard Poland's liberty and laws and prevent any disruption of Poland's domestic order. If these principles forced Russia to employ its army, this was not a whim,but a consequence of its fundamental interests, which outweighed those of all other courts.

Branicki's troops appeared at the dietine in Graudenz (in the Prussian province) to bolster his cause but were blocked by a Russian unit guarding the supply depots there. The Czartoryski party approved the Russian action, whereas their opponents loudly protested the intervention by foreign forces. On April 5 Lobkowitz complained about the intervention, saying the Polish protest was completely justified and the presence of Russian troops a major violation of Polish liberty.

The vice chancellor retorted that the Russian forces, which had left Graudenz, were forced to return to protect the supply depots from being seized in the popular upheaval. Lobkowitz was relying on the protest of just one side. Because it had just two hundred and twenty signatures, he should read the other side's manifesto which two hundred and seventy had signed. Major General Khomutov's corps had been in Graudenz for several years, not sent there for this purpose. The Viennese court did not protest that the presence of Russian forces violated Polish liberty when the Russian army acted on behalf of the empress-queen [Maria Theresa].

Lobkowitz responded that, although he had not seen the other party's manifesto, he doubted it was as credible as the first protest. Although he had no intention of discussing the past, his main concern was that Russian supply depots might appear where they never existed before. "In drafting an answer to Prince Lobkowitz," Catherine wrote on the report of this meeting, "it might not be bad to mention that we find it very strange we always are being interrogated."

In Vienna Kaunitz told Prince Golitsyn plainly that the Austrian court was totally unaware Branicki and other Poles were using force as the Russian court claimed, although it did know a large Russian corps had moved into Poland. "I wanted," Golitsyn wrote, "to ascertain this court's intentions in Poland in talking with Prince Kaunitz, but he was not very accommodating. The present ministry has displayed no frankness, and I expect none now."

Given the Viennese court's firm decision not to begin a war over Poland under any circumstances, this highly irritating "interrogation" was particularly strange. Maria Theresa said that she shuddered at the smallest spark in Poland, fearing it would burst into flame. In regard to the Saxon prince Xavier's ambitions for the Polish throne, she said "In my present financial state I can give him only one hundred thousand gulden. This is meager help! I cannot consider sending forces into Poland, for that might draw me into a new war when the wounds of the last war [Seven Years War] have not healed yet."[14]

FRANCE OPPOSES RUSSIA IN POLAND

St. Petersburg found France's conduct equally strange in as much as it constantly "interrogated" without firm resolution to oppose Russian aims. "Our letters from Vienna make it clear," Louis XV wrote at the beginning of the year, "that the court there will furnish Prince Xavier neither troops nor money. It promises him all possible good offices and urges him to declare his candidacy (for the Polish throne). In these circumstances any money we give will be wasted, and we do not have money to throw away. I think Spain will take the same attitude."

On February 3 the French *chargé d'affaires* Bérenger[15] told the vice chancellor Prince Golitsyn that every foreign power had the right to support its candidate, although not to violate Polish liberty arbitrarily by excluding all other powers. On March 1 Bérenger noted that Russia's exclusion of the Saxon princes contradicted Russian declarations about preserving the Commonwealth's rights and liberties. Prince Golitsyn replied that Russia obviously had a greater interest in preserving the Polish constitution than did the French court and proposed a Piast only because a majority, the sensible element of the population, wanted it.

On March 29 a note from the vice chancellor to all foreign ministers stated that attacks by Branicki and Radziwiłł might bring Russian forces into Poland. When Bérenger raised questions and commented on every point in the note, Prince Golitsyn told him to be satisfied with the note's contents and repeated that France's interests in Poland and its liberty were far inferior to Russia's. In Versailles the duke of Praslin[16] told the Russian minister Prince Dmitry Alexeevich Golitsyn[17] Russia should not intervene in Polish affairs and should withdraw its forces from Poland to deny the Poles any pretext for complaints. Panin's comment on this part of Golitsyn's report was "Meanwhile the Sejm was adjourned in order to leave our party in Poland defenseless and accelerate the buildup of Branicki's forces."

Praslin then told Golitsyn that France was very disturbed by the rumor the empress had ordered sizable forces to the Polish border. He said as a friend that France would be placed in a very awkward position were the Polish Commonwealth's rights and liberties unexpectedly violated and Poland formally asked France for help. At the end of April Praslin showed his disappointment when he told Golitsyn that Russian forces had entered Poland. First, Polish law forbade electing a king while foreign troops were in the Commonwealth. Second, the empress herself declared that she would not allow foreign forces to invade Poland. Third, many Poles now were complaining to his most Christian majesty,[18] requesting French assistance because the Russian empress was violating their rights by excluding foreign candidates and sending her troops into Poland.

In fact Count Branicki's and Prince Radziwiłł's attacks which provided the pretext for Russian military intervention, if there were any, were not that serious. Their enemies [Praslin continued] presented an exaggerated picture to Catherine in hopes she would cease protecting the two magnates. Branicki did not increase the royal army in the slightest when the king died.

The empress's best course of policy would be to order her forces from Poland, leaving the Poles to sort things out among themselves. In this event France would make a formal declaration neither to intervene in any way in Poland nor to send a single copeck there. "An obvious result," a note at this point in Golitsyn's report stated. "They [the French] are giving now, but see it is to no avail."

FRENCH RELUCTANCE TO INTERVENE

Praslin told Golitsyn candidly as a friend that he was very disturbed by Polish requests for help and that he was at loss what to do. "I readily believe," Golitsyn wrote to his court, "that Polish requests have put this court in a difficult position, less from any reluctance to intervene in Poland than from the realm's domestic problems. Besides, France will take its lead from the Austrian court, which is more involved than France in Poland."

According to a May 13 memorandum from Golitsyn, the French envoy in Warsaw the marquis de Paulmy[19] told his court that his feeble efforts on behalf of the Polish Commonwealth and inadequate protection of French supporters were arousing great dissatisfaction and damaging France's reputation. The [French] court took notice and recalled Paulmy. As he left Paulmy was supposed to announce that because the Commonwealth was in upheaval and foreign troops were on its soil, the king felt obliged to recall his ambassador until order was restored. "The present situation in Poland," Golitsyn wrote, "really is unusual and very painful for the ministry. The king and Choiseul [Praslin] have no intention of intervening in Poland and just now told the Austrian court this again. They emphasized that success was impossible because they could not send much money or dispatch forces. The dauphin and his wife[20] want to send troops, however, and blame Choiseul for France's indifference."

Later reports from Golitsyn indicated France was anxious to see the Polish interregnum end and, above all, feared a double election. This would pose great difficulties for France because it was unable to help the Czartoryskis' opponents, and failure to aid this party would cost France its standing in Poland. News finally arrived that Stanisław Poniatowski was chosen. The French queen[21] asked her father Stanisław Leszczynski[22] whether the new king might have the title Stanisław II to acknowledge the royal status of Stanisław I (Leszczynski). Were this impossible he could be called Stanisław August.[23]

FRANCE TRIES TO INCITE TURKEY AGAINST RUSSIA

France could not oppose Russian policy in Poland directly but word arrived from Constantinople that the French envoy there had not been idle. On January 4 the Porte sent Obrezkov a statement that it did not intend to intervene in Polish affairs or in the free election of a Piast and wished that other neighboring powers do likewise. It had heard that Russia in concert with the Prussian king planned to force the Poles to choose Count Poniatowski king. Although the report was not credible, the Porte asked the [Russian] envoy for some clarification. Obrezkov's reply was not to believe it, and the Prussian envoy Rixen[24] sent a note saying the same.

At the end of February Obrezkov wrote that when the French king saw the Porte consented to electing a Piast he managed to influence the sultan[25] through a Neapolitan physician serving in the women's section of the seraglio who had free access to the sultan. Thanks to this Neapolitan doctor the sultan sent a Porte interpreter to Obrezkov on February 7 to inquire about Polish affairs and learn the empress's final decision. When Obrezkov asked the reason for this unexpected questioning, the interpreter told him in strict confidence that the sultan had changed his mind about electing a Piast as king of Poland. The major cause of the shift was the French envoy, who flattered the sultan by suggesting the latter would encounter no difficulty in placing his choice on the Polish throne despite the efforts of any power to block him. He would gain eternal glory and enhance his empire's prestige. Since Obrezkov's experience with the Porte was that a milder response was better than an firm one, he answered that things could not have changed in Poland. As envoy he could assure the Porte, based on his empress's instructions, that she would not prevent the Poles from choosing a Piast. Yet, were malicious Poles or a foreign power to disturb the Polish Commonwealth's tranquillity, the empress could not remain indifferent and must do everything to safeguard Poland and restore order.

The Porte interpreter thought this reply would convince the sultan that an attempt to put his choice on the Polish throne would not be as easy as the French claimed, and that the sultan would refrain from actions which compromised the Porte. The response was effective. The Prussian envoy submitted another note to the Porte about the need to choose a native Pole. When the senior French interpreter Duval gave the chancellor [reis effendi] a statement that as children of the deceased Polish king the Saxon princes could be considered native Poles, the chancellor threw it in his face. Was not the [French] envoy ashamed to bother the ministry with such trifles? Did he think the Porte's officials were foolish children?

OBREZKOV DEFENDS RUSSIAN POLICY

We saw that from the outset of Catherine's reign Russia wanted to act in concert with Prussia in Poland and with Austria in Turkey. Clearly this dual policy was very difficult. Thus Prince Dolgoruky in Berlin was unsuccessful when he wanted to persuade the Prussian government not to conclude an alliance with Turkey. In Constantinople Obrezkov tried to enlist the Austrian internuncio [equivalent to minister plenipotentiary] to oppose the same Turkish-Prussian alliance, but his counsel and proposals were greeted coldly and contemptuously. "I think it is time to drop the matter," Panin noted on Obrezkov's report, "leaving the Viennese court to its fate. Russia will not be affected adversely by this alliance (between Prussia and Turkey), while Vienna has weakened its previous natural connection with us considerably. Why make others jealous of us by promoting Vienna's interests?"

In April the Polish resident Stankiewicz told the Porte on Hetman Branicki's behalf that the electoral Sejm could not be conducted freely unless the Porte promised to help the hetman and the Commonwealth. Russia had massive forces surrounding Poland on all sides as well as major supply depots in Poland guarded by sizable detachments, which now were being reinforced. The word throughout the kingdom was that the Russian empress would allow no one but Poniatowski to be elected, whereupon she immediately would marry him, thus uniting Poland to the Russian empire. Obviously this would be a great blow to Turkey.

Obrezkov adroitly countered Stankiewicz's proposals by approaching influential figures. He wrote that a Porte interpreter Grigore Ghica,[26] a favorite of the princes of Moldavia, gave him this advice on Poland. As soon as a Polish king acceptable to the empress was chosen, he should send the sultan and the vizier a formal announcement of his election and his desire to gain the Porte's favor. Showing deference to the Porte was the best way to achieve its cooperation with Russia and Prussia. Playing on its vanity would distract attention from the insult to Turkey's dignity caused by the Russian empress having single-handedly chosen the Polish king.

Obrezkov added that in his opinion Ghica's advice expressed the desires of the entire Turkish ministry, not merely his own. Ghica also assured Obrezkov he would serve the empress faithfully in Polish and other matters when he arrived in Moldavia. In response Obrezkov gave him a sable coat and one thousand rubles. "We definitely should hold on to him (Ghica)," Panin wrote on the report. "Perhaps your highness would agree to have her ambassadors in Poland instructed in advance to do so.

Also, Stankiewicz must be recalled as soon as possible, and when he returns made aware of the outrages he allowed himself to perpetrate." "It is so ordered," Catherine noted. "Obrezkov should be complimented appropriately for his zeal, skill and diligence, and may Almighty God henceforth bless our undertakings in like manner."

The rejoicing was premature. Obrezkov reported on July 15 that Branicki, the Crimean khan and the French ambassador greatly disturbed the Porte with news that Russia was promoting Poniatowski secretly because he was Catherine's fiancé. A Porte interpreter visited Obrezkov with a message from the vizier that Poniatowski's election would cool relations between Turkey and Russia. The vizier then had a statement sent to Obrezkov. "God alone knows," it read, "how I have striven for close friendship between Turkey and Russia. Still all my efforts will have been in vain if Poniatowski is elected king. The Porte does not fear his marriage to the empress because it accepts your assurances this will not happen.

"He is unacceptable, even so, to every power except Russia and Prussia. If he acceded to the throne he might marry an Austrian or Bourbon princess, thus making Poland dependent on one of these houses. In short, if Russia gave Poniatowski the Polish crown, there would be war with Turkey, and I would be powerless even if I kept my post. The choice may be anyone but Poniatowski, even his brother if he is of legitimate birth."

Here too Obrezkov could reassure the Porte. "My lot is a hard one," he wrote the empress, "and there is no respite." A letter arrived from the Crimean khan concerning the reply he received to a request for an evaluation of the Commonwealth. This document, signed by many castellans and military commanders, said the Czartoryski family in league with the primate held sole power in the Commonwealth. With Russian backing this family organized the Sejm using measures contrary to the Commonwealth's customs and extremely prejudicial to the entire kingdom, instead reflecting the views of the Russian court. The Czartoryskis' primary aim was to place the universally hated Poniatowski on the throne. Should the Porte not defend the Polish gentry their opponents' superiority would drive them into exile, leaving Poland at Russia's mercy.

At the same time as the khan's letter,there was a report from the pasha in Khotin that Prince Radziwiłł, defeated and pursued by Russian forces, had fled to Turkish territory, placed himself under the Porte's protection and brought complaints against Russia. The sultan flew into a towering rage and ordered his ministry to convey a reprimand to Obrezkov to make him realize the extent of the sultan's displeasure. Obrezkov described the reprimand he received on July 20 as coarse and rude in the extreme. It claimed Russia was behaving improperly and disrespectfully toward the Porte and that Obrezkov revealed himself to be a liar and a swindler.

Since experience had taught Obrezkov that the Porte's bark was worse than its bite, he sent a note the next day that such language was inappropriate in dealings between great powers and that the rebukes were unwarranted. Poland was an independent Commonwealth, therefore no single power had the right to complain no matter whom it chose as king. The previous war between Russia and Turkey was caused by similar reports which were given hasty credence, a war in which each side lost perhaps more than one hundred thousand men.

When the Porte interpreter translated Obrezkov's note he thought it quite outspoken and suggested changing some of the phrases. "The Porte is to blame," Obrezkov replied. "Nothing I have said is unnecessary or excessive. I would be willing to make changes if the Porte deleted all the coarse and insulting terminology from its reprimand." "The Porte is not requiring you to send this reprimand to your court," the interpreter noted. "I am not the Polish resident Stankiewicz," Obrezkov retorted. "It is my duty to report everything to the empress." Then the interpreter asked Obrezkov on behalf of the ministry not to forward the reprimand to St. Petersburg and on July 30, the following day, he and the Prussian envoy Rixen were summoned to meet with the grand vizier's chief secretary. The session was intended to counter the reprimand's impact by assurances the sultan desired friendship with Russia.

In response to instructions from St. Petersburg Obrezkov on September 2 had his interpreter tell the Porte's interpreter that rumors about the empress's marriage to Poniatowski after his election were "the basest kind of calumny." They were, moreover, direct insults, or better put, "blasphemies against her sacred person," not worthy of a response. She had full confidence that the Porte "would give no credence to such impious chatter."

There was no reason to fear Poniatowski would marry a foreign princess because Russia and Prussia had more incentive than the Porte to prevent Poland's dependency on a foreign power. Besides, there was a verified report that Poniatowski was betrothed to a prominent young Polish lady. Obrezkov told the [Turkish] chancellor the Sejm specified that if the new king were unmarried he could marry only a native Pole. "This is a total farce," the chancellor said with a laugh. "Say right out this means Poniatowski. Everyone knows already no one else will become king. I think he already has been chosen."

OBREZKOV SOOTHES TURKEY AFTER PONIATOWSKI'S ELECTION

French and Austrian maneuvers in Constantinople continued after Poniatowski's election with suggestions to the sultan that coercion had rendered it void. Were the Porte to refuse to recognize Stanisław as king the courts of Vienna and Versailles would do the same, and all Christian powers would follow their lead. The Porte was told that Russia and Prussia recommended Poniatowski and supported their choice with Russian troops, thus enabling the Russian party to dominate Poland.

These communications made a powerful impact. The chancellor was most upset when he received the Russian embassy's interpreter sent by Obrezkov. "A fine business," he began. "First the Russian and Prussian envoys [to Poland] recommended Poniatowski to the Sejm, then the Russian resident and the Prussian ambassador [in Constantinople] assured us orally and in writing that their courts had not presented a candidate. Your resident ruined me because I believed him and corroborated him, thereby making me responsible. Cursed be the moment I met him!

"When the Porte asked Russia if Poniatowski could be barred as a candidate for the Polish throne, Russia's response was that excluding anyone would violate promises of non-interference. If no individual can be barred, obviously none can be recommended, especially someone the Porte wants to veto. Is not the Porte justified in claiming this was done for spite and ridicule? Will not your enemies use this to your disadvantage? It is you who create and you who destroy!

"Let the resident submit a well-argued written answer to remove the manure which has cascaded on my head. I gave the resident a golden reputation, but he has turned his name and mine to mud. The Porte never will recognize the newly-elected king nor accept his documents. Deposing Poniatowski is the sole remedy, and unless the resident gives firm assurances that Russia will make every effort to do so, no further representations from him will be entertained."

The Porte decided in council that the Russian court's proposal of Poniatowski, supported by a large military force, totally contravened the Commonwealth's laws and Russia's solemn promises. To preserve its standing among the Christian powers the Porte must strive to dethrone Poniatowski, just as Austria and Russia had deposed Leszczynski after France installed him. Russia's haste in elevating Poniatowski to the throne meant it had some hidden and hostile agenda. If Russia made false promises to the Porte in such a public affair, what could be expected in its private bilateral negotiations? One possible response was construction of fortresses to be held by the Kabardians.[27]

Because such promises deserved no credence whatsoever, the Porte quickly must undertake necessary measures to protect itself from the Russian court's designs. When this decision was reported to the sultan he expressed a desire to do everything to depose Poniatowski. When the question whether the Porte might use force and if this would be beneficial was raised, an Islamic jurist and the clergy opposed it, and no decision was reached.

On September 2 the chancellor summoned Obrezkov and Rixen to complain about Russian and Prussian promotion of Poniatowski. The Turk *pressed* Obrezkov so hard (to use the exact words of the meeting's protocol) that he had to admit that either the Russian court did not honor its promises or that the Russian and Prussian ministers in Warsaw had exceeded their instructions. Agreeing to the former would be insulting to the Russian court. In the latter event the chancellor immediately would say that had the ministers acted contrary to the empress's will she would have no hesitation joining the Porte to depose Poniatowski.

In desperation Obrezkov answered that the three powers, Russia, Prussia and Turkey, had agreed a Piast would be elected freely as king of Poland with no one preferred and no one excluded. It was the Porte that took the first step by trying to veto Poniatowski, whom his fellow citizens favored. Russia and Prussia recommended the candidate the Poles wanted because a recommendation was the same thing as a veto. The chancellor was taken aback by this answer and at first did not know what to say. Upon reflection he replied that Branicki's candidacy was vetoed even earlier, whereupon Obrezkov showed there was no written or oral proof of this.

"Let bygones be bygones," the chancellor responded. "There is no point discussing the matter further although the Porte has legal grounds to complain that the Commonwealth elected as king the very man the Porte wanted to exclude." Obrezkov answered that the Poles were unaware of the Porte's desire to bar Poniatowski, and would not have believed it if they had known. Perhaps they would think that, given the Porte's well-known sense of justice, malicious suggestions by outsiders had prejudiced it against a man it scarcely knew. Here Obrezkov heaped praise on Poniatowski, concluding with the assurance the new Polish king would pay special respect to the Porte.

"The resident is a good officer," the chancellor said laughing, "who knows how to create a smokescreen. I do not know what decision his highness the sultan will make. I would like to know what the reaction of the Russian court would be were the vizier to send a letter to each Polish magnate inquiring about the present royal election. I wonder whether each would reply that it was free." "Poland is a sovereign power," Obrezkov replied. "Since the Porte has relations with it, you know what can be asked of the Poles, but I cannot venture how my court will regard this. This would be an unusual step, and the Poles might ask what right the Porte has to take it."

"The Porte hears from all sides," the chancellor said, "that the election was coerced and contrary to the majority will." Obrezkov responded that the Porte was inclined to listen to such reports and slanders from France and Austria, who had agreed to put the dauphin's brother the Saxon prince[28] on the Polish throne. Besides, Austria was angry that Russia distanced itself from their former alliance. Hence it was inciting Turkey against Russia with all its might to persuade the empress to renew the close alliance with the Viennese court. Here the chancellor told the Porte interpreter "Do you understand what I told you? Now you see that I am right." ("The chancellor is a shrewd fellow," Catherine wrote here on the report. "We should try to win him over.")

The Porte did not believe the news that the Russian empress would marry Poniatowski when he was crowned in Warsaw. It was disturbed by reports that major changes, particularly the abolition of the *liberum veto*, were planned in Poland. The chancellor asked Obrezkov and Rixen to have the Polish Commonwealth provide firm written assurance that no changes whatsoever would be made in the Polish constitution, especially the article on the *liberum veto*. The Prussian envoy wished to convey this request to his court, whereas Obrezkov thought it offended the Polish kingdom's dignity and brought no benefit to Russia. Hence he politely declined and persuaded Rixen to follow suit.

"This is further proof of Resident Obrezkov's political insight," Panin wrote on the report. "Such a declaration by Poland would enable the Turks to intervene in Poland. With solid guarantees from the Polish government they would share the role which Russia hitherto, albeit unwillingly, alone has played, one acknowledged by other powers."

DIPLOMATIC BLUNDERS IN THE CRIMEA

Kabarda's weak position in Asia, under the powerful influence of Russia and of the Crimean khan, echoed Poland's in Europe. In his efforts to control Kabarda the khan aroused its rulers' suspicions of Russian intentions, claiming he would protect them from impending disaster.

Simultaneously he complained about Kabarda to the Russian government, demanding satisfaction so as to incite Kabarda even more against Russia. The khan opposed Russia over Poland, sending hostile suggestions to Constantinople. Meanwhile he suggested to the [Russian] consul [Nikiforov] how powerful he was, and that Russia needed to respect him because he was in a position to help or harm it.

The College of Foreign Affairs ordered Nikiforov to rein in the khan. When the khan requested a falcon as a present, Nikiforov was directed to mention that the empress knew the khan was trying to weaken the friendship between Russia and Turkey instead of undertaking everything possible to strengthen it. He believed every slander against Russia and wanted the Porte to do the same. He was forfeiting great rewards by his behavior, and might expect Russian favors only by changing his ways completely.

Russia's first consul in Crimea was a failure. Nikiforov made such serious mistakes as urging the khan not to intervene in Polish affairs before the khan had raised the issue, thus suggesting that Russia needed the khan and was trying to ingratiate itself with him. He presented gifts directly in the name of the empress instead of that of the Kievan governor general and also was suspected of financial irregularities.

The consul's mishandling of a very delicate religious problem finally led to his recall. In October Nikiforov's fifteen-year-old serf, Mikhailo Avdeev, fled and became a Muslim. The consul and his men brought him back forcibly, claiming a violation of international law. The Tatars in turn demanded Avdeev's return since he now was a Muslim. "Although the consul came," one of the Tatar officials said, "our books and our law allow us to convert him to Islam."

When the consul's interpreter objected to this statement to the *kaimakam*, or khan's deputy, an Islamic jurist sitting there said "Even if your queen came here, we would convert her." Nikiforov's report of the affair earned him a strong reprimand from the College of Foreign Affairs. It called his action reckless and inexcusable because he should have known that renegades were as good as dead, and no one tried to have them returned. The Islamic jurist's insults to the empress were caused by the consul's carelessness.

FRANCE SUPPORTS THE SWEDISH CROWN AGAINST RUSSIA

On this occasion France exerted itself in vain in Turkey and left Poland to its fate, then made greater effort in Sweden, where it now changed its policy.[29] Hitherto France supported opponents of increased royal power, following the common wisdom that a weak monarchy enabled other powers to intervene in a country's affairs and exercise their own influence. Now France must decide between two courses of action. Was it better to spend large sums on its adherents and share influence in Sweden with Russia, or to strengthen royal power? The latter policy gave Russia an enemy close enough to be dangerous, one always ready to block unfriendly Russian moves against France.

The Polish example led to a quick French policy reversal in Sweden. "All Poles talk a good game," wrote the French envoy Paulmy to his court, "but few dare act, and when they do it turns out badly. Maintaining Polish liberty now entails defending an exposed location without a garrison, officers, military supplies, grain or fortifications." Versailles was unwilling to make these kinds of defense commitments in Sweden. "Owing to circumstances, France mistakenly promoted a weakened monarchy in Sweden," Choiseul's instructions to Breteuil[30] read. "This created an impotent government that existed only in theory. We wasted money on weak parties while Sweden steadily lost power and importance. Hence the king must be strengthened."

At the beginning of the year Ostermann[31] informed the empress that General Count Fersen[32] formed close ties with the French ambassador Baron Breteuil, who recently arrived in Stockholm. Fersen informed the queen[33] he was trying to persuade Breteuil to work with him in the next Riksdag to eradicate Sweden's endemic disorder. Breteuil promised to do so, and the Danish court also was inclined to cooperate. Hence the queen continued to be very friendly to Fersen, increased her favors to Breteuil and for the first time began to talk to the Danish envoy.

"It seems the Swedish queen is fated to be deceived by French ambassadors," Panin noted on Ostermann's report. "In my time the marquis d'Aurencourt promised he would everything he could for her before the Riksdag at which Count Brahe was beheaded. At a masquerade he inveigled her to tell him all her plans against the senators who were his creatures, then betrayed her to them.[34] Breteuil is much more furtive than d'Aurencourt."

Fersen confirmed that the French envoy was instructed not to follow the example of his predecessor d'Aurencourt, who had worked against the king and queen. "Apparently Breteuil has manipulated things very well," Panin wrote. "He has blamed the former envoy for everything that happened, and naturally the queen will be taken in. Her majesty does not recall that Breteuil was not sent to reconcile her with d'Aurencourt but to help the remaining French creatures in Sweden. As far as Count Fersen is concerned, he was the high priest who cut off Brahe's head when their Swedish majesties were defeated."

When Ostermann told reliable people that the queen's trust in Fersen and the French court was misplaced, they cited her firm assurances that she never agreed to join the French system. She had no trust in Fersen and even less in Senator Scheffer.[35] Because the French party was in power she must accept its favors. There was no other way to conduct business. This at least would provide protection, especially since neither the English nor the Russians told the queen exactly what form their aid might take. The French ambassador on the other hand promised a million livres for the next Riksdag, and if an extraordinary session were not held before the regularly-scheduled time, the French court would send another three million livres.

"This is all window dressing," Panin noted here. "It is further evidence of her majesty's dissimulation for the loyalists rather than a true expression of her sentiments. How can her demonstrated servility to the French party be reconciled with her haughty character and her obvious scorn for apparent danger when she has neither support nor any hope of it either at home or abroad?"

RUSSIA RESPONDS TO FRENCH INITIATIVES

Ostermann was instructed to maintain friendly relations with the court party and the loyal patriots and not provide any encouragement for convoking an extraordinary session of the Riksdag. As was their wont, the loyalists importuned Ostermann to specify exactly what form Russian aid would take so they could guard against sudden French initiatives and stay in the queen's favor. They promoted an extraordinary session of the Riksdag, claiming that otherwise arbitrary rule would become so entrenched that sooner or later it would lead to autocracy. If this did not occur during the king's lifetime, it would follow immediately upon his death.

"When the wise householder engages in commerce," Panin noted here, "he first determines the price based on his need, his resources and the benefit he expects to receive. This axiom goes for politics as well. It is in your majesty's [Catherine's] undisputed interest to act lest corruption totally discredit the Swedish government. It is impossible to determine your precise role because so far we have no idea what the outcome in Poland will be. The loyalists should not take decisive measures relying on hope alone unless absolutely necessary, for there is no indication Sweden is at this point yet."

Meanwhile Panin, who initially thought Breteuil was deceiving the queen, grew convinced the French envoy sought to establish autocracy in Sweden, which was the real French goal. "Breteuil's assurance he does not intend to intervene in domestic affairs is no cause for alarm," Panin wrote on Ostermann's March 19 report. "He will intervene at the Riksdag session, thus betraying the court party. The real fear is that after France employs all its defenders to reinforce the government against the king, Breteuil suddenly might make common cause with the court supporters of his own system. This would provide them an inconspicuous method of establishing autocracy, which is where the real present and future interest of France lies, if it really can attain it."

At the beginning of May Ostermann was instructed to try to prevent the king from falling into the French partisans' trap. At the same time he was to restrain the loyalists (Caps) from breaking with the court party prematurely. Ostermann responded that the court party assured him of the king's and queen's devotion to the empress, and that any dealings with the French partisans would be superficial at best. Because experience made the queen mistrust their enticements, she had total confidence in the empress's assurances, placing all her hopes in them no matter what the French party did to change her mind.

The loyal patriots viewed their only salvation to be the empress's protection and were grateful beyond measure for promises of Russian aid. They promised to follow the empress's magnanimous counsels, avoid the appearance of estrangement from the court party and solicit royal favor more actively.

At the beginning of June Ostermann reported that the queen expressed her special and unlimited loyalty to the empress and her ardent wish to merit her exalted friendship. Ostermann asked her to trust that the empress was favorably disposed towards her and the king, and put no credit in any overtures from the other side, concocted by those who envied Russia's good relations with Sweden. "You are right to speak of envy," the queen said here, "and I want you to believe that I give no credence to any overtures. As an indication of my devotion to the empress and my faith in you, I cannot conceal my grief at hearing the Danish and Viennese courts' hostile designs against the empress."

"I know nothing of these harmful designs," Ostermann answered. "I can assure your majesty that there is no danger, and that envy alone is the cause." "That is my hope also, said the queen, "but I feel close enough to you that I cannot hide my concern." Ostermann urged the queen not to believe anything she heard. Earlier she had told him how it pained her to learn of reports to the empress that she, the queen, disliked the empress whom she thought favorably disposed to the king but not to her.

RUSSIA PREPARES FOR AN EXTRAORDINARY SESSION OF THE RIKSDAG

On August 24 Ostermann described his conversation with the Prussian envoy Baron Cocceji,[36] who confirmed he had full authority from his sovereign to act in concert with the Russian minister. Cocceji told Ostermann that establishing autocratic rule in Sweden was contrary to Russian and Prussian interests, whereas restoring the king's rights and prerogatives at the next Riksdag session would benefit both courts. These included rights like those of the English king to declare war, conclude peace and make new commitments with foreign courts. Ostermann naïvely took this to mean Cocceji lacked instructions [from Berlin] on Swedish domestic affairs, relying instead on the court party's statements when discussing royal powers.

In the same report Ostermann described the decision to convoke an extraordinary session of the Riksdag. "All loyal patriots," Ostermann wrote, "expect great benefits from this decision if they receive the assistance your imperial majesty promised. If this early opportunity is missed, spending even twice as much later will not make up for it." The loyal patriots thought three hundred thousand rubles were needed, of which one hundred thousand should paid at once, with assignats to be redeemed over two years for the remainder.

The loyal senator Count Löwenhielm[37] told Ostermann he pressed the queen to observe strict neutrality in elections for the land marshal and other offices, but was unsuccessful. Löwenhielm noted that the queen trusted Count Fersen's advice and counted on his promise to obtain French funds for her use. On September 24 Ostermann reported an interesting conversation between Löwenhielm and the French ambassador Breteuil. Löwenhielm tried to convince the ambassador not to use bribery, which split the nation[38] into different factions, caused its entire woes and prevented it from benefiting the fatherland. If bribery persisted, the same evils could be expected, and the envoy would render his court more harm than good.

RUSSIAN AND ENGLISH BRIBERY IN SWEDEN

When Breteuil heard this he answered that he had no intention of following his predecessors' example, but that if his opponents used bribery naturally he must use the same weapons in self-defense. "Who are your opponents?"

Löwenhielm asked. "The English envoy Goodricke[39] and the Russian Ostermann," replied Breteuil. In fact Goodricke had offered Ostermann forty thousand pounds sterling for joint action.

Ostermann received fifty thousand rubles from Russia with these instructions. "It has been our long-standing and inalterable policy in Sweden consistently to safeguard the governmental liberties of 1720[40] and to oppose the introduction of autocracy. Therefore anyone whose sole aim is to restore the proper balance between the three [governmental] powers and to eliminate the disorder caused by arbitrary rule and a distorted theory of government, in our opinion is a loyal patriot.

"We will consider such restoration and the eradication of abuses complete if all senatorial interpretations and Riksdag decisions, especially acts promulgated by the 1756 parliament,[41] are nullified without exception. The proviso in the preamble specifying the basic form of government must be amended. At present it reads that 'at a general Riksdag state officials are accorded the right to interpret and amend the established form of government if this shall prove necessary.' The following wording should be substituted. 'If interpretation or amendment of the established form of government shall prove necessary, the state officials shall have the right to present a proposal at a general Riksdag to be promulgated to the entire nation. At the next Riksdag session deputies with the proper authority and instructions can approve the proposal, which only then will have the full force of law.'

"We enjoin you to render true and loyal patriots every possible assistance, money as well as counsel. You should try to form these patriots into an organized body, possible only if a single leader is chosen. Our choice is Count Löwenhielm since he is the wisest and most politically astute of the loyal patriots. Senator Count Horn, Colonel Rudbeck and State Secretary Duben should be his associates since they long have sympathized with our court.

"Tell them: (1) Our assistance is not meant for personal vendettas against members of the opposition party, nor is it to be used for the personal benefit of one or another of the loyal patriots, but solely for governmental reform and to bolster the entire loyalist party's standing with the people. Therefore they must not allow their friends to be enmeshed in private concerns. (2) They must make every effort to restrain the arrogance of the court party, especially its leader Colonel Sinclair.[42] At the same time they must avoid a total break with this party and try to convert it to loyalist views. (3) They must attempt to win over Senator Count Hepken and persuade him to return to the Senate. Meanwhile they should force Senator Scheffer to resign voluntarily. (4) They must try to place as many honest and capable people as possible on the Secret Committee.[43] (5) Thus they can exploit the Senate's own supporters' desire for independence from foreign powers. Further, they can begin to dismantle the French system by instructing their ministry to make no commitments to foreign courts, which could cost Sweden its neutrality should war break out in Europe."

Catherine wished to create her own independent party in Sweden or to revive the old Cap party. Such a party could oppose French influence while keeping the queen and the court party from trying to change the 1720 constitution. Of course the court party could not ignore this. At the end of October one of this party's leaders spoke with Ostermann, who concluded that its supporters wanted Russian and English money to go to the queen, who would form a single court party with the Caps totally dependent on it. This same member of the court party told Ostermann that a separate party, allied neither to the Senate nor the king, always would be impotent, citing the example of the 1747 Riksdag.

Ostermann assured him he had no intention of alienating the Caps from the court party. Since the unfortunate events at the Riksdag of 1747 were caused by French intrigues, he was inspired to urge the king and the queen to guard against them now. When their majesties' friendship with the empress led them to heed her counsel, there would be no separate party, and the alliance between Russia and Sweden would be strong enough to prevent any harm from French exertions.

Meanwhile one of the loyalists (this had to be Löwenhielm himself) told Ostermann about his conversation with the queen. Louisa Ulrika asked him to promote the reputations of Fersen and Sinclair among the people, claiming their intentions were honorable. The loyalist did not consent, responding that were he to follow her wishes she would gain nothing, and he would forfeit his own credit with the people.

At this point the loyalist begged the queen not to trust the French promises transmitted by Fersen and Sinclair, but rather the English and Russian assurances, which were more in accord with the national interest. "I still do not know," the queen answered, "what form Russian support will take. If, as I think, it means merely the restoration of the 1720 form of government, I see no great advantage in that. Naturally I favor those who promise me more."

A prominent leading member of the court party (Sinclair?) visited Ostermann on November 12. He said that at the next Riksdag session the king and queen would not introduce even the pettiest matter without first soliciting the empress's opinion from Ostermann. They would conform all their steps to her will. Ostermann responded with his set piece that above all their majesties should not believe suggestions from the French side, Count Fersen and his comrades. The guest swore that the king and queen did not believe the French party's statements and that, moreover, the court soon would break openly with it.

The delegate finally said that since the French side soon would begin to buy titles of nobility, their majesties would be thwarted unless they followed suit. Ostermann, realizing where the conversation was heading, replied that he hoped to receive instructions from the very highest authority very soon, without which he could make no response. As a sign of his concern for the welfare of the king and queen he gave the delegate twenty thousand daler (in copper coins), promising to provide the same amount at the beginning of the next week in concert with the English envoy. The money was designated to purchase titles. "The sum is quite insignificant," Panin noted on the report. "It was not bad to set the bait, but it is too soon to give more."

After the delegate received the Russian money he went to the English envoy Goodricke to ask how much the English had appropriated for their majesties' use and to request that it be paid. Goodricke demurred, saying that he could make no disbursements unless the Russian minister agreed, to whom the delegate should address himself. The delegate went to Ostermann to explain that no other measures were necessary if the empress intended to help the king financially. It would be sufficient if the two hundred thousand rubles requested were ready, for without them it would be improper for the king to become involved himself and urge others to act.

Ostermann answered that if the empress sent monetary assistance, naturally she must know how it would be spent lest it be wasted, as had happened on previous occasions. The English court was even more curious about the destination of the money. Its participation in Swedish affairs depended in large measure on early success in electing loyalists as land marshal and members of the Secret Committee. The delegate then said he would determine with three leading members of the loyalist party that same day the amount needed, then submit a request to Ostermann and the English envoy. He named the three members so Ostermann could ask them if he were telling the truth.

Since Ostermann saw the delegate was on the right path he gave him another four thousand instead of the fifteen thousand he had requested, and Goodricke promised to give the same amount. "There is an added benefit," Ostermann reported, "to this fine achievement. Their majesties are beginning to rely more on the assurances I have conveyed to them on your supreme authority and have deigned to show their great satisfaction with my conduct.

"The only remaining problem is that a court partisan and his accomplice Lord High Chamberlain Gyldenstolpe[44] have managed to acquire a standing with their majesties that no one can equal. His majesty expressed his heartfelt gratitude to your imperial majesty for the assistance promised and his great pleasure with me, your most humble servant. On this occasion he told me that should I have any communication for him I should address it to his majesty's faithful servant, Count Gyldenstolpe.

"His majesty's unexpected directive surprised me greatly. Your imperial majesty knows this individual, whom I used constantly as an intermediary since the beginning of my stay here. I am well aware of his devotion to your august court and to his majesty personally. I felt obliged to submit to the king's command, but also thought it absolutely necessary to employ someone else for this overture. Therefore I most respectfully requested his majesty's gracious permission to employ the same person I had previously.

"I explained that my devotion to his majesty, which always would be my guiding principle, meant I would employ Gyldenstolpe. The king's communications to your imperial highness formerly were conveyed to me by this person [Ostermann's previous intermediary] and naturally he would sense a lack of trust if Gyldenstolpe enjoyed your august confidence. This lack of trust would be completely undeserved since to my knowledge no one has been more devoted to his majesty.

"After listening graciously to my explanation, the king replied he had no reason to doubt this person's loyalty. He gave me permission to use him as before but said that Gyldenstolpe was a better intermediary since the other individual was involved with [state] affairs. I repeated my humble petition, taking the liberty to add that for greater secrecy his majesty might deign to consider employing this person since something might arise known to the king alone.

"His majesty graciously consented, and accepted my assurances of your highness's intention to cooperate to his satisfaction at the next Riksdag session. When your counsels are heeded, he will be pleased. He was certain of this, said the king, hoping that on occasion his advice would be followed as well. This was self-evident, I responded, since this was the only way the two sides could agree.

"Her majesty the queen was just as grateful, praising the distinguished member of the court party at length as a man of great skill and intellect, whereupon I added my compliments. Since well-known French supporters had learned about the matters under discussion, she asked whether I should continue treat them with civility at court receptions or break with them completely as recommended by some of the loyalists. I ventured that while I found such civility distasteful, there was good reason to accept it. It was enough that I had her majesty's word that she had no confidence in them."

Ostermann nonetheless was obliged to report, however, that the "member of the court party "so praised by the queen had proven false. He did begin consultations with the "Bonnets" (Caps) then quickly cut them off from Russian and English funds and began to insist on electing certain members of the French party to the Secret Committee. He would not consent to use some of the money for the Caps to pay the costs of poor deputies and began to avoid meetings with Cap members. The king was less open with him and began insisting that Count Fersen and the other leader of the French party, Baron Hermansson,[45] were loyal.[46]

RELATIONS WITH DENMARK

There was no cause for concern in Denmark. The Danish court endorsed Russian policy in Poland completely. At the end of June Korff[47] described a conversation with the minister of foreign affairs Baron Bernstorff,[48] who praised the actions of the Czartoryskis and Poniatowskis and expressed his amazement at Catherine's skillful handling of affairs. In her brief reign her far-reaching and salutary achievements at home and abroad were well-nigh incredible, a model for other courts. She succeeded in creating such harmony among the Poles at the electoral Sejm that they were emboldened to correct obvious defects in the Polish fundamental laws that for centuries they had not dared address, judging them impossible to rectify.

"Will not Poland be a danger to its neighbors," added Bernstorff, "when it achieves total harmony?" Korff praised his frankness, saying that since the phrase *total harmony* suggested how far Poland must journey before it became a danger to its neighbors, Bernstorff could rest easy. The empress was anxious to earn the title of peacemaker and was well aware that her interests were affected by the status of other powers. The primary focus of Polish legal reform was the Polish king's economic situation and civil law. The *liberum veto* hardly could be abolished, for it always could be used to block the king and the Commonwealth should their plans seem to threaten their neighbors.

KORFF PROPOSES NORTHERN SYSTEM

Baron Korff did not restrict himself in Copenhagen to Danish affairs. On February 25 he asked the empress's gracious permission to unveil a system he had been planning for more than two years. "Perhaps a prominent and powerful group of powers in the North should unite," the description ran, "to oppose the Bourbon alliance, now apparently augmented by the house of Austria. When the Viennese court continues as France's ally, England must abandon its previous role of maintaining equilibrium between them and will be forced to take sides. In this event its only recourse is to join the Northern powers, although this means reconciling a multitude of different interests! If there is merit in my suggestion, it offers your imperial majesty a great opportunity."

OBSTACLES TO THE NORTHERN SYSTEM

The proposed system was the famous "Northern Alliance, Northern Concert or [Northern] Accord" which so impressed Panin and which he espoused after Korff died. The difficulty in implementing the system lay in demonstrating its advantages to the other two suggested members, Prussia and England. Frederick II felt the bitter enmity of Austria and France and no longer was close to England. He sought refuge in a Russian alliance, realized thanks to events in Poland, and this for him was enough. Above all he wanted no part of any system with obligations to secondary powers he considered insignificant.

England as a *separate entity*[49] outside the common political life of the continent was even more opposed to any system which offered no immediate commercial benefit. It would impose obligations, including payments to various distant members, but offer no specific advantages the ministry could cite to parliament.

GROSS REPLACES VORONTSOV IN ENGLAND

We noted that Russia sought English financial help in Sweden and Poland.[50] Funds might be extracted with difficulty for Sweden because they would be used against the French enemy, but there was no soliciting England to throw pounds into a Poland of no concern to it and which already caused difficulties for the Russian ambassador in London, Count Alexander Vorontsov.[51] His failure to make headway with the current ministry inevitably led to Vorontsov's rapprochement with the opposition. The government's understandable displeasure raised the possibility of

Vorontsov's recall, a most agreeable prospect for Panin, who was no friend of the Vorontsovs.

On January 5 the English envoy the earl of Buckinghamshire[52] informed the vice chancellor [A.M. Golitsyn] there was no way his government could grant Russia a five-hundred-thousand-ruble subsidy for Poland. The London court might be pleased if Count Vorontsov were recalled since he, Buckinghamshire, had instructions to warn the Russian ministry against giving full credence to Vorontsov's incorrect reports on English domestic affairs. His ties with the party opposed to the court had been noted, and it could be said with assurance that its leaders were dictating his dispatches to him.

The vice chancellor replied that Vorontsov would be recalled at the pleasure of the English court, although his reports were an accurate reflection of the actual state of English affairs. There was no indication in them of ties with the party opposed to the court to the detriment of the current ministry. The obvious conclusion was that his links with the opposition leaders were no more than superficial courtesies.

Buckinghamshire then urged that treaties be concluded without delay. Golitsyn replied that the Russian side was anxious to complete an arrangement which benefited both powers, yet success was unlikely as long as the English ministry ignored Russian requests. It also took no interest in any of the continent's internal affairs, which might place the English crown in great danger. France was establishing a solid political system by increasing its naval forces in concert with Spain and strengthening its alliances with various courts, especially Vienna and Sardinia. Panin explained to Buckinghamshire that a treaty could not be negotiated unless England agreed to help Russia financially in Poland and Sweden. Although the Russian court had sent two million rubles to Poland, Russia's supporters wanted more because France was squandering huge sums there.

The famous Gross[53] was named Vorontsov's successor. In a meeting on February 3 Buckinghamshire claimed England would find him unacceptable because he was very committed to France. The vice chancellor replied that Gross was a man of proven loyalty, and that he had earned his court's praise and approval wherever he had been. During the last war,[54] like all Russian ministers, he was closer to the French than to the English envoys, but that was due to the former policy and not his personal conviction.

Buckinghamshire said nothing on this point but again complained of delays in concluding the treaties. He stated that his court preferred friendship with Russia, ignoring all other proposals, but must entertain them if the Russian side did not act. When Buckinghamshire on February 12 repeated his previous complaints about the slow pace of negotiations, Golitsyn ascribed the delay to a special commercial commission which was reviewing the question.

On March 1 Buckinghamshire said that his court intended to recall him because it reasoned that efforts to agree on alliance and commercial treaties had failed, the former Russian minister in London Count Vorontsov bearing the primary responsibility. A trade agreement benefited Russia more than England, which could manage without Russian products that could be replaced from its new American possessions.[55] The vice chancellor again blamed the failed negotiations on England, which neither agreed to Russian proposals nor provided the slightest opening to do so. The Russians remained convinced that trade was mutually advantageous, given that the English continued to reap the benefits of the old treaty after it expired.

PROPOSALS FOR ANGLO-RUSSIAN COOPERATION IN SWEDEN

Buckinghamshire's requests and Golitsyn's responses continued into autumn. On October 4 Buckinghamshire told the vice chancellor his court had instructed him to inform the Russian ministry of a report from the English minister in Stockholm, who was assigned to Sweden at the request of and for the benefit of the Russian court. In describing the present Swedish situation this minister said he needed forty thousand rubles at once to lay a solid foundation for Russian and English court policy in Sweden. This would reduce French influence markedly and shape the Swedish government at the Riksdag to conform with both courts' desires. He would need at least 120,000 rubles to complete this effort successfully. Hence, Buckinghamshire continued, the English court hoped the empress would be willing to provide half of this amount.

The vice chancellor replied that Swedish issues might persuade the Russian court to accept the English proposal, and that England might take them just as seriously. England should be concerned about reforming the Swedish government as well as destroying the dominant French party. In addition the Senate must be stripped of the royal power it had usurped, and equilibrium must be restored between the king and the Senate, both of whom were needed to declare war, conclude treaties and alliances, impose taxes and so on. England had, moreover, a special interest in thwarting the

French court's dangerous plan to conclude a naval treaty with Sweden, obligating it to give France ten warships in the event of war at sea. English subsidies to Sweden offered the only way to block this scheme.

TREATY NEGOTIATIONS WITH ENGLAND

Gross arrived in London on February 16 and three days later met with Lord Sandwich,[56] head of the Northern Department of the Foreign Ministry. Sandwich began by expressing the king's fervent wish that a commercial and alliance treaty between England and Russia finally be signed. The arrival of a new minister of acknowledged talent raised his hopes for success in the negotiations. Gross responded that English stubbornness was responsible for delay, the same thing Panin and Golitsyn customarily told Buckinghamshire in St. Petersburg.

Sandwich stated that England never could accept two points in the Russian project, one concerning Poland and the other Turkey. England's commercial interests prevented it from agreeing to assist Russia in the event of war with Turkey. Because the latest war had exhausted the treasury, subsidies for Poland also were impossible, for this would cause a general public outcry against the current ministry. England readily agreed to all the empress's other proposals.

A directive was sent to Lord Buckinghamshire to make every effort to negotiate the alliance and the commercial treaties. When he saw there was absolutely no hope of success, he could expect a letter of recall. When Gross asked whether a replacement would be sent if Buckinghamshire were recalled, Sandwich said a second-rank minister would be named. He added there was every indication the empress would succeed completely in Poland, where England's restraint deterred France from greater involvement in Polish affairs. "We have informed the English court about French troublemaking and intrigue in Poland," Panin wrote on the report. "It should be noted that English restraint here is a poor deterrent and is more likely to confirm French influence in the North."

England did not wish to deviate in the slightest from its *policy of restraint*. When Gross asked Sandwich about the instructions for Wroughton,[57] the English resident in Warsaw, Sandwich said Wroughton was directed to proceed in concert with the Russian ministers *to a certain point*. In conversations he was to mention that in the coming election for the Polish king his sovereign would be most agreeable to complete cooperation with the Russian empress's intentions, *if* liberty were respected.

This would be the English resident's policy. Gross pointed out the inconsistency in the last part. "Your imperial majesty can see for herself that no real assistance in Poland should be expected."

The signing of an alliance treaty between Russia and Prussia prompted Sandwich to speak to Gross in May. Were England invited to join the alliance, it would prefer to make a separate treaty with Russia since as a maritime power its commitments differed from those of the Prussian king. Gross's report suggested that Sandwich's words could be ascribed to envy of the Prussian king, "and to the unease the English are beginning to feel because as yet they do not have a definite system. Hitherto they did not want one, but when they become more aware of the new negotiations between the Bourbon houses[58] they will not haggle with us so much."

Panin was very pleased with Gross's report of June 1 describing his conversation with Sandwich the previous day, May 31. Gross asked whether the English ministry knew that negotiations between Spain, France and Austria were concluded. This meant Spain would adhere to the Treaty of Versailles[59] and the Viennese court to the Bourbon sovereigns' family treaty.[60] Sandwich said he had reason to believe such an agreement was made, adding that it made the English king more anxious to conclude an alliance treaty with Russia.

England was ready to accept all reasonable obligations if it could convince the nation they were mutually beneficial. The English side would not oppose a request that the Prussian king adhere to the treaty. Although the opposition party was spreading rumors of the ministry's displeasure with the treaty between Russia and Prussia, Lord Sandwich considered it a sound basis for the English ministry's commitments.

DIFFERENCES OVER POLAND AND SWEDEN

"I would be most offended, though," Sandwich added, "if Russia again proposed English involvement through subsidies in Polish affairs because the king's ministers cannot justify this before parliament." "This would be quite feasible," Gross remarked, "if it were made clear how England would suffer if France acquired influence in Poland at Russia's expense." "I know for a fact this argument will fail," Sandwich answered, "but I agree with you that Russia and England must be absolutely equal treaty partners, committed to money payments when land or naval assistance is impossible."

"A judicious and forceful policy could induce England to pay part of the Polish expenses," Panin noted on Gross's report. "Your imperial majesty herself has deigned to observe that prolonging the negotiations from our side has caused no harm and might produce great results in the future. Perhaps there will be a repetition of what your majesty saw when the Prussian king independently sought our main policy goal."

Gross's subsequent conversations with English ministers were similar to Buckinghamshire's with Panin and Prince Golitsyn in St. Petersburg. While the English ministers hoped for an alliance excluding the Turkish and Polish points, Gross replied these were absolutely essential. In July the English ministers began saying that if no alliance could be made with Russia, England must seek security through other alliances. "These are nowhere to be found," Panin wrote.

In September the English ministry stated that the king would modify his established policy of avoiding onerous military commitments on land to other powers. Because the English nation had an immediate interest in defeating such French plans as attempts to obtain warships from Sweden, it would not begrudge money for this important issue. Because Russia had an even greater interest and was the first to broach the topic it was only proper that Russia assume half the cost. "That is called negotiating like a real merchant,"[61] Panin noted.

FRANCE'S VIEW OF RUSSIA

Sandwich in strict confidence showed Gross two French documents acquired by the English government. The first was a letter from Breteuil, the French ambassador in Stockholm, to the duke of Praslin dated August 31, 1764. Bérenger the French *chargé d'affaires* in St. Petersburg, wrote that Catherine intended to establish a base in Finland the following year, a project Breteuil thought was meant to exert pressure on the Riksdag. "If," wrote Breteuil, "the Russian sovereign's plan is not thwarted, inevitably it will have disastrous consequences for Sweden. I am confident Swedish patriots will support me resolutely, yet the whole government is in such bad shape that any help they obtain will be inadequate.

"According to all reports from Russia discontent and opposition are increasing daily. Granted, they also say Catherine has redoubled her efforts and her vigilance, but tyrannical measures promote rather than suppress unrest. In a servile country great enterprises are not based on a reasoned consensus, something the general myopia and suspicion prevents. I speak from experience, since I personally saw how quickly sluggish and timid hearts and minds were inflamed to attempt the most dangerous exploits.

"Some who hope for a better future feel the hour has come to act quickly and decisively, and money soon would convince the soldiers as well. I see from Bérenger's letters that people whom I know deserve notice have approached him, promising their loyalty if they are protected in the event of failure and are given monetary assistance now. Undoubtedly he has sent you a report on the situation, and I can vouch that he responded to the proposals circumspectly to maintain the enthusiasm of his petitioners.

"I am certain he is more than competent to bring them along prudently, if you give him the assignment and when the king is willing to spend five or six thousand livres to try to overthrow Catherine and all her grandiose plans. He [Bérenger] is young, extremely zealous and honorable to a fault. I also think a capable *chargé d'affaires* is more suited for this kind of task than a minister or an ambassador. May I also say that, whatever the project's outcome, no one could hate France more than the haughty empress does."

When Bérenger sent Praslin the same information he received the following reply. "We found your assessment of the manifesto announcing Prince Ivan's death[62] quite astute. I would add only that the Russian empress should have kept the news out of official publications or announced it more discreetly. You are right to proceed very cautiously. You should concentrate on probing the nation's sentiments and intentions. Further, you are are to encourage those who have confided their secrets in you, but only to keep us informed, not venturing any advice in such a delicate matter.

"It is not surprising that the Prussian king and the Russian empress sometimes do not see eye to eye. Both are ambitious in the extreme and often have contradictory political views and interests. Their alliance is fundamentally unsound because it was based on passing circumstances rather than on a system both sides planned carefully. Perhaps they will fall to quarrelling over Poland. I will receive Odard[63] when he appears, although the manner in which he left Russia and the paltry benefit he derived from the great opportunities he had do him little credit. I doubt his majesty will be inclined to grant him a title which might be considered a reward for service. He never performed the service we expected nor accomplished anything for us."

This was England's revenge on Russia. Since Russia continually frightened England with the prospect of increased French power, England passed on information that the French government was sponsoring forces opposed to the empress and Russia itself, though subsequent negotiations between England and Russia were not affected.

DIFFICULT TREATY NEGOTIATIONS WITH ENGLAND

At the end of December Gross handed Sandwich the draft of a commercial treaty, complaining of Buckinghamshire's unwillingness to entertain the proposal. Sandwich replied that the imperial court already had the satisfaction of having Buckinghamshire recalled (Sandwich personally had a low opinion of Buckinghamshire's talent). He hoped that Buckinghamshire's successor Macartney[64] would be more successful.

When discussing the commercial treaty Sandwich asked if Gross had received instructions regarding the defensive alliance. Gross responded by asking whether the English court really wanted close ties with Russia. "There is nothing we desire more and nothing more compatible with our interests," answered Sandwich. "Then it is all the more surprising," said Gross, "that the earl of Buckinghamshire always insisted just on renewing the old alliance treaty. This was concluded to promote Austria's interests, but European relations now have changed completely.

"The empress hopes that when negotiations are resumed the English court clearly and unreservedly will express its wish to be her ally, thus doing its part to strengthen European equilibrium. This is why the draft of a defensive treaty submitted to you last year included two secret paragraphs dealing with Poland and Sweden. These are connected with the Northern System, which envisions an alliance between the Northern powers to create a stable counterweight in Europe to the Bourbon and Austrian houses."

After listening with satisfaction Sandwich asked "Can we expect to see the Prussian king a part of this system, since we fear his ambitious plans?" "I have no special instructions concerning the Prussian king," replied Gross. "Naturally his Britannic majesty will be very pleased with this proposal," Sandwich remarked, "but how will the problems with the previous draft be resolved?" When Gross said that Russia wanted five hundred thousand rubles from England as partial compensation for Russia's expenditures in the Polish royal election, Sandwich stressed that he dared not propose this to the royal cabinet since he knew its members' views. The treasury, moreover, was empty. He did favor a proposal that Russia receive five hundred thousand rubles if it went to war with Turkey, while England would get the same amount from Russia for a war with Spain.

A few days later Sandwich told Gross that the secret paragraph for a subsidy of five hundred thousand rubles for a Turkish war was unacceptable because the ministry would have to inform parliament, which must appropriate the funds. In this event the Porte and France would learn about the funds, to the detriment of English trade in the Levant. In addition, there was little chance of war with Spain. ("A merchant's excuse!" Panin noted here. "Nothing need be disclosed until the issue is raised. If it is, the nation will not rise up against the government over five hundred thousand rubles. They are haggling like shop clerks when it is time to win as much as possible.")

It would be much better, Sandwich continued, merely to renew the former treaty, inserting a general paragraph guaranteeing the favorable outcome of the Polish royal election and preserving the Polish Commonwealth's liberties and government structure. ("Even more petty haggling," Panin commented. "When we really needed them [the English] in Poland they begged off, instead claiming an interest in Sweden. Now they are saying just the opposite.")

"I cannot pretend that simply renewing the former treaty is desirable," Gross responded with amazement, "because circumstances have changed completely. When it was signed the Viennese court was Russia's principal ally, England assuming defense responsibilities to strengthen the bond. Now the empress desires a direct link with England to aid Russia against the Porte financially just as Maria Theresa was obligated to send military forces.

"We are proposing comparable assistance against Spain. This is more than sufficient since we have no quarrel with the Turks, who have made no move against us in eight years.[65] The Spanish king's[66] character, conflicting interests and the family treaty between France and Spain make war between England and Spain a much more likely prospect now. England may ignore all these considerations and decide to exclude the eventuality either of a Spanish or a Turkish war. In that case I must insist on payment of five hundred thousand rubles for expenses, as contained in my first proposal."

Sandwich objected that if the royal cabinet would not promise to pay some of the Polish expenses before the royal election, it would be less willing after its successful conclusion. He ended by saying that England did not like the treaty's eight-year term, and the nation and parliament would find it strange were the present alliance treaty to offer Russia more advantages than previously.

("The Russian empire would find it just as bizarre," Panin noted here, "if its concern for the general welfare and the sovereign's glory did not inspire the Russian court to negotiate the most beneficial treaties possible. Finally, the English, believing war unlikely, want to take advantage of the current situation. They are exploiting our problems to achieve what would be impossible were our situation equal. We must instead stand fast and be patient, for England's immediate need for our alliance may bring us success.")

Although England objected to the short duration of the new alliance treaty, Panin justified this decision in a November 12 letter to Gross. "It is apparent," he wrote, "that the general state of affairs does not remain constant, and that unusual and unexpected events occur frequently. These cause utterly unforeseen changes in the interests, policies and actions of great powers which ordinarily severely damage their entire system when they do not destroy it completely. This is why an eight-year term is proposed, during which ordinarily there will be changes as events unfold.

"Hence her imperial majesty, considering all her present and future allies and not just the English court, is pleased to limit her obligations to eight years. She is not hoping this short term means an occasion for furnishing assistance will not arise. Her intent rather is to provide it when required more eagerly and zealously than would be possible under other circumstances. She would have complete freedom to determine and to fulfill her responsibilities, thus rendering great service to her allies."

Panin reassured Gross concerning reports about the intrigues of Breteuil and Bérenger. "To put your mind at ease," he wrote, "I must tell you that we have nothing to fear from these scoundrels' deeds or plans. Wait instead for them to violate the law openly and thus trip themselves up. Bérenger is a fanatic for political details, while Breteuil is a clever and daring fop, who now realizes the extraordinary Riksdag session and the disorder in Sweden are threatening his future political career, so this reckless young man apparently planned to stir up some trouble in Russia to keep us occupied. He used Bérenger's personal loyalty and his own flair for petty politics to excite the French court's interest, in turn leading Breteuil to exaggerate his private delusions."

PROBLEMS ON THE CHINESE BORDER

Russia's vast size meant that the government must negotiate an alliance with a neighboring power in Western Europe while simultaneously taking precautionary measures on the Chinese border. In July Lieutenant General Springer[67] reported from the Ust-Kamengorsk fortress that reconnaissance found a large Chinese force at the frontier. As a result Villebois,[68] Panin, Count Zakhar Chernyshev, Count Ernst [von] Münnich,[69] Prince Alexander

Golitsyn, Weymarn and Olsufiev held a meeting and sent a report of its conclusions to the empress. "(1) Direct the Siberian governors and other authorities to improve the conditions in that remote region, prescribing the means for implementation. (2) Establish regulations for Chinese trade and customs. (3) Institute new defensive measures to protect the frontier against sudden attack. (4) As quickly and expeditiously as possible open negotiations with the Chinese to halt incursions, at least until there are enough weapons on hand to make Russian policy on the frontier credible."

The meeting proposed "(1) Siberia must be divided into two governments with governors stationed in Tobolsk and Irkutsk. At the same time hunting and trapping policies should be changed. This is a common way of life in this vast and sparsely settled region where much of the population is scattered in remote Northern districts. Under current policies these people are destitute, living almost like animals, facing certain ruin. The governors and other authorities must offer them incentives to persuade them to leave the arctic zone to settle in groups in the South. These colonists will benefit the frontier area and will derive far greater advantage from farming and other agricultural pursuits than from hunting and trapping, presently their only sustenance in the barren North.

"(2) The Chinese have transferred their trade from Kiakhta to Urga to force Russian merchants to go to a Chinese city, although they have backed down somewhat and again are beginning to allow commerce by way of Kiakhta.[70] The meeting nevertheless has decided that establishing a special independent company might benefit Russian merchants. Not only might this prevent inflated prices, it also would be to the company's advantage to halt smuggling and the consequent loss of customs duties.

"Until such a company is founded the meeting considers it necessary (1) To open trade to every Russian merchant, as was the case previously. (2) That the merchants gather in Selenginsk to choose brokers instead of going directly to Kiakhta. These would exchange wares in Kiakhta at set prices, thus preventing the merchants from undercutting each other.

"Eleven regiments are needed to defend Siberia. Field artillery should be sent to Omsk and Selenginsk, and some major generals added to the command structure. A lieutenant general would reside in Omsk or wherever circumstances dictate, with one major general in the Petropavlovsk fortress, a second in Ust-Kamengorsk, a third in Biisk and a fourth in Selenginsk. The regiments would be stationed in units ready to repel the enemy, but not in forward positions."

NOTES

Additional information on personalities and topics found in the text and notes is available in George N. Rhyne and Joseph L. Wieczynski, eds., *The Modern Encyclopedia of Russian, Soviet and Eurasian History* (MERSH) and its *The Supplement;* Harry B. Weber and Peter Rollberg, eds., *The Modern Encyclopedia of East Slavic and Eurasian Literatures* (MEESEL); Paul D. Steeves, ed., *The Modern Encyclopedia of Religions in Russia and Eurasia* (MERRE), and David R. Jones, ed., *The Military Encyclopedia of Russia and Eurasia.*

CHAPTER I

1. Prince Stepan Mikhailovich Meshchersky (1698-1775) was commander-in-chief (glavnyi kommandir) of Kronstadt from 1762 to 1763. He later attained the rank of admiral.

2. Pavel Petrovich (Paul I) (1754-1801) was only eight years old but already a pawn in the political maneuvering of Catherine's first years on the throne. Nikita Panin was named Paul's tutor and guardian by Elizabeth in 1760. He planned and supervised an excellent educational curriculum for his charge and naturally saw his post as an opportunity to advance his own career. Separated from his mother at birth on Elizabeth's orders, Paul never felt close to her, while Catherine realized he could be a rallying point for her opponents. Here Catherine is using Paul to strengthen her still tenuous position by invoking the memory of Peter the Great, a tactic she repeated frequently throughout her reign. See Hugh Ragsdale, "Paul I (Pavel Petrovich) (1754-1801)," *Modern Encyclopedia of Russian and Soviet History* (hereafter MERSH), Vol. 27, pp. 64-73 and his *Paul I. A Reassessment of his Life and Reign* (Pittsburgh, 1979). Peter III (1728-1762) was the husband of Catherine II who ruled as emperor for seven months, during which his erratic personality and unpopular policies left him vulnerable to a coup engineered by her in June 1762, shortly after which he was murdered. Naturally he casts a long shadow over this early part of Catherine's reign. As Soloviev describes in these pages, Catherine removed many of his associates from power while carefully reassessing the position of others, all the while attempting to forge her own policies and validate her own questionable claim to the throne. See entry by Lindsey A.J. Hughes, MERSH, Vol. 27, pp. 238-244; R. Nisbet Bain, *Peter III, Emperor of Russia* (London, 1902); and Carol S. Leonard, *Reform and Regicide. The Reign of Peter III* (Bloomington, 1993).

3. Here Catherine is invoking the memory of Peter the Great's famous role as "the grandfather of the Russian navy" who conquered the Baltic coast and tried to reach the Black Sea, constructed new ports, recruited foreign seamen and naval experts, built and dispatched warships and set an example for future generations by going to sea himself whenever possible. See Donald A. Mitchell, A *History of*

Russian and Soviet Sea Power (New York, 1974) and L.G. Beskrovnyi, *Russkaia armiia i flot v XVIII veke* (The Russian Army and Fleet in the Eighteenth Century) (Moscow, 1958).

4. Mikhail Mikhailovich Golitsyn (1681-1764) began his military career in 1703 and served at sea in the Great Northern War (1700-1721). After holding various government posts he assumed supreme command of the navy in 1748. In this position, which he held until his retirement in 1763, he was unable to prevent the decline of Russian naval power caused by the neglect of the service by Peter the Great's successors, but did achieve some construction in St. Petersburg. He died in 1764. See entry in MERSH, Vol. 13, p. 3.

5. *S.-Peterburgskie vedomosti* (St. Petersburg News), 1763, No. 3. (Soloviev's note)

6. Alexander Ivanovich Shuvalov (1710-1771) increased his power and influence rapidly after joining the court of the future Empress Elizabeth. She rewarded his support in the 1741 coup which brought her to the throne with a number of important posts during her reign, that of lieutenant general in 1744 and adjutant general in 1750. Shuvalov directed various investigations as a member and then head of the Secret Chancellery. He was a member of Elizabeth's Conference and chief steward of the court of Grand Duke Peter and Grand Duchess Catherine, whose enmity he incurred for his support for Peter as heir to the throne. His influence reached a peak in 1758 when he discovered his old rival A.P. Bestuzhev had secret dealings with Catherine. He was named senator in 1760. After his accession Peter III heaped more honors on Shuvalov, naming him general field marshal in 1761. Although apparently he switched allegiance from Peter to Catherine as her 1762 coup unfolded, she quickly pushed him aside, as Soloviev describes here. It is unclear how he spent the years before he died in 1771.

7. *S.-Peterburgskie vedomosti*, 1763, No. 9. (Soloviev's note)

8. Ivan Ivanovich Shuvalov (1727-1797) came from a noble family which first achieved prominence under Peter the Great. He received an excellent education in languages and European culture and, thanks in part to family support for Elizabeth's coup in 1741, quickly became a favorite of the new empress. Here he had a hand in every area of policy, particularly in foreign affairs, where he was instrumental in cementing the Franco-Russian alliance at the time of the Seven Years War. Shuvalov was most noted for his promotion of learning and the arts, supporting Lomonosov, overseeing the establishment of the Academy of Fine Arts, sponsoring the publication of Voltaire's life of Peter the Great, and, above all, planning and assisting the new Moscow University. Although Catherine cleared him of the charges of financial wrongdoing in connection with the university described here, his key position in Elizabeth's court drew him into the bitter rivalries of her last years, compromising him in Catherine's eyes. As a result he left Russia in April 1763 for travels in Western Europe, returning in 1777. Catherine's hostility cooled in the meantime, and he spent his remaining years as a respected elder statesman and patron of the arts. See entry by John T. Alexander, MERSH, Vol. 53, pp. 34-43.

9. Elizabeth (1709-1762) was empress of Russia from 1741 until 1762. As Soloviev describes in this volume, Catherine's initial policies were shaped in the context of Elizabeth's legacy. Catherine quickly replaced many of the leading figures of Elizabeth's time while continuing to promote many of her predecessor's interests, for example, Elizabeth's energetic support of arts and culture. Catherine also followed Elizabeth's lead in fostering economic development, carrying out a general census and attempting to reform the judiciary. Elizabeth initially restored the Senate to the leading position it had under Peter I, but later weakened it in favor of a Conference in 1756. Catherine strengthened the Senate again, restructuring it in hopes of improving government effectiveness. In other areas Catherine soon changed course. Elizabeth, personally devoted to the church, gave the Holy Synod control over the lands taken from the church in 1726, although these were put under lay administration in 1756, and encouraged aggressive evangelization of non-Orthodox in the East and North. Catherine, who in the words of one observer, "plays a pious role," brooked no opposition in establishing complete state control over the church and its holdings and tried to placate religious dissenters of all kinds, including Old Believers, with the general welfare of the state as her overriding goal. Another legacy from Elizabeth was the imprisoned Ivan VI (see below, Chapter II, Note 30) who became the unwitting focus of the Mirovich conspiracy. While Elizabeth restored the hetmanate in the Ukraine in 1750, Catherine moved quickly to replace it with direct government control in 1764. Both episodes are described in this volume. Catherine also had to deal with the chaotic international aftermath of the Seven Years War. Elizabeth was the main inspiration for the alliance with France and Austria against Frederick II of Prussia and England, only to have Russia's sacrifices go for naught when Peter III switched sides after her death in 1762. Soloviev describes how Catherine cautiously tried to put together a new foreign policy in concert with Russia's former enemies. Catherine also took a more active role in Polish affairs and against the Ottoman Empire. See entry by George E. Munro, MERSH, Vol. 10, pp. 178-185; R. Nisbet Bain, *The Daughter of Peter the Great* (London, 1899); and Tamara Talbot Rice, *Elizabeth, Empress of Russia* (New York, 1970). More recent is Evgeny V. Anisimov, *Empress Elizabeth. Her Reign and Her Russia, 1741-1761* (Gulf Breeze, Fla.: Academic International Press, 1995), an illuminating study. Consult as well the earlier volumes of this series.

10. Nikita Ivanovich Panin (1718-1783) won a powerful position under Elizabeth for his skillful handling of Russian interests at the courts of Denmark (1747-1748) and Sweden (1748-1760). Rewarded in 1760 with responsibility for education and upbringing of the future Paul I, he threw his weight on Catherine's side in the struggle between her supporters and those of Peter III. Thereafter he played a key role in Catherine's reign in such areas as administrative reforms, secularization of church lands, commercial development and, above all, foreign affairs. Panin was the architect of the so-called "Northern System," under which Russia abandoned its old ally Austria in favor of cooperation between Russia, Prussia, England and Denmark as "active" powers. They were to be supported by Sweden,

Saxony and Poland as "passive" powers. The Northern System's failure was the major reason for Panin's fall from power in 1781. Catherine also suspected him of partiality to Grand Duke Paul. See entry by David L. Ransel, MERSH, Vol. 26, pp. 215-18 and his *The Politics of Catherinian Russia. The Panin Party* (New Haven, 1975). Also see David M. Griffiths, "The Rise and Fall of the Northern System. Court Politics in the First Half of Catherine II's Reign," *Canadian Slavic Studies,* IV (1970), pp. 547-569.

11. Alexis Petrovich Bestuzhev-Riumin (1693-1766) combined brilliance, ambition, and a penchant for intrigue in an extraordinary career which spanned more than five decades, bringing him to the heights of power but also subjecting him to two separate death sentences, both later commuted. At this time Catherine frequently consulted him after raising him from his disgrace in the last years of Elizabeth's reign and under Peter III. He was in favor for most of Elizabeth's tenure, which allowed him to shape Russia's anglophile policy. He wanted to keep an important role under Catherine, but she soon bypassed him in favor of Bestuzhev's protégé, Nikita Panin. See entry by Munro, MERSH, Vol. 4, pp. 94-96.

12. Vasily Yevdokimovich Adadurov (1709-1780) after an outstanding student career worked as a translator and taught at the Academy of Sciences. In 1744 he became the Russian language tutor for the future Catherine II. Upon her accession she named him curator of Moscow University and president of the College of Manufactures. In 1764 he was made a senator. He worked on legislation regulating the governance of Russian universities and actively recruited Russians and foreigners for university positions. See entry in MERSH, Vol. 1, p. 26.

13. Ivan Shuvalov played a major role preparing for the formal approval of the university charter by Elizabeth on January 12, 1755 and was named by her as one of the two curators of the university, holding this position until his death in 1797. Shuvalov's defense of his stewardship as reported by Soloviev here emphasizes the unusual degree of autonomy the university was granted. It was independent of all state bodies except the Governing Senate, and professors had special tax exemptions and legal privileges. Most importantly it was governed by an appointed director and two curators who reported directly to the empress. The first director was A.A. Argamakov who, like Shuvalov, although in his case posthumously, became the target of complaints after the death of Shuvalov's protector, Elizabeth. Despite Shuvalov's claims, the number of students, especially from the nobility, remained relatively low in the university's early years. See entry by William L. Mathes, "Moscow University," MERSH, Vol. 23, pp. 121-26.

14. Sergei Pavlovich Yaguzhinsky (1731-1806) was the only surviving son of a statesman who rose from humble origins to prominence under Peter the Great. Although he attained the rank of lieutenant general by 1764 he was a dissolute wastrel who squandered his own and both his wives' fortunes, eventually being placed under a guardian. One wonders if, even with a receipt, the debt mentioned ever was collected.

15. Undoubtedly this is Mikhail Matveevich Kheraskov (1733-1807), a prominent writer who was associated with Moscow University since its founding in

1755. He was named one of its four curators in 1778, promoted Russian as the medium of instruction in place of Latin and German and was the first director of the university press. Kheraskov also edited various literary journals and wrote extensively in a number of genres. Perhaps his greatest achievement was to complete the first Russian epic, the *Rossiada* (1779), an account of Ivan IV's capture of Kazan. An active freemason, he cast many of his works as moral allegories with a strong didactic element. See entry by John M. Mohan, MERSH, Vol. 16, pp. 140-142 and Stephen Baehr's entry on him in Victor Terras, ed., *Handbook of Russian Literature* (New Haven, 1985), p. 222.

16. François-Marie Arouet, better known as Voltaire (1694-1778), had a profound impact upon Catherine, reflected in their voluminous correspondence, as well as on many educated Russians of her time. Such policies as the secularization of church lands Soloviev describes in this volume, the founding of the Free Economic Society or the partitions of Poland bear the stamp of Voltaire's call for moral and intellectual progress under the aegis of enlightened rulers and statesmen. See, for example "Vol'ter i vol'terianstvo v russkoi literature (Voltaire and Voltairianism in Russian Literature)," *Novyi entsiklopedicheskii slovar', Brokgauz-Efron* (New Brockhaus-Efron Encyclopedic Dictionary), Vol. 13, pp. 157-159, as well as the works on Catherine's era cited earlier.

17. Gavrila Romanovich Derzhavin (1743-1816) was the greatest poet of Catherine's age while also making his mark as a soldier and state official. Born to poor landowners in the Kazan government, he appears in Soloviev's account here as a soldier in the Preobrazhenksy Guards Regiment, which he entered in 1762 after an indifferent early education. His early poetic efforts attracted favorable notice during his distinguished military career, from which he retired in 1777 with the rank of lieutenant colonel and the grant of an estate. Derzhavin's skillful blending of classical and popular elements in the unsettled Russian language of his day won him even wider acclaim in the latter part of the century, and the empress herself became one of his greatest admirers. He served as governor of the Olonets and Tambov governments and briefly as minister of justice under Alexander I. Although at the end of his life he was a member of Admiral Shishkov's conservative literary circle, he acknowledged the young Pushkin's genius after hearing him declaim at the Tsarskoe Selo Lycée. See entry by Frank R. Silbajoris in Terras, *Handbook of Russian Literature*, pp. 98-100; and Pierre R. Hart, *G.R. Derzhavin. A Poet's Progress* (Columbus, 1978).

18. By this time freemasonry was well established in Russia. It attracted some support when it first arrived from England, probably about 1731, although its real flowering came in Catherine's reign. A large number of prominent court and literary figures were active freemasons until the final suppression of the movement in 1822. Like freemasons elsewhere, Russian lodges, which always included a large number of foreign members, promoted moral regeneration through brotherhood, the search for truth and promotion of education and learning. Russian freemasonry was more tolerant, less mystical and more imbued with Christian elements than its counterparts in Western Europe, especially France. Needless to

say it did not constitute the political and criminal threat that Derzhavin's aunt feared. See entry by James F. Clarke, "Freemasonry in Russia," MERSH, Vol. 12, pp. 14-18, Stephen Baehr's, "Freemasonry" in Terras, *Handbook of Russian Literature*, pp. 156-57, and his "The Masonic Component in Eighteenth Century Russian Literature," A.G. Cross, ed., *Russian Literature in the Age of Catherine the Great* (Oxford, 1976), pp. 121-40.

19. *Sochineniia Derzhavina* (Derzhavin's Collected Works), Vol. VI, p. 437. (Soloviev's note)

20. Nikita Yurievich Trubetskoy (1699-1767) played a prominent role in state affairs from the reign of Peter the Great on, beginning with military service in the 1720s and 1730s. He served as procurator general under Anna and was an early supporter of Elizabeth's coup in 1741. He continued as procurator general with a considerably expanded area of responsibility and a princely salary of three thousand rubles per year under Elizabeth. He carried out many other official commissions for her, including helping coordinate Russian foreign policy during the Seven Years War. A sign of her favor was his elevation to the rank of general field marshal in 1756. His talent for political maneuvering, which made him the frequent target of other courtiers, is demonstrated by the success with which he first quickly rose to high position under Peter III, then rallied to Catherine's cause in the middle of her coup. After he served as marshal for Catherine's coronation in Moscow in September 1762 she rewarded him lavishly upon his voluntary retirement, as Soloviev describes here. He died on October 17, 1767. See entry by Alexander, MERSH, Vol. 40, pp. 1-5.

21. Feofan Prokopovich (1681-1736) was born in Kiev and after completing theological studies with distinction at the Kievan Academy did equally well at the Jesuit-run Greek College of St. Athanasius in Rome. As a teacher and later rector at the Kiev Mohyla Academy from 1705 to 1716 he demonstrated his grasp of philosophy, theology, rhetoric and literature. He was well versed in Latin, Italian and Polish; he knew scholastic philosophy and baroque literature, and he could cite scriptural, patristic and Byzantine sources. He came to Peter I's attention as a brilliant and eloquent supporter both of Peter personally and of monarchical power in general, and the emperor summoned him to St. Petersburg in 1716. Prokopovich drafted the *Spiritual Regulation* which formally abolished the patriarchate and became the dominant figure on the Holy Synod which replaced it as the governing body of the church. He was keenly interested in the arts and literature and, in addition to his elegant and forceful speeches and sermons, wrote poetry and drama. He died in 1736. See entry by James Cracraft, MERSH, Vol. 11, pp. 103-05 and his longer article on Prokopovich in J.G. Garrard (ed.), *The Eighteenth Century in Russia* (Oxford, 1973), pp. 75-105.

22. Antiokh Dmitrievich Cantemir (or Kantemir) (1709-1744) was the son of a hospodar, or governor, of Moldavia who took refuge in Russia in 1711. He enthusiastically supported Peter the Great's westernization and, as Soloviev mentions here, was an associate of Feofan Prokopovich. He drew on his wide knowledge of Western European thought in a series of satires against the Russian

backwardness of his era. He translated Latin and French authors with extensive philological commentary and further developed traditional Russian syllabic versification. Kantemir also served as Russian ambassador to France and England. See entry by I.R. Titunik in Terras, *Handbook of Russian Literature*, pp. 214-215.

23. Mikhail Larionovich (or Ilarionovich) Vorontsov (1714-1767) was the son of a Rostov nobleman who rose in rank under Peter I. Attached as a teenager to the court of Grand Duchess Elizabeth in 1728, he was handsomely rewarded by her for his key role in the coup that brought her to power in 1741. His brothers, Roman and Ivan, also had great power under Elizabeth. As vice chancellor, second only to Chancellor A.P. Bestuzhev in the conduct of foreign affairs, he narrowly escaped disgrace in 1748 when Bestuzhev exposed the intrigues of Vorontsov's French associates. He replaced Bestuzhev as chancellor in 1758 and wielded broad influence during the early part of the Seven Years War in domestic as well as foreign policy. His position became weaker after the accession of Peter III in 1762, and he fell definitively from power after Catherine's coup because he opposed her openly. She let him keep the title of chancellor, although without duties, and he travelled extensively abroad until his death in 1767. See entry by Ransel, MERSH, Vol. 43, pp. 48-50 and his *The Politics of Catherinian Russia. The Panin Party* (Yale, 1975).

24. Baron Bernhard Wilhelm von Goltz was sent by Frederick II to represent Prussia in St. Petersburg just after Peter III announced in February 1762 that he intended to withdraw from the Seven Years War and return all Prussian territory Russia had taken. Peter's favoritism toward Prussia was so pronounced that Goltz actually drafted the treaty signed between the two powers on April 24/May 5, 1762. After Catherine seized power in June 1762 Count Victor Friedrich Solms replaced Goltz as Prussia's envoy.

25. Dmitry Vasilievich Volkov (1718-1785) came from obscure origins to the College of Foreign Affairs where he became a client of A.P. Bestuzhev in the 1740s. He played a key role coordinating policy during the Seven Years War and continued in power under Mikhail Vorontsov, Bestuzhev's successor as chancellor. His role was even greater under Peter III, when he was instrumental in drafting measures for the secularization of church lands which Soloviev describes in this volume, and in ending compulsory service for the nobility. He took special interest in removing restrictions on grain exports. Although he was arrested at the time of Catherine's coup and she never completely trusted him thereafter, she did give him a number of assignments, for example, as vice governor of Orenburg province, as president of the College of Manufactures and helping devise new taxes to finance the Turkish War of 1768-1774. He had a key role in combatting the Moscow plague epidemic of 1770-1771. Volkov held other government posts before retiring in 1782. He died in 1785. See entry by Alexander, MERSH, Vol. 43, pp. 9-14.

26. The Stroganovs, originally of peasant stock, became established in the Urals in the sixteenth century, with immense holdings in agricultural land, salt works, fishing, hunting and mining. They raised military detachments, founded

towns and spearheaded the conquest of Siberia. In the eighteenth century the Stroganovs took the lead in developing mines, smelters and foundries in the area. The family acquired noble status early in the eighteenth century, and a number made their mark in government service and as patrons of arts and culture. See entry by V.I. Buganov, "Stroganov Family," MERSH, Vol. 37, pp. 224-226 and Roger Portal, *L'Oural au XVIIIe siècle* (The Urals in the Eighteenth century) (Paris, 1950).

Alexander Sergeevich Stroganov (1733-1811) was the son of a leading figure in the court of Elizabeth, who sent young Alexander abroad to study Western art, culture and technology, which he continued to pursue and promote after his return to Russia in 1757. In 1757 he married Anna Mikhailovna Vorontsova, as described by Soloviev here. A major factor in their marital discord was her family's support for Peter III, while he was an early partisan of Catherine II. They separated in 1765, and she died in 1769 in the midst of divorce proceedings. He continued to take an active part in court life under Catherine but avoided politics and court rivalries, winning instead general acclaim by his lavish hospitality and his promotion of painting, belles lettres and education. He enjoyed the favor of Paul I and Alexander I and concluded his life in a fitting manner by supervising the construction of the Kazan cathedral, which was consecrated just before his death on September 15, 1811. His son, Pavel Alexandrovich Stroganov (1772-1817), was a trusted advisor of Alexander I and a member of his Unofficial Committee. See entry by Elmo E. Roach, MERSH, Vol. 37, pp. 217-219.

27. *Sbornik Russkogo istoricheskogo obshchestva* (Collection of the Russian Historical Society [hereafter SRIO]), Vol. 48, p. 580. (Soviet editor's note). See also Appendix III, which is a good example of the diplomatic minutiae which landed on Catherine's desk.

28. Zakhar Grigorievich Chernyshev (1722-1784) was the son of a prominent statesman under Peter the Great. He entered service in his teens, was posted to Vienna, then was assigned by Elizabeth to the court of the then Grand Duke Peter and Grand Duchess Catherine. He represented Peter at the Imperial Diet in Frankfurt on behalf of Holstein-Gottorp from 1745 to 1748. Out of favor from 1748 to 1750, he had a brilliant military career in the Seven Years War, commanding the Russian forces that captured Berlin in 1760. He continued to distinguish himself through the rest of Elizabeth's reign and under Peter III, who gave him command of Russian forces in Prussia at the end of the Seven Years War. After the temporary setback at the outset of Catherine's reign Soloviev describes here, Chernyshev went on to hold a variety of important positions. As vice president of the War College he supervised military reforms and wielded enormous power during the Turkish war of 1768-1774. He left the War College in protest against Grigory Potemkin's growing influence there, serving until 1782 as the first Russian governor for territories acquired from Poland in the First Partition, and finally as governor general of Moscow from 1782 until shortly before his death in 1784. See entry by Victor Kamendrowsky and David M. Griffiths, MERSH, Vol. 7, pp. 21-22.

29. SRIO, Vol. 7, pp. 336-38. It could be added that Chernyshev fell out of favor over the Khitrovo affair, which led to his retirement. (Soloviev's note) The Swedish papers for 1768 contain a translation of notes made by the Swedish ambassador to St. Petersburg Düben. "Generals Count Zakhar Chernyshov [sic], Rumiantsev and Panin were very insulted to learn that the youngest general, Prince Volkonsky, was named commander-in-chief of the corps assigned to Poland. That is why Chernyshov asked to be retired. His request was approved and his retirement promulgated in an order he found very insulting. He found himself in great difficulty and immediately made every effort to be taken back into service. After great exertions the Counts Orlov finally obtained this for him." (Soloviev's supplementary note)

30. Peter Alexandrovich Rumiantsev (1725-1796) was a military commander who administered Catherine's reforms in the Ukraine in the 1760s, served in the war against Turkey, and helped prepare the annexation of the Crimea in 1763. See entry by Alexander, MERSH, Vol. 32, pp. 15-19.

31. See Appendix IV.

32. Gottlieb Heinrich Todtleben (1710-1773) was born in Saxony. He entered Russian service under Elizabeth and fought in the Seven Years War. He was court-martialed for retreating as Frederick II approached his forces at Berlin, stripped of his rank, and exiled. His distinguished service in the Turkish war of 1768-1774 earned him a pardon.

33. Afanasy Romanovich Davydov (died 1763) was governor of Orenburg from 1760 to 1763.

34. SRIO, Vol. 7, pp. 278, 279. (Soviet editor's note)

35. Andrei Gudovich (1731-1808) was Peter III's adjutant general.

36. See Vol. 42 of this series, p. 135.

37. SRIO, Vol. 7, pp. 282, 283. (Soviet editor's note)

38. Andrei Gavrilovich Chernyshev (1720 or 1721-1797) entered service sometime after 1740. He attracted the favorable attention both of the future Peter III and then Grand Duchess Catherine, who found him a willing helper and an invaluable source of information. After being caught in what Empress Elizabeth considered a suspicious conversation with Catherine in 1746 Chernyshev was arrested, interrogated, kept under guard for two years, then sent to serve in the Orenburg garrison for fourteen years. Recalled by Peter III in 1762, he was promoted to adjutant general and stood by the emperor in Catherine's coup that June. Catherine nevertheless let him stay in service with a colonel's pay until he retired at his own request in 1763. As Soloviev mentions, he was given the rank of major general, also receiving a brigadier's pay of eight hundred rubles a year. Chernyshev returned to service in 1773 as commander-in-chief of the St. Petersburg fortress, rising to general-in-chief in 1796. He retired definitively in January 1797 and died the next month.

39. See Volume 40 of this series.

40. SRIO, Vol. 7, p. 298. (Soviet editor's note)

41. What Soloviev calls the "old system" emerged with the ascendancy of Betuzhev under Empress Elizabeth, its cornerstone opposition to Prussia. Although

Russia took the lead in forging the alliance which isolated Frederick II during the 1750s its allies, France and Austria, played a stronger role in the Seven Years War (1756-1763). Peter III abruptly switched sides upon his accession in 1761, enabling Frederick to outlast his opponents. By the Peace of Hubertusburg signed on February 15, 1763 between Austria, Prussia and Saxony, Prussia retained Silesia and evacuated the kingdom of Saxony. The "old system" failed in its main objective and Russia's position in the eyes of its erstwhile allies was compromised seriously. No wonder Panin believed an entirely new approach to foreign policy was needed.

42. Friedrich Christian (1722-1763) became elector of Saxony when his father August III died on October 5, 1763, but died himself on December 17, 1763. His son Friedrich August (1750-1827) succeeded him as elector of Saxony. As Soloviev describes here, there was some talk of promoting one of Friedrich Christian's brothers, Karl (1733-1796), just deposed as duke of Courland, or Xavier, as candidates for the Polish crown. Prince Franz-Xavier of Saxony (1730-1806) was the second son of August II. He had a distinguished military career in the Seven Years War. His sister, Maria Josepha, was married to Louis, the dauphin of France, who died nine years before his father, Louis XV. As administrator for Friedrich August, Xavier worked energetically to restore his devastated land. His strenuous efforts to acquire his father's other title of king of Poland were unsuccessful. He clashed with Friedrich August's mother and resigned as administrator just before his nephew came of age in 1768. Thereafter he lived luxuriously in Western Europe until he lost his properties in the French Revolution. Eventually he returned to Saxony, where he died in 1806. There were no hopes for the minor Friedrich August. His mother Maria Antonia nevertheless continued to dream of the Polish throne for her son and kept in secret contact with figures from Poland. Friedrich August did not renounce his claims to the Polish throne until 1796.

43. Count Victor Friedrich Solms (1730-1783) entered Prussian service after university studies. He represented Prussia in Stockholm before replacing Baron von Goltz as Prussian ambassador in St. Petersburg in 1762 upon Catherine's accession to the throne, a post he held for the next seventeen years. He won the trust of Catherine and Nikita Panin and contributed to the overall cooperation between Russia and Prussia which characterized this period, for example, in the First Partition of Poland.

44. Dispatch from Solms, January 9. (Soloviev's note) *Forschungen zur deutschen Geschichte* (Studies in German History), Vol. 9, pp. 67-69. (Soviet editor's note)

45. Panin helped Catherine draft the manifesto restoring Bestuzhev to his former ranks and honors when the latter returned from exile on August 31, 1762. See Ransel, *The Politics of Catherinian Russia*, p. 117.

46. Dispatch from Solms, August 12. (Soloviev's note) *Forschungen zur deutschen Geschichte*, Vol. 9, p. 80. (Soviet editor's note)

47. Soloviev undoubtedly refers to 1756-1757 when Empress Elizabeth's health deteriorated markedly at the time when Russia joined France and Austria against Prussia and England in the Seven Years War. Bestuzhev threw his

considerable support to Catherine as a counterweight to Grand Duke Peter, even planning a role for her in government when Peter succeeded Elizabeth. In 1757 Bestuzhev also tried to deflect Elizabeth from passing over Peter, and hence Catherine, in favor of Paul Petrovich as her heir. Bestuzhev was arrested in February 1758, when Elizabeth suspected he was involved in a plot to overthrow her. He was able to warn Catherine in time for her to burn her correspondence and maintain her admittedly tenuous standing with Elizabeth. See Volume 41 of this series.

48. *Dnevnik A.V. Khrapovitskogo* (Diary of A.V. Khrapovitsky), p. 481 (Soviet editor's note)

CHAPTER II

1. For example, shortly after her accession Catherine made arrangements to care for Peter III's mistress Elizabeth Vorontsova. On another occasion after an abortive conspiracy to dethrone her in favor of Ivan VI was discovered in the Izmailovsky Guards Regiment in the fall of 1762, Catherine ameliorated the sentences passed on the Khrushchev and Guriev brothers who were the ringleaders.

2. Arseny Matseevich (1696-1772) was educated in Poland and at the Kiev Mohyla Academy, where he took monastic vows before his graduation in 1723. After several years as a preacher in Kiev he filled various positions in Siberia, some of which Soloviev describes here. Arseny threw himself into every task wholeheartedly, whether attempting to convert Old Believers, punishing clerics suspected of doctrinal errors or, as a client of Amvrosy Yushkevich of Vologda, defending church prerogatives curtailed by Peter the Great. After becoming metropolitan of Siberia in 1741 and then of Rostov in 1742 he pressed the case for church control of ecclesiastical lands so forcefully that he clashed frequently with military and civilian authorities. Soloviev describes here how Arseny's crusade met its match in Catherine's determination to subordinate the church once and for all and to make Arseny an example for other potential opponents. On Arseny see entry by Samuel C. Ramer, MERSH, Vol. 2, pp. 115-117. For a discussion of the affair in the context of Russian church history, see Igor Smolitsch, *Geschichte der russischen Kirche, 1700-1917* (History of the Russian Church, 1700-1917) (Leiden, 1964), pp. 238-244, 261-268.

3. Since Kievan times the church, particularly the monasteries, accumulated extensive domains with a large number of attached peasants through pious bequests, government grants and its own expansion into frontier areas. These increased under Mongol rule thanks to tax exemptions. The victory of Joseph of Volokolamsk and the "Possessors" over Nil Sorsky in the sixteenth century confirmed the church's conviction that great material possessions not only were compatible with the monastic vow of poverty but even essential to its autonomy and spiritual mission. Although Peter the Great established effective state control of the church when he replaced the patriarchate with the Holy Synod and imposed

some taxes on and extended control over church possessions, he did not implement full-scale secularization of church lands. Encouraged by Empress Elizabeth's piety, the Holy Synod even argued that his laws protected traditional church control of its lands. As late as the middle of the eighteenth century the church possessed about thirteen percent of all peasants, approximately two million people, eighty percent of whom belonged to monasteries. The issue of church lands played a larger role than these figures might indicate because of chronic unrest among church peasants who envied their brethren under state control. Church peasants constituted half the labor force of the manufacturing enterprises in the central industrial region. The government's financial needs and the growing anticlericalism of educated Russians, including state officials, led to renewed calls for secularization in Elizabeth's time, although she shrank from confronting the Holy Synod directly, relying instead on extraordinary contributions. At Peter III's accession in January 1761 the Senate endorsed a comprehensive plan to send state officials to survey church holdings, gain control of church revenues and put church people on a fixed state payroll schedule. Personnel shortages and clerical resistance delayed effective implementation of the project before Peter was overthrown in June 1762. Catherine initially reversed Peter III's measures,but at the same time announced her intention to form a commission to "bring the entire matter of assessments to completion." The Commission on Church Lands was established on November 29, 1762 to review the whole issue of church property and support. It was to make a register of church lands and serfs, analyze the church's economic resources and recommend new methods to maintain the church and promote such social goals as education and poor relief. Her anticlerical and reformist convictions were well-known, and it was only a matter of time, in 1764, that Catherine took the decisive measures Soloviev describes here. See entry by Alan Ball, "Church Peasants," MERSH, Vol. 7 pp. 105-107; Leonard, *Reform and Regicide*, pp. 73-89; Smolitsch, *Geschichte der russischen Kirche*; and Volume 42 of this series.

4. Dmitry of Rostov (1651-1709) was born Daniel Savvich Tuptalo to a Ukrainian gentry family. Appointed metropolitan of Rostov in 1702, he tried to defend church autonomy after initially supporting Peter the Great's ecclesiastical policy. He wrote a lengthy compilation of saints' lives, a chronicle on the origin of the Slavs, a polemical history against Old Belief and numerous sermons and dramatic works. He founded a school in Rostov which taught Latin, Greek, Russian and other subjects, and even had its own theater. In his funeral oration Stefan Yavorsky called Dmitry a saint. Many miracles soon were attributed to him, and his body was uncorrupted when exhumed in 1752. He was canonized in 1757. In 1991 Dmitry's remains were returned with great ceremony to their original resting place in the Savior Yakovlevsk monastery in Rostov from the museum to which the Soviets had removed them. See entry in MERSH, Vol. 9, pp. 178-179.

5. Stefan Yavorsky (1658-1722) was born in the Ukraine and studied first at the prestigious Kiev Mohyla Academy and then, after a conversion of convenience to Roman Catholicism, at several Jesuit colleges in the Commonwealth. Back in Kiev in 1689 he returned to Orthodoxy, took monastic vows and applied his Jesuit education with great success as a teacher in the Kiev Mohyla Academy.

Peter the Great, struck by Stefan's oratorical talent, had him named bishop of Riazan in 1700 and "guardian of the patriarchal throne" when Patriarch Adrian died later that year. Although Stefan endorsed Peter's plans to educate the clergy further and took pride in Russia's military successes, increasingly he found himself opposing Peter's subordination of the church to state control and resisting what he saw as Protestant tendencies in government and church circles. By 1718 he was eclipsed by Peter's new ecclesiastical protégé, Feofan Prokopovich, whose elevation to the see of Pskov Stefan vainly tried to block. He became the first president of the Ecclesiastical College, soon renamed the Holy Synod, which replaced the patriarch as the supreme authority in the church, but poor health and Stefan's distaste for the new institution made his role here minimal. He died in 1722. His principal work, *Kamen very* (The Rock of Faith), was an exposition of Orthodoxy which used Jesuit neo-Scholastic methodology to challenge Protestant teachings. See entry by Paul D. Steeves, MERSH, Vol. 45, pp. 24-30. For an account of ecclesiastical policy under Peter the Great see James Cracraft, *The Church Reform of Peter the Great* (Stanford, 1971).

6. Anna (1693-1740) was the daughter of Ivan V who shared the throne for a time with Peter the Great. Educated both in traditional Russian spirituality by her mother and by Western tutors named by Peter, Anna was married in 1710 to Friedrich Wilhelm, duke of Courland. She remained in Russia after the duke died suddenly in 1711, until Peter sent her to Courland in 1717. She shrewdly exploited the succession crisis of 1730 to outmaneuver the Supreme Privy Council and take power in her own hands, ruling as empress until 1740. Her reign was marked by the emergence of a Cabinet of Ministers, greater recognition of noble status and partial emancipation from the degree of state service imposed by Peter the Great. She followed Peter's policy of intervention in Poland and expansion against Turkey, and the decade also saw a continuation of the economic development and westernization her uncle had begun. A strong German influence marked Anna's rule, personified in her favorite Ernst Biron. While a number of Germans held prominent positions in the military and civil service, a number of Russians also advanced. Charges that Anna and her associates constituted some kind of German conspiracy that threatened Russian national identity are grossly exaggerated. Biron fell shortly after her death and other Germans had at best individual roles under succeeding rulers. See entry by David M. Griffiths, MERSH, Vol. 2, pp. 8-16, Philip Longworth, *The Three Empresses. Catherine I, Anna and Elizabeth of Russia* (New York, 1972) and Anisimov, *Empress Elizabeth.*

7. Anna Leopoldovna (1718-1746) was the daughter of Karl Leopold, duke of Mecklenburg-Schwerin and the granddaughter of Ivan V, half-brother of Peter the Great. When her aunt Anna became empress of Russia in 1730 she moved to Russia and married a nephew of Charles VI of Austria in expectation that a son would be named heir to the Russian throne. Ivan Antonovich was born on August 12, 1740. Three months later Empress Anna died after naming her favorite Ernst Biron regent, but Anna Leopoldovna took his place in a coup a few weeks later. In her brief tenure as regent for the infant Ivan VI Anna managed to keep Russia out of

the War of the Austrian Succession and saw Russia ward off a Swedish threat in a war which began in 1741. She also attempted to divide the functions of the Cabinet of Ministers and supervise state finances more closely. Peter the Great's daughter Elizabeth meanwhile won the support of the Preobrazhensky Guards Regiment for her successful seizure of power on November 25, 1741. Anna and her family were arrested and confined in Kholmogory where she died in childbirth on February 28, 1746. See entry by William J. Stanton, III, MERSH, Vol. 2, pp. 16-19. See also below, Note 30.

8. Ernst Johann Biron (1690-1772) was born into a Baltic German noble family in Courland in 1690. In 1718 he joined the court of Peter the Great's niece Anna of Courland, who installed him as her favorite after she became empress of Russia in 1730. Though he lived well at court during Anna's reign, Biron's influence as the head of the so-called "German party" has been exaggerated by Russian nationalists. When Anna died in 1740 Biron briefly held supreme power as regent for the infant Ivan Antonovich (Ivan VI) but was arrested and sent into internal exile three weeks later when Ivan Antonovich's mother, Anna Leopoldovna, staged a coup. Biron remained in exile, although under more comfortable circumstances, throughout Elizabeth's reign. Peter III allowed him to return to St. Petersburg, and Catherine brought his career full circle by naming him duke of Courland when Russia regained control of the duchy in 1763. He abdicated in favor of his son in 1769 and died in Mitau in 1772. For Soloviev's description of Biron's installation as duke of Courland and his early tenure there see Chapter V in this volume. See entry by David M. Griffiths, MERSH, Vol. 4, pp. 178-182.

9. The Holy Synod was created by Peter the Great in 1721 to replace the patriarchate, vacant since 1700, as the chief ecclesiastical authority. Peter and his principal advisor on church affairs, Feofan Prokopovich, were impressed by the structures for state control of churches in Protestant lands, and Prokopovich drew upon the Swedish model in drafting the *Ecclesiastical Statute* of 1721 which defined the Holy Synod's role. The Synod consisted of clerics appointed by the crown under the direction, except between 1726 and 1741, of a lay official, the chief procurator. While Peter and his successors sincerely felt this body would be an effective instrument for church reform, any improvements were overshadowed by the church's well-nigh total loss of independence. Soloviev's description of the Arseny Matseevich affair in this volume is a good example of the ease with which Russian rulers used the Holy Synod to impose their will on the church. See entry by James Cracraft, "Holy Synod," MERSH, Vol. 14, pp. 75-77, his *The Church Reform of Peter the Great*, and Alexander V. Muller, trans. and ed., *The Spiritual Regulation of Peter the Great* (Seattle, 1972).

10. Old Believers broke with the official Russian Orthodox church in rejecting what they saw as ungodly innovations by Patriarch Nikon in the 1650s and 1660s. In addition to opposing changes in the texts and liturgical practices, such as the use of the three-fingered in place of the two-fingered sign of the cross, the Old Believers soon became convinced the official church, and the Muscovite state which enforced its rules, were illegitimate authorities to the point of being agents

of the Antichrist. Although open resistance eventually was suppressed in a series of bloody campaigns, many secretly adhered to the old rituals while nominally submitting to the official church. Others continued to profess Old Belief openly in remote areas, especially the Far North and Siberia. Old Belief, now fragmented into a number of sects, has persisted until the present day. Some rulers, like Peter the Great and Catherine II, took a more pragmatic attitude towards the Old Believers, granting them *de facto* toleration if they were loyal and productive citizens of the state. Others, like Nicholas I, sought in vain to coerce them into conformity. Old Belief did not receive legal status as a recognized confession until 1905. See entry by G. Douglas Nicoll, "Old Believers," MERSH, Vol. 25, pp. 228-237; Nickolas Lupinin, *Religious Revolt in the XVIIth Century. The Schism of the Russian Church* (Princeton, 1984); and Robert O. Crummey, *The Old Believers and the World of Antichrist. The Vyg Community and the Russian State, 1664-1855* (Milwaukee, 1970).

11. See above, Note 5.

12. See Volume 42 of this series.

13. This is St. Dmitry described in Note 4.

14. Adam Vasilievich Olsufiev (1721-1784) came from an old noble family. Enrolled in the Noble Cadet Corps in 1732 his intelligence, especially his gift for languages, was noticed early. In 1739 he was called from the Corps to join Field Marshal Münnich's campaign against the Turks with the rank of lieutenant. He transferred to the diplomatic service, serving first as secretary in the Russian embassy in Copenhagen, then in the College of Foreign Affairs in St. Petersburg. Through his brother-in-law Sergei Saltykov, Olsufiev came to the attention of Grand Duchess Catherine whom he helped correspond secretly with her mother, among other services, . Promoted to senior privy councillor in 1756, he assisted in the restructuring of the College of Foreign Affairs in 1758, the same year he was named private secretary to Empress Elizabeth. Olsufiev continued to gain power. It was he, for example, who drafted the manifesto relieving Bestuzhev of duty. He navigated the dangerous shoals of court politics successfully, keeping the good will of Elizabeth, Peter and Catherine simultaneously. After July 1762 when he, along with Teplov and Yelagin, was named state secretary to Catherine, he managed her personal financial affairs, sent secret instructions to governors and dealt with other important state business. In January 1763 Olsufiev became a senator in the First Department of the Senate, where he dealt effectively with a variety of issues for more than twenty years. That same year also saw him take an active role in negotiations for a new commercial treaty with England. As a member of the Legislative Commission of 1767 he ardently defended noble interests. His last major accomplishment was a comprehensive critique he drafted in 1784 of problems in the state theaters, the same year he died. As a senator and in his other government functions Olsufiev was noted for his tact as well as his intellect; he avoided controversy and steered clear of court intrigue. He took a keen interest in music, art and literature, translated foreign works and was an active member of such bodies as the Free Economic Society, the Academy of Sciences and the Academy of Fine Arts.

15. Julian the Apostate (331-363) was the son of Emperor Constantine's half-brother. Although he received a Christian education, Julian espoused a neo-Platonic form of paganism and tried to reverse his predecessor's pro-Christian policies after he became emperor in 361. Arseny undoubtedly is referring to Julian's revocation of the rights, immunities and lands the church received and his attempt to recover state funds given the church. Arseny hoped that Russia would imitate the example of Julian's successors by restoring the Constantinian alliance between throne and altar.

16. Vladimir Sviatoslavich, or St. Vladimir (died 1015), was the prince of Kiev who unified a number of Slavic tribes into an organized state, extended the power of Kiev far to the south and east and, most importantly, in 988 adopted Christianity in its Byzantine form for himself and his people. The first of the saintly princes in Russian history, Vladimir rightly is seen as a crucial figure who shaped the destiny of Kievan Rus and its successors religiously, culturally and politically. See the entry by Leopold Sobel in MERSH (Vol. 42, pp. 153-160), which emphasizes Vladimir's political and military role. For treatments of his religious and cultural significance, see the works by Vlasto, Schmemann, Fedotov and others.

17. Ivan Alexeevich Musin-Pushkin (1661-1729) served as military commander in Smolensk and later in Astrakhan, where his success in defeating rebellious cossacks and increasing government income won him Peter the Great's favor. He accompanied Peter on journeys and took part in the battle of Poltava in 1709. Named a count in 1710 and a senator in 1711, Musin-Pushkin directed the Monasterial Chancellery from 1710 to 1717. Later he held other positions such as director of the Chancellery for Book Publishing and the Mint.

18. St. Cyprian was a wealthy citizen of Carthage who became a Christian about 246. Shortly thereafter he was named bishop of Carthage where his tenure was marked by conflicts in the Christian community over doctrine, discipline and governance. He and his flock also had to face Roman persecution, and he was martyred in 258 in the manner Arseny describes here. A famous orator and pleader before his conversion, Cyprian's eloquent writings were read widely in his own time and later. Although he sold his property when he became a Christian, apparently friends bought it back and restored it to him. As bishop he used his riches freely to help the Christian community. No wonder Arseny saw him as a model for the Russian church of his time, particularly Cyprian's dramatic final act of largesse.

19. John 12:5.

20. Fedor Yakovlevich Dubiansky (died 1771) was born in the Ukraine, and after his father-in-law Konstantin Fedorovich Sharogorodsky died in 1735, succeeded him as the future Empress Elizabeth's confessor. Elizabeth's piety and personal liking for Dubiansky meant riches and influence for him, including a grant of hereditary nobility in 1761. He continued as Catherine's confessor until his death, a position which gave him considerable influence in church affairs.

21. Literally, stripped of his *klobuk* (monastic headdress).

22. Dmitry Sechenov was born in 1709 and educated at the Moscow Slavic-Greek-Latin Academy, where he taught oratory after his graduation in 1730. After

taking monastic vows in 1732 Dmitry became archimandrite of the Sviiazhsk monastery. Beginning in 1740 he directed a remarkably successful mission to Christianize Muslims and pagans in the Kazan and Nizhny Novgorod governments. Dmitry was named bishop of Nizhny Novgorod in 1742 but relinquished the post because of illness in 1748. He became a member of the Holy Synod in 1752 and archbishop of Novgorod in 1757. He played a prominent role in Catherine's coronation in Moscow in 1762 and was raised to the rank of metropolitan later that year. He served as a clerical delegate to the Legislative Commission in 1767, dying that same year. Dmitry was a celebrated orator, and Catherine often called upon him for sermons on important occasions, including her coronation.

23. Timofey Shcherbatsky was archimandrite of the Caves monastery in Kiev before serving as metropolitan of Kiev from 1747 to 1754, and metropolitan of Moscow from 1757 to 1767.

24. Gavriil, in the world Grigory Fedorovich Kremenetsky (1708-1783), was born in the Ukraine and studied first at the Kiev Mohyla then at the Moscow Academy. He taught at the Alexander Nevsky seminary after 1736, becoming prefect there in 1739. In 1748 he became archimandrite of the New Savior monastery and was named to the Holy Synod. Consecrated bishop of Kolomna in 1749, he moved to the diocese of Kazan in 1755, becoming archbishop of St. Petersburg in 1762. That same year he was named to the commission preparing the secularization of church lands. Although he was designated metropolitan of Kiev in 1770, illness prevented him from settling there until 1772. Upon his death in 1783 he was buried in the Kiev cathedral. He was known for his zealous defense of Orthodoxy, opposing, for example, accommodation with Old Believers, for his attempts to impose Great Russian standards on the church in the Ukraine and his scholarships for needy students.

25. Gedeon Krinovsky (1726-1763) was born in Kazan where he studied at the local seminary. He taught for while there and became a monk. In defiance of his bishop's orders he went to the Moscow Theological Academy in 1751 to further his education. After Ivan Shuvalov and Empress Elizabeth heard him preach Gedeon rose rapidly, becoming a court preacher in 1753, archimandrite of St. Sabbas the Guardian monastery in 1757 and the following year a member of the Holy Synod and archimandrite of the Holy Trinity-St. Sergius monastery. Although he was named bishop of Pskov in October 1761, his duties at the Holy Synod and his attendance at court kept him from his diocese for all but three months between then and his death in June 1763.

26. Amvrosy, in the world Andrei Stepanovich Zertis-Kamensky (1708-1771), studied from 1720 to 1728 in the Epiphany monastery in Kiev, from 1728 to 1733 at the Lvov Theological Academy and from 1733 to 1736 at the Slavic-Greek-Latin Academy in Moscow. He then taught at the Alexander Nevsky monastery until 1743 when he was named archimandrite of the New Jerusalem monastery of the Resurrection. Amvrosy became bishop of Pereiaslavl and Dmitrov in 1753, transferred to the diocese of Saray and the Don and was designated archbishop of Krutitsa in 1764. Archbishop of Moscow after 1768, he was entrusted by Catherine with renovation of the Kremlin cathedrals. Amvrosy was murdered in the Don

monastery during the Moscow plague epidemic of 1771 by an angry mob, which accused him of stealing church funds. Catherine called the death of this "learned and meritorious man" a "catastrophe."

27. Afanasy Volkhovsky (died 1776) studied in Kharkov and at the Kiev Theological Academy. At the Holy Trinity-St. Sergius monastery, where he took monastic vows in 1745, he served as prefect, rector, professor of theology and, after 1753, as archimandrite. The following year, 1754, he became a member of the Holy Synod. Consecrated archbishop of Tver in 1758, he was transferred in 1763 to the diocese of Rostov , where he died and was buried. He was the author of several theological works.

28. Misail (died 1764) was archimandrite of the New Savior monastery. In 1758 he refused a nomination to serve as bishop of Voronezh.

29. This must be one of the otherwise unidentified "prominent persons" mentioned in the synodal report quoted elsewhere in this chapter.

30. Ivan Antonovich (Ivan VI, 1740-1764) was the nominal emperor of Russia from October 17, 1740 to November 25, 1741. He was named emperor as a newborn infant by Empress Anna shortly before her death, but was imprisoned after Elizabeth's coup in 1741. His life was spent in confinement, and he was executed by his guards after an abortive attempt to free him in 1764. See entry by Karl W. Schweitzer, MERSH, Vol. 15, pp. 61-63. See Soloviev's description of his death in Chapter IX, section "Eyewitness Testimony."

31. See above, Note 22.

32. St. John Chrysostom (c. 347-407) was born in Antioch and studied law and rhetoric before forsaking a worldly career to devote himself to prayer and bible study after converting to Christianity in 370. Ordained a priest in 386, John won widespread fame for his fiery sermons, penetrating insight into the scriptures, denunciations of luxury and calls for reform. His zeal and eloquence continued unabated as patriarch of Constantinople after 398, earning John many enemies, including the empress Eudoxia. He was exiled, recalled, and exiled definitively in 404, dying in Pontus in 407. It is easy to see how John could appeal to Arseny, who could imagine that he too someday would be vindicated and honored.

33. St. Cyril of Belozero was born late in the fourteenth century and died in 1427. At the age of sixty he left the Simonov monastery in Moscow to found a new monastery on the shore of the White Lake, (Belozero) in the region of Vologda. This became an important spiritual and cultural center, and until the confiscation of church lands played a major economic role in the region. The monastery, now known as the St. Cyril-White Lake monastery, was closed after the Bolshevik Revolution and later made a museum. Negotiations are being conducted to reestablish a monastic community in part of the enormous monastery complex. Cyril wrote extensively on spiritual and secular subjects and advised several of the princes of his time. Concerning St. Cyril, see the entry in MERSH, Vol. 17, p. 27 and concerning the monastery, see entry by Lupinin, pp. 27-29.

34. Peter Ivanovich Shuvalov (1710-1762) was the son of a prominent statesman of Peter the Great's time. As pages he and his brother Alexander were close to then Grand Duchess Elizabeth, and like the rest of the family rose rapidly after

her successful coup in 1741. His talent, a marriage to one of the empress's favorites and Elizabeth's friendship brought him the rank of lieutenant general and a place in the Senate in 1744 with further honors and gifts thereafter, for example, the title of count of the Russian empire in 1746. He strove simultaneously and successfully to promote economic development, increase state revenue and enrich himself. Shuvalov founded Russia's first savings bank, attempted to reform the coinage, raised vodka taxes and fought to eliminate internal tariffs. He was able, over Elizabeth's objections, to restore the death penalty as part of his campaign to crack down on lawlessness. In maintaining and expanding his dominant position in internal matters Shuvalov frequently extended his reach to foreign affairs as well, clashing repeatedly with Bestuzhev in the process. He pushed through measures to settle and fortify New Serbia, a policy Bestuzhev labelled "foolishness." Starting in 1749 he promoted increasing the size and improving the quality of the army, particularly the artillery. Although in 1758 he managed to secure the fall of his old enemy Bestuzhev, his own illness and the death of Elizabeth in 1761 meant the end of his influence. While Peter III treated him with deference and respect, his days were numbered, and he died in January 1762.

35. See above, Note 3.

36. A common term for the reign of Peter the Great.

37. *Chteniia v Obshchestve istorii i drevnostei rossiiskikh* (Readings at the Society of Russian History and Antiquities), III (1862), Section V, pp. 234-294. (Soviet editor's note) Catherine wrote an interesting note to Prince [Alexander Alexeevich] Viazemsky. "Since G.P. von Benckendorff now has been appointed commander-in-chief in Reval, please write him to supervise Vral as Thiesenhausen did. Unless Benckendorff is given instructions, I am afraid Vral will play some trick or other during the change of command and that he will not be supervised as strictly. This could create new problems for us." Arseny died on February 28, 1772 after he had confessed and communicated. (Soloviev's note)

38. Alexander Ivanovich Glebov (1717-1790), the son of a general and senator of the Petrine era, served in the army from 1737 to 1749, then entered the civil service. After his marriage to Empress Elizabeth's niece he was named high procurator of the Senate in 1756, winning the favor of the future Peter III and the powerful Peter Shuvalov. He was opposed by the Vorontsovs and Yakov Petrovich Shakhovskoy, who forced him from the procurator's post in 1760, although he still had enough standing to become chief commissioner of war that year. Upon his accession in 1761 Peter III reappointed Glebov chief procurator of the Senate while continuing as chief commissioner of war, promoted him to lieutenant general and named him to a new war commission. He played a key policy role in Peter's short reign in such issues as the toleration of Old Believers, plans to secularize church lands, and the emancipation of the nobility. Although he retained his positions for a time after Catherine's seizure of power in 1762, Glebov was too corrupt and too wedded to established government practices to survive Catherine's reform efforts, as Soloviev describes in this volume. He made a brief return to government service

as governor of Smolensk and Belgorod in 1775 after he drafted the report for the commission that tried Pugachev and his associates. He was removed almost immediately after once again being caught in embezzlement and played no public role thereafter. See entry by Robert E. Jones, MERSH, Vol. 12, pp. 193-194, and Carol S. Leonard, *Reform and Regicide.*

39. SRIO, Vol. 7, pp. 287-288. (Soviet editor's note)

40. June 28, 1762 was the date of the coup which deposed Peter III and brought Catherine to the throne.

41. Grigory Grigorievich Orlov (1734-1783) was one of five brothers who had a key role in Catherine's successful coup of 1762 and enjoyed the empress's favor thereafter. He served at court, held various military positions and supervised the Plague Commission of 1771. See entry by Alexander, MERSH, Vol. 26, pp. 107-109.

42. Alexis Grigorievich Orlov (1737-1808) was the third of the five Orlov brothers who achieved prominence under Catherine after aiding in her seizure of power. He directed naval operations in the 1768 war with Turkey and was showered with honors after leading the Russian fleet to victory at Chesme in 1770. See entry by Munro, MERSH, Vol. 26, pp. 103-106, and Volume 46 of this series.

43. Ivan Perfilievich Yelagin (1725-1794), who served in the Infantry Cadet Corps, began writing poetry as a teenager. He was implicated in the 1758 plot on behalf of then Grand Duchess Catherine and exiled to Kazan government. After Catherine's accession he was showered with honors despite the Orlovs' dislike of him. He held a number of official positions such as lord high steward of the court and director of court dramatic and musical performances. As director of theaters from 1766 to 1779 Yelagin made a significant contribution to the development of Russian drama. He translated foreign works and collaborated with Catherine on some her literary efforts. Yelagin took a passionate interest in freemasonry, which earned him the empress's disfavor after the 1770s. See entry by Brigitte Agna in Terras, *Handbook of Russian Literature*, p. 119.

44. Nikita Ivanovich Roslavev (1724-1785) followed a military career after starting in the Noble Cadet Corps. In 1761 Empress Elizabeth named him chamberlain, a title confirmed in 1762 by Peter III. As first major in the Izmailovsky Guards Regiment Roslavev was able to aid decisively in Catherine's coup in 1762. Although Catherine rewarded him with land, money, titles and a high place in the new court, his jealousy of the greater role played by the Orlovs led him to join Khitrovo's plot as Soloviev describes here. For this he and his family were sent to the St. Elizabeth fortress, from which they were allowed to return after Ivan Yelagin's intercession. He was retired from service in 1765 with the rank of lieutenant general.

45. SRIO, Vol. 7, p. 234. (Soloviev's note)

46. Vasily Ivanovich Suvorov (1705-1775) began service as a translator and personal servant of Peter the Great. After a trip abroad to study fortifications, knowledge he later used to instruct his son, the famous field marshal, Suvorov pursued a military career. As a magistrate in Siberia in the 1730s he had a hand in

the interrogation and torture of the exiled Ivan Dolgoruky. After his return to St. Petersburg in 1741 he served for ten years as procurator general of the College of Mines, then as a procurator in the Senate and as a member of the War College with the rank of major general. Suvorov was given important assignments in the Seven Years War, including the post of governor general of Russian-occupied Prussia. After serving as governor of Siberia under Peter III he returned to the Senate under Catherine II where, as Soloviev describes here, he investigated the Khitrovo affair. He spent the spent the last years of life in retirement in Moscow, retaining the rank of senator until his death in 1775.

47. Ivan Vasilievich Nesvizhsky (died 1806) served in the Horse Guards and was an active participant in the coup that brought Catherine to power. After leaving active duty he was named chamberlain and privy councillor. Later he was awarded the title of high cupbearer.

48. Mikhail Nikitich Volkonsky (1713-1788) was a general who served as ambassador to Poland from 1757 to 1759, as governor in 1758 of Prussian territory conquered in the Seven Years War and as a member of Peter III's state council in 1762. In 1764 he commanded the Russian corps sent to Poland to ensure the choice of Stanisław August in the royal election that year. From 1771 to 1780 he was governor general of Moscow.

49. The Cherkasskys were descended from a Kabardian princely family.

50. Kirill Grigorievich Razumovsky (1728-1803) was the son of a Ukrainian cossack who rose to power under the patronage of his brother Alexis, a favorite of Empress Elizabeth. In 1746 he was named president of the Academy of Sciences, a post he held until 1798, but did not play an active role in it, especially in later years. He served as hetman of the Ukraine from 1750 until the position was abolished in 1764, as Soloviev describes in Chapter XI, section "Abolition of the Hetmanate." He was given the title of general field marshal that same year and was a member of the State Council from 1768 to 1771. See entry by R.V. Ovchinnikov, MERSH, Vol. 30, p. 214.

51. Peter Ivanovich Repnin (died 1778) served in the Noble Infantry Cadet Corps, then in various military posts until his marriage in 1741 to a relative of Count Golovkin opened doors to a career at court. As chamberlain to the young court of Grand Duke Peter and Grand Duchess Catherine after 1748, Repnin won their friendship and Empress Elizabeth's favor. Named Russian minister plenipotentiary to Spain in 1762, he had to leave in 1764 when relations between St. Petersburg and Madrid soured, although Catherine expressed her gratitude for his efforts. Repnin was appointed grand master of horse in 1765, a post he held until 1768, but his less than onerous duties left him time to participate in masonic circles and pursue a number of unsuccessful financial interests in iron foundries and the like.

52. Peter Bogdanovich Passek (1736-1804) as a lieutenant in the Preobrazhensky Guards Regiment enthusiastically supported the conspiracy that brought Catherine to power in 1762. In fact it was his arrest on June 27 that spurred his comrades to strike the next day, Catherine herself freeing him that morning. Not surprisingly rewards and honors soon followed, including on August 3 the rank of

captain and twenty-four thousand rubles. He retired for health reasons in 1765 as a lieutenant general with fifteen thousand rubles "to pay his debts." He returned to service as governor of Mogilev from 1778 to 1781, and after a few months in the First Department of the Senate, as governor general of Mogilev and Polotsk from 1782 to 1796. When Paul I acceded to the throne in 1796 Passek immediately was removed from office and banned from St. Petersburg and Moscow. After Alexander I allowed him to return to St. Petersburg in 1801, he took no part in public life until his death in 1804.

53. Grigory Nikolaevich Teplov (1717-1779) by this time had a successful and often stormy public career. He received his early education under the patronage of Feofan Prokopovich and after study in Prussia made his mark as a botanist at the Academy of Sciences. A second trip abroad from 1743 to 1746 as tutor to Kirill Razumovsky not only broadened Teplov's knowledge of western European learning, it also gave him a powerful patron. He played a dominant role in the Academy of Sciences from 1746 to 1751 when Razumovsky was its nominal director, and exercised similar power in the Ukraine when Razumovsky was named its hetman in 1751. Peter III had him arrested for supposed disloyalty in 1762, but Teplov rose to new prominence after supporting Catherine's coup in 1762. As Catherine's secretary he had an active hand in many of the policies of her reign, including topics described in this volume such as the secularization of church lands and the abolition of the Ukrainian hetmanate. A specialist in economics, he promoted the Panin party's reform efforts, emphasizing the need for careful collection and analysis of data as the basis for government action. He also tutored the future Paul I and continued to pursue intellectual and cultural interests. Among other things he encouraged the study of philosophy and published the first collection of Russian songs. See entry by Wallace L. Daniel, MERSH, Vol. 38, pp. 240-244, and his *Grigorii Teplov. A Statesman at the Court of Catherine the Great* (Newtonville, Mass., 1991).

54. Ivan Sergeevich Boriatinsky (or Bariatinsky) (1740-1811) and Fedor Sergeevich Boriatinsky (1742-1814) were guards officers who supported Catherine in her 1762 coup. Catherine appointed Ivan as a companion to Grand Duke Paul, who spent much of each day with the heir. Named lieutenant general in 1779, Ivan served from 1773 to 1786 as minister plenipotentiary to France. After Catherine's accession Fedor held a number of court positions and accompanied the empress on journeys. Paul allowed Fedor as lord high marshal of the court, a title he was granted in 1796, to participate in the funeral of Catherine II, then promptly banished him to his estates and forbade him to visit the capital.

55. Sergei Khovansky was named lieutenant general in 1759 and served in the Seven Years War.

56. Peter Fedorovich Apraksin (1728-1813) was a lieutenant general who distinguished himself in the Seven Years War.

57. This was the imprisoned Ivan Antonovich who as former emperor was a possible claimant to the throne. See above, Note 30.

58. Catherine Romanovna Dashkova (1743-1810) was a princess who used the prominence she gained for helping Catherine seize power in 1762 to exercise major

political and cultural influence throughout the empress's reign. She received an excellent education in her uncle Mikhail Ilarionovich Vorontsov's home, and while still a teenager found in the then Grand Duchess Catherine a personal and intellectual soulmate. While Dashkova's later claims of playing the key role in the 1762 coup are exaggerated, her part was significant, and Catherine initially rewarded her handsomely. It is not surprising that two such intelligent and strong-willed women would clash on a number of issues. On several occasions Dashkova retired to her estates or travelled extensively abroad. Whether in public life or not she took every opportunity to further her own education and that of her children while encouraging art and culture in Russia. She was active in the Free Russian Assembly (Volnoe rossiiskoe sobranie), and as director of the Academy of Sciences and president of the newly-founded Russian Academy from 1783 to 1794 she promoted an impressive range of scholarly and literary activity by almost every major figure of the age. In 1794 she resigned her posts when Catherine objected to Dashkova's publication of a play by Ya.B. Kniazhnin which the empress judged anti-monarchical. Her ties with Catherine ensured her disfavor under Paul I (1796-1801), and she spent the years until her death in 1810 in retirement, although in 1801 Alexander I invited her to resume her positions. Near the end of her life she dictated her memoirs, a vivid depiction of her times and one of the few eyewitness accounts of the 1762 coup, to a young Anglo-Irish protégé, Martha Wilmot. See entry by David M. Griffiths, MERSH, Vol. 8, pp. 190-197.

59. Vasily Onufrievich Brylkin was the brother of Ivan Onufrievich Brylkin. See the following note.

60. Ivan Onufrievich Brylkin (born 1709) began his career as a page under Empress Anna and advanced under Elizabeth, who named him chief procurator of the Senate in 1741. He served for a time as governor of Astrakhan after 1745, then returned to the Senate. For a while he directed the Pauline Hospital. Assigned by Catherine to the Sixth Department of the Senate in January 1764, Brylkin retired from service that December and died sometime in the 1770s.

61. Catherine's correspondence with Suvorov is published in SRIO, Vol. 8, pp. 289, 292-294. It was Dashkova rather than Panin who prevented her uncle Vorontsov from explaining himself to the empress. She says that Rzhevsky informed Orlov of the project. (Soloviev's note) *Zapiski kniagini E.R. Dashkovoi* (Notes of Princess E.R. Dashkova) (London, 1859), pp. 84-85. (Soviet editor's note)

62. *Polnoe sobranie zakonov* (Complete Collection of Laws [hereafter PSZ]), Vol. 16, No. 11, 843. (Soloviev's note)

63. Alexis Semeonovich Kozlovsky (1707-1776) was chief procurator of the Holy Synod from 1758 to June 9, 1763. Under Elizabeth and Peter III he was the major voice urging state control of the church in the name of reform.

64. Alexis Petrovich Melgunov (1722-1788) served in the Noble Infantry Cadet Corps, then as page of the chamber under Elizabeth and adjutant to the future Peter III. Under Catherine he was governor of New Russia, then senator and president of the Treasury College. As governor of Vologda and Yaroslavl after 1777 Melgunov opened an orphanage and a navigation school. An active freemason, he

studied German literature and published a literary magazine. Catherine once called Melgunov "a man most useful to the state."

65. Schlüsselburg was a military fortress originally built by the Swedes to control the passage from Lake Ladoga to the Neva. Important prisoners frequently were housed there such as Ernst Biron and Tsar Ivan VI, as well as Decembrists and other nineteenth-century revolutionaries.

66. The letter and the records are in the State Archive. A letter written by Nikolay Roslavev from the St. Elizabeth fortress on August 12, 1763 to Yelagin is in the Moscow Archive of the Ministry of Foreign Affairs. "Dear Sir, my old pal, Ivan Perfilievich! If, my pal, you would like to help the poorest and most unfortunate of men, I beg you in the name of humanity to send me away from here, though I would die soon, even in Moscow. I am very sick, my throat is oozing blood and I cannot get out of bed. No one can cure me. The doctor is incompetent. My wife is poor, sick and also pregnant," and so on. (Soloviev's note)

CHAPTER III

1. SRIO, Vol. 7, pp. 291-292. (Soviet editor's note)
2. PSZ, Vol. 16, No. 11, 855. (Soloviev's note)
3. PSZ, No. 11, 845. (Soloviev's note)
4. Peter Spiridonovich Sumarokov (1709-1780) was a page of the chamber under Catherine I. In 1730 he eluded efforts by the Supreme Privy Council to keep the future Empress Anna from learning of its plans to limit her powers. She rewarded him with the post of stablemaster in 1742 and that of grand stablemaster in 1752. Sumarokov was named to the Senate in 1761 then became embroiled in the franchise dispute Soloviev describes here and retired at his own request in 1764.
5. SRIO, Vol. 7, pp. 235-237. (Soviet editor's note)
6. SRIO, Vol. 7, p. 324. (Soviet editor's note)
7. In the fall of 1762 Panin proposed a permanent imperial council drawn from top administrative officials to advise the sovereign, but in December of that year Catherine decided not to implement the plan. In February 1763 she appointed a Commission on Noble Emancipation consisting of the same members Panin had nominated for the council. This body also was charged with planning reform of the Senate.
8. SRIO, Vol. 7., pp. 279-280. (Soviet editor's note)
9. PSZ, Vol. 16, No. 11, 989. (Soloviev's note)
10. Fedor Grigorievich Orlov (1741-1796) was the fourth of the five Orlov brothers who were rewarded with important assignments during Catherine's reign for their key role in her 1762 seizure of power. Fedor served in the Seven Years War, then after Catherine's accession was named chief procurator of the Senate as Soloviev describes here. Later he participated in Spiridov's expedition which set out in 1769 for the Mediterranean, during which he won several naval victories

over the Turks. Catherine erected a column ornamented with ships' prows in his honor at Tsarskoe Selo.

11. SRIO, Vol. 7, p. 286. (Soloviev's note)

12. PSZ, Vol. 16, No. 11, 869. (Soloviev's note)

13. The Arshenevsky family, of Lithuanian origin, came from the Smolensk area. It is not clear which member is mentioned here.

14. SRIO, Vol. 7, pp. 286-287. (Soloviev's note)

15. SRIO, Vol. 7, p. 285. (Soloviev's note)

16. Yakov Petrovich Shakhovskoy (1705-1777) began his career in the Semenovsky Guards Regiment. Through his uncle A.I. Shakhovskoy he developed close ties with influential figures in the capital, surviving the fall of successive patrons in the turbulent period from the end of Anna's reign to Elizabeth's seizure of power in 1741. As chief procurator of the Holy Synod from 1741 to 1753 he won the enmity of the clergy but the support of the empress in his efforts to establish greater state control over the church. Named chief of the commissary in 1753, he fought for honesty and efficiency in military affairs, with even greater responsibilities during the Seven Years War. After the fall of his arch-rival P.I. Shuvalov in 1760 Shakhovskoy gained even more power as procurator general of the Senate, but was removed immediately when Peter III succeeded Elizabeth in 1761. Catherine appointed him to the Senate upon her accession in 1762, and lent an attentive ear to his proposals for reform, such as sending inspectors general to the provinces. In 1766 he retired in poor health, spending his last years writing an informative memoir of his public career. See entry by Robert E. Jones, MERSH, Vol. 34 pp. 142-144.

17. Martyn Karlovich Skavronsky (1714-1776) was the son of prominent court figure, but his youth was made difficult by a brush with the Secret Chancellery and by Empress Anna's enmity to his family. His fortunes changed after Elizabeth's accession in 1741, and Skavronsky advanced rapidly in rank, including to that of senator, and received lavish grants of land and serfs. His years in the Senate were undistinguished, although contemporaries praised his decency and good nature. He was a deputy for the Kolomna nobility at the 1767 Legislative Commission.

18. Porfiry, in the world Kraisky, was bishop of Kolomna from 1755 until his death in 1768. Previously he was bishop of Suzdal and of Belgorod. He studied at the Moscow Theological Academy, where he later served as teacher and rector. He was a renowned preacher.

19. Ivan Orlov also served as a member of the War College.

20. See Volume 41 of this series.

21. SRIO,Vol. 1, pp. 218-252. (Soviet editor's note) For Glebov's unsuccessful effort to justify himself see SRIO, Vol. 7, pp. 340-345. (Soloviev's note)

22. Alexis Mikhailovich Pushkin (dates of birth and death unknown, fl.1700-1775) studied abroad during the reign of Peter the Great, then held various government posts under Empress Anna. He was governor of Archangel from 1744-1745, then served in diplomatic posts in Sweden and Denmark before becoming governor of Voronezh in 1747, a office he held until 1760. Summoned to St.

Petersburg in June, 1762, he was retired from service with the rank of privy councillor.

23. Alexander Alexeevich Viazemsky (1727-1793) enjoyed Catherine's confidence and held a number of important positions during her reign. As procurator general he controlled the Senate and the domestic affairs of the empire more effectively than his predecessors. He had a major role in the Legislative Commission of 1767, gradually achieved more order in imperial finances and was able to exercise greater control over provincial authorities. His success was due in large part to his hard work, attention to detail and avoidance of factions. See entry by Jones, MERSH, Vol.42, pp. 76-79.

24. The foundries, like many of the industrial enterprises of the time, relied on the labor of assigned peasants. These were attached to particular firms, often working under the harsh conditions Soloviev describes here. The purchase of workers for the factories reduced the agricultural labor force to the point that the practice was forbidden between 1762 and 1798. See Madariaga, pp. 104-107 and Portal, *L'Oural.*

25. The native tributary people, or *iasachnye*, lived mainly in Siberia or the Urals and paid the state a tax in furs (yasak, from the Mongol word for tribute). This practice began with the Russian conquest of the region and was an important source of government revenue in the seventeenth century.

26. Tax rolls (skazki or revizskie skazki) listing the number of souls (dushi), or adult males, were submitted by landlords or local officials to the government. These rolls were the basis for the taxes levied by the state, particularly the soul tax (podushnaia podat') instituted by Peter the Great which soon became the major source of state revenue.

27. A hundredman (sotnik) was responsible for a territorial unit called a hundred (sotnia).

28. The Votiaks, today called Udmurts, were absorbed by Russia in the fifteenth and sixteenth centuries. They speak a Finno-Ugric language and live in the area of Voronezh. An autonomous region was created for them in 1920 and an autonomous republic in 1934.

29. See above, Note 27.

30. The Russian expression used is *muzhik-gorlan.*

31. Under the municipal administration established by Peter the Great in 1721 each city was governed by a magistracy (magistrat) consisting of a president, two magistrates (burmistry) and four aldermen (ratmany). Initially the city magistracies, or *ratushy,* were subject to the Chief Magistracy (glavnyi magistrat), but this was abolished in 1727 and supervision exercised by the military governors.

32. The institutions of municipal government in medieval Novgorod were the arena for vigorous, often bloody, struggles for control among the leading boyar families of the city. The Boretskys mentioned by Soloviev here held power in Novgorod before Ivan III of Moscow defeated and annexed the city in 1477-1478. See George Vernadsky, *Russia at the Dawn of the Modern Age* (New Haven, 1959) and Henryk Birnbaum, *Lord Novgorod the Great. Essays in the History and Culture of a Medieval City State* (Columbus, 1981).

33. Free homesteaders (odnodvortsy) were descendants of Muscovite servicemen who settled on the southern and eastern frontiers. They had some freedom to dispose of their land and could own serfs, but like peasants had to pay the soul tax. Many lived in the Orel government. See Jerome Blum, *Lord and Peasant in Russia from the Ninth to the Nineteenth Century* (Princeton, 1961).

34. Peter Semeonovich Soltykov (or Saltykov, 1698?-1772) came from an old boyar family. He was enrolled in a guards regiment, studied several years in France and with his father and other relatives helped Anna gain the throne in 1730. Except for a brief tenure as adjutant general and senator under the regency of Anna Leopoldovna from 1740 to 1741, Soltykov held a number of military posts, winning the rank of field marshal for his victory over Frederick II at Kunersdorf in 1759 as commander-in-chief of Russian forces at the time. His military prowess earned him the favor both of Peter III and Catherine, who named him governor general of Moscow in May 1763. Here he enjoyed unrivalled authority, including the power to conduct investigations on his own and report directly to the empress. Catherine took a close interest in his work and for a time expressed her confidence in him, but had her doubts by 1770 and removed him from office when he failed to control the plague outbreak of 1770-1771 and the turmoil it unleashed. See entry by Alexander, MERSH, Vol. 33, pp. 49-53.

35. Ivan Ivanovich Yushkov (died 1781) was a chief justice of the Chancellery of Justice in 1753, president of the Treasury College in 1760, gendarme general of St. Petersburg and civil governor of Moscow.

36. Ivan Larionovich (or Ilarionovich) Vorontsov (1719-1786) was a member of the Commission on Church Lands in 1762, a member of the College of Hereditary Estates in Moscow, first secretary of the Moscow Senate Bureau and attained the rank of lieutenant general.

37. See Volume 39 of this series.

38. The term used is *pripisnye goroda.*

39. Peter III issued the Manifesto of Freedom for the Nobility on February 18, 1762. Peter I required nobles to serve for life. This obligation gradually diminished after he died, and there was growing sentiment to define the rights, privileges and duties of the nobility as the century progressed. Peter III's manifesto allowed nobles to request release from service under certain conditions and also permitted service abroad, but neither specified noble privileges clearly nor defined their legal status exactly. Although Catherine tried to deal with these issues at various times yet they never were resolved satisfactorily then or later. See Marc Raeff, "The Domestic Policies of Peter III and his Overthrow," *American Historical Review,* Vol. 75 (1970), pp. 1289-1310 and Soloviev, *History of Russia*, Volume 42 of this series, pp. 6-10

40. SRIO, Vol. 7, pp. 232-233. (Soviet editor's note)

41. Alexander Mikhailovich Golitsyn (1723-1807) was a diplomat who served in Germany (1749-1754) and as minister plenipotentiary in Great Britain (1755-1762) before becoming vice chancellor (1762-1775). Although nominally he was

second only to Nikita Panin in foreign affairs, in practice others close to Catherine often eclipsed him.

42. Dmitry Mikhailovich Matiushkin (1725-1800) was the son of a prominent general of the Peter the Great's time. Catherine may have been irked in part because in 1762 Matiushkin was named a count of the Holy Roman empire for no other reason than his family name.

43. This came in response to a petition on behalf of over seventy thousand Old Believers who fled to Poland to escape persecution. They were encouraged to settle in Siberia and promised protection from church officials. See Leonard, *Reform and Regicide*, pp. 20-21.

44. SRIO , Vol. 7, pp. 234-235. (Soviet editor's note)

45. *Sobranie postanovlenii po chasti raskola, sostoiavshikhsia po vedomstvu Sinoda* (Collection of Resolutions Concerning the Schism, Compiled under the Auspices of the Synod) (St. Petersburg, 1860), Vol. 1, pp. 598-599. (Soviet editor's note)

46. Boris-Leonty Alexeevich Kurakin (1733-1764) educated his son Alexander and Grand Duke Paul together. Kurakin served as president of the new college until his death a year later.

47. PSZ, Vol. 16, Nos. 11814, 11844. (Soviet editor's note)

48. See above, p. 27.

49. The reference is to the coup of June 28, 1762 which overthrew Peter III and brought Catherine II to power.

50. Grigory Alexandrovich Potemkin (1739-1791) reaped the benefits of his support for Catherine in 1762 throughout her reign. He won glory as a field commander against Turkey in 1769 and 1770. After Grigory Orlov's fall from favor he was installed in the palace as Catherine's lover and principal advisor. Although he too was replaced in his former role by 1776, Catherine continued to value his counsel. He served as military commander and governor in the areas conquered from the Turks in the south until his death in the field in 1791. See entry by Munro, MERSH, Vol. 29, pp. 123-128, and George Soloveytchik, *Po-temkin. Soldier, Statesman, Lover and Consort of Catherine of Russia* (New York, 1947).

51. SRIO, Vol. 7, p. 316. (Soviet editor's note)

52. These representatives elected by the peasants also served as auxiliary agents for the authorities, in this case the factory proprietors.

53. PSZ, Vol. 16, No. 11, 790. (Soviet editor's note)

54. See above, Chapter III, section "Reorganization of Other Government Bodies."

55. Peter Ivanovich Panin (1721-1788) was the younger brother of Nikita Panin. After a successful military career he held a number of important government positions under Catherine. His distinguished military and administrative record, plus his brother's influence, gained him a place on the government council established at the outbreak of war with Turkey in 1768. From here he was named to command the Second Army where he captured the fortress of Bendery and contained the Crimean Tatars. Disillusioned at what he considered inadequate

recognition of his accomplishments, he retired from public life and levelled criticism at Catherine and her favorites. Catherine recalled him in 1774 to put down the Pugachev uprising, after which he retired permanently. He kept in contact with his brother's circle and had some influence on Paul I's plans for government reform. See entry by Ransel, MERSH, Vol. 218-221, and his *Politics of Catherinian Russia*.

56. Town governors also were responsible for the surrounding countryside.

57. The reference is to the era of Tatar rule when the horde was a political and territorial unit.

58. The Legislative Commission of 1767 was the result of Catherine's oft-stated intention to reform the Russian state on the basis of enlightened principles. Its theoretical foundation was the *Great Nakaz* she issued in 1766, which argued that Russia was a European state under a centralized monarchy where rational laws and policies would insure the welfare of all its subjects. The Commission, whose 564 members were drawn from various elements of the free population throughout the empire, first met on July 30, 1767. Although there was some interesting debate over reports and recommendations the deputies brought from their constituencies, the overall results were negligible. Plenary sessions ended in December 1768 without a single resolution being adopted, although some sub-committees continued to meet until 1773. The Legislative Commission is discussed in treatments of Catherine's reign. See the entry by L.V. Milov, MERSH, Vol. 19, pp. 147-48; and Madariaga, *Russia in the Age of Catherine the Great*, pp. 139-83.

59. SRIO, Vol. 7, pp. 321-322. (Soviet editor's note)

60. Literally "making himself my equal."

61. *Russkii arkhiv* (Russian Archive) 1865, 2nd. ed. (Moscow, 1866), pp. 484-485. (Soviet editor's note)

62. SRIO , Vol. 7, p. 234. (Soloviev's note)

63. PSZ, Vol. 16, No. 11, 988. (Soviet editor's note)

64. A large salt lake about eighty-five miles northeast of Tsaritsyn.

65. Ivan Ivanovich Nepliuev (1693-1773) rose from obscure origins to fill a variety of state positions with distinction from the reign of Peter I to that of Catherine II. Sent abroad for naval studies in 1716, he went from a naval post in St. Petersburg to Constantinople in 1721, where he served until 1735 as Russian resident. Appointed governor of Kiev in 1739, he fell briefly from favor when Elizabeth seized power in 1741. As governor of Orenburg from 1742 to 1758, he administered his vast and restless territory admirably. He built a chain of fortresses, the Uzh line, refounded the city of Orenburg on its modern site, placated local cossacks and earned the respect of the Bashkirs and other Muslim peoples of the region, despite their resentment at Russian efforts to Christianize and settle them. In 1760 Elizabeth named him to the Senate and as a member of the conference she established to reform government structures. Nepliuev supported Catherine in her 1762 coup, and she rewarded him lavishly when blindness forced him to retire in 1764. He spent his last years compiling his memoirs, which remain an important source for his era. See entry by Munro, MERSH, Vol. 24, pp. 147-151.

66. *Russkii arkhiv* 1884, No. 1, p. 261. (Soviet editor's note)

67. Count Burckhardt Christoph Münnich (1683-1767) was born in Oldenburg and after service in the French, Hessian, Imperial and Polish armies entered Russian service in 1721. Between 1723 and 1732 he supervised construction of the Ladoga canal, which greatly increased the flow of commerce to St. Petersburg. He had a major impact on military policy under Anna, whether establishing Russia's first corps of engineers, founding the Imperial Cadet Academy in 1731, reforming military law or introducing heavy cavalry units. Münnich undertook diplomatic assignments and commanded forces against Poland and Turkey in the 1730s. He made an abortive bid for power in 1740 by unseating Ernst Johann Biron as regent for the infant Ivan VI with the boy's mother Anna Leopoldovna, but in turn was deposed and sent to exile in Siberia when Elizabeth seized power. Allowed to return to St. Petersburg by Peter III in 1762, Münnich unwisely backed him against Catherine but soon was reconciled. In the last stage of his remarkable career he was director of the Baltic ports, wrote a lengthy treatise on government and advised Catherine on the division of the Senate into departments as Soloviev describes in this volume. See Munro, MERSH, Vol. 23, pp. 182-188.

68. Alexis Mikhailovich (1629-1676), who was tsar from 1645 to 1676, had his own problems with copper money. To pay for the lengthy war with Poland which began in 1654, the government increased the proportion of copper to silver in coins and finally resorted to copper alone. Despite efforts to maintain face value, rapid inflation, widespread shortages and poverty ensued. The new copper coinage sparked a mass protest on July 25, 1662. Thousands marched on the tsar's residence at Kolomenskoe outside Moscow demanding lower taxes and punishment of counterfeiters and speculators. Although there was little bloodshed, a number of merchant warehouses were looted. The disturbances were put down that afternoon, and harsh reprisals followed. See entry by Hugh F. Graham, "Copper Revolt," MERSH, Vol. 8, pp. 58-60. For a full discussion of Alexis's reign see Joseph T. Fuhrmann, *Tsar Alexis, His Reign and His Russia* (Academic International Press, 1981).

69. Ivan Ivanovich Betskoy (1704-1795) was the illegitimate son of Field Marshal Prince Ivan Yurevich Trubetskoy. Born in Sweden, he entered Russian service in Paris in 1722 and advanced in rank after joining his father as aide-de-camp back in Russia in 1726. After a brief stint as chamberlain to the future Peter III, he fled court intrigue in 1747 for extensive travels in Western Europe. He spent the years abroad studying European thought and public institutions, especially educational, until Peter III recalled him in 1762. He kept his court position under Catherine, who named him director of the Academy of Fine Arts and acting director of the Cadet Corps in 1763. Betskoy also drafted plans for a comprehensive educational system under the strong influence of Locke and Rousseau. He argued that boarding schools run by the state were the best means to form enlightened and virtuous citizens. Soloviev describes the founding of the Moscow Foundling Home at Betskoy's initiative. Institutions modelled on the same principles were established for girls from the nobility and the middle ranks, while

the Cadet Corps was restructured along the same lines for noble boys. He also inspired the establishment of a gymnasium attached to the Academy of Fine Arts and a commercial school for boys from the merchant class. The comprehensive network Betskoy envisioned never materialized, but several institutions, such as the Smolny Institute for girls, the Cadet Corps and the foundling homes survived until 1917. See entry by Mary West Case, MERSH, Vol. 4, pp. 102-106.

70. PSZ, Vol. 16, No. 11, 908. (Soviet editor's note) Betskoy presented his ideas on education in the third chapter of *Prosveshchenie v Rossii ot osnovaniia Moskovskogo universiteta do konchiny Lomonosova (1755-1765)* (Enlightenment in Russia from the Founding of Moscow University to the Death of Lomonosov 1755-1765). (Soloviev's note)

71. Alexander Ivanovich Cherkasov (1728-1788) was the son of a cabinet secretary of Empress Elizabeth. At the age of fourteen he was sent with his brother to Cambridge University, entering the Preobrazhensky Guards Regiment upon his return. He retired with the rank of guards captain due to illness in 1761, but in 1762 his education and long experience led him to be chosen to organize the College of Medicine. As Soloviev describes here, Cherkasov was named its first president, a post he held until 1775, and was given the rank of high chamberlain. He strove with limited success to improve hospital medical training and to encourage Russians to enter a medical profession hitherto dominated by foreigners. It was through his intercession that the celebrated Dr. Thomas Dimsdale came from England in 1768 to vaccinate Catherine and Grand Duke Paul against smallpox. He retired in 1778 with the rank of senior privy councillor, living in the country until his death in 1788.

CHAPTER IV

1. The Yakuts are a Turkic-speaking people who moved from the steppe to the middle reaches of the Lena river in the middle ages, retaining some of their traditional nomadic ways. Like other Siberian peoples, the Yakuts periodically rose unsuccessfully against the extension of Russian rule and the imposition of the fur tribute in the seventeenth century. Many were converted to Orthodoxy after the Irkutsk diocese was established in 1731. The Tungus, today called the Evenki, are a Northeast Siberian people whose language is part of the Manchu group. Even today some still follow a life of hunting and reindeer herding. Many of the Tungus also were converted to Orthodoxy. The Chukchi, who speak a paleo-Siberian language, led a subsistence existence in the northeastern tip of Siberia. In recent years there has been considerable contact between them and closely-related native peoples on the American side of the Bering Strait. The Buriats are a Mongol people living around Lake Baikal. Originally animists, most were converted to Buddhism by Tibetan and Mongolian missionaries at the beginning of the eighteenth century. Their life historically was based on nomadic herding, but the presence of numerous monasteries and the introduction of a written language early in the nineteenth century made them more developed than many of the other Siberian peoples.

2. PSZ , Vol. 16, No. 11, 749. (Soviet editor's note)

3. Starting about 100 B.C. Roman generals and dictators established special colonies for their soldiers (coloniae militum), often using lands seized from opponents. Marius, Sulla, Julius Caesar and Augustus followed this practice, the latter setting up some twenty-eight such settlements in Italy alone.

4. Catherine endorsed the accepted eighteenth-century doctrine that the greater the population, the greater the power and wealth of a state. Although the appeal described here was directed at Europe in general, many governments would not allow it to be published. Most foreign colonists came from the small states of southern and western Germany and the free cities of the Holy Roman empire. Professional recruiters were compensated in land or cash for persuading settlers to come. Some twenty-five thousand Germans answered Catherine's call, growing over time to some three million so-called Volga Germans, because their largest concentration was on the lower Volga. Although, like every other grandiose scheme in Russian history, the initial colonies were beset with problems, later travellers marvelled at the orderly and prosperous German villages and towns that were established. The Volga Germans were summarily deported to Siberia and Central Asia by Stalin when Hitler invaded Russia in 1941. Although over a million citizens of the former Soviet Union still are listed as of German nationality, the language is disappearing, and many are emigrating to Germany. See entry by Joseph L. Wieczynski, "Volga Germans," MERSH, Vol. 42, pp. 230-32 and Roger P. Bartlett, *Human Capital. The Settlement of Foreigners in Russia, 1762-1804* (Cambridge, 1979).

5. The Treaty of Nystadt, signed on August 30 1721, confirmed Peter the Great's victories over Sweden in the Great Northern War (1700-1721). Russia gained considerable territory on the Baltic, including Livonia, Estonia, Ingria, part of Karelia and the islands of Øsel and Dago. See entry in MERSH, Vol. 25, p. 154.

6. PSZ, Vol. 16, Nos. 11, 879, 11, 880. (Soviet editor's note)

7. New Serbia was founded by Elizabeth on the upper course of the Ingul river to settle Orthodox refugees from Turkish rule in the Balkans. The Turks protested in vain that the Russians were prohibited by treaty from sheltering fugitives.

8. See Volume 41 of this series.

9. *Mémoires de la princesse Daschkoff* (Memoirs of Princess Dashkova), Vol. 1, p. 90. (Soloviev's note)

10. PSZ , Vol. 16, No. 10, 861. (Soviet editor's note)

11. The Yaik Cossack army was formed when cossacks from the Don and Volga settled on the Yaik, now the Ural, river at the end of the sixteenth century. Early in the seventeenth century they came under Muscovite authority but preserved considerable autonomy, including the right to enroll fugitives in their ranks. The Yaik Cossack army fought bravely for the sovereigns of the seventeenth and eighteenth centuries but strove to defend their cherished independence against the gradual extension of government authority, joining enthusiastically, for example, Stenka Razin's revolt in 1669-1671. Matters came to a head in Catherine's reign after the events Soloviev describes here. An uprising in 1772 sparked by

opposition to the cossack leader Borodin mentioned here was put down harshly, and most of the army's remaining autonomy was abolished. After the suppression of the Pugachev revolt of 1773-1775, which almost all of the Yaik Cossacks joined, the last vestiges of cossack liberties disappeared amid bloody reprisals. In 1775 the name Yaik with its rebellious associations was expunged, and the Yaik river, the town of Yaitsk and the Yaik Cossack army were renamed the Ural river, Uralsk, and the Ural Cossack army. See entry by Edward D. Sokol, "Yaik Cossacks," MERSH, Vol. 44, pp. 144-151.

12. Until the early Soviet period the designation Kirghiz was used for the Turkic people now called Kazakhs. They first appeared in Russian sources in the sixteenth century as nomads in the vast steppes east of the Caspian Sea. By this time they had broken off from the Uzbek khanate under their own khan, later dividing into three hordes, each made up of a loose confederation of clans. Russia began to move into the area early in the eighteenth century, establishing a line of fortresses based in Omsk, Semipalatinsk, Irtysh and Orenburg. Trade links developed, and leaders of the three hordes swore allegiance to Russia between 1731 and 1742. Clan leaders treated these acts more as temporary alliances which did not prevent them from seeking Manchu protection later in the century. Russian rule was not firmly established until the nineteenth century, and the nomadic peoples of the steppes not settled until Stalin's time. See Andreas Kappeler, *Russland als Vielvölkerreich. Entstehung, Geschichte, Verfall* (Russia as a Multinational State. Rise, History and Decline) (Munich, 1992), pp. 154-159 and George V. Lantzeff and Richard A. Pierce, *Eastward to Empire. Exploration and Conquest on the Russian Open Frontier to 1750* (Montreal, 1972).

13. The Kalmyks are a West Mongolian people who moved into the steppe north of the Caspian Sea in the early seventeenth century. As lamaist Buddhists they stood out among their Islamic Turkic neighbors. Nomadic shepherds and disciplined warriors, the Kalmyks were grouped in hordes or clans and formed a powerful khanate on the middle Volga. Until the death of the powerful Khan Ayuki in 1724 the Russian state treated the Kalmyks as a sovereign entity, signing treaties and military alliances with them. As Soloviev indicates here, the Russians now treated the Kalmyk khans more and more as puppets, and governors of Astrakhan and officials increasingly intervened in Kalmyk affairs. In 1771 more than two-thirds of the Kalmyks answered a Chinese invitation to return to their ancestral homeland. Those who remained were integrated thoroughly into the Russian administrative structure. See Michael Khodarkovsky, *Where Two Worlds Met. The Russian State and the Kalmyk Nomads, 1600-1771* (Cornell, 1992).

14. See Volume 40 of this series.

15. The Kabardians are the eastern branch of the Cherkess who settled at the foot of the mountains near the Terek river. They are Muslims who speak a Caucasian language and are divided into numerous clans with a strong warrior ethos. In the middle of the sixteenth century some Kabardian princes sought Muscovite protection, a tie that was strengthened when Ivan IV married the Kabardian princess Kucheney (Maria Temriukovna). Some entered Russian

service, and it is from these that the prominent noble Cherkassky family is descended. Resistance to the extension of Russian rule lasted well into the nineteenth century; in this period many Kabardians emigrated to Turkish territory.

16. The Cherkess are an Islamic Caucasian people occupying the western part of the Caucasus to the coast of the Black Sea. They held out longer against Russian expansion than related peoples in the eastern Caucasus. See also the previous note.

17. See Volume 42 of this series.

18. SRIO, Vol. 48, p. 522. (Soviet editor's note). See Appendix V.

19. Bogdan Khmelnitsky (1595-1657) was the son of a minor noble who was educated in the Jesuit college of Lvov, then fought for Poland against the Turks and the Russians. Named hetman of the Zaporozhian Cossacks during the great 1648 rebellion to throw off Polish rule, Khmelnitsky pledged loyalty to Moscow at Pereiaslavl in 1654, working thereafter to win the cossacks over to their new masters. Not surprisingly he has continued to arouse controversy. Both tsarist and Soviet Russia praised him for furthering the "natural" unity of the Ukraine with Russia. A large statue of Khmelnitsky was erected in front of the Ukraina Hotel in Moscow on the three hundredth anniversary of Pereiaslavl, and he also is the central figure in the massive sculptural group celebrating the union erected in Kiev. Ukrainians often have seen him as a traitor, and he is a powerful but malevolent character in Henryk Sienkiewicz's romantic nationalistic novels of the period. See the entry in MERSH, Vol. 16, pp. 154-155; George Vernadsky, *Bohdan, Hetman of Ukraine* (Yale, 1941) and Volume 19 of this series.

CHAPTER V

1. Matthias von Simolin (1720-1799) was a career diplomat who had served in Copenhagen and Vienna before becoming Russian resident at the Imperial Diet in Regensburg. Later he was successively Russian ambassador in Denmark, Sweden, Great Britain and France.

2. Karl (1733-1796) was a younger son of August III of Poland (August I of Saxony) who ruled Courland from 1758 until Russia deposed him in favor of Biron in 1763 as Soloviev describes here. See also Chapter I, Note 42.

3. Tadeusz Lipski (1725-1796) was named royal chamberlain in 1748, major general in the royal army in 1760 and castellan of Brest in 1761. In 1763 he became castellan of Łęczyca and a commissioner of the Royal Treasury, also serving that year as a deputy to the Sejm and to the Royal Tribunal. He opposed Russia as a member of the Confederations of Radom and Bar, a stance he maintained until the bitter end. In 1792 he urged Stanisław Poniatowski to resist the Second Partition and participated in the uprising of 1794.

4. The Sejm, or diet, was the legislative body of the Polish-Lithuanian Commonwealth. Its two houses were the Senate, consisting of high church and state officials, and the Chamber of Deputies, whose members were selected by local

diets or "dietines" (sejmiki) of the Polish gentry. It jealously guarded the prerogatives of the gentry against actual or potential encroachment by the crown. By the eighteenth century the Sejm had become the instrument of great magnates who controlled groups of lesser gentry and also an arena in which foreign powers jockeyed for influence in Poland. See Norman Davies, *God's Playground. A History of Poland* (2 vols., Oxford, 1981). Vol. 1. *The Origins to 1795*, pp. 322-339.

5. Józef Zabiełło (died 1794) became marshal of the Permanent Council in 1786 and was a delegate to the Four Years Sejm. Later he became marshal of the Confederation of Targowica which supported Russia in 1792, and was named Lithuanian hetman.

6. Count Hermann Karl von Keyserling (1696-1765) was born in Courland and educated at German universities. He owed his early success to the patronage of the future Empress Anna and Count Biron, who took him to Russia and in 1730 made him vice president of the College of Justice for Livonian and Estonian Affairs, a post he held until 1735. In 1733 he served as president of the Academy of Sciences. He then embarked on a diplomatic career that took him to Poland (1733-1744), the Imperial Diet in Regensburg (1746-1747), Prussia (1747-1748) and Austria (1752-1761). After Catherine's accession in 1762 Keyserling, together with Panin and Bestuzhev, was one of the key advisors on foreign affairs, siding mostly with Panin in disputes. In December 1763 he arrived in Warsaw, where he took a leading role in the political conflict, as Soloviev describes here. He died there in September 1765, only three weeks after the coronation of Stanisław Poniatowski marked the victory of Russian policy, a fitting culmination to a life spent in service of Russia.

7. Catherine, of course, meant to prevent the king from carrying out any policy not in Russia's interest. As Soloviev describes here, Russia already had cultivated strong supporters among the gentry who could be used to advantage in the Sejm.

8. August III of Poland (Friedrich August II of Saxony) (1696-1763) succeeded his father as elector of Saxony immediately upon the latter's death in 1733, but it took somewhat longer for him to gain his father's other title of king of Poland. With the support of Russia and Austria he was able to oust his French-backed rival Stanisław Leszczynski and be crowned in Warsaw in 1734. While Polish culture flourished during his reign, August III allowed the authority of the central government to wither, a gap filled by the great magnates such as the Czartoryskis. His foreign policy was just as passive, as he readily accepted Russian tutelage and allowed Russian and Prussian forces to march across the Commonwealth at will during the Seven Years War.

9. Jan Jędzry Józef Borch (1715-1780) worked with the Czartoryskis to further their reform plans during the reign of Stanisław August. He became vice chancellor in 1767, participated in the delegation that met with Russian representatives at the time of the Partition Sejm of 1773 and served as chancellor in the last year of his life.

10. The French term used in the original is *en avocat*.

11. Fryderyk-Michał Czartoryski (1696-1775) was an uncle of Stanisław Poniatowski and a leader of the powerful Czartoryski faction, known simply as the

"family." He became Lithuanian chancellor in 1752. Under August III the Czartoryskis initially supported the court in hopes of promoting reform, then later passed into the opposition. Despite their intellectual ability and ideals the "family" contributed to Poland's decline by factional politics, even, as Soloviev describes here, seeking outside, in this case Russian, allies.

12. Stanisław August Poniatowski (1732-1798) was the last king of Poland, reigning from 1764 to the dissolution of the Commonwealth in the Third Partition in 1795. The scion of a prominent noble family, he received an excellent education, including time with leading figures of the European enlightenment in Paris. He went to St. Petersburg in 1757 as secretary to the British ambassador, where for a time he was a lover of the then- Grand Duchess Catherine. In this volume Soloviev provides an lengthy account of Catherine's vigorous and successful campaign to put him on the Polish throne with the help of Prussia, England and Poniatowski's powerful Czartoryski relatives. He soon disappointed his Russian patrons by supporting reforms in what was a vain attempt to strengthen royal power and preserve Polish independence. In the face of overwhelming international, particularly Russian, pressure and resistance from Polish noble factions, he was forced to acquiesce in the three partitions which dismembered his country and led to his abdication in 1795. While his talent and intelligence are unquestioned, historians are divided between those who call him weak and those arguing he did what he could in an impossible situation. On Stanisław August in particular and Polish affairs in general in this period, see Davies, *God's Playground*, Vol. 1, Chapter 18.

13. Władysław Lubienski (1703-1767) was a partisan of the king until his sudden death in 1767.

14. Teodor Potocki (1664-1738) became primate of Poland in 1722. Initially he favored August II then switched his support from the Saxons to Stanisław Leszczynski in the election of 1733.

15. Michał Massalski (died 1768) supported the Czartoryskis during the 1763-1764 interregnum, partly because his Radziwiłł rivals in Lithuania opposed them. Later he turned against them and what he saw as harmful Russian influence. In the Sejm of 1766 he spoke against Russian-sponsored proposals to extend dissident rights.

16. Jan Klemens Branicki (1689-1771) was the leader of a family that long opposed the Czartoryskis. As crown hetman his overriding goal was to defend the privileges of his and other traditional offices in the name of "republican" principles. In the chaotic struggle following the death of August III the Potockis, the Radziwiłłs and the Saxon party supported him for the royal title against Stanisław Poniatowski. Forced to flee the country after Poniatowski's election Branicki, by now somewhat disillusioned with the king, for a time in 1767 negotiated with the Russians in hopes they would support restoration of traditional rights. When it became clear the Russians really wanted full control of Poland, Branicki and his associates looked variously for help from France, Saxony or Turkey. His estate at Białystok rivalled Versailles in splendor.

17. Although Keyserling uses the term *senatus consilium* (Senatorial Council), the body he describes more likely is the Senate itself. The Senatorial Council

consisted of sixteen "resident" senators chosen by the full Senate of one hundred forty members. With the king it conducted business between regular Senate sessions. The Senate, which developed from the old Royal Council, was made up of prominent ecclesiastical and lay officials and was the upper chamber of the Sejm or diet of the Polish-Lithuanian Commonwealth. For a fuller description of the governmental structure of the Commonwealth, see Davies, *God's Playground*, Vol. 1, pp. 321-372.

18. The *pacta conventa* was the formal agreement between a newly-elected king and the Sejm binding the monarch to certain policies and procedures in return for the Sejm's approval of his coronation. The first such formal agreement was drafted in 1573 at the election of Henry of Valois, with additional provisions attached at the accession of Stephen Bathory in 1576. Although properly speaking the term Henrician Articles referred to the 1573 agreement, and the *pacta conventa* to that of 1576, both were used interchangeably thereafter. See Davies, *God's Playground*, 1, pp. 334-335.

19. Sigismund III had aroused gentry opposition by his Germanic tastes, narrow piety and foreign adventures, most notably the expedition to put the False Dmitry on the throne of Moscow. In addition, his advisors talked openly of establishing a hereditary monarchy, giving the king more taxing authority and establishing a standing royal army. Michał Zebrzydowski led an armed rebellion against the king, the so-called Sandomierz rebellion, to defend gentry rights. Although the rebels were defeated in battle, the leaders of the uprising were treated leniently and efforts to strengthen royal authority abandoned. Keyserling exaggerates by calling this check on the king's authority a "constitution," but naturally it was in Russia's interest to keep royal power weak in 1763 as well.

20. As part of the price for Russian support in his bid for the Polish crown after the death of August II in 1733 August III promised Courland to Empress Anna's favorite, Biron. The "Pacification Sejm" of 1736 recognized August III and the commitments he had made.

CHAPTER VI

1. The Sejm, the dietines and royal elections all adhered to the *liberum veto*, or the right of any single member to nullify decisions taken. The gentry came to regard it as essential to their cherished liberties. The opportunities it offered to Russia and other foreign powers seeking to influence Polish politics are obvious. See Davies, *God's Playground*, 1, pp. 338-39, 344-48.

2. The confederation was a time-honored Polish institution giving formal and legal recognition to the right of an individual, a group or an entity to resist a perceived injustice. An armed league met at an appointed time and place to swear solemnly to fight together until their demands and grievances were satisfied. The confederation ended when justice, as it saw it, was served or the confederation defeated in battle. Eighteenth-century confederations, often abetted by foreign powers as Soloviev describes here, were used frequently by great magnates to

advance their causes, a practice that undermined the central government and contributed to the demise of the Commonwealth. See Davies, God's *Playground*, Vol. 1, pp. 339-45.

3. The exploits of Philibert de Grammont (1621-1707) were the basis for Anthony Hamilton's *Mémoires du comte de Grammont* (Memoirs of the Count of Grammont) to which Keyserling alludes. As Hamilton portrayed him, Grammont bitterly opposed Cardinal Mazarin's tutelage over Louis XIV while proclaiming his loyalty to and affection for the king. See Appendix VI.

4. The Seven Years War. See above, Chapter I, Note 41.

5. A town in Saxony.

6. The letter, written in French, concludes with a phrase in German, "the Poles will love the Haidamaks [Ukrainian cossacks]." (Soloviev's note)

7. See Appendices VII-VIII. Jan Jerzy Flemming (1699-1771) also held a number of military posts, including that of Pomeranian military commander after 1766. A strong supporter of the Czartoryskis, he was married successively to two daughters of Michał Czartoryski, and his daughter married another Czartoryski. Although he supported the confederation summoned by Radziwiłł in 1764, he took no part in those of Radom and Bar. Prince Karol Stanisław Radziwiłł (1734-1790) became Wilno military commander in 1762. He was the greatest magnate in Lithuania and a staunch defender of the liberties of the old gentry. He left the country after Poniatowski's election, returning in 1767. At Repnin's urging he became marshal that year of the Russian-inspired Confederation of Radom.

8. Friedrich Christian. See above, Chapter I, Note 42.

9. The Piasts were the first dynasty of Poland, beginning with Mieszko I in the tenth century. Although the direct line had died out long before, the term Piast is used here to designate a native Pole in contrast to the recent Saxon kings and the various foreign candidates then being advanced.

10. Adam Kazimierz Czartoryski (1734-1823) was the only son of Prince August Czartoryski (see following Note). As a youth he acquired an excellent education and travelled widely in Western Europe. He succeeded his father as general of the Podolian lands in 1756. Later he attracted the sympathy of Grand Duchess Catherine during a trip to Russia in 1759. Although the Czartoryskis preferred him as the royal candidate, the Russians passed over him in favor of Stanisław Poniatowski. Adam then supported his cousin's election, later helping form a corps of cadets. In the 1770s he broke with the king to join his family's old enemies, the Potockis, in resisting royal initiatives. Adam worked to promote education in the last years of the Commonwealth.

11. August-Aleksander Czartoryski (1697-1782) was the brother of Michał (See above, Chapter V, Note 11) and the father of Adam (See previous note). His marriage in 1731 to the wealthy Zofia Sienawska enabled the Czartoryskis to exercise a powerful influence on Polish politics over the next several generations. August and his relatives first supported August II, then under August III promoted reforms against the strong opposition of the Potockis. Catherine II's accession to the Russian throne in 1762 raised their hopes for power in Poland because of her previous liaison with August's and Michał's nephew Stanisław Poniatowski.

While Catherine worked with the Czartoryskis to put Poniatowski on the throne as Soloviev describes in this volume, she later urged him to break with his uncles because she felt they were making him a less than pliant Russian tool. August became general crown hetman in 1764.

12. See above, Chapter I, Note 42.

13. See above, Chapter I, Note 42.

14. The term Greek often was used to describe any Orthodox.

15. The Uniates in the Commonwealth were former Orthodox Christians who preserved their rites and traditions when, with considerable encouragement from the Polish authorities and the Jesuits, they accepted the authority of Rome in the Union of Brest (1596). The Russians always regarded the Uniates either as traitors or victims of Western chicanery. They never achieved full equality with Roman Catholics within the Commonwealth but, as the passage here indicates, were perceived by the Russians as favored over Poland's Orthodox subjects.

16. Louis (1729-1765) was the son of Louis XV who died before he could ascend the throne. At this time his wife was Maria Josepha of Saxony.

17. Frederick II the Great (1712-86) was directly involved in many of the foreign policy issues treated in this volume, especially those related to Poland. When Peter III succeeded Elizabeth in 1762, he pulled Russia out of the alliance with France and Austria that at one point threatened the existence of the Prussian state. By the Peace of Hubertusburg, signed February 15, 1763 between Prussia, Austria, and Saxony, Austria was forced to renounce all claims to Silesia, which Frederick had seized in the War of the Austrian Succession (1740-1747). He in turn evacuated Saxony. An alliance with Prussia was the basic component of Panin's Northern System and, as Soloviev describes in this volume, Frederick found Poland a mutually beneficial area of cooperation. Twice during Frederick's reign and once during his successor's, Russia and Prussia carried this cooperation to its logical conclusion through the partitions of Poland. In addition to their fundamental agreement on most foreign policy issues, Catherine and Frederick developed a close personal rapport over the years based on similar intellectual interests and a common commitment to a style of rule that came to be called enlightened despotism.

18. Maria Theresa's son Joseph, who succeeded his father as Holy Roman emperor in 1765 and his mother as emperor of Austria in 1780, married Isabella of Bourbon-Parma in 1763, although she died that same year. Prince Wenzel Anton von Kaunitz-Reitberg (1711-1794) began his diplomatic career in 1740, and by 1749 had won Maria Theresa's endorsement of his plan to abandon Austria's previous dependence on England and The United Provinces for an alliance with France and Russia. In 1753 he was named head of the state chancery, from which position with the empress's blessing he had almost sole control of Austrian foreign policy until her death in 1780. Although his power diminished somewhat after the accession of Joseph II, who admired Frederick II greatly, Kaunitz continued to exercise considerable influence until the reigns of Leopold II and Francis II. He resigned in 1792 and died in 1794. See Karl A. Roider, Jr. *Austria's Eastern Question, 1700-1790* (Princeton, 1982).

19. The ruling house of Prussia.

20. Although Peter the Great supported August II against the Swedish-backed Stanisław Leszczynski, he spent some time in Poland in 1706 and 1707 considering other candidates when August deserted his throne. In 1715 he initially backed the Confederation of Tarnogrod against August, then supported him only after Peter's envoy, reinforced by eighteen thousand Russian troops, forced the king and the Sejm to accept what amounted to a Russian protectorate. The parenthetical query is Soloviev's.

21. Charles of Lorraine (1712-1780) was the youngest son of Leopold, duke of Lorraine, whose eldest son Francis married Maria Theresa, later becoming Holy Roman emperor. In 1744 Charles married Maria Theresa's sister, although she died shortly thereafter. His military record as an Austrian officer was mixed, culminating in a crushing defeat by Frederick II at Leuthen in 1757. As governor of the Austrian Netherlands he had more success, introducing some enlightened reforms.

22. Friedrich II (1720-1785) became count, or landgrave, of Hesse-Cassel in 1760. His conversion to Catholicism, a step which did not affect his subjects, made him more attractive as a candidate for the Polish throne. Later he sent twelve thousand of his soldiers to fight in the American Revolution in return for a British subsidy, money he applied to the cultural and intellectual development of his principality.

23. Nikolay Vasilievich Repnin (1734-1801) was the son of an old princely family who distinguished himself in the Seven Years War, earning the rank of major general in 1762. Despite his lack of success as minister plenipotentiary in Prussia (1762-1763) he was appointed ambassador to Poland in 1764, thanks to the influence of his wife's uncle, Nikita Panin. During his tenure in Poland (1764-1769) Repnin forcefully promoted Russian interests, not hesitating to use bribery and force to do so. He was recalled in 1769 because of widespread Polish resistance to his methods. He then returned to active military service against Turkey. Following a trip abroad he participated in negotiations for the Treaty of Kuchuk-Kainardji (1774) and served as extraordinary envoy to Turkey (1774-1776). His masonic connections and the eclipse of his mentor Panin caused him to be shunted off to governor-generalships in the western provinces between 1778 and 1791. He saw military service again in the second Turkish war (1787-1791) but clashed with Potemkin. From 1792 to 1798 he was governor general of Livonia and Estonia. He returned to Poland as commander of Russian forces there, imposing harsh rule in the territories acquired in the Third Partition. Although Paul I initially favored him, giving him the rank of field marshal he long had desired and entrusting him with special assignments, he was forced to retire definitively in 1798. See entry by Ransel, MERSH, Vol. 31, pp. 26-28.

24. Maria Theresa (1717-1780) became empress of Austria in 1740 but immediately faced opposition from Bavaria, France, the Spanish Bourbons and Prussia. In the War of the Austrian Succession (1740-1747) she was able to gain control of the lands she had inherited with the important exception of Silesia,

which Frederick II of Prussia seized and retained in the peace settlement. Her efforts to regain the province in alliance with France and Russia against England and Prussia in the Seven Years War (1756-1763) failed. Maria Theresa's hostility to Prussia and its king was a major, if not the major, element shaping Austrian policy in this period. In this volume Soloviev shows how Russia's closer cooperation with Prussia inevitably led to conflict with Austria which, even so, was drawn into participating in the First Partition of Poland in 1772 with Russia and Prussia.

25. Kazimierz Poniatowski (1721-1800) was Stanisław's older brother. He served as lord high chamberlain from 1742 to 1773. He played a key role in the first years of his brother's reign in efforts to create a royal party independent of the Czartoryskis. He withdrew from politics at the time of the First Partition.

26. Andrzej Poniatowski (1735-1773) was a younger brother of the future king. He served in the Austrian army as a young man and attained the rank of lieutenant general in 1760. In the period 1765-1766 he was involved in projects to arrange a marriage between his brother and an Austrian archduchess. His son Józef Antoni Poniatowski fought brilliantly for Napoleon and was named a marshal of France in 1813.

27. Michał Poniatowski (1736-1794), Stanisław's brother, became primate of Poland in 1784. As a member of the Educational Commission he actively promoted culture and learning during his brother's reign. He committed suicide in the midst of the 1794 insurrection.

28. Ignacy Ogiński (1698-1774), held various offices in the grand duchy of Lithuania and participated in two Polish delegations to St. Petersburg.

29. Ignacy Massalski (1729-1794), who became bishop of Wilno in 1762, cooperated closely with the Russians after the First Partition in 1772. He took an active role in the Confederation of Targowica which the Russians inspired in 1792 in opposition to the reform constitution of 1791. Not surprisingly he was regarded as a traitor and was lynched during the nationalist uprising of 1794.

30. See above, Note 7.

31. Pawel Mostowski (died 1781) became a major general in the royal army in 1754, and was named a lieutenant general and Pomeranian military commander in 1758. He was a partisan of the Saxon house, but in 1764 supported the Czartoryski reforms and the election of Stanisław Poniatowski. Mazovian military commander after 1766, he turned against the king, calling for Poniatowski's deposition in favor of the Saxon elector. He was a member of the Confederation of Radom.

32. Andrzej Zamoyski (1716-1792), a member of one of Poland's most powerful families, worked closely with the Czartoryskis. He served as crown chancellor from 1764 to 1767 where he tried to limit the *liberum veto* and promote local reform. He resigned in protest in 1767 when the Russian ambassador Nikolay Repnin seized members of the Sejm who opposed Russian policy. During the Confederation of Bar he advised the king to resist Russia and not to antagonize the confederates. He withdrew from public life in 1780.

33. Stanisław Lubomirski (1719-1783), a strong supporter of the Czartoryski party in the first years of Poniatowski's reign, became lord high marshal in 1766.

In 1768 he worked to reconcile Stanisław Poniatowski with the Confederation of Bar, which was formed in 1768 to protest growing Russian pressure on Poland. Before the First Partition he was part of the magnate opposition protesting the king's cooperation with Russia. He also worked on civic improvements in Warsaw.

34. See Note 7, above.

35. Wacław Rzewuski (1706-1779) was one of four outspoken opponents at the Sejm of 1768 arrested and deported to Russia on Repnin's orders.

36. Franciszek Bielinski (1683-1766) was the Chełm military commander after 1736, becoming high crown marshal in 1742. Under his energetic direction the Warsaw Street Commission paved streets and made other improvements to beautify the city.

37. Jerzy August Mniszech (1715-1778) was court marshal from 1742 to 1767. He organized the court party and opposed the Czartoryskis. Later he angered Russia by opposing rights for religious dissidents and was a leader in the Confederation of Radom, organizing provincial confederations to support it in Great Poland.

38. Kajetan Sołtyk (1715-1788) was arrested along with three others on Repnin's orders at the Sejm of 1768 for opposing dissident rights, and was sent in chains to Kaluga. Released that year, he was one of the handful who protested openly against the First Partition at the Sejm of 1773.

39. Adam Krasiński (1714-1800) was a guiding force behind the anti-Russian Confederation of Bar formed in 1768 and acted as its chief diplomatic agent.

40. Józef Sosnowski (died 1783) was the grand referendary of Lithuania. Later he opposed Poniatowski and Russian influence, then supported the king when he pursued a more independent policy towards St. Petersburg.

41. Florimundus Claudius, count of Mercy-Argenteau (1727-1794), came from a family in Lorraine that long had served the Habsburgs. After diplomatic posts in Turin and in 1762-1763 at St. Petersburg, Mercy became minister and later ambassador to France from 1766 to 1790. Marie Antoinette's marriage to the future Louis XVI in 1770 put him at the center of French court life and politics. After the revolution began he strove energetically to rally support for the royalist cause from the Austrian Netherlands and as Austrian ambassador to London.

42. See above, Chapter I, Note 41.

43. Frederick II habitually referred to himself (in the third person) as "the king."

44. Vladimir Timofeevich Dolgoruky (or Dolgorukov) (1720-1803) was the son of a Russian diplomat, accompanying his father to France and Constantinople. As a major in the engineers he helped win military support for Catherine at her coup in 1762 and that same year was named ambassador to Prussia with the rank of colonel. He held this post for almost twenty-five years, winning the favor of Frederick II in the process, retiring to Moscow when the Prussian king died in 1786.

45. See above, Note 20.

46. Gédéon de Benoît served as Prussian resident in Warsaw after 1758.

47. Karl Wilhelm, Count Finck von Finckenstein (1714-1800), was the son of a Prussian general field marshal. He was a childhood playmate of the future

Frederick II because his father was the crown prince's tutor. After studies in Geneva and travel in Western Europe he entered the Prussian civil service. He served from 1735 to 1740 as minister in Stockholm. After Frederick's accession in 1740 Finckenstein rose rapidly. After serving as envoy to Denmark, England and a second time to Sweden, in 1747 he was named a state minister and ambassador to Russia. As a cabinet minister after 1749 Finckenstein was one of Frederick's closest advisors, and the king often turned to him during the Seven Years War. He held sole responsibility for foreign affairs from 1760 to 1763 and continued to exercise considerable influence on the king thereafter. He died on January 3, 1800.

48. Karl Adolf von Rixen (or Rexin)'s real name was Gottfried Fabian Haude. A Silesian by birth, he had promoted Austrian interests in Istanbul until switching his allegiance to Prussia after 1740. After an absence he returned to Istanbul in January 1757 and attempted to stir the Porte to action against Russia, then Prussia's opponent in the Seven Years War. After Peter III's alliance with Prussia early in 1762 Rixen devoted the same energy to encouraging Turkey to oppose Austria. He spent one million thalers between 1757 and 1762 trying to influence Turkish policy.

49. Ahmed Resmi Efendi (1700-1783). For an account of his career, which includes Resmi's account of his mission, see Virginia H. Aksan, *An Ottoman Statesman in War and Peace. Ahmed Resmi Efendi (1700-1783)* (Leiden, 1995).

50. At the time of Peter III's accession to the throne in December 1761 Russia and its allies France and Austria were on the brink of decisive victory over Frederick II. At one point Russian troops occupied Berlin, but the new tsar was enamored of all things Prussian, particularly its king, and in February 1762 unilaterally issued a declaration of peace. By a peace treaty signed with Prussia on April 24/May 5, 1762 Peter returned all the territory Russia had taken, and shortly afterwards concluded an alliance with Prussia against Austria, both parties agreeing to remain neutral if either went to war with another power. Frederick also agreed to support the duke of Holstein's claims on Courland and the recovery of Schleswig from Denmark. While Catherine used Russian resentment at Peter's partiality to Prussia both in foreign affairs and in his domestic style of rule to advantage in her successful coup in June 1762, this treaty helped pave the way for Catherine's close cooperation with Prussia later in her reign. One clause, for example, which was a portent for the future, promised Russian and Prussian protection for Protestant and Orthodox dissidents in the Polish Commonwealth.

51. Freiherr von Ried followed a military career before becoming Austrian ambassador to Berlin.

52. *Forschungen zur deutschen Geschichte*, Vol. 9, pp. 11, 12, 66, 67, 89-92, 99-105. (Soviet editor's note)

53. See above, Chapter I, Note 41.

54. Prince Dmitry Mikhailovich Golitsyn (1721-1793) served as Russian *chargé d'affaires* in Paris from 1760 to 1761, then as ambassador to Austria from 1761 to 1792.

55. Prussia wanted Austrian acceptance of its conquest of Silesia in the War of the Austrian Succession (1740-1747). The hope of regaining Silesia was Maria Theresa's primary goal in the Seven Years War.

56. Dmitry Alekseevich Golitsyn (1734-1803) served in the Russian embassy in Paris from 1754 to 1768, where he became a close friend of Voltaire, d'Holbach and other prominent figures of the Enlightenment. He continued his keen interest in contemporary European thought after being named minister extraordinary to The Hague in 1768, holding the rank of ambassador there from 1770 to 1782. Golitsyn published voluminously on literature, philosophy, history, economics and the natural sciences. His son later had a notable career as a Catholic missionary priest on the Pennsylvania frontier under the name of Demetrius Gallitzin. See G.K. Tsverava, *Dmitry Alekseevich Golitsyn. 1734-1803* (Leningrad, 1985).

57. A common title of the French king.

58. Louis-Auguste Le Tonnelier, baron de Breteuil (1730-1807), came to the attention of Louis XV after military service. After diplomatic assignments in Copenhagen and Cologne, he was sent to Russia in 1760. From there he went to Sweden, Holland and Naples. He was France's envoy to Austria from 1775 to 1783, when he returned to Paris. There he had responsibility for the department of Paris and the *maison du roi*, leaving his mark as a strong supporter of royal power. He continued to be involved in diplomatic negotiations in exile after 1789, returning to Paris in 1802, where he died poor and forgotten in 1807.

59. Louis XV (1710-1774) succeeded his great-grandfather Louis XIV as king of France in 1715. His marriage in 1725 to Marie Leszczynska, the daughter of the deposed king of Poland Stanisław Leszczynski, helped keep his attention focused on his wife's homeland throughout his reign, for example French intervention in the War of the Polish Succession (1733-1735). Later he attempted to promote the Prince de Conti for the Polish throne. His broader goal was to maintain a strong French role in the east by supporting France's traditional allies, Sweden, Poland and Turkey, but his penchant for secret diplomacy often led to a muddled and ineffective policy in practice. From Soloviev's account in this volume it is obvious how the approach adopted by Louis clashed directly with Russian interests.

60. See above, Chapter I, Note 42.

61. Louis-François de Bourbon, prince de Conti (1717-1776), early distinguished himself by his bravery on the battlefield. At twenty-seven he commanded the Army of Italy which conquered Nice and crossed the Alps, then served in Germany and Flanders. Leaving military service in 1747, Conti became a patron of the arts. He expressed interest when a Polish delegation encouraged his candidacy for the Polish crown in 1747. He and Louis XV preferred the traditional policy of alliances with Turkey, Poland and Sweden, whereas some French ministers preferred to support the house of Saxony in Poland together with Prussia. Louis XV used him as a secret agent in international affairs, and for a time after 1750 he controlled the direction of French foreign policy, although the failure of French efforts in Poland after 1756 led to his disgrace. The death of August III in

1763 gave him brief hope of gaining the Polish crown, but as Soloviev describes in this volume, Louis XV refused to take a strong position in Poland. In the last years before his death in 1776 Conti was a determined opponent of efforts to reform the French monarchy.

62. Count Étienne-François de Choiseul, duc de Praslin (1719-1785, more usually referred to by his comital title), was French foreign minister until 1766, then served as minister of war from 1766 until 1770. From 1761 to 1770 he also was minister for the marine. He rebuilt French military power after the reverses of the Seven Years War and promoted an active French role in international affairs. This meant frequent confrontations with Russia as Catherine energetically promoted its interests in Sweden, Denmark, Poland, Turkey and elsewhere. No wonder she later described Choiseul as "the cursed enemy of my state and my person."

63. The Treaty of Oliva (1660) ended the long Polish-Swedish War of Succession (1600-1660). Sweden retained its Livonian holdings while the Polish king Jan Casimir renounced any claims on the Swedish crown beyond his own lifetime. Oliva also confirmed the Treaty of Wehlau (1657) by which sovereignty over Ducal Prussia was transferred from the Polish crown to the elector of Brandenburg.

64. The Turkish council of ministers.

65. The Russo-Turkish War of 1735-1739 was one more test of arms in Russia's ongoing contest with the Turks. With a friendly King August III installed on the Polish throne in 1735, Russia's flank was secured for a major campaign directed at Azov and the Crimea. Although Russian forces twice broke into the Crimea, and they and their Austrian allies made temporary gains in Moldavia, Austria's surrender of Belgrade without a battle in August 1739 left it and Russia no alternative but to end the war on most unfavorable terms. Austria lost territory acquired earlier in Serbia and Wallachia, while Russia had to abandon Khotin, raze the fortress of Azov and agree not to send its ships into the Black Sea, although Russian merchants were allowed to trade freely in the Ottoman Empire. See entries by Samuel C. Ramer, "Belgrade Treaty of 1739," MERSH, Vol. 3, pp. 206-07, and Karl A. Roider, Jr., *The Reluctant Ally. Austria's Policy in the Austro-Turkish War, 1737-1739* (Baton Rouge, 1972).

66. Catherine refers to the Russo-Turkish War of 1735-1739 when Russia was forced to abandon many of its gains when its Austrian ally concluded a separate peace with Turkey. In 1761 Turkey signed an alliance with Prussia. Given Peter III's partiality for Prussia, Russia hardly could take any action against the Porte.

67. Laurent Bérenger, previously secretary of the French legation in St. Petersburg, assumed the role of *chargé d'affaires* when Breteuil left to become ambassador to Sweden in 1763.

68. *Correspondence secrète de Louis XV* (Secret Correspondence of Louis XV), Vol. 1, pp. 288, 290; *Études diplomatiques et littéraires par M. Alexis de S. Priest* (Diplomatic and Literary Studies by Monsieur Alexis de St.-Priest), Vol. 1, pp. 73, 85-95. (Soviet editor's note)

CHAPTER VII

1. Alexis Mikhailovich Obrezkov (or Obreskov, 1718-1787) was a diplomat who spent most of his career on Turkish affairs. He served as Russian resident in Constantinople from 1751 to 1768. His arrest and imprisonment by the Porte in 1768 was the occasion for the war with Turkey that began that year. He played a key role in negotiating the Treaty of Kuchuk-Kainardji in 1774 which concluded the war on terms very favorable to Russia. See entry in MERSH, Vol. 25, pp. 169-170.

2. Although Montenegro was conquered by the Turks in 1499, Istanbul never established effective control over the warlike clans there beyond occasional payment of the soul tax and some military help against the Venetians in neighboring Dalmatia. What central authority existed was exercised by the bishop of the Cetinje monastery. For a time early in the eighteenth century Venice had some influence in the region. Beginning with Peter the Great Russia supplanted it as the dominant outside element by stressing Orthodox solidarity with the Montenegrins and dispatching subsidies and Russian agents. If Catherine and her advisors periodically were exasperated by what they saw as the ignorance, feuding and venality of various secular and ecclesiastical Montenegrin leaders, they continued to try to incite Montenegro against the Turks. See Barbara Jelavich, History of *the Balkans,* 2 vols. (Cambridge, 1985), Vol. 1, pp. 84-88.

3. The Orthodox in Montenegro followed the same Byzantine rite and used the same Church Slavonic in the liturgy, but there was no juridical connection.

4. That is, in union with Rome and presumably subject to Venetian ecclesiastical authorities.

5. The patriarch of Constantinople, or ecumenical patriarch, held ecclesiastical jurisdiction over the Orthodox in question.

6. Khan Kirim-Girey ruled as khan of the Crimea from 1758 to 1769 under what by this time was nominal Turkish sovereignty. He eagerly answered the Ottoman call to arms against Russia in 1768 and conducted a successful raid of Elisavetgrad province early in 1769 but died shortly thereafter, the last truly independent ruler of the Crimea. Although Crimean independence was prescribed in the Treaty of Kuchuk-Kainardji (1774) which concluded the war, from the outset there was a strong Russian presence which culminated in annexation by Russia in 1783. See Alan W. Fisher, *The Russian Annexation of the Crimea, 1772-1783* (Cambridge, 1970) and *The Crimean Tatars* (Stanford, 1978).

7. In the 1740s the Kievan governor Leontiev sent Nikiforov to the Crimean capital Bakhchisaray to be accredited as resident consul, or agent, but the khan sent him home. In 1763 he returned, and this time was accepted. Although the khan refused to discuss the various issues Nikiforov raised, in 1764 he did permit him to build a house. When Nikiforov took an aggressive role, for example pressuring the Crimeans not to become involved in Polish affairs, he wore out his welcome. In 1764 Selim-Girey replaced Kirim-Girey as khan by promising the divan he would throw Nikiforov out, and so the Russian was expelled in 1765.

8. Köse Bâhir Mustafa Pasha. Earlier he was grand vizier from 1752 to 1755.

9. Charles Gravier, comte de Vergennes (1717-1787), began his diplomatic career in Lisbon in 1740, serving in Frankfurt from 1741 to 1745, and again in Portugal between 1745 and 1750. He became minister plenipotentiary and later ambassador to Turkey in 1754, where he remained until 1767. Here he played a key role in calming the sultan's fears when France joined Turkey's traditional enemies, Russia and Austria, in the Seven Years War. As Soloviev describes here, Vergennes worked energetically to pursue Choiseul's policy of pressuring Turkey to support Polish independence from Russia. Ironically, his superiors, angered by the failure of French policy there, recalled him just before Turkey went to war with Russia in 1768. He returned to the task of trying to curb Russian power in 1771 as ambassador, first to Sweden and then to Denmark. Named minister of foreign affairs in 1774, he resigned himself to the partition of Poland and to further Russian gains at Turkey's expense, concentrating his efforts on forging alliances against England, for example, with vigorous support for the American Revolution. In the last years of his life Vergennes took an active role in debates on the growing governmental financial crisis.

10. Philip of Bourbon (1720-1765), duke of Parma from 1748, was the son of Philip V of Spain and the son-in-law of Louis XV of France.

11. Archduke Joseph (1741-1790), the fourth child and eldest son of Maria Theresa, in 1760 married Isabella of Bourbon-Parma, who died of smallpox November 27, 1763. He succeeded his father as Holy Roman emperor and his mother as ruler of Austria in 1765.

12. The governors of Moldavia and Wallachia held the title of hospodar. The hospodar was chosen by the Porte from the Greek elite of the empire (Phanariots) in return for a large cash payment. They lived well from the revenues of the principalities and presided over lavish courts. For the history of the principalities in the hospodar period see R.W. Seton-Watson, *A History of the Roumanians from Roman Times to the Completion of Unity* (Cambridge, 1934) and Barbara Jelavich, *History of the Balkans* (Cambridge, 1983), Vol. 1, pp. 99-112.

13. Ivan Andreevich Ostermann (1725-1811) was the son of Heinrich Johann Friedrich Ostermann, who made his career under Peter I and Anna, only to fall from power under Elizabeth. Ivan served as Russian ambassador to Sweden from 1760 to 1774 after travel abroad and a tour at the Russian embassy in Paris. After his return to St. Petersburg in 1774 he enjoyed the favor of Catherine and later of Paul I. He was vice chancellor from 1775 to 1776 and chancellor from 1796 until he retired in 1797.

14. The death of Karl XII (1682-1718) and the Russian victory in the Great Northern War (1700-1721) brought an end to Sweden's century as a great power, caused a major realignment of Sweden's political structure and opened the door to continued foreign interference in its domestic affairs. In 1720 reaction against the autocratic rule of Karl XII and his predecessors forced the acceptance of a constitution which gave the four estates of the Riksdag or parliament extensive power over the king and the royal council. Soloviev and many other foreign commentators use the terms Senate and senators for the royal council and its

members. A parliamentary Secret Committee made up of nobles, clergy and burghers, but excluding farmers, handled foreign affairs, finance and all other important matters of state. The estates dominated Swedish politics until a coup by King Gustav III regained control for the crown in 1772. Queen Louisa Ulrika unsuccessfully attempted to undo the 1720 constitution and reassert royal power in 1756. The Riksdag's central role during what Swedes call *frihetstiden,* or age of liberty, led to the emergence of two disciplined parties, nicknamed the Hats and the Caps. The Hats, who drew much of their strength from the upper aristocracy and wealthy commercial classes, tended to favor mercantilist policies and an active role in international affairs. The Caps had closer ties with the lower aristocracy, clergy, farmers and some courtiers, although both parties opposed a strong monarchy. Policy differences usually were less important than personal and party loyalties. Divided authority, bitter partisan rivalry, strict observance of secrecy in parliamentary proceedings, Sweden's relative poverty and the expense of attending parliamentary sessions fostered corruption on a grand scale. Foreign powers used the opportunity to gain leverage in the weakened but still strategically important nation. Here Russia played the key role. It upheld the 1720 constitution to keep a once threatening neighbor divided, cultivated the Caps and looked for chances to expand into Karelia and Finland. Just before the period Soloviev treats here, the Hat party, which had long-standing ties with France and held power since 1739 lost considerable support for introducing Sweden into the Seven Years War on the French side, a step which brought Sweden no benefit and great losses. Catherine kept her diplomatic options open by renouncing Peter III's alliance with Prussia but also staying aloof from Russia's previous allies, France and Austria. In this volume Soloviev describes the initial workings of Nikita Panin's Northern System in Sweden, as Ostermann in coordination with England and Prussia attempted to bolster support among the Caps to counter the Hats and their French patrons. Although, as noted earlier, Russia opposed strengthening royal power, it saw a chance to influence King Adolf Fredrik (1710-1771), who ascended the throne in 1751, through his talented and energetic queen, Louisa Ulrika (1720-1784), a younger sister of Frederick II of Prussia. For a general survey of Sweden for this period see Franklin D. Scott, *Sweden. The Nation's History* (Minneapolis, 1977), pp. 237-267 and for a detailed treatment of the interaction of domestic and foreign policy see Michael F. Metcalf, *Russia, England and Swedish Party Politics, 1762-1766* (Stockholm, 1977).

15. General Fredrik Axel von Fersen (1719-1794), a leading member of the Hats and a lifelong friend of France, had a distinguished military career. Although he long defended the rights of the aristocracy against the crown, erosion of Hat power in the Riksdag session of 1760-1762 in which he served as land marshal led him to make an extraordinary overture to the queen. If she helped him bring the session to a satisfactory close, he would support reform of the 1720 constitution, a prospect that understandably alarmed Ostermann.

16. Baron Matthias von Hermansson (1716-1789) was secretary of state for foreign affairs and a leading member of the Hat party who joined Fersen's approach to the queen. See also previous Note.

17. Colonel Fredrik Carl Sinclair (1723-1776) was a confidante of the queen and a leader of the court party who sought opportunities to strengthen the crown in the confused competition between the Hats and Caps and their French and Russian patrons.

18. Panin refers to Russia's victory over Sweden in the Great Northern War (1700-1721), marking the end of Sweden as a great European power. Thereafter Sweden had to face strong opposition in the Baltic and, as Soloviev describes here, growing foreign involvement in its domestic affairs.

19. Soloviev does not specify the monetary unit.

20. Johann Albrecht, Baron von Korff (1697-1766), was president of the Academy of Sciences from 1734 to 1740, Russian representative to the Hanseatic cities and the district of Lower Saxony from 1740 to 1741, envoy in Sweden from 1746 to 1748 and ambassador to Denmark from 1748 to 1766.

21. Catherine's deposition of Peter III in 1762 paved the way for friendly relations with Denmark. In his brief tenure on the Russian throne Peter concluded an alliance with Prussia to wrest his old duchy of Holstein-Gottorp from Danish rule. Catherine abandoned this policy immediately upon her accession. Soloviev's account reflects the key role Count Johann Hartwig von Bernstorff (1717-1781) played in Danish politics from 1751 to his fall from power in 1770 when Johann Friedrich Struensee (1737-1772), the king's physician and the queen's lover, briefly came to power. During his tenure Bernstorff was a staunch supporter of Russian policy, with the empress publicly expressing her regret at this departure. In addition to directing foreign affairs, Bernstorff had a hand in almost every public and private enterprise in Denmark.

22. See previous Note.

23. This is an obvious reference to the Great Northern War (1700-1721) between Russia and Sweden. Russia emerged victorious and acquired the Baltic provinces in the Treaty of Nystadt (1721) but only after initial setbacks, substantial expenditures of men and resources and warding off Karl XII's daring invasion of the Ukraine.

24. See above, Note 14.

25. Baron Adolf Siegfried von der Osten (1726-1797) represented Denmark in St. Petersburg after 1755, becoming ambassador there in 1757. Here he became the intermediary in Catherine's love affair with Stanisław Poniatowski. He continued in this post until 1766, except for a brief time in Poland in 1761. While under Peter III (1761-1762) Osten had to guard against Peter III's plans to regain the part of his Holstein-Gottorp duchy claimed by Denmark, relations improved after Catherine's accession. After serving as Danish ambassador to Naples from 1766 to 1770, Osten was named foreign minister and director of the Sound tolls in 1770. He left these posts in 1773, later serving as a local prefect and on the supreme court. See also above, Note 21.

CHAPTER VIII

1. John Hobart, second earl of Buckinghamshire (1723-1793) served as a member of Parliament for Norwich and comptroller of the royal household before becoming England's ambassador to Russia from 1762 to 1765. From 1776 to 1780 he was lord lieutenant of Ireland. Although Soloviev and other writers often refer to him as Buckingham, this term is more properly used for a separate line of earls, marquesses and dukes. His half brother George Hobart, who eventually became third earl, accompanied him as secretary to the embassy.

2. See Volume 42 of this series.

3. See Appendix IX.

4. In 1581 Elizabeth I granted a charter to the Turkey Company after the sultan gave English merchant William Harborne trading privileges. In 1592 it was amalgamated with the Venice Company under the new name of the Levant Company, which carried on an active trade in the eastern Mediterranean for over two centuries.

5. Alexander Romanovich Vorontsov (1741-1805) served in the Izmailovsky Guards Regiment, then in 1759 was sent by his uncle Mikhail Vorontsov to a military school in Strasbourg, later accompanying him to Paris and Madrid. In 1761 he was named *chargé d'affaires* in Vienna and in 1762 minister plenipotentiary to England, where he served until the unhappy departure Soloviev describes here. Although he became a senator and president of the College of Commerce, he remained aloof from court affairs and was forced into retirement in 1791. He returned under Alexander I as chancellor, a post he held until his retirement in 1804. Here in concert with his anglophile brother Semeon (1744-1832), longtime ambassador to England, he promoted Russian rapprochement with England and Austria, and had a major hand in Alexander's break with Napoleon in 1803. In this period Vorontsov also contributed to the reorganization of the Senate and the establishment of ministries. See Patricia Kennedy Grimstead, *The Foreign Ministers of Alexander I* (Berkeley, 1969), pp. 91-103.

6. George Montagu Dunk, second earl of Halifax (1716-1771), took an active interest in colonial development, helping found the city of Halifax, Nova Scotia, which bears his name. Lord lieutenant for Ireland from 1761 to 1763, he also for a time served in 1762 as first lord of the Admiralty. He was secretary of state for the Northern Department, which included Russia, from 1762 to 1763 and again in 1771. He also held the post of secretary of state for the Southern Department for a time after 1763 and was briefly lord privy seal.

7. William Pitt, first earl of Chatham (1708-1778), was the most prominent English politician of his generation. A leading spokesman for the Whig cause since his entry into parliament in 1735, Pitt as a member of the opposition energetically and brilliantly promoted a world campaign against France in the War of the Austrian Succession between 1741 and 1747. Appointed to form a government by

popular demand in 1756 after England's fumbling policy at the outbreak of the Seven Years War, Pitt successfully orchestrated a comprehensive military and diplomatic strategy that created the British empire confirmed by the Treaty of Paris in 1763. By this time he was out of office for two years after clashing with George III in 1761 and remained out of power until his death, except for leading an unsuccessful all-party ministry from 1766 to 1768. Nevertheless he was a powerful and commanding figure, as Panin acknowledges here.

8. The text reads "Polish ministry," but this is obviously a mistake.

9. Thomas Wroughton represented England in Warsaw from 1762 to 1769 as resident, and from 1769 to 1778 with the rank of minister plenipotentiary. He owed his position to his acquaintance with Catherine when he was in Russia before her accession to the throne.

10. John Montagu, fourth earl of Sandwich (1718-1792), served on the admiralty board and as first lord of the Admiralty before becoming secretary of state for the Northern Department in 1763, a post he held until 1765, and again from 1770 to 1771. Although he was first lord of the Admiralty again from 1771 to 1782, his career suffered from England's reverses in the American Revolution. In 1778 James Cook named the Sandwich Islands (now known as Hawaii) in his honor. For his role in foreign policy during this period, see Michael Roberts, *Splendid Isolation, 1763-1780* (Reading, 1970) and Metcalf, *Russia, England and Swedish Party Politics, 1762-1766.*

CHAPTER IX

1. The Academy of Sciences was planned by Peter the Great but the first meeting was not held until November 1725, some months after Peter's death. It was intended to be, and at least up through Soviet times has remained, the guiding force behind research and scholarship in all areas of knowledge. In its early years the members of the academy were overwhelmingly foreigners, most of them Germans. By the latter part of the eighteenth century Russian scholars such as Lomonosov began to hold their own. See entry by William H. Hill, "Academy of Sciences," MERSH, Vol. 1, pp. 20-23 and Wayne Vucinich, *Science in Russian Culture,* 2 vols. (Stanford, 1963-1970).

2. Jakob von Stählin (1709-1785) was born in Swabia and studied at the University of Leipzig. An engraved allegorical tribute to August III, the new king of Poland, earned him an invitation to join the Russian Academy of Sciences as an assistant in 1735. There he wrote poems for public occasions, soon was named professor of elocution and given supervision of engraving for the academy. At Empress Elizabeth's coronation Stählin staged *La Clemenza di Tito* (The Clemency of Titus) with a prologue of his own composition, *La Russia afflita e reconsolata* (Russia Afflicted and Reconsoled), and planned fireworks for the occasion. Elizabeth named him to direct the education of the future Peter III, although Stählin had little success with his wayward pupil. He continued to write

poems, plan public spectacles and teach at the academy, where after 1748 he also was responsible for publishing its *Vedomosti* (Proceedings). In 1763 he accompanied Catherine to Moscow to plan the coronation festivities there. In 1765 he replaced Gerhard Müller as the Academy's conference secretary, a post he held until 1769, and in 1766 was elected a member of the Free Economic Society, where for the next thirteen years Stählin was secretary for foreign correspondence. His responsibilities at the Academy were reduced after Princess Dashkova began to play a major role there, and he died of dropsy in 1785.

3. Mikhail Vasilievich Lomonosov (1711-1765) was Russia's most prominent man of science and letters in the eighteenth century. Born the son of a fisherman in the North, he enrolled in the Slavic-Greek-Latin Academy in Moscow in 1731, was admitted to the Academy of Sciences in 1736 and immediately sent to study mining and chemistry at Marburg and Freiburg in Germany. During his five years abroad he avidly pursued literary as well as scientific subjects and quickly attained a major role both at the Academy and in Russian intellectual life in general after his return to St. Petersburg in 1741. Pushkin's famous description of Lomonosov as Russia's first university captures the breadth of his interests and the importance of his contributions in almost every branch of learning. In addition to research in chemistry, physics, astronomy and geography, Lomonosov paid special attention to Russian language and history, also writing poetry and dramas. Strong-willed and energetic, Lomonosov was embroiled in a number of professional and personal controversies, notably his vehement attacks on the "Scandinavian" thesis of the origins of the Russian state. He had an active hand in the administration of the Academy and helped plan the university which opened in Moscow in 1755 and which today bears his name. See entry by Taylor Stults, MERSH, Vol. 20, pp. 130-132, and by Frank R. Silbajoris in Terras, *Handbook of Russian Literature*, pp. 264-265.

4. See Chapter II, Note 30.

5. See Chapter II, Note 65.

6. See Volume 42 of this series.

7. Karl XII (1682-1718) was the king of Sweden who shortly after ascending the throne in 1697 initially defeated both Russia and the Saxon king of Poland, August II, in the first stages of the Great Northern War (1700-1721). Although he succeeded in placing his candidate Stanisław Leszczynski on the Polish throne in 1706, Karl's daring invasion of the Ukraine ended in disaster with his defeat by the Russians at Poltava in 1709. After escaping to Turkey he returned to Sweden in 1714 and attempted to renew the struggle. By this time August II had regained the Polish crown with Russia's help, and the tide turned definitively in Peter's favor. Karl was killed in action in Norway in 1718.

8. Ivan Stepanovich Mazepa (1639-1709) came from a Ukrainian gentry family which remained under Polish sovereignty after Moscow acquired Left Bank Ukraine in 1654. Ivan received an excellent education and later travelled widely in Western Europe under the auspices of the king of Poland. After his capture by Zaporozhian Cossacks in 1674 Mazepa carved out a successful career under the

aegis of Moscow, taking a major role, for example, in V.V. Golitsyn's campaign against the Crimean Tatars in 1687. That same year Mazepa was elected hetman with Golitsyn's blessing. After Peter I deposed the regent Sophia and Golitsyn in 1689, he relied on Mazepa as a military commander and advisor for the southern region. Although Peter showered him with land grants and honors, as early as 1705 Mazepa contemplated betraying Peter to create an independent cossack state. Initially Mazepa thought of seeking Polish protection for this entity, but saw in Karl XII's invasion in 1708 an alternative to the Ukraine's powerful neighbors and suddenly joined the Swedes to Peter's complete surprise. Mazepa went down in defeat with Karl XII at Poltava in July 1709 and died two months later in his Turkish refuge. See entry by Cracraft, MERSH, Vol. 21, pp. 151-154, which includes an excellent survey of the historical controversy Mazepa continues to inspire, and Orest Subtelny, *The Mazepists. Ukrainian Separatism in the Early Eighteenth Century* (New York, 1981).

9. Pavel Leontievich Polubotok (1660-1724) was the son of a Ukrainian lieutenant who, despite some early differences with Mazepa, was named Chernigov colonel by him in 1705. Of the ten colonels, Polubotok was one of four who remained loyal to Moscow in 1708. Despite, or perhaps because of, his reputation for intelligence, Peter chose Skoropadsky over him as hetman that year, although awarding him villages in compensation. Polubotok's growing wealth, power and pretensions over the next few years increasingly led people to see him as a future hetman, particularly in contrast to the ailing and ineffectual Skoropadsky. When Skoropadsky died in 1722 Polubotok was allowed to function as regent until 1724, but Ukrainian autonomy already was restricted by Peter's establishment of a Ukrainian College to exercise more direct Russian control. Polubotok's efforts to stir opposition to the College in particular and Russian rule in general led to his arrest and imprisonment in 1724. He died that year in the Peter and Paul fortress in St. Petersburg. See also below, Chapter X, Note 4.

10. Catherine I (1684-1727) was a Lithuanian peasant girl who caught the eye of Count Boris Petrovich Sheremetev, then of Prince Alexander Dmitrievich Menshikov, and finally of the tsar himself. He had two daughters by her, Anna and Elizabeth, before marrying her in 1712. Peter crowned Catherine empress in 1724 but did not formally designate her his successor before his death. She owed her accession to the support of Menshikov and other close associates of Peter. In her brief tenure on the throne Catherine's failing health and agreeable personality led her to continue Peter's general course, but in much milder form. This made her popular yet left Russia without either a firm policy direction or a designated successor when she died on May 6/17, 1727. See entry by Munro, MERSH, Vol. 6, pp. 112-118.

11. See Chapter I, Note 9.

12. The Secret Chancellery was established by Peter the Great in 1718 to investigate the possibility of a treasonous conspiracy centered on his son Alexis. It soon became more important than the Preobrazhensky Chancellery, the other bureau responsible for political investigations. It was abolished in 1762 by

Catherine II, who transferred its functions to the Secret Investigative Office (Tainaia Ekspeditisiia) under the Senate.

13. Vasily Yakovlevich Mirovich (1740-1764) was twenty-four years old at the time.

14. See Chapter I, Note 18.

15. June 28, 1762, when Catherine and her supporters deposed Peter III and seized power.

16. That is, on the northern shore of the Neva across from the major government centers.

17. See Chapter II, Note 48.

18. See Chapter II, section "Catherine Goes to Rostov."

19. See Chapter II, Note 41.

20. Since the Middle Ages Germans controlled the political and economic life of the Baltic provinces. Peter the Great confirmed their privileges when he annexed the region in the Great Northern War, and succeeding rulers continued this policy until late in the nineteenth century. The Baltic Germans, as they were called, were prominent in the military, the court and in intellectual life until the end of the empire.

21. Obviously inspired by the title "Father of the Fatherland (Pater Patriae) often used to honor Peter the Great.

22. See Chapter III, Note 65.

23. See Chapter I, Note 10.

24. A Russian affirmation for a solemn oath.

25. Cf. Job 9:10.

26. Ivan Ivanovich Weymarn (1722-1792) was born on the island of Øsel to an old Baltic German family. After education in the Noble Cadet Corps he pursued a military career. In 1756 he was given a handsome reward for his success in convincing the Poles to permit Russian forces passage through Poland to aid Austria. He served as quartermaster general in Apraksin's army during the Seven Years War, was promoted major general in 1759 and assigned to a command in Siberia. In 1764 Weymarn, now a lieutenant general, was assigned to investigate the Mirovich conspiracy as Soloviev describes here. That same year he was named to a special conference to assure the security of the Chinese border, discussed by Soloviev in Chapter XIII, "Problems on Chinese Border." Later he commanded a corps in Lithuania, which was transferred to Poland. In 1772 the Russian ambassador Saldern's displeasure with what he considered Weymarn's indecisiveness led to the latter's recall.

27. See Chapter II, Note 53.

28. See Chapter III, Note 23.

29. See Chapter II, Note 38.

30. See Appendix X.

31. See Chapter II, Note 8.

32. Peter Alexeevich Soimonov (1737-1800) later served as director of court theaters from 1789 to 1791 and president of the College of Commerce, 1796-1799.

His daughter Sophie Swetchine converted to Catholicism, later emigrating to France where she presided over a salon which included many prominent Catholic intellectuals of the mid-nineteenth century.

33. See Chapter III, Note 71.

34. See Chapter II, Note 14.

35. Karl Ivanovich Emme began his career during Anna Leopoldovna's tenure as regent. In 1741 he became a state secretary to Count Münnich and was named to a commission to review the new Livonian law code. That December he was one of those appointed to investigate opponents of Elizabeth's successful coup, and also was designated vice president of the College of Justice for Livonian, Estonian and Finnish Affairs, becoming president of that body under Catherine II. In 1764 he served on the commission investigating the Mirovich conspiracy, as Soloviev describes here.

36. See Chapter I, Note 17.

37. A.S. Stroganov described Mirovich's last minutes in Poroshin's *Zapiski* (Notes). (Soloviev's note) S.A. Poroshin, *Zapiski, sluzhashchye k istorii e. i. v. i velikogo kniazia Pavla Petrovicha* (Notes for a History of His Imperial Highness and Grand Duke Paul Petrovich) (St. Petersburg, 1844), p. 53. (Soviet editor's note)

CHAPTER X

1. See above, Chapter III, "Glebov's Disgrace."

2. See Chapter II, Note 34.

3. SRIO, Vol. 7, (1871), pp. 345-347. (Soviet editor's note) Here as elsewhere Catherine was fond of comparing herself to the good shepherd of the Gospel. Cf. John 10:12.

4. Ivan Iliich Skoropadsky (1646-1722) was hetman of the Left Bank Ukraine under Peter the Great. A protégé of Ivan Mazepa, Skoropadsky remained loyal to Moscow when his master supported Karl XII's invasion of the Ukraine and was rewarded with the hetmanate by the tsar in 1708. Skoropadsky's tenure was marked by growing Russian dominance in Ukrainian affairs, culminating in the establishment of the Ukrainian College staffed by Russian officers in 1721, as well as by arbitrary exactions by cossack commanders nominally under his authority. By nature amiable and submissive, Skoropadsky alternately is criticized for weak leadership and defended as doing the best he could for his people in an impossible situation. His wife Anastasia Markovna, née Markovicha, was as assertive during his life as Soloviev portrays her here, exercising considerable influence over her husband's decisions and garnering choice appointments for her relatives. See entry by Sokol, MERSH, Vol. 35, pp. 176-182. Also see above, Chapter IX, Note 9.

5. See Chapter III, Note 67.

6. Jakob Johann Sievers (1731-1808) began his career as a copyist in the College of Foreign Affairs, served in Russian embassies in Copenhagen and London and took part in the Seven Years War. Named governor of Novgorod in 1764,

Sievers worked tirelessly and effectively to improve the economic and social conditions in his primitive northern domain. He promoted transportation, forestry, agriculture and mining, also building schools and defending serfs against oppressive landlords. In 1776 he also assumed control of the governments of Tver and Pskov. Alexander I later named the canal he built between the Volkhov and Msta rivers in his honor. After retirement between 1781 and 1789 Sievers was named minister plenipotentiary to Poland where he took an active part in the Second Partition. Definitively retired after 1794, Sievers was named senator in 1796 and awarded the rank of count in 1798. He has a well-deserved reputation as one of the most capable and effective statesmen of Catherine's era. See entry by Jones, MERSH, Vol. 35, pp. 124-27, and his *Provincial Development in Russia. Catherine II and Jakob Sievers* (Rutgers, 1984).

7. See Chapter II, Note 43
8. See Chapter II, Note 51.
9. Lev Alexandrovch Naryshkin (1733-1799) was stablemaster from 1773 to 1799.
10. Catherine uses the terms *domostroistov* and *domostroistvo*, recalling the popular sixteenth-century guide for householders, the *Domostroi* or The Household Manager.
11. SRIO, Vol. 7, p. 404. (Soloviev's note)
12. PSZ, Vol. 16 (St. Petersburg, 1830), pp. 672-674. (Soviet editor's note)
13. Count Nikolay Alexeevich Golovin also served as master of heraldry from 1765 to 1769.
14. Yakov Matveevich Yevreinov (died 1772) was vice president of the College of Commerce from 1745 to 1759 and president from 1759 to 1762.
15. PSZ, Vol. 16, No. 12, 037, p. 530. (Soviet editor's note)
16. The Demidovs rose from obscure origins in the seventeenth century to become Russia's leading manufacturers in the eighteenth century. Nikita Demidov, a craftsman at the Tula Arms Factory, so impressed Peter the Great by his skill that the tsar gave him land, contracts and eventually a patent of hereditary nobility. Later he and his descendants expanded to the Urals, Siberia and elsewhere, and developed enormously profitable factories in copper, gold, silver and other minerals in addition to the iron that was the basis of the family fortune. See entry by Hugh D. Hudson, Jr., "Demidov Family in the Eighteenth Century," MERSH, Vol. 9, pp. 46-51 and Portal, *L'Oural.*
17. Fedor Ivanovich Sukin was vice president of the College of Manufactures from 1766 to 1772. He served as a delegate to the Legislative Commission of 1767.
18. See Chapter I, Note 25.
19. In Russian *Nadezhda blagopoluchiia.*
20. PSZ, Vol. 16, No. 12,009, p. 491. *Sankt-peterburgskie vedomosti*, No. 2, January 7, 1765. (Soviet editor's note)
21. PSZ, Vol. 16, No. 12,150, pp. 739-740. (Soviet editor's note)
22. See Chapter IV, Note 13.
23. See Chapter VI, Note 7.

24. See Volume 32 of this series.
25. See Chapter III, Note 16.
26. See Chapter I, Note 28.
27. See Chapter III, section "New Census Proposed."
28. SRIO, Vol. 7, p. 351. (Soviet editor's note)
29. PSZ, Vol. 16, No. 12,137, pp. 716-720. (Soviet editor's note)
30. PSZ, Vol. 16, No. 12,181, pp. 799-800. (Soviet editor's note)
31. See Chapter II, Note 3.
32. PSZ,Vol. 16, No. 12,060, pp. 549-569. (Soviet editor's note)
33. A lieutenant in the Guards was the equivalent of a captain in regular army units.
34. Soltykov or Saltykov. See Chapter III, Note 34.
35. SRIO, Vol. 7, p. 375. (Soviet editor's note)
36. In 1716 Peter the Great ordered all Old Believers to register with the government and pay double the amount of the soul tax normally levied on people of their social class. Catherine eventually repealed this burden and removed most of the other special restrictions on Old Believers. See Robert O. Crummey, *The Old Believers and the World of Antichrist* (Madison, 1970).
37. See Volume 39 of this series.
38. See Chapter II, Note 27.
39. Mefody (died 1776) became archimandrite of the Transfiguration monastery in Astrakhan in 1731 and bishop of Astrakhan in 1758.
40. Old Believers would not have recognized the validity of Dmitry's canonization in 1752, long after their rejection of the official church.
41. *Sobranie postanovlenii po chasti raskola, sostoiavshikhsia po vedomostu Sinoda* (Collection of Resolutions Concerning the Schism, Compiled under the Auspices of the Synod), Vol. 1 (St. Petersburg, 1860), pp. 600-604. (Soviet editor's note)

CHAPTER XI

1. In other words cease wanting to escape Russian rule.
2. See above, Chapter IV, section "Trouble over Succession to the Hetmanate."
3. See Chapter II, Note 50.
4. Teplov did not mention the most questionable aspect of this description of peasant flight to Poland. Obviously serfs ran away to escape oppression by the landlords, but why would free peasants flee? (Soloviev's note)
5. The Russian term used is *podsudsedki.*
6. The memorandum was printed in the second volume of *Zapiski o Yuzhnoi Rusi* (Notes on Southern Russia), but without the explanation given here that it refers to Empress Elizabeth's reign. (Soloviev's note) *Zapiski o Yuzhnoi Rusi,* Vol. 2 (St. Petersburg, 1857), pp. 169-196. (Soviet editor's note)

7. SRIO, Vol. 7, p. 375. (Soviet editor's note)

8. Semeon Vasilievich Kochubey (died 1779) was colonel of the Nezvinsk regiment before becoming quartermaster general of the Ukrainian army in 1762.

9. Vasily Grigorievich Tumansky (1723-1809) also was a Little Russian general judge, then lieutenant to the administrator of the Novgorod Seversk Province.

10. Ivan Matveich Zhuravka was named a lieutenant general in the Ukrainian Army in 1759. He was a member of the Ukrainian College until 1780.

11. Daniel Petrovich Apostol was a grandson of the Hetman Daniel Petrovich Apostol.

12. See Chapter I, Note 30.

13. Yakov Ilarionovich von Brandt (died 1774) was given direction of the government of New Russia in 1765, continuing to serve in this post when he also was named governor of Kazan in 1772. Here Yemilian Pugachev was in his custody briefly in 1773, but escaped and the following year returned with his army and captured the city, killing Brandt in the attack.

14. Platon Stepanovich Meshchersky (1713-1799) served as president of the Ukrainian College during Rumiantsev's absence between 1769 and 1775, as governor general of Viatka from 1785 to 1792 and after 1796 as military governor of Kazan.

15. The Zaporozhian Cossacks were one of the oldest and most important cossack groups. They lived on the lower course of the Dnieper river where they played a crucial role in the continuous competition between Poles, Russians, Turks, Tatars and local elements for control of the region. The events Soloviev describes paved the way for definitive Russian domination of the Ukraine and the consequent suppression of local autonomous bodies. Catherine abolished the Zaporozhian Host in 1775. See entry by Sokol, MERSH, Vol. 45, pp. 164-170 and Philip Longworth, *The Cossacks* (New York, 1969).

16. PSZ, Vol. 16, No. 12,277, pp. 961-962. (Soviet editor's note)

17. SRIO, Vol. 7, pp. 376-390. (Soviet editor's note)

18. *Sochineniia imperatritsy Ekateriny II* (Collected Works of Empress Catherine II), Vol. 3 (St. Petersburg, 1850), p. 187. (Soviet editor's note)

19. The reference is to Judas's betrayal of Jesus in the garden. See Matthew 26:48.

20. See Chapter III, Note 55

21. See Chapter II, Note 64.

22. PSZ, Vol. 16, No. 12,099, pp. 657-667. (Soviet editor's note)

23. PSZ, Vol. 16, No. 12,221, pp. 842-843. (Soviet editor's note)

24. PSZ, Vol. 16, No. 12,293, pp. 1003-1007. (Soviet editor's note) The Settlement Ukraine government had its roots in the Slobodskie Cossacks of the northeastern Ukraine, so-called from the numerous *slobodas,* or settlements, established in the region by refugees from Poland. In the seventeenth century Moscow organized the often unruly cossacks into regiments. Although Slobodskie

Cossacks served bravely in eighteenth-century wars, corruption among cossack officers and their oppression of ordinary cossacks, as well as an influx of Russian and other non-cossack immigrants, convinced Catherine to abolish what remained of cossack self-government by reorganizing the area as the Settlement Ukraine government, as described by Soloviev here. See entry by Sokol, "Slobodskie Cossacks," MERSH, Vol. 35, pp. 241-244.

25. Alexander Ilich Bibikov (1729-1774) was the son of a prominent general whose own military exploits in the Seven Years War earned him the rank of major general. He quickly won Catherine's favor, shown in the important assignments she gave him. In 1763 he was sent to put down disturbances among factory serfs, in 1765 sent to inspect defenses on the western frontier and then consulted by the empress during her preparations for the Legislative Commission of 1767, in which he served as marshal. In 1771 Bibikov helped subdue anti-Russian confederate forces in Poland, and when the Pugachev uprising broke out in 1773 he organized the forces that repulsed the rebel attack on Kazan. He was rewarded with the Order of St. Andrew and the rank of senator, but died suddenly of a fever on April 9, 1774. See entry by Kamendrowsky, MERSH, Vol. 4, pp. 126-29.

26. See Chapter III, Note 25.

27. See Chapter IV, Note 1.

28. Denis Ivanovich Chicherin (1720-1785) was governor of Tobolsk from 1763 to 1781.

29. Vitus Jonassen Bering (1681-1741) was born in Denmark and entered the Russian navy in 1704. He retired after service in all naval theaters during the Great Northern War, but was recalled to active duty in 1724. Just before his death Peter the Great commissioned Bering to search for America and learn if it were joined with the eastern tip of Siberia. His expedition of 1728 made significant discoveries, but did not sight American soil. The honor of being the first Europeans to discover America from the west fell to Mikhail Gvozdev and Ivan Fedorov in 1732. On a second voyage (1741-1742) with Alexis Chirikov, Bering did reach the Aleutians and the Alaskan coast, but died after his ship was wrecked on what today is named Bering Island in his honor. See entry by Allen F. Chew, MERSH, Vol. 4, pp. 39-42, and N.N. Bolkhovitinov, *Rossiia otkryvaet Ameriku, 1732-1799* (Russia Discovers America, 1732-1799) (Moscow, 1991).

30. Martin Spanberg was a Dane who sailed with Bering on his first voyage. See also previous Note.

31. Vasily Alexeevich Miatlev (1694-1761) was governor of Tobolsk from 1752 to 1757.

32. This was the Treaty of Nerchinsk signed August 27, 1689. Russia lost Albazin and the Amur river valley but gained the right to trade directly with China. The Treaty of Kiakhta (October 21, 1727) defined the Russian-Chinese border running west between Siberia and Mongolia. See entry by Clifford M. Foust, "Chinese-Russian Relations to 1917," MERSH, Vol. 7, pp. 56-63, and his "Nerchinsk, Treaty of (1689)," MERSH, Vol. 24, pp. 156-160. Also see Joseph

Sebes, S.J., *The Jesuits and the Sino-Russian Treaty of Nerchinsk* (Rome, 1961) and Vincent Chen, *Sino-Russian Relations in the Seventeenth Century* (The Hague, 1966).

33. Between the signing of the Treaty of Kiakhta in 1727, and 1756, several large official convoys carried goods between Russia and China, and a large private trade developed through the border point of Kiakhta. See Foust, "Chinese-Russian Relations to 1917."

34. See Appendix XI.

CHAPTER XII

1. See Chapter I, Note 11.
2. See Chapter V, Note 6.
3. See Chapter VI, Note 23.
4. See Chapter V, Note 12.
5. See Chapter VI, Note 17.
6. See Chapter V, Note 16.
7. See Chapter VI, Note 7.
8. Franciszek Salezy Potocki (died 1772), the richest magnate of his time, became Kievan military commander in 1756. Initially he and his family opposed August III, but became reconciled with the court after the king broke with their old enemies, the Czartoryskis. Not surprisingly his opposition to Stanisław Poniatowski continued after his coronation.
9. See Chapter VI, Note 33.
10. Władysław Lubienski. See Chapter V, Note 13.
11. In other words, Lubomirski was unfit to be king.
12. See Chapter V, Notes 11, 12; Chapter VI, Notes 10, 11.
13. The recently-deceased Polish king, August III, was also the elector of Saxony and as such had Saxon forces at his disposal in Poland. See also Chapter V, Note 8.
14. Nikolay Khomutov was a major general in the Smolensk Division. From 1730 to 1762 he directed the Chancellery for Provisions in St. Petersburg.
15. See Chapter VI, Note 41.
16. Mikhail-Kondraty Ivanovich Dashkov (1736-1764) held the rank of chamberlain. He married Catherine, daughter of Roman Ilarionovich Vorontsov, in 1759. For Catherine Romanovna Dashkova see Chapter II, Note 58.
17. Antony Kazimierz Ostrowski (1713-1784), bishop of Kujawy, supported Russian policy in this period. He was a signatory of a 1766 treaty with Russia defending dissident rights.
18. See Chapter VI, Note 32.
19. For August see Chapter VI, Note 11; Michał, Chapter V, Note 11; Adam, Chapter VI, Note 10. Stanisław-Kostka Czartoryski (died 1766) became master of

the royal hunt for Lithuania in 1742. As a representative in various Sejms he supported the family's reform plans. He endorsed the election of Poniatowski in 1764 and in 1765 was one of the delegates who negotiated with the Prussians and Russians. Józef-Klemens Czartoryski (1740-1810) was a son of Stanisław, and like him, supported Poniatowski's election in 1764. He then was sent to Rome to obtain papal approval for the new king. He took no further part in politics until the late 1780s, instead promoting cultural and economic projects.

20. August Sułkowski (1729-1786) was the son of a Saxon minister. He held various military and diplomatic posts, and after Poniatowski's election was named a royal secretary and commander of the Cadet Corps. He supported Russia on the dissident issue and kept his position as Gniezno military commander thanks to Ambassador Repnin's protection. Sułkowski also was a member of the Permanent Council and a promoter of educational reform.

21. See Chapter VI, Note 46.

22. A Prussian decoration.

23. The order of Saint Apostle Andrew the First-Called was the oldest of the Russian orders, instituted by Peter the Great in 1698.

24. The Protestants and Orthodox in Poland often were described collectively as dissidents.

25. Wacław Rzewuski (1706-1779) was a supporter of the Potockis in opposition to the Czartoryskis. He and his son Seweryn (1743-1811) were among the four Poles deported to Russia on Repnin's orders in 1768 after protesting too vehemently against Russian influence. He also made a reputation as a man of letters.

26. See Chapter V, Note 18.

27. Marie-Thérèse Geoffrin (1699-1777) presided over a Paris salon in the Hôtel de Rambouillet which became the city's most famous rendezvous for men of letters, artists and other prominent figures between 1749 and 1777. She particularly encouraged the *philosophes* and helped subsidize the publication of the *Encyclopédie*. She struck up a lifelong friendship with Stanisław Poniatowski during his stay in Paris, sometimes even paying his debts and visiting him in Warsaw in 1766. She also corresponded with Catherine the Great. See Dena Goodman, *The Republic of Letters. A Cultural History of the French Enlightenment* (Cornell, 1994).

28. Geoffrin undoubtedly was thinking of Aeneas's vision in the underworld of the future greatness of Rome as portrayed by Virgil in Book VI of the *Aeneid.*

29. See above, Chapter XII, section "Russia Promotes Poniatowski's Candidacy."

30. See above, Chapter IX, sections "Catherine Leaves St. Petersburg" and "Catherine's Reaction."

31. See Chapter VI, Note 28.

32. Georgy Konissky (1717-1795) was archbishop of Mogilev and White Russia. For his salute to Catherine as a savior of her people at her coronation, see Volume 42 of this series, pp. 124-125.

33. Soloviev undoubtedly means that Konissky's case would have to wait until the general guidelines of Russian policy in Poland were set.

34. Arseny, in the world Alexis Mogiliansky (1704-1770), taught at the Tver seminary and the Moscow Theological Academy. His rhetorical skill earned him the favor of Empress Elizabeth, who named him a court preacher in 1743. In 1744 he became archimandrite of the Holy Trinity-St. Sergius monastery, where he also directed the seminary. Named archbishop of Pereiaslavl in 1744, he retired from this post in 1752. He became metropolitan of Kiev in 1757 and made major improvements in the Kiev Mohyla Academy during his tenure. Arseny also wrote on spiritual themes.

35. See Chapter VI, Note 15.

36. In 1599 the Protestant and Orthodox communities of Poland made a formal agreement of mutual assistance through the Confederation of Wilno. Although the Sejm did not ratify the agreement, it was used by Prussia and Russia thereafter as a pretext for intervention, as Catherine does here.

37. In 1686 King Jan Sobieski signed a treaty with Russia abandoning all Polish claims to Ukrainian territory that remained in Russia's possession at the Treaty of Andrusovo in 1667. One of the provisions obligated Poland to grant its Orthodox subjects freedom of worship.

38. Johann Christoph von Stoffeln (1718-1770) saw action in all of Russia's major wars from 1738 on. He was named quartermaster general in 1757 and took an active part in the campaigns of the Seven Years War. Stoffeln, by then a lieutenant general, led a large force in successful attacks against the Turks in the Danubian principalities. He died of the plague in Jassy in 1770. See Volume 46 of this series, pp. 99-104, 106.

39. Johann Dietrich Rennenkampf (born 1732) entered military service in 1749. In 1765 he became commander of a corps formed in Lithuania and participated in the Turkish campaign of 1770. As a deputy to the Legislative Commission of 1767 and of several of its committees in the following years he staunchly defended Livonian privileges. He retired in 1771.

40. *Correspondence inédite du roi Stanislas-Auguste Poniatowski et de madame Geoffrin (1764-1777)* (Unpublished Correspondence between King Stanisław August and Madame Geoffrin, 1764-1777) (Paris, 1875), pp. 101-104, 115, 135, etc. (Soviet editor's note) F. Raumer, *Beiträge zur neueren Geschichte aus dem britischen und französischen Reichsarchive* (Essays on Recent History from British and French Government Archives) (Leipzig, 1839), Vol. 3, pp. 353, etc. (Soviet Editor's note)

CHAPTER XIII

1. Stanisław Kostka Gadomski (1718-1797) held posts in the Prussian army and during the reign of August III supported the Potockis. He also served as Łęczyca military commander. Gadomski continued to support Prussia as a delegate

to the 1764 convocation Sejm, but later joined the court party and worked together with the Czartoryskis.

2. See Chapter VI, Note 44.
3. See Chapter I, Note 42.
4. See Chapter VI, Note 47.
5. See Chapter I, Note 43.
6. See Chapter VII, Note 1.
7. *vains et lâches.*
8. Calchas was a soothsayer who accompanied the Greeks during the Trojan War. He correctly predicted the duration of the siege and suggested constructing the Trojan horse.
9. See Chapter VI, Note 46.
10. Sir Andrew Mitchell (1708-1771) began his career in the Scottish government service. Appointed Great Britain's envoy to Prussia in 1756, he quickly developed a close personal rapport with Frederick II, often accompanying him on campaigns. After English subsidies to Prussia were reduced in 1762, Frederick's friendship cooled somewhat, and Mitchell was recalled for a time. He represented England in Prussia again from 1766 until his death in Berlin in 1771.
11. See Chapter VI, Note 51.
12. *F orschungen zur deutschen Geschichte* (Studies in German History), Vol. 9. (Soviet editor's note)
13. Prince Joseph Maria Lobkowitz (1725-1802) had a distinguished military career, including service in the Seven Years War, before becoming Austrian ambassador to Russia, a post he held until 1777. He took an active part in negotiations for the First Partition of Poland.
14. *Correspondence secrète inédite de Louis XV* (Unpublished Secret Correspondence of Louis XV), Vol. 1, (Paris, 1866), pp. 312-313. (Soviet editor's note)
15. See Chapter VI, Note 67.
16. See Chapter VI, Note 62.
17. See Chapter VI, Note 56.
18. A common title of the French king.
19. Antoine-René Voyer, marquis de Paulmy d'Argenson (1722-1787), followed a military career before holding various diplomatic posts. He represented France in Poland from 1762 to 1764. He was one of the great bibliophiles of his age, amassing a personal library of one hundred thousand volumes.
20. See Chapter I, Note 42; Chapter VI, Note 16.
21. Maria (Marie) Leszczynska (1703-1768), only daughter of the deposed king, married Louis XV in 1725. The match was arranged as part of a long-range plan to bring the Polish succession into the Bourbon line. An obvious precondition for success was restoration of Marie's father to the throne, a policy France avidly pursued in this period. Her marriage sparked France's involvement in the War of the Polish Succession and helped win the duchy of Lorraine for France. Although she bore Louis nine children, the marriage was not a happy one, and Louis directed his attention to long series of mistresses.

22. Stanisław Leszczynski (1677-1766) was first elected king of Poland in 1704 under the patronage of Karl XII of Sweden, but was deposed by his predecessor August II in 1709 as a result of Russian intervention. He briefly recovered the Polish crown in 1733 with French help, only to be removed definitively in 1738 after the War of the Polish Succession. He spent the rest of his life as duke of Lorraine and Bar in France and is remembered fondly to this day by the citizens of Lorraine's capital, Nancy, for the magnificent palace he built there.

23. F. Raumer, *Beiträge*, Vol. 3, pp. 215-216, 319, and ff. (Soviet editor's note)

24. See Chapter VI, Note 48.

25. Mustafa III (1717-1774) became sultan of Turkey in 1757. He saw the necessity of westernization, enlisting French and Prussian assistance in improving finances, upgrading the military and even contemplating a Suez canal. Despite a preference for peace, he went to war with Russia in 1768 to block Catherine's ambitions, but Russians defeated the Ottoman forces soundly on both land and sea.

26. Grigore Ghica was from a Phanariot family that became romanized over time. He was hospodar of Moldavia as Grigore III from 1764 to 1767.

27. See Chapter IV, Note 15.

28. See Chapter I, Note 42.

29. See Chapter VII, Note 14.

30. See Chapter VI, Note 58.

31. See Chapter VII, Note 13.

32. See Chapter VII, Note 15.

33. Louisa Ulrika. See Chapter VII, Note 14.

34. Panin was Russian ambassador to Sweden from 1748 to 1760. In 1756 the struggle between the king and the Riksdag reached a climax. When the royal council threatened to override the king's veto of bills passed by the Riksdag and promulgate them on its own authority, Queen Louisa Ulrika organized a coup to reassert royal power. It failed, and eight of the ringleaders were beheaded publicly, including Count Erik Brahe. See also Chapter VII, Note 14.

35. Baron Carl Fredrik Scheffer (1715-1786) was a senator, and as a leading member of the Hats promoted Sweden's alliance with France in the Seven Years War in return for French subsidies. He also had close ties to the Danish foreign minister Bernstorff. In the period Soloviev describes Scheffer explored cooperation with the court party to promote governmental reform. For him this entailed clear delineation between the legislative and executive branches in the spirit of Montesquieu. He and other Hats were forced out of the Royal Council by the resurgent Caps in August 1765. See also Chapter VII, Note 14.

36. Baron Johann Friedrich Cocceji served as Prussian ambassador to Sweden after 1764.

37. Count Karl Gustav Löwenhielm was a member of the court party which opposed the Hats. Thus he was open to cooperation with England and Russia against France.

38. Nation (natsia) here is used in the sense of the *natio politica*, that part of the population which participated in politics. In Sweden, as almost everywhere else in

Europe, this was a small group, hence the distinction between "nation" and "fatherland" (otechestvo).

39. England sent John Goodricke as extraordinary envoy to Sweden early in 1764. In the period Soloviev describes and later he worked closely with Ostermann to counter the French and their Hat allies.

40. See Chapter VII, Note 14.

41. See above, Note 34.

42. See Chapter VII, Note 17.

43. See Chapter VII, Note 14.

44. Nils Filip Gyldenstolpe was personal secretary to Queen Louisa Ulrika.

45. See Chapter VII, Note 16.

46. F. Raumer, *Beiträge*, Vol. 3, No. 1, pp. 215-216, 319, etc. (Soviet editor's note)

47. See Chapter VII, Note 20.

48. See Chapter VII, Note 21.

49. The Russian is *otrezanny lomot*, literally a slice that has been cut off.

50. See above, Chapter VIII, section "Negotiations for an English Alliance."

51. See Chapter VIII, Note 5.

52. See Chapter VIII, Note 1.

53. Friedrich Ulrich Gross (1729-1796) served briefly as ambassador to Great Britain from 1764 to 1766. From 1767 to 1796 he represented Russia in Lower Saxony and the Hanseatic cities.

54. The Seven Years War (1756-1763) in which Russia, France and Austria were allies opposing Prussia and England.

55. England had just acquired Quebec and the Ohio territory from France at the conclusion of the French and Indian War.

56. See Chapter VIII, Note 10.

57. See Chapter VIII, Note 9.

58. Meaning France, Spain and Naples.

59. Soloviev alludes to the third of three treaties relating to the Seven Years War signed at Versailles. The first, a defensive alliance between France and Austria signed in 1756, was the basis for their campaign against Frederick II of Prussia. Russia joined the alliance in the Second Treaty of Versailles in 1757. In the third treaty, signed in 1759, France reaffirmed the Austrian alliance but reduced some its previous commitments on the continent to focus its energy more on England.

60. Although there was a family compact in 1733, the treaty signed between France and Spain in 1743 was more important. The two would cooperate to their mutual benefit in Italy, France opposing Sardinia and Spain attempting to regain Milan. In the third family treaty, signed on August 15, 1761, France and Spain agreed come to each other's aid against any enemy. They would act jointly and not sign a separate peace. The king of Naples, a son of the Spanish king, would be allowed to join, but no non-Bourbon would be admitted. A secret convention

specified that if France were still at war with England on May 1, 1762, Spain would go to war against England. London's discovery of this provision led to England's declaration of war on Spain on January 4, 1762.

61. *C'est qu'on dit negocier en vrai marchand.*

62. See above, this section.

63. Michel Odard (died 1773) was born in Piedmont. After coming to Russia he became a secretary to Empress Elizabeth, but soon left the post because he knew no Russian. He participated in Catherine's 1762 coup as a messenger between conspirators. Later he served as a librarian for Catherine, then was assigned to collect material on trade and commerce. He helped prepare the commercial treaty with England Soloviev discusses here. Odard left Russia in 1764, dying in Nice in 1773.

64. George Macartney (1737-1806) was appointed envoy extraordinary in 1764 to conclude the commercial treaty with Russia which Soloviev discusses here. He returned to England in 1767, refusing an offer to resume his post in Russia. From 1769 to 1772 he was chief secretary for Ireland, captain general, then governor, of the Caribbee Islands in 1775-1779, and governor general and president of Fort George in Madras from 1781 to 1786. In 1793-1794 he led an embassy to China, and ended his career as first English governor of the Cape of Good Hope Colony. He was elevated to the rank of earl in the Irish peerage in 1792 and became a baron in the English peerage in 1796, but the title became extinct on his death.

65. Only four years later, in 1768, a major war broke out between Russia and Turkey. See Volume 46 of this series.

66. Charles III (1716-1788), first cousin to Louis XV, was duke of Parma from 1731 to 1735, king of Naples and Sicily from 1735 to 1759 and reigned as king of Spain from 1759 to 1788. In the spirit of enlightened absolutism he curbed the power of the church, promoted economic development, strengthened colonial administration and increased the role of the central government.

67. Johann (Ivan Ivanovich) von Springer (died 1771) entered military service in 1738. From 1762 to 1771 he was commander of the troops of the Siberian Line. He was named lieutenant general in 1763.

68. Alexandre Guillemot de Villebois (Alexander Nikitich) (1717-1781) was quartermaster general from 1756 to 1757 and again from 1762 to 1765. He was a deputy to the Legislative Commission of 1767.

69. Count Ernst von Münnich (1708-1788) was the son of the famous field marshal, Burchard Christoph von Münnich. He served as ambassador to France 1731-1732 and as lord high marshal of the court in 1740 and 1741. In 1763 he was named to supervise customs collections, which hitherto were farmed out to private contractors. He was an influential member of the Commission on Commerce established in 1760 and revived by Catherine in 1763.

70. See Chapter XI, Note 33.

APPENDICES

I. DIPLOMATS MENTIONED IN THE TEXT
(dates in office when known)

In Russian Service

Chancellor:
Count Alexis Petrovich Bestuzhev-Riumin (1744-1763)

Senior Member, College of Foreign Affairs:
Count Nikita Ivanovich Panin (1763-1780)

To Austria:
Prince Dmitry Mikhailovich Golitsyn (1761-1792)

To China:
Bratishchev (1756-1758)

To the Crimea:
Nikiforov (1763-1764)

To Denmark:
Baron Johann Albrecht von Korff (1748-1766)

To England:
Count Alexander Romanovich Vorontsov (1762-1764)
Heinrich von Gross (1764-1766)

To France:
Prince Dmitry Alexeevich Golitsyn (1754-1768)

To the Imperial Diet in Regensburg:
Johann Matthias von Simolin (1762-1771)

To Persia:
Ilia Igumnov (Consul)

To Poland:
Davydov (Consul)
Count Hermann Karl von Keyserling (1762-1765)
Prince Nikolay Vasilevich Repnin (1764-1769)

To Prussia:
Prince Valdimir Timofeevich Dolgoruky (1762-1768)
Prince Nikolay Vasilievich Repnin (1762-1763)

To Sweden:
Count Nikita Ivanovich Panin (1748-1760)
Count Ivan Andreevich Ostermann (1760-1774)

To Turkey:
Alexis Mikhailovich Obrezkov (1751-1768)

In Austrian Service
Foreign Minister:
Prince Wenzel Anton von Kaunitz-Reitberg (1753-1780)

To Prussia:
Ried

To Russia:
Count Florimundus Claudius Mercy d'Argenteau (1762-1763)
Prince Joseph Maria von Lobkowitz (1764-1777)

In Danish Service
Foreign Minister:
Count Johann Hartwig von Bernstorff (1751-1770)

To Russia:
Baron Adolf Siegfried von der Osten (1755-1766)

In English Service
Secretary of State for the Northern Department:
George Montagu Dunk, earl of Halifax (1761-1763)
John Montagu, earl of Sandwich (1763-1765)

To Poland:
Thomas Wroughton (1762-1769)

To Prussia:
Andrew Mitchell (1756-1771)

To Russia:
John Hobart, earl of Buckinghamshire (1762-1765)
George Macartney (1764-1767)

To Sweden:
John Goodricke (from 1764)

In French Service
Foreign Minister:
Étienne-François de Choiseul, duke of Praslin (1758-1770)

To Poland:
Antoine-René Voyer, marquis de Paulmy d'Argenson(1762-1764)

To Russia:
Louis Le Tonnelier, baron de Breteuil (1760-1763)
Laurent Bérenger (from 1763)

To Sweden:
d'Aurencourt (1750s)
Louis Le Tonnelier, Baron de Breteuil (from 1763)

To Turkey:
Charles Gravier, comte de Vergennes (1757-1764)

In Polish Service
To Turkey:
Stankiewicz

In Prussian Service
Foreign Minister:
Karl Wilhelm, Count Finck von Finckenstein (1760-1763)

To Poland:
Gédéon de Benoît (from 1758)

To Russia:
Baron Bernhard Wilhelm von Goltz (1762)
Count Victor Friedrich Solms (1762-1779)

To Sweden:
Baron Johann Friedrich Cocceji (from 1764)

To Turkey:
Karl Adolf von Rixen (from 1757)

In Swedish Service
Secretary of State for Foreign Affairs:
Baron Matthias von Hermansson

To Russia:
Count Carl Wilhelm von Düben (1763-1765)

In Turkish Service
To Prussia:
Ahmed Resmi Efendi (1763-1764)

II. COURT AND MILITARY TERMS

Russian	*English*	*Class in Table of Ranks*
ad"iutant	adjutant	
admiral	admiral	II
asessor	assessor	VIII
ataman	hetman	
baron	baron	
brigadir	brigadier	V
bunchukovskii	standard bearer (cossack)	
burgomistr	burgomaster	
burmistr	mayor	
deistvitel'nyi kamerger	high chamberlain	
deistvitel'nyi tainyi sovetnik	senior privy councillor	II
deloproizvoditel'	chief secretary	
diak	clerk	
diuk	duke	
dofin	dauphin	
dofina	dauphine	
esaul general'nyi	lieutenant general (cossack)	
fel'dmarshal	field marshal	I
general	general	II
general-ad"iutant	adjutant general	
general-admiral	admiral general	I
general-anshef	general-in-chief	II
general-feldtseikhmeister	quartermaster general	II
general-gubernator	governor general	
general-kvartermeister	quartermaster general	II
general-reketmeister	general master of petitions	V
general'nyi fel'dmarshal	field marshal general	I

genral'nyi sud'ia	general judge	
general-maior	major general	IV
general'nyi pisar'	general clerk (Ukr.)	
general-politseimeister	gendarme general	
general-poruchik	lieutenant general	III
general-prokuror	procurator general	
gerol'dmeister	master of heraldry	V
gertsog	duke	
getman	hetman	
glavnyi kommandir	commander-in-chief	
glavnyi sekretar'	chief secretary	VII-VIII
gofmeister	court tutor	
gorodskii nachal'nik	town governor	
gospodar	hospodar	
gosudarstvennyi sekretar'	state secretary	
graf	count, earl	
grazhdanskii gubernator	civil governor	
gubernator	governor	
imperator	emperor	
imperatritsa	empress	
internuntsii	internuncio	
kamerger	chamberlain	
kameriunker	chamberlain	
kamerpazh	page of the chamber	
kantsler	chancellor	I
kapitan	captain	IX
kapitan-kommandor	captain commander	V
kashtelian	castellan	
khan	khan	
khorunzhii general'nyi	general standard bearer (cossack)	
kniagina	princess	
kniaz	prince	
kollezhskii sovetnik	collegiate councillor	VI
komendant	commandant	
konferents-sekretar'	conference secretary	
konsul	consul	
korol	king	
koroleva	queen	
koronnyi kantsler	crown chancellor (Pol.)	
kurator	curator	
kurfiurst	elector	
kurfiurstina	elector's wife	
lowczy wielki koronny	master of the royal hunt (Lith.)	
maior	major	VIII
markiz	marquis	

marshal	marshal	
marshal seima	marshal of the Sejm (Pol.)	
ministr	minister	
ministr inostrannykh del	minister of foreign affairs	
nadvornyi marshal	court marshal (Pol.)	
nadvornyi sovetnik	court councillor	VII
naslednaia printsessa	crown princess	
naslednik	heir to the throne	
ober-burggraf	chief burgrave	
ober-egermeister	grand master of the hunt (Lith.)	
ober-kamerger	lord high chamberlain (Pol.)	
ober-komendant	commander-in-chief	
ober-prokuror	high procurator	
oer-rat	chief alderman	
ober-sekretar'	senior secretary	X-XII
obershenk	high cupbearer	
oboznyi	quartermaster (Ukr.)	
oboznyi general'nyi	quartermaster general (Ukr.)	
piatidesiatnik	lieutenant(cossack)	
pisar'	high notary (Pol.)	
pisar' koronnyi	high crown notary (Pol.)	
podpolkovnik	lieutenant colonel	VII
podporuchik	second lieutenant	XIII-XIV
podpraporshchik	subaltern	XIV
podskarbii velikii	high crown treasurer (Pol.)	
podstolii	steward (Pol.)	
polkovnik	colonel	VI
poruchik	lieutenant	XII-XIII
portovykh tamozhen' direktor	customs director	
poslannik	minister, ambassador	
poverenny v delakh	chargé d'affaires	
praporshchik	ensign	XIV
president	president	
primas	primate	
prints	prince	
printsessa	princess	
prokuror	procurator	
referendar'	referendary (Pol.)	
registrator	registrar	XII-XIV
sekund-maior	second major	IX
resident	resident	
senator	senator	
serzhant	sergeant	
shtab-ofitser	staff, field grade officer	
shtalmeister	stablemaster	

sovetnik	councillor	II-VII, IX
starshii tainyni sovetnik	senior privy councillor	III
starshina	officer (Cossack)	
starshina iz komandy	unit officer	
starosta	prefect (Pol.)	
stats-sekretar'	secretary of state (Eng., Swed.)	
statskii sovetnik	state councillor	V
stolnik	table attendant	
strazhnik koronnyi	crown frontier commander (Pol.)	
subaltern-ofitser	subaltern officer	
sultan	sultan	
tainyi kabinetskisovetnik	privy cabinet councillor	III
tainyi sovetnik	privy councillor	III
tituliarnyi sovetnik	titular councillor	IX
tsar	tsar	
tsaritsa	tsaritsa	
tsesarevna	princess	
velikaia kniagina	grand duchess	
velikii getman koronnyi	high crown hetman (Pol.)	
velikii kniaz	grand duke	
velikii vizir	grand vizier	
velikii marshalok koronny	high crown marshal	
vitse-admiral	vice admiral	III
vitse-gubernator	vice governor	
vitse-kantsler	vice chancellor	II
vitse-president	vice president	
vizir	vizier	
voevoda	military commander	
voenny gubernator	military governor	

III. Count A.P. Bestuzhev-Riumin's Note to Empress Catherine II

For her imperial highness's information and most gracious consideration. Doubtless the College of Foreign Affairs has sent your imperial highness a report about the Dutch ambassador's intervention on behalf of a certain merchant Reingold. At issue was a contract ("which are sacrosanct throughout the world," Bestuzhev wrote in the margin) the College of Commerce made for tar. The aforementioned ambassador asked Alexis Bestuzhev-Riumin about it several times and finally submitted a memorandum. Since Count Bestuzhev is not in a position to make a decision, he most humbly presents his recommendation. Perhaps her imperial majesty would to deign to have the Senate issue a short resolution after considering the matter and satisfy the merchant's request.

The empress's remarks. I saw the petition and sent it to the Senate. Monopolies are recognized evils, and not taking one city's special privileges away will set a precedent for others. If a concession is made in one case, there will be many others. I will listen to the Senate's discussion of the matter. Society as a whole benefits when particular grievances are ignored.

IV. Handwritten Letter From Catherine to Rumiantsev Moscow, January 13, 1763 Archive of the Ministry of Foreign Affairs

SRIO, Vol. 7, pp. 102-103. (Soviet editor's note) The conclusion of the letter reads "I await another letter from you informing me whether you will fulfill your family's ardent desire to see you or confirm what your previous letter stated. In either case I remain your steadfast well-wisher, Catherine." This was the empress's second letter to Rumiantsev. The first, preserved in the same archive, is signed but not written by her, and dated August 5, 1762. In reply to Rumiantsev's letter informing her of his illness, Catherine gave him permission to live in the country or to take the waters for his recovery.

V. Empress Catherine II's Note June 1, 1763

SRIO, Vol. 48, p. 522 (Soviet editor's note) I think there is a ready response to the Kirghiz-Kasak khan's demand for permission to cross the Yaik [river] with his herds. Since he has submitted to Russian authority, he should be ignored and not take his herds to forbidden places. No Russian subject can go anywhere without permission. If the Kirghiz need fodder for their herds, they should be advised to buy it, trade for it or stockpile it for winter. If they intend to settle down permanently they should have what they need to live. Tevkelev has some good ideas on this. He suggests inviting them to build a fortress and attempt to persuade other local peoples to come to it. But since he has intrigued against Davydov, it would not be a bad idea for Vice Chancellor Prince Golitsyn to summon Tevkelev and explain that I ordered Golitsyn to consult with him about these matters.

Tevkelev will be pleased if Prince Alexander Mikhailovich [Golitsyn] shows great patience when they meet. Golitsyn should say further that he is ready to show his willingness to endorse Tevkelev's ideas, that Tevkelev has a lot of useful information in addition to the unbounded confidence of the local peoples. After the meeting I want to know the opinion of the vice chancellor and the College of Foreign Affairs so we can deal with them [the Kirghiz] more systematically. This could be a model for dealing with similar peoples, for hitherto we have acted on a day-to-day basis.

VI. Keyserling's Report from Warsaw March 26, 1763

I made several attempts to persuade the Lithuanian hetman Massalski to a accept a pension, but to no avail since he refuses to take anything. I am confident that he and his son the bishop of Wilno are loyal, a belief confirmed by their conduct at the last Senatorial Council. Neither signed the [Council's] resolutions. The bishop consistently and resolutely opposed the Senatorial Council, and the hetman left for Wilno before it adjourned. I know the Massalski family is anxious to buy the Dombrowenski lands at the right price. These used to belong to Prince Menshikov but now are owned by the Sapiehas. A legal case over the property is pending. The outcome is uncertain because the judges for the tribunal hearing the case have not been chosen. If Prince Menshikov could be persuaded to convey his claims on the property to Massalski for the right price, I would send a letter relinquishing his claims for his signature. (Catherine made a note here. "The chancellors could discuss this with Prince Menshikov, but I do not want to force or compel him to agree. On the other hand money is better than empty pretensions.")

Perhaps a pension should be offered Hetman Branicki to bring him over to your imperial majesty's side. His credit is not that great, and his rank in the army, which consists of gentry, is his only source of power. He is fickle, indiscreet and totally subservient to Prefect Torżyński's wife, as well as to some clergyman. The clergy's loyalty to France is well known. Under these circumstances it is doubtful he will be on our side, nor can he be trusted to keep our affairs secret. I use the money sent only when needed, and I cannot predict good results in every case. The sower does not know if all his seeds will sprout.

VII. Handwritten Instructions from Empress Catherine II to Colonel Puchkov, 1763

SRIO, Vol. 48, pp. 287-288 (Soviet editor's note)] Secret instructions to Colonel Puchkov. (1) You are to go to Wilno in Lithuania. (2) You will be given eight thousand rubles from the College of Foreign Affairs. (3) The chancellor Count Vorontsov will give you a letter for Count Flemming, the Lithuanian grand crown treasurer, who will aid and advise you. (4) Your commission will be as follows. The royal party is trying to strengthen its position throughout the Commonwealth. It seeks to establish a tribunal in Lithuania under its control and will continue its efforts to do so. On its authority the Wilno military governor will choose as deputies both those who have been allowed to swear allegiance and those who have not. He intends to give his side the advantage by reserving one seat for young

Prince Radziwiłł. As we saw it, most of the nobles met in Wilno on April 4 (15) to accomplish our plans fully but opposed the Polish court over the Courland border disputes between us and the domestic Polish authorities. Since our Russian party must gain the upper hand, you are being sent eight thousand rubles which in consultation with Count Flemming you can use to improve your standing with the authorities. Since lies and insults directed against Russia are circulating among the lesser gentry throughout the region, you must do your best to counter them. Catherine.

VIII. Handwritten Letter from Empress Catherine to Count Keyserling

Peterhof, July 6, 1763. Count Keyserling: In regard to your secret reports sent to me personally, I already have informed you of my intentions. I will lend a helping hand to a confederation in Poland only when the king dies. I am not surprised at my friends' obvious eagerness, evident from their earnest proposals, to achieve this goal [a confederation] before then [the king's death]. Their cause is just as great, and their opinions just as important as they seem to be, and so the public will justify any methods they use. It is different for me. It doubtless will harm my true glory if I help dethrone a friendly neighboring prince only because he perhaps put too much confidence in a weak and deceitful minister (who also has one foot in the grave) who is as daring in planning undertakings as he is cowardly in executing them.

Initiating a confederation and maintaining it until his [the king's] death for an indeterminate period might cost me a considerable sum and affect my standing in the eyes of others. Certainly it will be difficult to evaluate the cost [of supporting or not supporting a confederation] in terms of the benefit to my empire after a national king is elected. I see no need to tell you here what the political effect on my empire would be if a brief confederation reestablished good order in the country's domestic affairs (if a government like that can accommodate good order).

Since I know only too well, Count Keyserling, that you are an enlightened and faithful minister, I have not the slightest doubt of your zeal for and commitment to the principal and permanent interests of my empire. A party supported by the intrigues and resources of its court can exercise a kind of casual despotism. Eventually this party can develop into a monarchical government which genuinely alarms its neighbors. Thus the existing despotism should be considered an extension of underlying anarchical principles and an aberration rather than the ordinary state of the nation.

I give you these preliminary ideas merely as a guide so you can understand the principles behind the latest orders I sent you. Restrain my friends from a premature confederation, while at the same time giving them the most positive assurances that we will support faithfully all reasonable action on their part until the king dies. Then we definitely will take their part.

I felt more obligated to write you this letter after I read in your dispatch No. 47 of the 9/20 of this month that those of enemy party are making great efforts to arm themselves and their troops. I compared this information with the news in your previous private report to me, that our friends enthusiastically and energetically are taking up arms and enrolling everybody. It is as if already they had my approval to put a confederation in the field. I find it reasonable that the other party believed our party's reckless enthusiasm put it at a disadvantage.

Four of my regiments now are moving into Poland. How they march in and how they behave may stir people up even more. It is your obligation to exercise supervision according to my orders. I thought it wise to have you supervise both aspects with your customary prudence and wisdom. Restrict yourself to soothing those of our party who might find the Wilno tribunal's conduct insufferable. The response we make to their requests should be limited lest their actions cause an open split before the proper time. For the same reason I want you to keep our regiments' stay there as brief as possible and have them take the route back to their barracks that will create the least disruption. You are well aware that all my orders to you are intended to prevent a confederation contrary to my interests. [Original in French]

IX. Handwritten Letter from Empress Catherine II to Count Keyserling

SRIO, Vol. 48, pp. 550-551 (Soviet editor's note). I am writing you this letter to solicit your advice. England is importuning me unduly to conclude alliance and commercial treaties. I want to know beforehand what course European affairs are taking. That is why under various pretexts I have avoided listening to their proposals. Since I have no more good pretexts, I have directed that the English ambassador's proposals be considered. The College of Foreign Affairs has produced a draft treaty for a defensive alliance, but I want to know your opinion before proceeding.

I have ordered the Viennese and Prussian courts informed in confidence that England has proposed an alliance treaty and that I did not enter into it without letting them know. I did this to prevent these two courts from taking umbrage and for them to allow me to propose a treaty of friendship. I wrote the [English] king about this eight days ago. I will tell you pointblank that my goal is friendly ties for defensive purposes with all powers. I want to be able at all times to stand by those most oppressed and thus be the arbiter of Europe. I am enclosing the College's draft. [Original in French]

X. Handwritten Note from N.I. Panin "Excerpt from My Letter to Lieutenant General Weymarn"

Yesterday evening I received the usual express dispatches sent from Riga on the tenth, including a most gracious letter to me from her imperial highness. With sure judgment she expressed her wish "to get to the bottom of this desperate and foolhardy enterprise to find out how far the foolishness has spread. Thus, if possible, it can be stopped immediately to protect innocent ordinary people." Then her highness recalled and deigned to remark that more than twelve instances of the same sort of insults had been discovered since Great Lent. During her absence last month a guards ensign assigned to an army regiment (I already have spoken to your excellency about him) heard the same kind of foul lies in taverns.

Supposedly Ivan was living in a village near Schlüsselburg, and many army staff officers had sworn allegiance to him and many people had come from the city to do him homage. Her highness has expressed the wish "to investigate if real evildoers are the source of these disclosures," and there can be little doubt of this. Your excellency therefore should condescend to determine by interrogation,and occasional torture when necessary, when, how, where and among whom these cockles have been sown to induce people to participate in their villainy.

XI. N.I. Panin's Letter Concerning the Eastern Frontier

Most gracious sovereign! I received Lieutenant General Springer's reports to the Senate which you sent me by the hand of Prince Viazemsky. Although I do not think our present situation is very dangerous, it nevertheless appears necessary to collect from various sources all the affairs and projects entrusted to different people at various times. Once they have been categorized here, it now should be determined what the future prospects are and how to attain them. Distance makes it harder to regulate customs than other government business, and both the customs and we will be exposed to disorder and interference if action is not taken. This is the case especially when the planners are in one place, while most of those who implement the plans rely completely on resolutions taken here and simply wait for these, but most of the resolutions have not been decided, and decisions always arrive late.

In evaluating these considerations, I most humbly venture to propose that your highness summon Lieutenant General Weymarn to the meeting today. He was the commander in the region and both knew about and dealt with many of the failed projects from that time. Hence he is in a position to provide a lot of basic information for the meeting.

"Summon Weymarn," Catherine wrote, "and let God *guide your thoughts for the best* to resolve everything."

INDEX

THE EDITOR AND TRANSLATOR

Daniel L. Schlafly, Jr. is Associate Professor of History and Director of Russian and East European Studies at Saint Louis University in St. Louis, Missouri. Born in St. Louis, he earned an A.B. degree at Georgetown University, then studied at the University of Munich. He received an M.A. degree, a Certificate of the Russian Institute, and a Ph.D. from Columbia University. He has published articles in the *Cahiers du monde russe et soviétique, Études sur le XVIIIe siècle, Communio* and *The Modern Encyclopedia of Russian and Eurasian History*, as well as having translated and edited a previous volume in this series (Volume 46). He lives in St. Louis with his wife and two daughters.